RIVERSIDE · SOCIAL STUDIES SERIES

Our Latin

UNDER THE EDITORSHIP OF

Clarence H. Haring

ROBERT WOODS BLISS PROFESSOR
OF LATIN AMERICAN HISTORY AND
ECONOMICS · HARVARD UNIVERSITY

American Neighbors

Harriett McCune Brown
WASHINGTON IRVING JUNIOR HIGH SCHOOL
LOS ANGELES, CALIFORNIA

Helen Miller Bailey
EAST LOS ANGELES JUNIOR COLLEGE
FORMERLY OF
MANUAL ARTS HIGH SCHOOL
LOS ANGELES, CALIFORNIA

HOUGHTON MIFFLIN COMPANY
The Riverside Press Cambridge

COPYRIGHT, 1952
1944, 1945, 1947
by Harriett McCune Brown and Helen Miller Bailey

ALL RIGHTS RESERVED INCLUDING THE RIGHT TO REPRODUCE
THIS BOOK OR PARTS THEREOF IN ANY FORM

HOUGHTON MIFFLIN COMPANY

The Riverside Press Cambridge

PRINTED IN THE U.S.A.

Contents

Part Five

THE CARIBBEAN IS THE HOME OF NINE SMALL REPUBLICS

Part Six

BOLÍVAR'S REPUBLICS BECOME MODERN NATIONS OF LATIN AMERICA

Part Seven

THE NATIONS OF TEMPERATE SOUTH AMERICA ARE VIGOROUS
AND PROGRESSIVE

Part Eight

THE GREAT NATION OF BRAZIL FACES A FUTURE OF PROMISE

Part Nine

THE GOOD NEIGHBORS WORK TOGETHER TOWARD A FINER CIVILIZATION AND A PERMANENT PEACE

Maps

To the Readers of This Book

You have all heard of Latin America. Newspapers and magazines carry stories about the Pan-American Highway which forms such an important link between the United States and Latin America. Tourist agencies advertise trips to fascinating places such as Acapulco, Rio de Janeiro, or the Chilean Lakes. You frequently see news items dealing with events connected with one country or another south of the Rio Grande. The President of Chile visits the President of the United States. The Uruguayan soccer team wins the world championship at Rio de Janeiro. Two Americans win a race in Mexico, traveling from El Paso, Texas, to the Guatemalan border. Indeed, there are references to Latin America on every hand.

But what do American high-school students of today really know about Latin America? Perhaps they know it as the place where people dance the rhumba or the conga, where orchids grow wild, or where the gauchos ride the range. Others may remember that certain South American Indians hunt human heads and dry them for curios to sell to tourists. Some may believe that Mexico is a country where armed bandits hold up visitors, or that all Latin American women are dark-eyed beauties who wear lace veils and go to bullfights. Some regard Latin America as a land of opportunity where a bright young American can make a fortune without knowledge of the language or the customs. Others, unfortunately, dismiss it with a sweep of the hand as a wild, undeveloped jungle. There may be some truth in all these statements, but is this a fair picture of Latin America?

On the other hand, the South Americans have a great many strange ideas about us. Some believe that our only interest is in making money and in driving as sharp a bargain as we can. From the movies which we send them they get the impression that all "North Americans," as they call us, own yachts, spend their time in night clubs, or chase Indians in the Wild West! They consider it dangerous to travel in the "United States of North America" because gangsters shoot people down on public streets. Many well-educated South Americans have been genuinely afraid of the military power of the United States. They are not at all sure that the United States would not gladly conquer them and make South America our empire. Is this a fair picture of our country?

You can see that there is a great deal of misunderstanding on both sides. The first thing we need to understand is what Latin America means. The word "America," of course, applies to both the continents in the Western Hemisphere, and "Americans" are citizens of the countries in both continents. A citizen of Brazil is just as much an American as is a citizen of the United States. The term "Latin" is used to distinguish those people who speak languages descended from Latin, such as Spanish, Portuguese, French, and Italian. It would be wrong to say "Spanish America," for in Brazil, the largest country in South America, Portuguese is spoken. In Haiti, an independent republic in the Caribbean, the people speak French. So we use the term "Latin America" to apply to all the countries south of the Mexican border.

Latin America is not a country; it is a convenient name for a group of countries. Do you know their names? Just south of us is the important country of Mexico. Below Mexico are the six republics of Central America: Guatemala, El Salvador, Nicaragua, Costa Rica, Honduras, and Panama. To the east of Central America in the Caribbean Sea are the three island republics of Cuba, Haiti, and the Dominican Republic.

There are ten republics in South America. Argentina and Brazil are the largest countries on that continent. Uruguay and Paraguay are two small nations in the south. In the west are Chile, Bolivia, Peru, and Ecuador; on the north coast are Venezuela and Colombia. When we use the term "Latin America," we mean the twenty republics we have named — ten in South America, seven in Mexico and Central America, and three island republics in the Caribbean.

It is very important for the United States and the Latin American countries to be on friendly terms. We need their trade and they need ours. We want to sell them manufactured goods and buy from them such products as coffee, tin, and rubber. We also need their co-operation in helping to maintain a world at peace. If we are to have the co-operation of the

Latin American nations, we must be a good neighbor to them.

It should not be difficult for us to be a good neighbor to Latin American countries, for there are many ties that bind us. In the first place, we all live on the same land mass which is tied together by the Isthmus of Panama. The Indians, who were the original "one-hundred-per-cent Americans," lived in both the Americas. Both continents were explored by adventurers from Europe, and became colonies of European nations. Both English and Spanish colonies had the same complaints against the mother countries, and both waged wars for independence. They won their freedom after years of bitter struggle, in which great national heroes led the people to victory. In both Americas, heroes became presidents of free republics and are still honored on national holidays.

As you see, we have much in common with the republics of Latin America. But our differences in language, customs, and background have made it difficult to understand each other. The distance between North and South America and the lack of transportation facilities have until now held us apart. But the new Pan-American Highway and the excellent air service to any part of South America will make it easy to get acquainted with our southern neighbors.

We hope the study of this book will help young Americans to know and understand our Latin American neighbors better than their parents and grandparents have. First, you will learn about the geography and physical appearance of Latin America. Then you will read the story of the ancient Indian people who lived there before the Spaniards came. In order to know our neighbors, it is important for you to appreciate the Indian contributions to Latin American civilization. The history of Spanish and Portuguese explorers and colonizers which follows is worth knowing because it helps you to realize why their influence is so strong in the civilization of today. You ought also to know the story of the heroes who fought for Latin American independence as George Washington fought for ours.

As young American citizens, you will be interested in the sections on the modern nations as they are today. We have tried to give you an understanding of the people and the land they live in, how they earn their living, and what kind of music, art, and literature they enjoy. We hope you will feel the charm of these countries and learn to appreciate their customs, their interesting Spanish towns and cities, and the artistic hand-work of the Indian people.

In the last section of the book you will learn what the United States is actually doing in order to be a good neighbor. We hope that you who read this book will take away with you a knowledge of and an admiration for the Latin American people. For then, indeed, may we become, in the words of the late President Roosevelt, a "family of nations."

MT. ACONCAGUA, mighty monarch of the Western Hemisphere, is only one of the thrilling sights you will see on the trip by clipper ship which is described in the first part of our book.

Pan American Airways

Part One · THE GEOGRAPHY OF LATIN

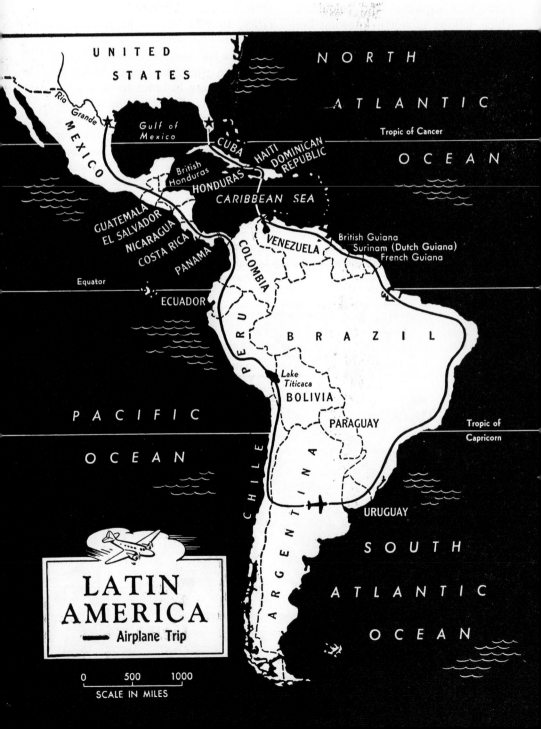

UNITED STATES

Rio Grande

MEXICO

Gulf of Mexico

NORTH ATLANTIC

Tropic of Cancer

OCEAN

CUBA

HAITI

DOMINICAN REPUBLIC

British Honduras

HONDURAS

CARIBBEAN SEA

GUATEMALA
EL SALVADOR
NICARAGUA
COSTA RICA
PANAMA

VENEZUELA

COLOMBIA

British Guiana
Surinam (Dutch Guiana)
French Guiana

Equator

ECUADOR

PERU

BRAZIL

Lake Titicaca

BOLIVIA

PARAGUAY

PACIFIC

OCEAN

CHILE

ARGENTINA

URUGUAY

Tropic of Capricorn

SOUTH

ATLANTIC

OCEAN

LATIN AMERICA
— Airplane Trip

0   500   1000
SCALE IN MILES

AMERICA IS THE KEY TO ITS HISTORY

BEFORE we start the story of the Latin Americans, let us find out what kind of land they live in. As you know, the geography of any country has a great deal to do with its history. Suppose we make a "non-stop" flight over the homeland of our twenty neighbors to the south.

First our plane will take us over Mexico and Central America, then it will continue down the Pacific coast of South America and return by way of the Atlantic coast of that continent. Below us the scenes will shift from snowy grandeur of majestic mountains to the verdant beauty of tropical forests. We shall become familiar with the physical face of Latin America — its mountains, highland plateaus, and great rivers; its lakes, deserts, and jungles. We shall learn the kinds of climate our neighbors live in, what natural resources they have, and what crops they raise. In short, our "air view" will give us the key to a better understanding of the Latin America of yesterday and of today.

Before we start our trip let us look at the map on the opposite page. How many continents does Latin America occupy? Trace the route the plane will take. Can you name the twenty independent republics of Latin America? Can you also name four colonies of European countries? South America is in reality what direction from North America? Can you find the Caribbean Sea? Turn to the map on page 17. Can you find the Andes Mountains, the Amazon River, the Orinoco River, and La Plata River?

Now you are ready to board the "Mexico Flyer" at Brownsville, Texas. As you look down upon the constantly changing scenes below, keep the following questions in mind. They will help you to focus your attention on important ideas to be gained from the trip:

1. Why is geography responsible for many of the differences between the countries of Latin America?

2. In what ways are the mountain slopes and valleys of tropical Latin America important?

3. Does altitude have any effect on the climate and products of the tropical countries of Latin America?

Chapter 1

We Look at Mexico and Central America from the Air

OUR PLANE takes off from Brownsville, Texas, and in no time we are over the border and flying south of the Rio Grande River. The homeland of our neighbors, Mexico and Central America, lies in the southernmost tip of North America. Like a great letter "Y," this land tapers from a northern border over 1800 miles long to a mere fifty miles at the Isthmus of Panama. The waters of the Pacific lap its western shore; on the north and east lie the warm Gulf of Mexico and the Caribbean Sea. We soon see from the plane the sparkling waters of the Gulf. The sandy shore appears and here and there are a few coco palms which look like giant feather dusters growing upside down.

MOST OF LATIN AMERICA LIES IN THE TORRID ZONE

When we have traveled south a little more than an hour, we cross the Tropic of Cancer and are above the hot Torrid Zone in which most of Latin America lies. This zone is a belt around the center of the earth which is hot all the year around. As you know, the earth is tipped on its axis so that, as it rotates about the sun, first the northern half, then the southern half, receives the more direct rays of the sun. This causes the sum-

mer and winter seasons. But the zone around the middle of the earth is not affected by this change of seasons, because here the sun's rays always strike directly or almost so. Since direct rays of the sun give the most intense heat, you can understand why lands in the Torrid Zone are hot in both summer and winter.

The northern limit of the Torrid Zone is marked by the Tropic of Cancer, which we have just crossed at a latitude of 23° 27'. Below the Equator the Tropic of Capricorn marks the southern boundary at the same degree of latitude. The Torrid Zone is often called "the tropics" because of these two boundary lines.

IN THE TORRID ZONE HEAT PLUS RAIN EQUALS JUNGLE

Mosquitoes and malaria, suffocating heat, tropical diseases, continual rain — these are all part of the tropical jungle which we see stretching for miles along the eastern coast of Mexico. The moist northeast trade winds blow in from the Atlantic and bring heavy rainfall throughout the year. The combination of continuous rain and intense heat produces a dense jungle.

Behind the sandy beach and palm trees are lagoons and swamps. Be-

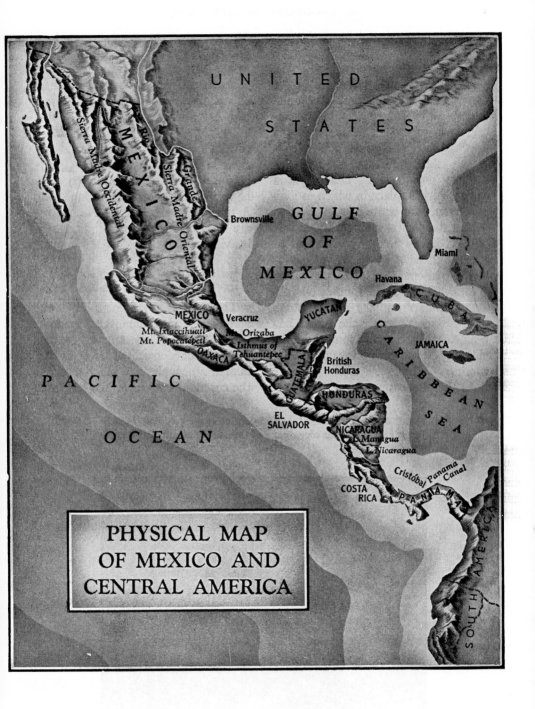

PHYSICAL MAP
OF MEXICO AND
CENTRAL AMERICA

yond the swamps, the jungle begins. Trees and creepers grow in tangled confusion, defying man to enter. Monkeys and parrots abound in the trees, snakes and alligators are hidden in the depths of the jungle. More discouraging to human beings than the heat and the dense growth are the millions of biting insects and malaria-carrying mosquitoes. The jungle is not a healthful place in which to live, particularly for white men.

You may be wondering whether this tropical jungle is of any use at all to man. Indeed it is! This hot, suffocating atmosphere is the natural home of the banana. Coconuts, vanilla beans, and pineapples are at home here, also. Wherever the jungle has been cleared away, this land produces valuable crops which grow only in the tropics.

As the plane turns toward Central Mexico now, the ground rises in a gradual slope. We see the jungle of smaller trees giving way to a tall, dense forest. Precious woods, such as ebony, rosewood, and mahogany, grow here between sea level and 2000 feet above. Rainfall is heavier and more continuous on this windward slope than in the flat coastland. This is because the trade winds rise to cross higher land and drop more moisture. A tropical forest such as the one we are looking at always indicates a heavier rainfall than does the jungle.

THE MOUNTAINS OF MEXICO ARE PART OF THE BACKBONE OF THE AMERICAS

The ground is rising rapidly now, and we see high mountains looming ahead of us. They are the eastern range of the Sierra Madre (see-ay'rah mah'dray) Mountains, which separate the coastlands we have just left from

THIS TROPICAL JUNGLE makes a human being appear very small indeed! Jungle growth like this covers much of the coast of Mexico and Central America.

Galloway

the interior of Mexico.[1] The mountains of Mexico are a continuation of the Rocky Mountains in western North America. They form a part of the great Rocky Mountain-Andes system that runs like a huge backbone the entire length of the Americas, from Alaska to the southern tip of South America. The Spanish word for a chain of mountains is *cordillera* (cor-dee-yay'rah). This name is now commonly used to mean the entire mountain system of both North and South America.

The cordilleras of Mexico are divided into two ranges which cut off the east and west coasts from the central region. The eastern range over which we are now flying is the Sierra Madre Oriental. If we had flown from Los Angeles along the west coast, we should have crossed the much steeper Sierra Madre Occidental. The western cordilleras rise above the coast 10,000 to 12,000 feet, which is two or three times higher than our Appalachian Mountains. The eastern and western ranges meet south of Mexico City in a jumble of high peaks and deep valleys.

It may seem that between impassable jungles and high mountain ranges, Mexico has little to attract man. Remember that you have not seen all of Mexico yet. These mountains, which appear to be only barriers, hold great treasure in their rocky depths. If you could look into the canyons cut by streams in the mountain-side, you would find a treasure-house of precious metals. Gold, zinc, and copper are hidden there. Silver exists in fabulous quantities. For four hundred years Mexican silver mines have furnished silver to the world, yet scientists say that the silver deposits have barely been touched.

THE PLATEAU OF MEXICO OFFERS A COOL CLIMATE IN A TROPICAL LAND

The mountains are thinning out below us now, and green valleys appear here and there. Ahead, spreading out as far as the eye can see, is a great, rolling valley. You are looking at the high central plateau of Mexico, thousands of feet above the sea. In the distance is Mexico City, the beautiful capital of Mexico. To the east, west, and south are mountains cutting the plateau off from the rest of the country. At this southern end the plateau is almost 7500 feet above sea level. There is sufficient rainfall here during the summer months to grow crops of wheat, barley, corn, and beans. Farther north, the plateau slopes downward and the amount of rainfall decreases. At the northern border of Mexico it joins the dry grasslands of the southwestern United States.

Since the plateau of Mexico is in the Torrid Zone, you might expect to find the hot climate of the tropics. July is the hottest month of the year in Mexico City, and the temperature is about 65 degrees! In fact, it is wise for tourists who plan to visit Mexico City in the summer to bring warm coats with them, for the nights are always chilly. Think of the broiling summer temperatures of some of our cities in the United States!

There is a reason for this cool climate in the tropics. That reason is altitude. Did you know that for every 330 feet one travels above sea

[1] The names of Latin American nations have not been given in Spanish pronunciation because their English form is already well known to you.

Sawders

THIS AIRVIEW OF MEXICO CITY shows its wide streets and its beautiful National Theatre. This building is easily recognized from the air by its roof of colored tile. To the left is one end of the famous park, the Alameda.

level the temperature lowers one degree? A little figuring will make it clear why two thirds of the people of Mexico prefer to live on this plateau. The important cities are situated here, too, in spite of the difficulty of reaching the plateau. In the early days before railroads, the trip inland from the coast meant a long and arduous journey. It is said that people who lived on the plateau so dreaded the heat of the lowland that one of the worst possible punishments was banishment to the coast.

TROPICAL MEXICO HAS THREE CLIMATES

We have now traveled over three distinct climatic zones in Mexico. The Mexicans refer to the coastal lowlands as *tierra caliente* (tee-ay'rah cah-lee-en'tay).[1] This is the home of the mosquito as well as of the banana. The mountain slopes of the Sierra Madre and parts of the plateau are *tierra templada* (tem-plah'dah) or temperate land. This land lies between 2000 and 6000 feet above sea level and is often called the land of perpetual spring. The mild climate of these slopes makes them ideal for raising coffee. The cold land, *tierra fria* (free'ah), begins above 6000 feet. Here, where the average temperature is about 60 degrees, grow wheat, barley, and potatoes.

[1] The Spanish spoken in Latin America is somewhat different from that spoken in Spain, so if you have studied in school the pronunciation used in Spain, do not pronounce *c* or *z* like *th*, but like *ss*. Double *l* is usually not pronounced like *l-y* but like *y* with no *l* sound at all. *Ella* is pronounced *ellya* in Spain, but *eh-ya* in Spanish America.

VOLCANOES HAVE MADE THE RICH SOIL OF MEXICO'S HIGHLANDS

We say good-bye to the plateau now and fly toward the mountains that border its southern end. Ahead of us we see a high snowcapped peak with a curl of smoke rising from its top. This is the live volcano, Popocatépetl (poh-poh-cah-tay'peh-tal), or "smoking mountain," which is a familiar sight to those who live in Mexico City. Farther west are the three snowy peaks of another volcano, Ixtaccihuatl (ees-tahk-see'whah-tal), named "white woman" because of its resemblance to the figure of a woman clothed in white. Beautiful Orizaba (oh-ree-sah'bah), highest of all, rises in snow-crowned majesty to a height of 18,209 feet above the sea. The whole southern end of the Sierra Madres is a series of volcanoes, most of them extinct, but a few still active. Although these volcanoes have had serious eruptions in the past, they have more than paid for any damage done. They have given a rich and fertile soil to the plateau region of Mexico. The volcanic ash and lava, which poured out from time to time in the past onto the floor of the plateau, have been more valuable than the finest fertilizer.

Flying beyond the mountains that fringe the plateau in the south, we come to another highland region. It is separated from the main plateau by the deep valley of the river Balsas. These highlands of Oaxaca (wah-hah'-cah) differ from the plateau in two respects. They are not so high, nor do they have the fertile soil left by volcanic outpourings. In the highlands there are many separate valleys made by streams cutting into the mountains. We see the thatched roofs and green fields of the Indian villages which abound in the valleys.

IXTACCIHUATL, the "white woman," slumbers peacefully above this Indian farmer and his livestock. Can you see also the snowy tip of Popocatépetl below the clouds far to the left?

Galloway

As Mexico narrows down at the Isthmus of Tehuántepec (tay-whahn′-tay-pek), the lowland of the east coast widens to form a dense and almost impenetrable forest extending many miles inward. This part of Tehuántepec has over 120 inches of rainfall a year, and in its dripping heat the tropical forest flourishes. When we consider that 30 to 40 inches of rainfall a year is sufficient to grow crops, we realize that 120 inches is a great deal of rain! This is an ideal climate for the vanilla vine, which is grown in large quantities where the forest has been cleared.

THE PENINSULA OF YUCATAN IS PART DESERT AND PART JUNGLE

The Yucatan Peninsula extends northward into the Gulf of Mexico. It is a flat plain of limestone which was at one time sea bottom. The northern end of this plain is semidesert with scanty soil and scantier rainfall. The Indians of this region get a bare existence from their crops of corn and beans. Northern Yucatan has two advantages. First, there are no mosquitoes in this dry region to bring malaria. Second, the arid land produces one profitable crop. This is the agave (ah-gah′veh) or century plant, whose hempen fiber is in great demand for twine.

Farther south on the peninsula the rainfall and the vegetation increase. Scrubby bush, then jungle, then dense forest show where the rain becomes heavier. A look at the vegetation in a tropical lowland will tell you the amount of rainfall. No part of this peninsula seems to be a desirable place in which to live. Yet you will discover in a later chapter that the dry plain of Yucatan was once the home of a great people.

THE GEOGRAPHY OF CENTRAL AMERICA IS SIMILAR TO THAT OF MEXICO

Suddenly, with no change in the mountainous scenery below us, we

THE VOLCANO, ATITLÁN, rears its cone-shaped head above lovely Lake Atitlán high in the mountains of Guatemala. In the foreground are Indians in bright-colored native costumes.

Gendreau

Acme

COFFEE–DRYING TIME is an important season in Central America. The berries are spread out on platforms and turned over to dry in the hot tropical sun. Coffee is one of the chief crops of our Central American neighbors.

have left Mexico behind and are flying over Central America. The six countries of Central America are located on the narrow finger of land which connects North and South America. Their whole area is not so large as the state of Texas. Since national boundaries are not visible from a plane, let us consider Central America as one region and leave the story of the separate nations until later.

Here is a land of volcanoes! As our plane crosses the highlands, the odd cone-shaped peaks of one volcano after another appear on the horizon to the right of us. The mountains appear to be a chain of beautiful volcanic cones. There are over thirty in Guatemala alone, and they continue in spectacular succession almost the entire length of Central America.

As in Mexico, the cordilleras of this region form a long backbone of mountains and plateaus. They lie along the

Pacific coast, leaving a wide lowland on the Caribbean side and a much narrower lowland on the western side.

CENTRAL AMERICA IS A REGION OF HIGHLANDS AND LOWLANDS

We are passing over slopes and plateaus high up in the mountains which are like the plateau of Mexico. Here, too, is the happy combination of warm climate, rich volcanic soil, and sufficient rainfall for crops. For mile after mile we look down on the beautiful green of great coffee plantations which flourish in these countries. The best coffee land is on the mountain slopes and valleys which lie from 1000 to 4000 feet above the sea. This is the *tierra templada* of Central America.

The capital cities and the bulk of the population are located in the highlands away from the heat and the mosquitoes. The Spanish colonists

13

who wished to reach the plateaus often crossed the Isthmus and took ship up the Pacific coast of Central America. From the Pacific side they had to transport themselves and their goods by pack-mule or oxcart up the difficult mountain trails. The jungle was so dense on the Atlantic side that it was sometimes easier to take this longer trip than to attempt crossing it.

The air route lies over the highlands of Central America between the capital cities. Beyond the mountains on the Caribbean side lies the hot and suffocating eastern coastland. This is another *tierra caliente* like the east coast of Mexico. Large portions of the jungle here have been cleared to make way for the banana plantations. From the air the banana trees look like fields of spinach! In another chapter you will learn how men have conquered the mosquito. This is an important problem when the trop-ical lowland is used for making a living.

WE REACH THE PANAMA CANAL

We continue to fly south. As the plane passes over a break in the mountains we see below us two beautiful lakes, set like jewels in the landscape. These are Lake Managua (mah-nah'-gwah) and Lake Nicaragua. In Lake Nicaragua, the larger of the two, is an island with a smoking volcano rising from it.

The land grows more and more narrow as we fly over Panama. Suddenly we see oceans to the right and left of us. Now we fly directly over a bit of territory occupied by the United States, the Panama Canal. In only twenty minutes we travel from the Pacific end of the Canal to the Atlantic end. We arrive at Cristóbal (crees-toh'ball) in the Canal Zone, and the first part of our trip comes to an end.

PANAMA CITY passes beneath the plane as we finish the first lap of our trip. This picturesque capital of the little republic of Panama lies at the Pacific end of the Panama Canal.

Are You a Careful Reader? Test Yourself:

Now you are ready to test yourself to see how carefully you read and remember what you read. Tests I and II should not take you more than ten minutes. *Don't write in this book but write your answers on a separate sheet of paper.*

I. Can you complete each of these statements correctly?

1. The parts of Latin America which are located on the continent of North America are .... and ....

2. The mountains of Mexico are a continuation of our .... , and are called the ....

3. The boundaries of the Torrid Zone are the Tropic of .... on the north and the Tropic of .... on the south.

4. The heavy rainfall on the east coast of Mexico and Central America is caused by the ....

5. Both .... and .... are needed to produce a tropical jungle.

6. The capital cities and most of the population of Central America are located in the .....

II. Select the statement from the right-hand column which best explains each word in the left-hand column. Match the letter with the number. There will be two statements not used in the right-hand column.

1. cordillera	*a.* the narrowest part of Mexico
2. tierra caliente	*b.* a peninsula of Mexico jutting into the Caribbean Sea
3. Popocatépetl	*c.* the capital of Mexico
4. Tehuántepec	*d.* Panamanian city where first part of the air trip ends
5. Yucatan	*e.* the highest mountain in Mexico
6. Lake Managua	*f.* highland country south of Mexico City
7. tierra templada	*g.* temperate region
8. Oaxaca	*h.* Spanish word for backbone range of mountains
9. Orizaba	*i.* Spanish word for cold country
10. Cristóbal	*j.* geographic feature of Nicaragua
	k. warm tropical region
	l. volcanic peak named "Smoking Mountain"

Food for Thought and Discussion

Here are some questions which will test whether you can understand and apply some of the important ideas in the chapter. Answer them as completely as you can in class discussion or as part of your written work.

1. Can you explain clearly why there are no winter and summer seasons in Torrid Zone lands?

2. What causes the three climatic zones in Mexico?

3. In what ways are the mountains valuable to Mexico and Central America?

4. Did you find the answers to any of the questions given in the unit preview on page 5?

Chapter 2

We Fly Over the Pacific Coast of South America

WE ARE NOW on the Isthmus of Panama, that narrow finger of land connecting the two Americas. Our trip over South America will be more interesting if we know a little about this great continent before we start. South America extends over the Equator like a huge fist with one finger pointing to the South Pole. Its territory is two times as large as that of the United States. This continent does not lie directly south of North America as you may have believed, but far to the east as well. If you wish to go from New York City to the east coast of South America, you must travel eastward halfway across the Atlantic Ocean! In fact, the large cities on the east coast are nearer to Spain and Africa than they are to New York.

Let us look at the map of South America on page 17. You can see three mountain regions, one on the west, two on the east, and three large river systems. You can see that there is a great lowland region in the center of South America made up largely of the basins of these rivers. The mountains which run the full length of the Pacific coast are the Andes. They are part of the huge mountain chain which

forms the backbone of the two Americas. The Brazilian Highlands on the east coast and the Guiana (gee-ah'-nah) Highlands to the north are mere hills compared to the Andes. Notice that the important rivers of South America all empty into the Atlantic Ocean. The Orinoco and the Amazon Rivers are in the northern half of South America, and the Plata River system is in the southern half. Nearly two thirds of South America is made up of the lowland drained by these rivers and their tributaries. We shall learn more about the rivers, mountains, and lowlands as we look at them from the air.

Notice that the greater part of South America is in the Torrid Zone, for the location has an important effect on the climate, the products, and the way the people live. If you look at the coastlines of the continent, you can see that there are few indentations on the Pacific coast except far to the south, and that the Atlantic coast has many natural bays and inlets. This explains the greater number of harbors on the Atlantic coast.

Now we are ready to follow the famous Panagra route of the Pan American Airways, from Cristóbal down the west coast of South America to Chile, then across the Andes and

CARIBBEAN SEA

ATLANTIC

OCEAN

Isthmus of
Panama

CARACAS

Lake
Maracaibo

Orinoco River

Guiana

BOGOTÁ

Llanos

Highlands

Magdalena River

Cauca River

QUITO

Mt. Cotopaxi

Mt. Chimborazo

Guayas
River

Muranon River

Iquitos

Amazon River

LIMA

Ucayali River

Andes

Cuzco

Lake Titicaca

LA PAZ

Mato Grosso

Brazilian Highlands

São Paulo

RIO DE JANEIRO

Santos

Gran Chaco

Paraguay River

PACIFIC OCEAN

Mt. Aconcagua

Valparaiso

SANTIAGO

Uspallata Pass

Paraná River

Uruguay River

BUENOS AIRES

MONTEVIDEO

ATLANTIC

Pampa

La Plata River

OCEAN

Patagonia

Punta Arenas

Straits of Magellan

Tierra del Fuego

PHYSICAL MAP
OF
SOUTH AMERICA

north along the Atlantic coast. We shall visit the islands of the Caribbean and finish our trip at Miami, Florida. The clipper takes off and soon we are flying over western Colombia.

THE MOUNTAINS OF COLOMBIA ARE THREE GREAT RANGES

The Republic of Colombia straddles the Isthmus of Panama with an ocean on two sides, the Pacific on the west and the Caribbean on the north. We are looking down upon the peaks of the Andes, much loftier and grander than the mountains of Central America. They extend like three giant fingers over western Colombia to form the western, central, and eastern cordilleras. The central cordillera is separated from the other two ranges by the wide valley of the Cauca (cow'-cah) River on the west and by the Magdalena (mahg-dah-lay'nah) River on the east. In the cool plateaus and valleys of the central and eastern mountains live most of the people of Colombia. Like the Central Americans, they cannot live safely or comfortably in the tropical climate of the coast.

COLOMBIA HAS THREE NATURAL REGIONS

You will find that the tropical countries on the Pacific coast follow the same geographical pattern. Each one has three distinct regions: the coastal strip, the mountain and plateau region, and the eastern lowlands. The mountain area which we have just described covers only about two fifths of the area of Colombia. Along the Pacific and the Caribbean coasts are the hot, damp lowlands you would expect to find in a tropical country where there is plenty of rain. There is a wide, low area in northwestern Colombia where the Cauca and the Magdalena join in their trip to the Caribbean. Much of the jungle near the coast has been cleared for banana plantations. So well do bananas thrive in the damp heat and rich soil that Colombia has become the leading South American nation in the production of this fruit.

If we could see eastward beyond the mountains, a great tropical plain would come into view. This plain is a vast area of grasslands, or *llanos* (yah'nos), as the Spanish call them. The rainfall is not heavy enough for the jungle to grow, so we find the grassland of the drier tropical regions. There are some cattle raised here, but the *llanos* are so cut off from the highlands by lack of roads that few people live here. This lowland region, too, is infested with mosquitoes and fevers.

THE RIVERS OF COLOMBIA ARE ITS HIGHWAYS

The beautiful valley of the upper Cauca shows wide and green among the mountains. On the fertile slopes are coffee and sugar plantations, far above the heat of the coast. In some places there are cattle grazing on such steep slopes that we wonder how they keep their footing. They are used to it, and, like mountain goats, become so agile that they rarely slip.

Rivers are important in this land of mountains, for they serve as highways. River steamers can travel up the Magdalena and the Cauca for hundreds of miles. The people who live on the cool plateaus must depend largely on river transportation for their goods. Railroads are short, being used mostly to connect the highland towns with navigable streams.

Severin — Black Star

ALONG THE LOWER MAGDALENA in Colombia the jungle crowds down to the river's edge. The plane whose shadow you see in the water leaves the slow river boats far behind as it wings its way to Colombia's capital.

For instance, Bogotá (boh-goh-tah'), the capital of Colombia, is only about 600 miles from the coast, but it is a mile and a half above the sea. To reach this city it is necessary to travel about 400 miles up the Magdalena River by steamer, then the rest of the way by rail. This journey takes about a week. Of course, travelers can reach Bogotá by air in a few hours, but this is an expensive way to carry goods.

ECUADOR IS THE LAND OF THE EQUATOR

The beautiful, forested mountains of southwestern Colombia pass rapidly by and soon we are crossing the boundary between Colombia and her southern neighbor, Ecuador. A little farther south we pass over the center of the earth at the Equator, and are now in the Southern Hemisphere. If we were on a cruise ship crossing the "Line," as the Equator is called, there would be a celebration on board in honor of the event. There is usually a King Neptune who "initiates" unsuspecting travelers by dousing them with water!

It means something very definite to be in the Southern Hemisphere, because the seasons are reversed below the Equator. To the South Americans, a day in June means a day in midwinter! What is the reason for this reversal of the seasons? We have noted that the earth is tilted on its axis as it rotates about the sun, so that the northern half of the earth is tipped away from the sun for half the year, producing the winter season. At the same time, owing to the tilting of the earth, the Southern Hemisphere is tipped toward the sun, causing the summer season. For this reason our winter months, December, January, and February, mean summer to the South Americans who live below the Equator.

In Ecuador, the Andes look bleak and barren from the plane, with deep gorges and forbidding white peaks. We cannot imagine man's living here. But soon plateaus and valleys begin to show among the mountains. We are approaching the highland region where most of the people of Ecuador prefer to live.

THE CAPITAL OF ECUADOR IS SURROUNDED BY MAJESTIC VOLCANOES

A beautiful, cone-shaped valley lies below us now. Here is Quito (kee'-toh), capital of Ecuador, over 9000 feet above the sea. Wherever you look beyond Quito, you can see a snowy mountain peak. Ahead is the volcano, Cotopaxi (coh-toh-pahk'zee), said to be the highest living volcano in the world. Flame and smoke issue

from its peak, rising 19,000 feet high among the clouds. Highest of all the peaks in this region is Chimborazo (cheem-boh-rah'so), monarch of all he surveys. In ancient Indian tongue, the name means "rays of the sun through clouds above the snow." Towering upward almost four miles, this mighty monarch is indeed wreathed in everlasting snow.

THE AMAZON REGION OF ECUADOR IS UNEXPLORED

Ecuador is not all mountains. Like other Andean countries it has a trans-Andean region, which means "across the Andes." If we could fly east beyond the cordilleras, we should see the vast forested lowland of Ecuador called the Oriente (oh-ree-en'tay). Very little is known about the damp, dark forests of the Amazon. In fact, few people from the highlands have ever seen this region, so completely is it cut off by the lofty Andes. There are only steep mule trails up the east side of the Andes connecting it with civilization. In the few settlements on the rivers it is so damp that salt dissolves and matches will not light if exposed to the air for any length of time.

THE FERTILE COAST OF ECUADOR PRODUCES TROPICAL CROPS

As our plane goes toward the Pacific, we are amazed to see a railroad zigzagging up the dizzy heights between Quito and the coast. Before the railroad was built, the only means of reaching the highland region was by mule, for the rivers of Ecuador are not navigable as far inland as those of Colombia. We look far out over the Pacific and down at the wide coastlands. They are covered with the dense green of tropical forests except where clearings have been made for cultivation. To the south is the wide valley of the Guayas (gwah'yahs) River, broadening out to a distance of two miles where the river joins the ocean. Thousands of cacao trees are planted in the lowlands about the river. The cacao beans produced by these trees are the source of our cocoa and chocolate and the most important product of Ecuador.

THE COASTAL REGION OF PERU IS A COOL, DAMP DESERT

As we fly toward the state of Peru, the coastal region loses its green and gradually becomes narrow and desert-like. Trees disappear and there is mile after mile of sandy plain. Brown, barren mountains rise from the desert, occasionally sending a spur down to the ocean. Here and there, plantations of green stand out against the yellow sand, where a river makes a fertile spot.

We imagine that this coastal desert must be a region of intense heat. To our surprise, we find that the climate is cool and damp with an average temperature of about 60 degrees! The tropical heat of the coast of Peru is lessened by a cold ocean current, called the Humboldt Current, which flows along its shores from the south. Westerly winds blowing across the 150 miles of this current become cool and moist so that they reduce the heat of the coast by several degrees.

Strangely enough, the current which keeps the coast cool also makes it a desert. For the cooling winds bring no rain, since their moisture is absorbed in the warmer air over the land. Indeed, rainfall is unusual on this desert. One place has the repu-

Gendreau

RAILWAYS IN THE ANDES are built under unbelievable difficulties. They must cross great gorges, tunnel through mountains, and climb along rocky ledges cut into steep canyon walls.

tation of having rain only once in seven years. There is enough moisture in the air to cause heavy mists and fogs, which hang over the coast for several months of the year.

The Humboldt Current has provided a valuable resource for Peru. Its fifty miles of moving water are teeming with fish of all kinds, which furnish food for millions of sea birds. The birds inhabit the thirty-eight rocky islands off the coast. For centuries their droppings have accumulated there, undisturbed by rain. The guano, as it is called, is an excellent fertilizer. At one time it was Peru's most valuable export. Today, under government supervision, the guano is used to enrich the land in the coastal valleys.

As we fly toward Lima (lee'mah), the capital of Peru, the city is hidden in fog. It is another surprise to find a large city near the coast instead of up in the highlands as we should expect it to be. In fact, Lima is the only capital on the west coast not in the highlands. As we feel the cold mist, we do not have to look far for the reason. There is no need for people to seek the coolness of higher altitudes.

In spite of the lack of rainfall, some parts of the coast produce crops. Cotton and sugar cane flourish in the fertile river valleys farther back from the coast where the cold fogs do not reach. In many places water from the rivers is used to irrigate, and here the crops are abundant. Wide belts of green mark the river valleys and irrigated lands.

EASTERN PERU HAS AN ATLANTIC SEAPORT

Our plane is now soaring over the Andes toward the region of fertile river valleys between the mountains which in Peru is called the *sierra*. Be-

yond the mountains lies the *montaña* (mohn-tahn'yah), the great tropical region which forms two thirds of Peru. The little town of Iquitos (ee-kee'tohs) is located on a branch of the Amazon in the *montaña*. This town is the Atlantic port of Peru. Imagine an ocean port 2300 miles away from the ocean! The Amazon is so deep that ocean steamers can make this long trip across the continent to Iquitos. Here they pick up the tropical products of the *montaña*. There are balls of crude rubber which the Indians have collected from the rubber trees; there are Brazil nuts and valuable woods from the forests. These have been brought down the river to Iquitos by launch or Indian rafts or canoes, after a trip by mule trail from the almost inaccessible forests on the mountain slopes. We understand why the goods are not sent over the mountains to a Pacific port when we learn that the journey

OLD SPANISH CHURCHES like this one in the ancient city of Cuzco, Peru, are a common sight in the cities of Latin America. Notice the blanketed Indians and their patient burros in the foreground.

Sawders

over the Andes to Lima takes seventeen uncomfortable days by steamer, steep mule trail, and finally by rail.

THE HIGHLANDS OF PERU ARE THICKLY POPULATED

We turn our attention now to the scene below us as we fly inland toward the *sierra*. We no longer see the green irrigated coastal valleys. There are only bare brown mountains reaching high and higher until their peaks are wrapped in clouds and snow. The cordillera here in Peru is one of the highest mountainous regions in the world. The peaks tower three and even four miles into the heavens. If we fly eastward from Lima, we see a railroad climbing over gorges and through tunnels up to the rich mining regions in the Andes three miles above the sea. Here are the copper mines which have made Peru famous. Gold and silver, too, are mined in the same region. As our plane passes over, we see holes on the mountain-side marking the mines, and zigzag trails leading down to the mountain valleys. The ore is carried to the railroad on the backs of llamas or mules, or frequently, where roads have been built, by truck. The llama, looking like the camel without a hump, is a valuable pack-animal in all the Andean countries.

If we fly south above the high Andes of Central Peru we see below us a series of narrow green valleys which are almost 3000 feet higher than the plateau of Mexico. Millions of Indian people live in these highland valleys, making a living by farming and grazing. On the downward slopes of the surrounding mountains, we see huge flocks of sheep and strange-looking animals resembling long-necked sheep. These are alpacas, raised for their wool, which is extra long and fine.

LAKE TITICACA IS THE GATEWAY TO BOLIVIA

Ahead we soon see the shimmering waters of a large lake. This is Lake Titicaca (tee-tee-cah'cah), situated between Peru and Bolivia and believed to be the highest fresh-water lake in the world. It is also the largest lake in the Americas south of the Great Lakes. As we approach, we see that no trees grow around this lake as we might expect; there are only reeds and rushes. It is too cold on this high plain for trees. There are many small boats on the water, built by the Indians out of the reeds and rushes growing along the shore, and used for fishing and for transportation to various parts of the huge lake.

When we have crossed Lake Titicaca, we are in Bolivia, for the boundary line runs through the middle of the lake. Bolivia is the only Andean country which does not have a sea-coast. Nature has divided it into two regions, the highland section in the west and the great lowland of the north and east. The westerly part is the real Bolivia, where three fourths of the population live. Notice on the map on page 17 how the Andes widen in Bolivia. Between the lofty east and west ranges is the vast plateau of Bolivia covering 40,000 square miles, which is about the size of the state of Ohio. It is believed that Lake Titicaca at one time filled this whole region and later shrank to its present size, leaving this huge, flat tableland. The Bolivian plateau averages 13,000 feet above the sea and is considered the highest civilized district in the world.

Sawders

INDIAN BALSA BOATS on Lake Titicaca are propelled by sails made of reeds. While a steamboat carries today's traveler across this lake, tomorrow's traveler on the Pan-American Highway may take an auto ferry!

HIGHLAND BOLIVIA IS A COLD AND BARREN REGION

We see La Paz (lah pahs'), the highest capital in the world, set in a magnificent canyon a thousand feet below the rest of the plateau. Here it is sheltered from the cold winds and snowstorms of the region above. Low barren mountains rise around the city, and in the background Mount Illimani (ee-lee-mah'nee) looks down from its snowy heights nearly two miles above La Paz. A railroad on the plateau above La Paz connects the city with both Argentina and Chile.

Perhaps you are wondering just how cold it gets up here. The Indians in this region wear knitted caps with earlaps! Actually, the temperature averages about 50 degrees, only 18 degrees above freezing, which means that sometimes it is much colder and sometimes much warmer than that temperature. Although the sun may be warm in the daytime, the nights are cold. Even in summer, it is chilly if you step out of the sun into the shade or into the house.

The plateau above La Paz is a cold and bleak country where only shepherds and miners live. Mining is an important industry of the plateau. Many people think of tin when they think of Bolivia, for this country is second in the world in tin production. Tin is found in the eastern range of the Andes, and is being mined in the same region which has been famous for its silver throughout four hundred years.

EASTERN BOLIVIA IS A HUGE TERRITORY

About three fifths of Bolivia is made up of the forested slopes and lowland plains of the eastern section. On the east side of the cordilleras are valleys with an altitude of 5000 to 8000 feet above sea level, where some agriculture is carried on. These valleys are like the *tierra templada* of Mexico, with abundant moisture and springtime climate.

The largest part of eastern Bolivia is a lowland plain suitable for little else than grazing. During the rainy season much of the level land is flooded by the rivers and becomes a great swamp. When the water drains off into the rivers, the deep grass grows to make a rich pasture land. To the southeast the land is dry, with only stubby grass and shrub for the cattle pastured here. To the far north is the wet, unhealthful Amazon jungle.

CHILE IS THE "SHOESTRING REPUBLIC"

Now our plane swings southwest over the plateau and across the western mountain range of Bolivia toward Chile. When we cross the Tropic of Capricorn south of Bolivia, we shall be leaving the Torrid Zone and entering the South Temperate Zone. We should keep in mind that there will be winter and summer seasons here as there are in the United States. Remember, too, that the seasons are reversed in South America. When we speak of winter in these countries, we mean June, July, and August. Christmas comes in summer in temperate South America.

Let us find Chile on the map. Doesn't it look like a mere sliver of territory? It has been called the "Shoestring Republic," which is a good description of its 2700 miles of length and its width of 50 to 200 miles between the ocean and the Andes. It

C. H. Haring

LOFTY LA PAZ cannot be seen from the plateau unless you stand on the edge of the canyon and look down. It is an amazing sight to see a large city at the bottom of a great hole in the earth.

THIS INDIAN SHEPHERD of the Bolivian plateau keeps his ears warm as he plays his flute! His ancestors were playing flutes like this one long before our ancestors set foot in America.

Sawders

is almost as long as the United States is wide, while its width could be covered by a drive of three or four hours in a car. Notice that the Andes run the full length of Chile and cover a third of its width. They rise very high in the central region and taper off into the sea in the south. In the northern half of Chile a coast range rises from the sea in a high bluff. You may be wondering where people can live in this strip of land. Between the coast range and the Andes is a depression which in the north is a low, dry plateau and in central Chile is a

CHILE'S COAST rises bleak and barren above one of its northern ports. Notice the white bags of flour in the barge, brought in to feed a desert community.

C. H. Haring

long, fertile valley. This is where most of the Chileans live.

RAIN IS A CALAMITY IN NORTHERN CHILE

Our first glimpse of Chile is not encouraging. We are flying over a gray land with not one living thing appearing on it, no trees, no grass, not even cactus. It seems to be a complete desert, with here and there great holes like giant pockmarks. To the west is the rocky, brown bluff of the coast range. To the east loom the Andes with several snowy volcanoes standing guard over the desolate scene.

Strangely enough, this earth which appears so dead is the source of life and growth when used on plants. For here in northern Chile is a 500-mile deposit of nitrate of soda, the rich fertilizer which has made Chile famous and wealthy. The holes we see are the old workings where the nitrate has been removed. Some of the largest copper mines in the world are also located here.

We are looking at the driest region known to man. There is one section on this desert where only six tenths of an inch of rain has fallen in twenty-one years! This is one place where rain is not wanted, for it would wash out the nitrate beds and bring ruin to the nitrate industry.

In Chile, as in Peru, the Humboldt Current keeps this coast dry and rainless. But once in a great while something goes wrong with this cold current from the south. It moves out to sea and warm waters from the north flow in between it and the land, bringing heavy rains. Millions of fish die in the unaccustomed warm waters, and millions of sea birds starve, or are killed from eating the dead fish. At one time water for drinking had to be brought into Chile's northern desert by ships; now it is piped down from the Andes. If you lived in one of the cities of the nitrate coast, you would find it difficult to have a lawn or a flower garden. Water is too scarce for such luxuries.

THE CENTRAL VALLEY OF CHILE IS A GARDEN PARADISE

Narrow, green river valleys here and there show us that we are coming to the end of this northern desert region. After we pass Valparaiso, the beautiful, fertile central valley of Chile stretches out beneath us. This valley, about 500 miles long and 20 or 30 miles wide, is one of the richest agricultural districts in the world. It is the heart of Chile, containing 90 per cent of its population and much of its wealth. In climate and products it resembles California, which is not surprising because they lie in about the same latitude. Orchards of apples, oranges, figs, and olives flash by; grape vineyards and fields of wheat, barley, and corn appear and are gone.

Many streams tumble down the west wall of the Andes, cross the valley, and disappear into the coast range. At the southern end of the valley is the Chilean lake region, a spot so beautiful that few visitors wish to miss it. Set like jewels in the green foothills of the Andes, these lakes are making Chile famous as a vacation land.

SOUTHERN CHILE IS A CHAIN OF ISLANDS AND FIORDS

We have seen all of Chile except the southernmost region. The smooth western coast of the continent is broken in the south by numberless islands. At some time in the past, the southern coast of Chile sank into the sea, leaving a chain of islands, and numerous fiords to mark where the coast range had once been. The lofty Andes as we have known them all the way down the coast have disappeared; the mountains of this land are lower and covered with forest. Southern Chile is as wet as northern Chile is dry, for it is in the path of the westerly winds from the Pacific which keep it

TIERRA DEL FUEGO with its majestic glaciers offers an amazing contrast to Chile's northern coast. The Straits of Magellan, too dangerous for sailing ships, were not used until the invention of the steamboat.

Sawders

drenched with rain as they rise to cross the mountains.

Note on the map where the Straits of Magellan cut through the southern tip. A little later you will learn how the daring Magellan made his way through these winding straits on his trip around the world. This cold land of snow and glaciers south of the strait was called Tierra del Fuego (tee-ay'rah del foo-ay'go), or "Land of Fire," by the explorer because of the many Indian campfires which glowed along the shores. Glacier-covered mountains rise up from the fiords in glistening beauty. Much of the land is covered with grass in summer and makes good pasture for sheep. The city of Punta Arenas (poon'tah ah-ray'nahs) has the distinction of being the farthest south of any city in the world.

We shall now take a plane from Santiago in central Chile and fly toward the Andes and Argentina; from there we shall start our journey over the Atlantic coast of South America.

Are You a Careful Reader?   Test Yourself!

I. Choose the best answer:

1. It is winter in Chile when it is summer here because: (*a*) the Southern Hemisphere is tipped away from the sun during June and July; (*b*) it is nearer the South Pole; (*c*) the rays of the sun never hit Chile directly.

2. Living is difficult for the people in the highland valleys of the Andes because: (*a*) all woolen clothes must be woven from llama wool; (*b*) the rivers are the only means of transportation; (*c*) not many crops grow at high elevations.

3. Rain is a calamity in northern Chile because: (*a*) all agriculture depends on controlled irrigation; (*b*) the valuable nitrates would be dissolved; (*c*) the people live in adobe huts which dissolve under heavy rain.

4. The people of the Andean countries live in the highlands because: (*a*) they prefer the cool climate; (*b*) they cannot make a living in the lowlands; (*c*) they are protected from their enemies.

5. The coast of Peru is cool because: (*a*) it is not in the Torrid Zone; (*b*) it is located in a high altitude; (*c*) it is cooled by the Humboldt Current.

II. Match these words and statements:

1. Oriente	*a.*	highest peak in Peru
2. La Paz	*b.*	river in lowland Ecuador
3. Punta Arenas	*c.*	region east of the Andes in Amazon Valley
4. Titicaca	*d.*	river of Colombia
5. Magdalena	*e.*	farthest-south city in the world
6. Bogotá	*f.*	mountain region of Peru
7. Ecuador	*g.*	highest capital in the world
8. Chimborazo	*h.*	lake between Bolivia and Peru
9. Guayas	*i.*	Peruvian port on the Amazon
10. Iquitos	*j.*	capital of Colombia
	k.	mountain peak in Ecuador
	l.	west coast country which is crossed by the Equator

Food for Thought and Discussion

1. What are the three geographical regions of the Andes and why do they differ in climate, population, and products?

2. Can you explain why the products of the Oriente and the *montaña* are not exported from Pacific ports?

3. Why are the crops of Chile similar to those of the United States?

4. Did your reading in this chapter help you to answer any of the questions given in the unit preview on page 5?

Chapter 3

We See the Eastern Coast of South America from the Air

WE FLY OVER THE ANDES TO BUENOS AIRES

WE ARE READY to cross the Andes and see the countries of eastern South America. The plane leaves Santiago and heads for the famous Uspallata (oos-pah-yah'tah) Pass. This historic route through the mountains has been used for hundreds of years, first by the Indians and then by the Spanish colonists. Today both railroad and plane use this break in the huge spine of the Andes to cross from Chile to neighboring Argentina.

Our plane climbs to 10,000 feet, then to 15,000, and finally levels off to cross between the mightiest peaks of the Andes. We look out upon snowy grandeur. To the north, Aconcagua (ah-kohn-cah'gwah), monarch of the Western Hemisphere, rears its snowy crown into the heavens to a height of over four miles! Near the summit of the Andes, we see the great statue known as "The Christ of the Andes." With cross lifted high in air above the border of Chile and Argentina, it commemorates the peaceful settlement of a boundary dispute between the two countries.

The pass between the mountains broadens out as the plane gradually lowers and starts the long trip down the east slopes of the Andes. We get our last sight of the great backbone of the continent which has been so important a part of every country whose map we have unfolded from the air.

Galloway

"THE CHRIST OF THE ANDES" was dedicated with this solemn pledge: "Sooner shall these mountains crumble to dust than Argentines and Chileans break the peace sworn to at the feet of Christ the Redeemer."

As we descend above the brown foothills, we look out upon a land entirely different from any we have seen so far. Let us consider for a moment the important features of Argentina so that we can understand what we shall see from the air.

ARGENTINA IS A LAND OF VARIETY

Almost as long as Chile, but many times wider, the wedge-shaped Republic of Argentina occupies most of the temperate land in South America. It is more like the United States in climate and products than any other country of this continent. Argentina extends over many more degrees of latitude than does the United States, reaching from the warm lands of the Torrid Zone on the north to the cold lands of Tierra del Fuego far to the south below the Straits of Magellan. We shall not be surprised to learn of wet tropical forests in the north, or of vineyards in the foothills of the Andes, as well as fields of corn and wheat in the central plains. The temperature of most of Argentina is like that of the United States and Canada except that the seasons are reversed. In the Torrid Zone of the north, of course, the climate is that of the tropics, but for most of the country, January is hot and July is cold.

With the Andes behind us, we look down upon an endless gray-green plain. We see miles and miles of fruit orchards and vineyards. Knowing that westerly winds from the Pacific cannot cross the mountains without losing their moisture, we wonder how this green garden can flourish here. Rivers rising among the melting snows of the Andes run through here, and are used to irrigate the vineyards. The grapes and fruit of this section ripen in the fall, and since this is springtime in the United States, the fruit is much in demand. North of this fruit region is another irrigated region where sugar is grown.

As we travel eastward, the plain becomes greener and soon an immense, grassy prairie stretches in all directions as far as our eyes can see. We are looking at the famous pampa (pahm'pah), the heart of Argentina. Thousands of cattle are grazing in the tall grass below. Here and there ranch houses and a cluster of trees break the monotony of the flat plains. As we fly nearer to Buenos Aires (bway'nohs eye'rays), cultivated fields of wheat, alfalfa, and corn appear. Although the pampa occupies only one fourth of the area of Argentina, it contains the largest part of the population and many of the important cities. This region furnishes about one tenth of the world's wheat, two thirds of the exported corn, and four fifths of the chilled or frozen beef.

On our way eastward we cross a beautiful hilly region called the *Sierra de Córdoba* (kor'doh-bah), a favorite summer resort of the Argentine people. Farther north lies the Gran Chaco (grahn chah'ko), or "great hunting ground," which continues beyond Argentina into western Paraguay. It is a flat country covered with scrub and forest, with alternating wet and dry seasons. Cotton is grown here, and lumbering is an important industry. Notice that northern Argentina is near the tropics and grows the same products as our own South. South of the pampa in Patagonia, the plain becomes barren, cold, and dry. In the summer there is enough scrubby grass for sheep, and millions of them are raised for wool.

THE ARGENTINE PAMPA is famous for its fine beef cattle. Some of the finest stock in the world is raised on this vast prairie. The climate of the pampa is so mild that no shelter is needed for the cattle.

Sawders

BUENOS AIRES, one of the most beautiful cities of the Americas, boasts modern buildings, wide boulevards, and many parks. This picture shows Colón Park with its tree-lined avenues.

THE PLATA RIVER SYSTEM DRAINS FOUR COUNTRIES

As our plane flies farther east, we see that the farming region of the pampa becomes more thickly settled, and cities and villages grow numerous. We are over the suburbs of Buenos Aires, the "City of Good Airs," on the Río de la Plata (ree'oh day lah plah'tah). This city is the capital of Argentina and third largest in the Western Hemisphere. Look at the map on page 17 for the Plata River system, which drains northeastern Argentina, southern Brazil, and Uruguay and Paraguay. This is the southernmost of the three great river systems of South America. The two

rivers which you see flowing into the Río de la Plata near Buenos Aires are the Paraná (pah-rah-nah') and the Uruguay. They and the Paraná's great tributary, the Paraguay River, rise far to the north in Brazil and flow through a territory of over a million square miles.

The Plata itself looks like a huge arm of the sea, but a taste of its water would prove that it is not, for the water in this river mouth is fresh, not salt. In flood season its muddy current can be seen far out in the ocean. The length of the Plata is about 100 miles. At Buenos Aires it is only 23 miles wide, but at the mouth it is about 130 miles across.

32

Here is one river wider than it is long!

PARAGUAY AND URUGUAY ARE NEIGHBORS OF ARGENTINA

Our route by air does not take us over the little country of Paraguay, tucked in between Brazil, Argentina, and Bolivia. Although this country is warm and fertile, only a small part of it is cultivated. There is a belt along the east side of the Paraguay River where sugar cane, tobacco, and cotton are raised. The most valuable product of Paraguay is Paraguay tea, or *yerba maté* (yer'bah mah-tay'). This beverage, made by pouring boiling water over the dried leaves of a tree resembling our northern laurel, is a drink of millions of South Americans.

Many people touch Paraguay on their way to see the famous Iguassú (ee-gwah-soo') Falls on a branch of the Paraná River. These spectacular falls are not only higher and wider than Niagara, but are believed to excel Niagara in beauty.

We set out now along the coast of South America, flying down the wide Plata and over Montevideo (mohn-tay-vee-day'oh), the capital of Uruguay. This smallest of South American republics occupies a little corner between Brazil and Argentina. As the country unrolls below us, we see neither jungle, desert, nor mountains. Uruguay is a land of green rolling plains which make excellent grazing for cattle and sheep. Although there is some farming done, most of the country is given over to stock raising, Uruguay's chief industry.

THE PANHANDLE OF BRAZIL IS IN THE TEMPERATE ZONE

Continuing north, we look down upon the Temperate Zone lands of southeastern Brazil. This section, sometimes called the "panhandle," has the same fertile plains and rolling

THE IGUASSÚ FALLS are among the scenic wonders of the world. Located on the Iguassú River between Brazil and Argentina, this great fall of water stretches in majestic beauty for over two miles.

Gendreau

woods we have passed in Uruguay. We see the same unending herds of cattle. This section of Brazil counts its cattle and sheep by the millions and equals the other Plata countries in the production of meat and hides.

Gradually the scene below us changes. The green coast becomes sandy, palm trees appear, and soon we recognize the familiar coast lands of the tropics. Before more of this fascinating land of Brazil appears, let us look at the map on page 17.

BRAZIL IS HALF HIGHLAND, HALF JUNGLE

It is not difficult to find the country which occupies nearly half of South America! Brazil touches every country on the continent except Ecuador and Chile. This country alone is larger than the United States. If we placed a map of Brazil on a map of Europe, it would hide the whole continent. It is difficult to talk about Brazil without using the words "richest," "greatest," and "largest." For in addition to its size, Brazil has been blessed by Nature with an enormous variety and extent of natural resources.

People are inclined to think of Brazil as a huge jungle. It is true that the greatest jungle in the world lies in the Amazon valley in the north. But that is not all of Brazil. Over half of the country is made up of a second very important region, the Brazilian Highlands. A high tableland or plateau rises above the sea in the southeast to a height of 1000 to 3000 feet. There is a coastal range of mountains on the edge of the plateau which makes travel into the interior difficult. Like the other tropical highlands we have seen, the highlands of Brazil have a pleasant climate, with warm days and cool nights.

Below the plateau over which we are now flying is a narrow coastal lowland. On this coast and in the highlands are the important cities of Brazil, as well as nine tenths of the population. Unlike the Pacific coast of South America, there are excellent harbors on the Atlantic side. The heat of the coast is tempered by the southeast trade winds from the sea.

BRAZIL IS THE COFFEE–POT OF THE WORLD

Santos (sahn'tohs), the world's greatest coffee port, appears below us now. The highlands of Brazil inland from Santos are ideal for growing coffee. The billion trees planted here furnish over 65 per cent of the world's coffee, a large part of which is shipped from Santos. Santos is connected by railroad through the mountains with São Paulo (sow pow'loo), the highland city in the heart of the coffee district, half a mile above the ocean. From São Paulo you can travel for miles over the famous coffee plantations of Brazil.

Farther inland where there is less rainfall are the scrub and grasslands of Mato Grosso (mah'toh groh'soh), a low plateau most of which is uncultivated. This is the great frontier of Brazil. Today because of its remoteness very few people live there, but in the future it may provide a home for countless numbers of pioneer settlers.

Next our northbound clipper takes us over the city of Rio de Janeiro (ree'oh day zhah-nay'roh), which has one of the most unusual and beautiful harbors in the world. Black, jagged mountains surround the city and a few even rear up in the bay beyond.

Guillumette

RIO DE JANEIRO with its magnificent harbor presents a view of breath-taking beauty when viewed from the hills above the city. The famous Sugar Loaf stands guard at the harbor's entrance.

One of them, the Sugar Loaf, is a noted landmark of Rio de Janeiro.

The coastal area widens as we fly north and there are hundreds of miles of sugar, corn, and cotton plantations. It is only from the air that we can get a picture of the immensity of the productive lands of Brazil. Although most of us do not know it, Brazil has more land suitable for cotton than our well-known southern states. Cotton growing in the São Paulo region has increased enormously in recent years. We pass coast cities where the products of Brazil are loaded on ships from all over the world.

THE AMAZON REGION IS THE LAND OF TOMORROW

As we round the east corner of Brazil, we leave the highland region and approach the great lowlands of the Amazon. One traveler has called the Amazon River basin the "Land of Tomorrow" because it has great possibilities for the future. Its millions of moist and fertile acres could be made to supply tropical products for the whole world if Nature's obstacles could be removed. Today malaria, floods, jungles, and terrific heat make development almost impossible.

It is hard to appreciate the size of the Amazon basin. Notice on the map the great network of rivers flowing from the north, west, and south to join the Amazon. These rivers drain over two million square miles in northern Brazil, an area equal to two thirds of the United States. The Amazon itself is the largest river in the world. It is so wide that in many places you could travel on it without seeing the trees on either bank. It is so deep that ocean vessels can run to Iquitos near the Pacific coast. Any

one of its large tributaries carries more water than the Mississippi. It carries so much more water than the Mississippi that if we should put the Amazon in the Mississippi basin, the central part of the United States would probably become a huge lake!

Why is the Amazon such a large river? Because the rainfall is very heavy in tropical Brazil and the excess water drains off into the rivers. During the season of heaviest rainfall, some of the rivers rise from 30 to 40 feet, overflowing their banks until the surrounding lowlands stand deep in water. The Amazon lowlands, like the east coast of Central America, lie in the path of the northeast trade winds. These winds become heated as they blow over the hot basin of the Amazon. When they rise, as hot air does, they strike the cooler air above and their moisture condenses in torrents of rain.

THE AMAZON JUNGLE IS LARGELY UNEXPLORED

As we have observed before in our travels, excessive heat and moisture cause the tropical rain forest to flourish. The forests of the Amazon are called *selvas* (sel'vahs) and, except for a few cleared places along the river, cover the whole region. The sun never reaches the interior of this dark forest. Plants that need the sun must struggle to stretch above the other vegetation.

Many parts of the valley are unknown land. The Amazon region does not welcome exploration into the interior. To travel by land, trails must be hacked out of the dense growth, and are soon overgrown again. Heat, tropic fevers, burrowing insects, and mosquitoes lie in wait for those bold

Sawders

CLEARING THE AMAZON JUNGLE is back-breaking labor. These workers are felling trees on a Brazilian rubber plantation which is being run as an experiment by Henry Ford.

men who dare venture into the jungle. A few Indians who seem to be immune to tropical diseases live along the river, hunting and fishing for a living.

Hidden in the jungle are wondrous sights. Creepers and vines grow as large as trees and countless ferns carpet the floor of the forest. There are monstrous spiders and butterflies nine inches across. The jungle is also the home of huge snakes like the boa constrictors, anacondas, and rattlers. The armadillo with its armored coat, the long-nosed anteater, and the sloth who hangs upside down are included among the citizens of the forest.

We have already described the Amazon from the Andes down to the sea. The wide expanse of yellow waters we now see below us is the king of rivers. Its muddy waters are visible far out to sea, as though this great old river disliked to lose itself in the ocean.

VENEZUELA IS THE LAST COUNTRY WE VISIT

Our plane now heads for Venezuela. On the way we pass over the three Guianas — French, Dutch, and British — which are colonies of those three nations and are not considered part of Latin America.

The Republic of Venezuela on the Caribbean has much more in common with the Andean countries than it has with Brazil. It has the three regions we found in most of the Pacific countries: the tropical coast, the highland region, and the hot interior lowlands. For good measure, Venezuela has another highland region far in the interior. In area not so large as Colombia, this republic has much the same resources and geography.

As we fly beyond the Guianas, we see huge mud flats cut through by streams of water. This is the delta of the Orinoco, one of the three large rivers of the continent. If we could fly up this river, we should see the central lowland of Venezuela, drained by the Orinoco and its tributaries. There would be vast stretches of grassy pasture land which are part of the *llanos* we saw in Colombia. Some cattle are raised here, but the *llanos* are not developed like the pampa of Argentina. This is partly because of the intense heat of these tropical pastures and partly because they are flooded in the rainy season. During this time the cattle must be moved to higher ground. It is such disadvantages as these that have hindered the development of tropical countries.

Like other navigable rivers of South America, the Orinoco and its branches take the place of roads. Large ships go 200 miles up the river to pick up cattle. Smaller boats can travel way into Colombia. The extreme southern portion of Venezuela is part of the Guiana Highlands. It is almost uninhabited and difficult to reach.

Let us continue along the coast to the northern part of Venezuela. The eastern range of the Andes in Colombia continues on into Venezuela along the rim of the Caribbean. As in the other Andean states, the mountains furnish cool and healthful plateaus high above the hot coast. Here are coffee and sugar plantations and fields of corn and wheat. The capital of Venezuela, Caracas (kah-rah'kas), is only 3000 feet above sea level. It is connected with the port on the coast by a concrete highway. Around

Lake Maracaibo (mah-rah-kye'boh) in northwestern Venezuela is one of the world's greatest oil-producing areas. When you read the story of Venezuela, you will learn more about this oil region.

HISPANIOLA AND CUBA COMPLETE OUR AIR–VIEW

We shall now leave the continent of South America and head for Miami, Florida, the end of our route. We shall go by way of the islands that border the Caribbean on the north and east — the West Indies. The West Indies are made up of three groups of islands, the Lesser Antilles, the Greater Antilles, and the Bahamas. On the map on page 4 you can see how the Lesser Antilles describe a graceful arc on the eastern edge of the Caribbean, the tiny islands set like stepping stones from Venezuela to Puerto Rico. You can see also that the Greater Antilles are a group of much larger islands with Puerto Rico at the eastern end, Cuba at the western, and Jamaica and Hispaniola in between. The Bahamas lie in the Atlantic, north of the Greater Antilles.

Our route takes us north from Lake Maracaibo over the sparkling waters of the Caribbean to Hispaniola. This tropical island, with its luxuriant green fields and snow-topped mountains, reminds us of the small countries of Central America. The trade winds water the north coast, but the high mountains in the center prevent the rain from reaching the southwest coast. We see sugar plantations on the lowlands, coffee plantations in the upper valleys. In the dry interior of the island, cattle and sheep find pasture land. As in other tropical countries with plenty of rain, there are forests of valuable woods.

Leaving Hispaniola, we fly westward toward Cuba. Our first impression of Cuba, as we see it from the eastern end, is that it is another mountainous island. But the high peaks soon disappear and Cuba becomes a low, rolling plain. Much of the island is covered with forest. Miles of pale green sugar fields flash past beneath us. The soil, climate, and abundant rainfall combine to make Cuba the leader of the world in the production of cane sugar. Can you imagine a pile of sugar weighing 6,000,000 tons? That is the amount Cuba produces in a year! Tobacco is the next most important crop of Cuba. As we pass over Havana, the beautiful capital of Cuba, we bid farewell to the tropics. Once more we cross the Tropic of Cancer and enter the Temperate Zone of the United States. In a short time we land at Miami, and our air-view of the Latin American countries is over.

Are You a Careful Reader?   Test Yourself!

I. Supply the correct word for each blank:

1. The lowlands of the Orinoco River valley in Venezuela are called the . . . . .
2. New York and Chicago are the only cities in the Western Hemisphere larger than . . . .
3. A river system which drains four South American countries is called the . . . . .
4. The greatest coffee-growing region in the world is in . . . . .
5. . . . . is one of the largest meat- and grain-producing countries in the world.

II. Match these words and statements:

1. pampa	*a.*	lake in Venezuela where oil is produced
2. Tierra del Fuego	*b.*	river rising in Brazil and flowing into the Plata
3. Uspallata	*c.*	highest peak in the Andes
4. Gran Chaco	*d.*	historic pass between Argentina and Chile
5. Montevideo	*e.*	plains of Venezuela in the Orinoco Valley
6. Paraná	*f.*	Argentine prairies where cattle are raised
7. Cuba	*g.*	capital of Venezuela
8. Maracaibo	*h.*	southernmost province of Argentina
9. Caracas	*i.*	Caribbean island famous for its sugar and tobacco
10. Aconcagua	*j.*	capital of Uruguay
	k.	"great hunting ground" on Argentine-Paraguay border
	l.	land south of the Straits of Magellan

Food for Thought and Discussion

1. Can you give good reasons why the Amazon region is not developed?
2. Why are the products of Argentina, Uruguay, and southern Brazil much alike?
3. Why are there larger cities and more trade on the east coast of South America than on the west?

Looking Backward

We have now completed the air-view of our Latin American neighbors. As you read, did you keep in mind the questions given in the preview on page 5? Can you answer them now? If not, you need more study on this part of the book. Be ready to use the questions as your teacher directs, either for discussion in class or as written work.

How to Find Material for "Interesting Things to Do"

When you have finished studying each one of the parts of this book, you will be ready to work on projects which will help you to learn more about the material in the chapters. At the end of each part you will find a list of suggested projects under the heading INTERESTING THINGS TO DO. For many of these activities you will need to look up additional information. Your success will depend in part on how skillfully you use the library. The following suggestions may help you to locate the information:

1. *Magazines.* The *Readers' Guide to Periodical Literature*, an annual publication, lists articles about Latin America which are published in all current magazines. The index of the National Geographic Society lists by topic all of the articles which have ever been published in the *National Geographic Magazine*. The magazines called *Modern Mexico* and *Américas*, the latter of which is listed in the *Readers' Guide*, contain information which will be especially helpful to you. Remember to look in more than one volume of the *Readers' Guide* in order to get all the articles which have been published on your subject. Then find out what bound volumes of magazines are available in your own school library or your local library.

2. *Books.* The books available in a library are usually listed in a *card index* or *catalogue.* The books are listed both by author and by subject. Using the author's name, look in the card catalogue of your library for the books listed in the bibliography at the end of each part. Since you will probably not know the names of other authors who have written on Latin America, you will then need to use the subject index.

In looking for a particular subject, such as "the beef industry of Argentina," remember to look under several different headings for key words, such as these: cattle, beef, livestock, Argentina, pampa, gaucho, South American industry, agriculture of Argentina, trade at Buenos Aires, etc.

If your library has the Dewey Decimal system of numbering books, you can soon learn to find books by their call number. Here is a list of general types of books which you may use and their Dewey Decimal classifications:

> South American travel books, 918
> Mexican and Central American travel books, 917.2
> South American history books, 980
> Mexican history books, 972
> History of colonial times, 970
> World geography books, 909–910

If you understand this classification you can go quickly to the library shelves and get books which contain helpful material. Remember that the index of a book lists alphabetically all the topics that are mentioned in the book. Be sure to look for key words in the book index just as you did in the card catalogue of the library.

For general use any good up-to-date encyclopedia provides a great amount of valuable information on Latin American countries.

3. *Pamphlets.* A committee may write the Pan American Union in Washington, D.C., for pamphlets or recent bibliographies on any phase of Latin America. Other good sources of information are: the consulates of Latin American nations in the nearest large city, the chambers of commerce in large cities, travel agencies, and companies like the United Fruit Company which import products from Latin America.

Interesting Things to Do

1. Make a relief map of clay or papier mâché showing the mountains, rivers, river valleys, coastal lowlands, and plains of Latin America.

2. Draw picture maps showing native plants and animals of the tropical jungles, the Andean region, or the pampa.

3. Be a nature-study explorer. Report to the class on animals or birds found either in the jungle, in the Andes, or on the pampa.

4. Read and report on the work of the following naturalists in Latin America: Baron von Humboldt, William Beebe, Charles Darwin, Wilson Popenoe.

5. Using a globe, explain to the class the reversal of the seasons in the Southern Hemisphere or explain the formation of the cordilleras by volcanic action.

6. Find out all you can about one of the famous volcanoes mentioned in Part I.

7. Look up and report to the class about the constellation, the Southern Cross. Why can it not be seen in the United States?

8. Make a language survey to find out what Spanish classes are offered at your school, how many members of your class study Spanish, whether they use Castilian or Latin American pronunciation.

9. Find out what radio programs are broadcast from Latin America to which members of your class can listen. If possible, listen in on a Latin American program.

10. Plan an airplane trip to Latin America. Send to the Pan American Airways or other tourist agency for literature and write your itinerary.

11. Start a correspondence with a "pen chum" of your own age in Latin America. Write to the Pan American Union for a list of agencies which arrange correspondence in English with Latin American students.

12. There are many Spanish words used in your text. Keep a list of them in your notebook with their meanings. An occasional spelldown will keep you up-to-date.

Interesting Books to Read

For Further Information

Carlson, Fred, *Geography of Latin America.* Prentice-Hall. One of the most usable geography reference books.

Davies, Howell, ed., *South American Handbook.* Wilson. Factual information published yearly.

Hager, Alice Rogers, *Wings Over the Americas.* Macmillan. Geography told as an airplane trip.

Goetz, Delia, *Neighbors to the South.* Harcourt. Interesting general account.

Rothery, Agnes, *South American Roundabout.* Dodd Mead. Geography and travel combined.

For Pleasure

Halliburton, Richard, *New Worlds To Conquer.* Bobbs Merrill. A "hitch hiker's" trip covering the route described in this unit.

Lamb, Dana, *Enchanted Vagabonds.* Harpers. A canoe trip along Latin America's tropical west coast.

Saint-Exupéry, Antoine, *Night Flight.* Appleton. A famous aviator's account of the air trip to Buenos Aires.

Tschiffely, Aimé, *Tschiffely's Ride.* Grosset. A three-year horseback trip covering the same route.

Part Two · THREE GREAT INDIAN

FLOURISHED IN

Pueblo
Indians

ATLANTIC

GULF OF

OCEAN

MEXICO

Tropic of Cancer

Teotihuacán
Tenochtitlán · L. Texcoco

Uxmal · Mayapán
· Chichén Itzá

AZTEC EMPIRE
Mitla ·
(Zapotecs)

MAYAN

EMPIRE

C A R I B B E A N   S E A

P A C I F I C

Chibcha
Indians

O C E A N

Equator

QUITO

Chimu
Kingdom

Chan Chan ·

Machu
Picchu

Great Wall
of Chimus

· Sacsahuamán

Cuzco ·

· L. Titicaca
· Colla People
Tiahuanaco

Tropic of Capricorn

GREAT INDIAN
EMPIRES

|||| 1st Mayan Empire
300 BC · 600 AD

━━ 2nd Mayan Empire
600 AD · 1400 AD

//// Aztec Empire
controlled by Montezuma

\\\\ Aztec Empire
paying tribute

0   500   1000

SCALE IN MILES

CIVILIZATIONS ONCE

LATIN AMERICA

As you looked down upon Latin America during the air trip, did you wonder how these twenty countries came to be what they are today? Historians, you know, are fond of saying, "The roots of the present are deep in the past." This is another way of saying that if we wish to understand the present we must first know something about the people and the events which have gone before. As we shall see, the roots of the Latin American republics are indeed buried deep in the past.

The past of Latin America reaches back to a time long before any Europeans set foot upon this hemisphere. In the following chapters we shall turn back the clock a few hundred years and visit the same land we have just seen from the air. We shall find the face of the land much the same, but the people and the cities very different. The inhabitants of Latin America five hundred years ago had never seen a European. Completely unaware of the Old World and its history, they had achieved their own civilization on the American continents. Their great stone cities, irrigated fields, and fine handicraft gave proof of the culture they had developed.

Before we visit these civilized Indians, suppose we learn a little about where and when they lived. Can you locate the Inca Empire on the map opposite? On what continent is it located? Find also the empires of the Mayans and the Aztecs. In what part of Latin America did they live? Which tribe had the largest territory?

The time chart on the following page is included to give you a clear picture of the rise and fall of the Indian civilizations. It also shows at a glance the relationship in time between the Spanish and English colonies and the Indian empires. Can you tell which Indian empire was established first and which last? What caused the downfall of these civilizations?

As you read Part II, try to keep these questions in mind:

1. How did we learn the story of the Indian empires?
2. How far did the Indians actually advance in civilization?
3. Why was the science of astronomy so highly developed by the Indians?

Time Chart Showing Rise and Fall of Great Indian Empires

Date	INCA EMPIRE	MAYAN EMPIRES	AZTEC EMPIRE	EARLY SPANISH EMPIRE	EARLY ENGLISH EMPIRE
Before A.D. 500		Rise of first Mayan Empire in Guatemala			
500–1000	Colla people establish kingdom near Lake Titicaca	First Mayan Empire at height; Mayans migrate to Yucatan	Toltecs establish home in Valley of Mexico		
1000–1100	Inca tribes near Cuzco start conquest of neighboring Indians	Second Mayan Empire at height; League of Mayan cities established			
1100–1200	Incas conquer land farther north and southward to Lake Titicaca; First Inca emperor	Civil war starts between Mayan cities; Toltecs from Mexico conquer warring Mayan cities	Toltecs control Valley of Mexico; Build Teotihuacán; Send warriors to Yucatan		
1200–1300	Incas learn to build with stone; Fight wild tribes from east of Andes; Cross Andes to west coast	Mayans accept Toltec leaders; Adopt Toltec religion and worship Quetzalcoatl	Aztecs still wandering tribes in northern Mexico		
1300–1400	Incas extend conquests south into Chile and Argentina	Continued civil war	Aztecs settle in Valley of Mexico; Build city of Tenochtitlan		
1400–1500	Inca Empire reaches its height; Kingdom of Chimus conquered	Toltecs depart; Mayan cities decay	Aztecs form confederacy; Capture many tribes; Montezuma I becomes ruler of Aztec Confederacy	Columbus discovers America	
1500–1600	Inca Empire divided into two kingdoms; Empire ends when Pizarro kills Atahualpa and conquers Incas	Mayan cities are conquered by Spaniards	Aztec Empire reaches height under Montezuma II; Empire ends when Cortez conquers Aztecs	Spanish explorers and conquerors claim great empire for Spain; Empire extends from Mexico to Argentina	Sir Francis Drake sails around world, claims California for England
1600–1700				Spain's empire grows in size and wealth; Great cities reflect Spanish culture; Trade brings wealth to Spain	First English colonies founded on Atlantic coast; Life still primitive; No large cities

Chapter 4

Ancient Cities Reveal the Story of Great Indian Civilizations

THE INDIANS WERE THE FIRST AMERICANS

HAVE YOU VISITED the cliff dwellings in the southwestern United States, or seen the staircase houses of the Pueblo Indians who live in New Mexico today? Perhaps some of you have visited Mexico City and have seen the great pyramids. Even in your own community there may be Indian mounds or relics of ancient Indian villages. The Indian people were the original inhabitants of the Americas. Ruins of their villages and cities are scattered from our own United States as far south as Chile. Many of these Indian civilizations had risen and fallen before white men ever saw the Western Hemisphere.

A RUINED CITY TELLS ITS STORY

Long ago, before Europeans knew the Americas existed, there was a great city in South America called Chanchan (chahn-chahn). It was the capital city of the Chimu (chee'-moo) Indians, who are often given this name because their king was called Chimu. They lived in a fertile river valley between the mountains and the sea in northern Peru. Chanchan extended over seven square miles. Perhaps 100,000 people lived within its gates, protected by a great wall from neighboring mountain tribes. On this wall forts were built at regular distances and armed warriors stayed on guard to ward off attack.

Chanchan was a colorful city, for gay figures adorned the walls of the terraced buildings. Stone was not used in this city, because the quarries were too far away in the mountains. The Indians used sun-baked mud, plastered the walls, and decorated them with bright designs. In the center of the city was the Chimu's palace. Its walls were decorated with beautiful paintings. There was also a great temple in Chanchan where the Chimus worshiped. Busy people thronged the streets, dressed in the vivid colors the Indians loved.

Outside the city, roads paved in stone led in all directions to outlying villages and farms. Llamas and their drivers filled the roads, carrying goods from farm to city. The fertile soil grew many crops, among them cotton, which they used for cloth. Since they lived in desert country where rainfall was scarce, the Chimus had a system of irrigation ditches and canals to bring water from the rivers to their farms. Some of them made a living in the near-by sea, fishing from rafts which they had built.

The Chimus made their bowls and

CHANCHAN was divided into blocks or compounds, each containing streets, courts, and dwellings. This aerial photograph shows the construction of one of these blocks much more clearly than archeologists can see it from the ground.

dishes and drinking vessels of pottery. These artistic people were not content to leave their utensils plain and undecorated, so they painted scenes from their daily lives on bowls and vases. There were dancers, armed warriors, fishermen, swimmers, and women decked in bright clothing. Sometimes they even molded the faces of their friends on the pots, shaping in clay a mischievous boy or a man with bad teeth and a big nose.

The Chimus liked to wear gay colors. Their women used dyes of red, blue, and yellow to make cloth with colored patterns. Their cloth of llama wool was closer and finer than any our machines can make today. They made thread by twisting a fiber of wool or cotton in their fingers with the help of a spindle.

In spite of their great wall and their warriors, the Chimus were conquered by a tribe from the highlands. From then on Chanchan became less and less important. When the Spaniards came, they tore up the city in search of the treasure they had been told was buried there. Today Chanchan, the pride of the Chimus, stands in ruins.

The Chimus never learned to write, so they left no written records. How, then, do we know about their city and their civilization? Because they have left behind them evidence which tells their story almost as clearly as if it had been written. The very walls of this ruined city reveal secrets today that have lain hidden from the eyes of man for centuries. Buried ornaments, heaps of broken pottery, graveyards — all have information to give those who are trained to interpret it.

ARCHEOLOGISTS READ THE EVIDENCE LEFT BY ANCIENT INDIANS

The scientists who study the ruined cities of early civilizations and the buried relics of ancient people are called archeologists. Their science is archeology, which means in Greek "study of old things." It was the archeologists working in the ruins of Chanchan who pieced out its story.

Chanchan is only one of many ancient Indian cities whose ruins have recently been studied. Many of the cities had been swallowed by the jungle; vines and creepers covered their massive stone walls; lizards and reptiles inhabited the streets where once the Indians walked. Native Indians, descendants of the men who built these cities, knew of the ruins, but thought only that the gods had put them there.

In Italy archeologists have been excavating for several hundred years the ruins of a Roman city called Pompeii, which was buried under the ashes of a volcanic eruption. It seems strange that the wonderful cities of the Americas, which were flourishing when Pompeii was buried, have received so little attention. For hundreds of years after the Spaniards came, no one paid any attention to these mute reminders of a vanished civilization. The Spaniards themselves considered the Indians an inferior race from whom they could learn nothing. They were not interested in their remarkable culture. In search of treasure, they often destroyed whole cities and the people in them. Any records they kept of the Indians and their civilization were sent to Spain, where they gathered dust with other government papers. Those few Spaniards who did realize that they were destroying a remarkable civilization went unheeded. In fact, it was not until the late 1800's that historians and archeologists turned their attention to the ancient Indian cities. Governments and scientific societies became interested and furnished funds for further investigations.

From the cliff dwellings north of the Rio Grande to the great stone ruins in Peru and Bolivia, archeologists have carried on their painstaking work. Braving warlike Indians, mosquitoes, malaria, and tropic heat, they visited sites of Indian culture to dig

ANCIENT CHIMU POTTERY has been dug from the ruins of Chanchan. These pieces were used as water bottles. Notice the silly one at the left and the man who is thinking. Or perhaps he has a toothache!

Sawders

and sift in the ruins. Every scrap of pottery, bone, or cloth, every weapon or utensil has its bit to add to the history of early America. Little by little, the archeologists fitted their information together until the long-hidden story of the first Americans emerged to take its rightful place in our early history. The history of the Americas before Columbus is a story of a savage people who came to the American continent thousands of years ago and built great civilizations here when much of Europe was still uncivilized.

THE FIRST AMERICANS WERE NOMADS FROM SIBERIA

Modern archeologists believe that the Indians in America, from the wild Comanches of our western plains to the Chimus of Peru, entered America from Siberia via the Bering Strait and Alaska. How long ago this crossing took place, and how long it took them to spread over two continents, has not yet been determined. Until the last few years the Indians were thought to have been here from 10,000 to 20,000 years. But recently evidence has been unearthed to disprove this. Flint darts, made of course by man, have been found in the remains of a buffalo known to have become extinct many thousands of years ago. Although we are uncertain when the Indians came to the Americas, we do know that they were nomads, that is, men who wandered from place to place hunting and fishing for their food. We also know that they were broad-faced people with copper-colored skin and straight black hair.

Let us imagine these people making their way into North America in small groups for hundreds of years. From Alaska they wandered over all of North America, and the wilderness gradually became peopled with hundreds of Indian tribes such as the Algonquins and the Iroquois. Into Central and South America, too, these wanderers ventured. Centuries must have passed while they spread over the two Americas. Perhaps they followed rivers to new regions or skirted the coasts of South America in dugout canoes. At any rate, these brown-skinned people inhabited the whole hemisphere and became the first Americans.

THE INDIANS LEARN TO BUILD PERMANENT HOMES, WEAVE CLOTH, AND GROW CROPS

We do not know how many centuries it took for the Indians to settle in villages. Probably family groups first built huts of grass, as savages on the upper Amazon still do today. Huts of earth followed these, like those the tourist sees in the Navajo Indian reservations in Arizona. When they had learned to make bricks of adobe or pile stones together to make permanent homes, they were ready to settle down. Some Indians never

SIBERIA

Bering Strait

ALASKA

BERING SEA

Aleutian Islands

BERING STRAIT

0   300   SCALE IN MILES

Lanks

THESE INDIAN HUTS in Peru have probably changed very little since ancient times. In fact, the Indians who live in them have not made much progress since the days when their ancestors learned to build stone huts.

advanced beyond the grass-hut stage; others became builders of great cities. Certainly our North American tribes never reached the degree of civilization of their relatives farther south.

At the same time, some Indian groups were taking other great steps toward civilization. They learned to weave, to make pottery dishes, and to plant seed for crops. The first step in weaving was the crisscrossing of weeds and grasses to make baskets. Centuries later, perhaps, they twirled animal hair or plant fibers in their fingers to make thread. The thread was woven into cloth in basket-weave method until there was a solid fabric. Ancient Indians also learned to mold sticky mud into bowls and bake it before a fire until it was hard enough to hold water.

Most important of all was the discovery that if seeds of a wild grass were planted, more grass would grow. The Indians who planted grass learned to save only the best seeds to plant the next year, until their plants were no longer wild grass with a small grain, but tall cornstalks with full ears of corn. Archeologists say that Indians have been planting grain for 20,000 years, because that is the time it would take modern grain to develop by primitive methods from a wild grass.

Their corn fields were farmed by the most primitive means. The Indians plowed by digging holes with a bent stick and breaking up the clods with their hands. Backbreaking hand labor was necessary in order to plant and harvest, for there were many tools of civilization which the Indians had not yet developed. They had not thought of the wheel, so they had no wagons. They had not even

Galloway

TAOS, NEW MEXICO, is the home of Pueblo Indians who still use the pueblo type of architecture. This is a fine example of the adobe "apartment houses" which were built by the Indians of our Southwest a thousand years ago.

learned to harness animals to help them carry loads.

Agriculture was as hard work for Indians in ancient America as it was for ancient Egyptians in the Nile Valley. In our dry Southwest, irrigation ditches had to be built. In the Andes in South America, the sides of hills had to be cut down in level terraces. In tropical Central America, land had to be constantly cleared of jungle. The inhabitants knew little about fertilizing the fields and could get plant-food back into the soil only by allowing fields to lie idle every other year.

THE INDIAN MAKES USE OF NATIVE PLANTS

The Indians learned to use many plants they found growing here. Potatoes, both white and sweet, were eaten by the first Americans. The Irish potato did not see Ireland until centuries after it was developed in South America. Tomatoes, pumpkins, and beans were used, as well as pineapple, strawberries, avocados, peanuts, and coconuts. The Indians learned that the turnip-like roots of the cassava made good food. They squeezed out the juice and baked the pulp on hot stones.

Tobacco was harvested and dried, then smoked in religious ceremonies. Hemp fiber was grown to make ropes. Cotton with long fibers was used by the Indians for spinning. They discovered rubber and played a rubber-

50

ball game which will be described in a later chapter. Common medicines, such as quinine, cascara, and cocaine, were known to the ancient people.

INDIAN CULTURES DEVELOP IN THE AMERICAS

Those Indians who had learned to plant crops and harvest them were sure of a food supply through the winter. They no longer had to spend their free time hunting wild game and wild food plants in the mountains and jungles. They had spare hours in which to make pottery or fashion ornaments from stone or metal for their own entertainment. There was leisure to honor their native gods in elaborate religious ceremonies. As time went on, they learned to build stone and adobe palaces for their rulers and temples for their gods.

In our Southwest, the Pueblo Indians built apartment houses of stone and adobe which housed 800 families! The upper houses were reached by ladders. In the Valley of Mexico, a tribe called the Toltecs built great pyramids out of stone on which they reared their temples. A city of stone and adobe which had been buried under lava for hundreds of years has recently been uncovered by archeologists. In the Valley of Oaxaca 300 miles south of Mexico City, a people called the Zápotecs (zah'poh-teks) built a city called Mitla, whose buildings were decorated by strange mosaic patterns in stone. In tombs at Monte Alban, another ancient city some thirty miles away, beautiful golden ornaments have been found by archaeologists. In the highlands of Colombia, the Chibchas had

THE RUINS OF MITLA, ancient city of the Zápotecs, reveal a civilization far more advanced than that of the Pueblos. The designs in relief can be seen today in the weaving and basketry of the modern Zápotecan Indians.

Lanks

become a civilized race who planted foods, wove cotton into cloth, and fashioned beautiful ornaments of gold.

More important than any of these Indian tribes are the three great civilizations which developed in the Americas. In the next three chapters you will read the story of the Incas in Peru, the Mayans in Central America, and the Aztecs in Mexico.

Are You a Careful Reader? Test Yourself!

I. Supply the correct word for each blank:

1. A person who studies the ruins of ancient cities is called an . . . . .
2. The first Indian people probably arrived in America from . . . . by way of the . . . .
3. One plant commonly believed to have been developed in the British Isles, but actually a native of South America, is the . . . . .
4. The Indians took the first steps toward civilization when they learned to . . . . , to . . . . , and to . . . .
5. The Indians could not lighten their work by using carts, because they had not invented the . . . . .

II. Are the following statements true or false?

1. Chanchan was an ancient city of the Chimus in coastal Peru.
2. Nomads are wandering tribes who live by hunting and fishing.
3. We know a great deal about the Chimus because they left written records.
4. The Pueblo Indians of New Mexico were nomads.
5. The Chibchas were semi-civilized people of the Colombian Highlands.
6. The Toltecs were early inhabitants of the Valley of Mexico.
7. Scientists believe that corn has been planted in America for 20,000 years because people in Europe had corn over 20,000 years ago.
8. Indians were able to settle permanently in villages when they learned to plant and harvest corn so they were sure of a food supply.
9. Indians learned to develop handicrafts when they no longer had to spend all their time in hunting and fishing.
10. Agriculture was difficult in the Andes because the jungle growth had to be constantly cleared from the fields.

Food for Thought and Discussion

1. What were the advantages to the Indians of settling permanently in villages?
2. How can archeologists reconstruct a vanished civilization if no written records are left?
3. Why did the Indians of temperate North America never reach the degree of civilization achieved by the Aztecs, Incas, or Mayans?

Chapter 5

The Incas Build an Empire in Peru

O SUN! Thou who art in peace and safety, shine upon us, keep us from sickness, and keep us in health and safety. We beseech thee that thy children the Incas may be always conquerors, since it is for this that Thou hast created them.[1]

AN INCA PRIEST in flowing robes faces eastward and greets with these words the first rays of the sun. The time is any year between A.D. 1000 and 1500. The place is somewhere in the mountains of Peru. The priest is an Indian belonging to the great tribe of the Incas. What do we know about these Indians who worshiped the sun so many centuries ago in South America?

THE PLATEAUS OF THE ANDES WERE INHABITED BY INDIANS BEFORE A.D. 1000

We do not know a great deal about the Indians of South America before A.D. 1000. Archeologists have discovered that parts of the coast and most of the high valleys, where the people of Peru, Ecuador, and Bolivia live today, were inhabited in the early days by Indian tribes. You have read about the Chimus, who lived near the coast in northern Peru. In the high Andean valley where Lake Titicaca lies was the mountain king-

dom of Tiahuanaco (tee-ah-whah-nah'coh). It was inhabited by people called the Collas. Like the Chimus, these highland people built a fortified city to protect themselves from other tribes. Their buildings were made, not of adobe, but of great blocks of stone. The ruins of Tiahuanaco still stand to remind travelers that an ancient people once lived there. The Collas learned to tame the llamas which they found roaming in the mountains. They discovered that they could weave cloth from their wool to keep themselves warm in the cold climate of the Bolivian plateau. The Tiahuanaco kingdom became very strong; later, for some reason which we do not know, its power declined.

Other Indian people lived on the coast below the Andes. They raised cotton in the river valleys which they traded to the mountain people for wool. We know that there were Indian tribes living in the Amazon region across the Andes. Each of these little settlements had its own chieftain and lived independently on its own territory. It is believed that the Indians of South America had been established here for two thousand years before the Spaniards came.

[1] From Hiram Bingham, *Inca Land*. Houghton Mifflin.

Galloway

ANCIENT MACHU PICCHU was lost to the world for centuries until an American archeologist stumbled on a hidden trail which led to this forgotten city.

THE EARLY INCAS LIVED IN FORTIFIED CITIES

Probably centuries after the decline of the Tiahuanaco kingdom, another mountain tribe grew strong in the highlands of Peru. These were the Incas. More is known about the early Incas than about other tribes because they were the ruling group in the Andes when the Spaniards came to South America. Archeologists have added to our store of knowledge by studying some of their early cities.

Machu Picchu (mah'choo peek'-choo) was one of the earliest known cities of the Incas. It was situated high on a mountain in the Peruvian Andes, and could be reached only by a stony path zigzagging up from the valley below. There were hundreds of stone houses built on terraces cut out of the mountain-side. Steps hewn out of the rock connected each level. It is still possible to see where farms had been built by terracing the mountain-sides. When we realize that the Incas had to carry soil for their farms from the valley below, we feel sure they must have feared attack from neighboring tribes. Otherwise they would have built their city in the valley where living would have been easier. In Machu Picchu, 4000 to 5000 people lived in safety.

The Incas also had a strongly fortified city in the valley of Cuzco (koos'-koh). Here can still be seen an enormous fort called Sacsahuamán (sahx-ah-whah-mahn'). It was furnished with supplies of food and water so that the people of Cuzco could retreat there in time of war. In the walls of old Cuzco buildings, stones have been found 38 feet long, 18 feet wide, and

6 feet thick. Can you picture a slab of stone like that? It is no wonder that Cuzco has resisted the earthquakes which tore down old Spanish and modern Peruvian buildings alike. Cuzco became the capital of the Inca people. We do not know when it was built, but the Spaniards found a flourishing city there when they arrived in the 1500's. It is an important city of Peru today.

THE INCAS CONQUER THE INHABITANTS OF THE PLATEAUS AND FORM AN EMPIRE

The story of how the Incas conquered the other Indian tribes and built an empire was written by the son of a rich Spaniard who had married an Inca princess. He grew up in Cuzco and heard from old Inca warriors the glorious history and the legends of his mother's people. When he was an old man, he recorded the story as it had been told to him. The Incas believed that their empire was founded by a divine being called Manco Capac. The story goes that Manco Capac was a child of the Sun who came to earth to instruct man. He became the founder of the line of Inca chiefs. By force or persuasion these divine descendants of Manco Capac gradually brought the neighboring tribes under their rule. They received tribute in the form of llamas, wool, pottery, and corn.

The Incas, made bold by their success, conquered the Colla people living around Lake Titicaca far to the south. Over a period of several hundred years their rulers added one mountain valley after another to their growing empire by military conquest. The tribes on the coast were also conquered when they refused to join the Incas. It is believed that the Incas cut off the water which supplied the irrigation ditches of the Chimus, thus forcing them to surrender. We know that Chanchan was a part of the Inca

INCA STONEWORK still forms the foundation for buildings in the old city of Cuzco. These great stones were cut without metal tools and fitted so carefully that even today a knife blade cannot be inserted between them.

Sawders

empire before 1500. The Incas also added the kingdom of Quito in Ecuador to their nation after a bloody struggle. The territory of the conquerors was gradually extended in this fashion until by the 1500's the Incas had an immense empire reaching from Quito in Ecuador to central Chile. It was larger than the area of the thirteen colonies in 1776 and contained perhaps 20 million people.

The Inca empire was at its height in the 1400's. It had two capitals, the original capital at Cuzco and a new one at Quito in the northern half of the empire. The cities were 1200 miles apart and separated by some of the roughest mountain country in the Western Hemisphere. The very fact that wise rulers were able to hold such an empire together is considered by one historian to be the greatest achievement in government made by any Indian people.

INCA MEANS "GOD–RULER"

The Incas spoke a language called Quechua (kay'choo-ah), and in that language the word "Inca" means ruler. The ruler himself as the descendant of the Sun God was believed to be a superior being. He became all-powerful, having the final word over his millions of people. But it was the tradition of the Inca to rule wisely for the good of his people.

The Inca at first took pride in visiting and inspecting every settlement in person and in establishing friendly relations with the chiefs of the conquered tribes. But as the empire grew, the tours of inspection took longer and longer until the Inca could visit his whole empire only at the beginning of his reign. He decided to appoint his kinsmen to assist him in inspecting and governing the empire. These kinsmen and their descendants became the nobility or ruling class, with luxuries and power not allowed to the common people. The boys of the nobility were educated in Cuzco and trained in warfare.

There was also a large class of officials or supervisors who lived in the various settlements and carried out the laws of the Inca, punishing those who deserved it. An official was responsible to the Inca for the welfare of the people, and if there was hunger in his province he was punished.

UNITY WAS THE CORNERSTONE OF THE INCA EMPIRE

With such a large territory and so many people, the wise Incas knew that they must bind their empire together by every possible means. They realized that they could not have a united empire unless the many tribes under their rule were loyal to them. Therefore, the loyal neighboring tribes who knew the Incas and their ways were moved to newly conquered regions and the new Inca subjects were transplanted to Cuzco or other loyal sections until they learned loyalty to the empire.

Common language was necessary for a united empire, so the chiefs of all the conquered tribes were required to learn the Quechua language. They in turn were required to speak to their people in that tongue only. Thus, as the empire grew, the language spread, and when the Inca made his tour from town to town he never needed an interpreter. Even today, archeologists in Peru are advised to learn the dialect of the present-day Quechuas, for through them ruins have been discovered which might not otherwise have been found.

The Inca used still another means

Sawders

THESE DIRT TERRACES on the mountainsides were built in the time of the Incas and are still used by the Indian farmers in the valley below Cuzco.

of uniting his people. He brought representatives from the twelve divisions of his empire and settled them in twelve wards in his great capital city of Cuzco. The groups wore the costume of their own people and must have made a colorful addition to the city. It was probably considered a great honor to be sent to Cuzco. These people would return home to teach loyalty and Inca customs to their own people.

So successful was the ruler in uniting his people in loyalty to him that the Quechuan word for unity was used by the Incas to describe their empire — *Tahuantinsuyo* (tah-whahn-teen-soo′yoh).

THE SUBJECTS OF THE INCA WORKED FOR THEIR COMMUNITY

The people of Inca land did not worry about keeping their jobs or providing for old age. Each head of a family was given a piece of land to farm, but he could not own it because it belonged to the community. If the family had a son, it was allowed more land, which the boy took over when he married. If parents died without sons, the land went back to the community. The villagers also worked part of the time on lands whose crops were set aside for the support of the Inca and of the priests. Part of these crops were stored in case of famine or other calamity in the village. Potters, metal-workers, and weavers for the community shared their work in the same way. There were markets for carrying on an exchange of products where craftsmen brought pottery, thread, metal-work, or cloth and received in return potatoes and corn.

Boys and girls began to work at the age of sixteen. They spent four

Galloway

ROPE BRIDGES similar to this one in Peru were crossed by the Indians and their llamas hundreds of years before burros like these were brought from Spain.

years as apprentices, learning farming, weaving, pottery-making, or the duties of a housewife. At the end of four years they were expected to marry, and all the couples who finished their apprenticeship in a certain year were paired off in one big village ceremony. From that time until they were fifty, the Inca people worked for their families and for the state. Those between the ages of fifty and sixty taught the youth of the community their trades, and after reaching sixty, they were cared for by the community.

A strong sense of being a part of the empire was built up in every subject because he shared in the support of the empire. Every community had to help care for the huge herds of llamas and alpacas owned by the government, and in turn the members of the community received meat and wool for their own use. When roads had to be built or wild tribes driven out, all men except skilled craftsmen were drafted.

ROADS AND RUNNERS UNITE THE EMPIRE

The roads built by the Incas extended all over the kingdom. They were so well paved with stone blocks that some of them are still in use today. Bridges of rope, which swayed dangerously when used, were built across deep canyons. Rest-houses, barracks for soldiers, and storehouses for corn and potatoes were set up at regular intervals. Llama caravans carried food and handmade articles along the roads from one town to another.

Runners were used to take news and messages for the government. They could travel the 1200 miles from Quito to Cuzco and back in twenty days by running in relays of ten miles each. Since there was no written

58

language, important messages had to be remembered and passed on accurately to the next runner. To help in remembering numbers, the runner would sometimes carry a bunch of knotted cords representing numbers into the hundreds of thousands. This was called a *quipu* (kee'poo). Of course the runner had to remember, as he carried the cord over the stone-paved roads of the empire, what he was counting — llamas, bushels of corn, marriageable couples, the number of soldiers needed for the army, or the days to elapse before the Inca ruler would come to visit. It is said that the Inca could call out at any time 200,000 trained men, all armed with bows, arrows, darts, or copper battle-axes. Think what a job it would be to keep track of the battle-axes alone without a device like the *quipu*!

THE INCAS WORSHIP THE SUN AND LEARN ASTRONOMY

The Incas were sun worshipers. When we recall the cold climate of the Andean plateaus, we can understand how the Incas would look to the warm sun as a god. They not only built great temples to the sun, but they observed its travels in the heavens and knew the exact day when the sun was highest in the sky. The priests of the Incas may have placed their temples with reference to the sun. At any rate, in the temple at Quito was a pillar which when it cast no shadow marked high noon of the longest day in the year. The Incas believed the Sun God himself descended at that time to sit on the columns of the temple.

The Incas also learned to divide the year into twelve months, to correspond to periods of the full moon. The various months and days of the year had special meaning and were celebrated by festivals. The first month began on the longest day, with a solemn feast to the sun. It was attended by officials from all over the empire. Special bread of fermented corn was made by the maidens who served in the sun temple. Processions through the streets lasted for three days and were led by the Inca himself. Animals, and sometimes people, were sacrificed in a holy fire to the Sun God. To start this fire, the priest would take a cup of highly polished gold, focus the sun's rays in one spot and ignite a tuft of cotton, much as Boy Scouts would do today with a magnifying glass.

During the following months there were other religious rites to celebrate plowing, planting, and the growing season. The seventh month was important to all the young men and women who had finished their four years of apprenticeship. Contests of strength were held among the boys and handicraft competitions among the girls. The Inca or one of his representatives gave them ear plugs to wear and then they were considered adults. In the twelfth month the harvest was celebrated. In this fashion, religion, science, and social events were all combined for the Incas.

THE INCAS WERE SKILLED IN HANDICRAFT

Those of you who have seen in museums the beautiful things that archeologists have found in Inca graves know how much time and skill they must have put into their handicraft. The weavers and the pottery-makers devoted their lives to creating beauty. We realize that our machine-made pots and pans and fabrics suffer in comparison with articles made by

American Museum of Natural History

THIS INCA HANDICRAFT shows the contrast between the work of Inca and pre-Inca craftsmen. The crude, though interesting, pottery vessels (*upper left*) were made long before the period of the Inca Empire. The other three articles show us what Inca artisans could do. Perhaps some Inca nobleman wore the poncho of fine wool with a silver thread. The little alpaca is made of silver.

the Inca craftsmen. Although the Spaniards plundered all the gold they could lay their hands on, gold was valuable to the Incas chiefly because they could easily mold it into figures and ornaments. In the palace of the Inca every dish was made of gold or silver and the Inca sat upon a golden chair.

Cloth was more valuable to them than gold because so much time went into its making. It is possible that the Incas learned to make their most beautiful cloth from the Colla people, whose weaving we have already mentioned. Both wool and cotton dresses

in bright-colored patterns have been found in thousands of graves. Each woman spun and wove enough for her own family from wool and cotton granted her by the government. The looms were tied at one end to a tree or post and at the other end around the waist of the weaver, as the Indians of Guatemala and Mexico do today. We know that dolls for the children were made of cloth because an unfinished doll was found in a grave.

The pottery found in Inca graves is not so picturesque nor so life-like as the Chimu portrait jugs we described. The patterns used by the Incas were plain geometric designs like the vase in the picture on page 60. Pottery was made by working the clay into long coils and then laying one coil upon another to form the desired shape. The outside was then smoothed with a gourd or a shell. Water jars as large as four feet in height and three feet in diameter have been unearthed.

The Peruvian peoples worked with other materials than clay. Stone and wood were used to make corn-grinders, wooden spoons, and spindles. The Incas combined tin from their mines with copper to make bronze. They did not have bellows to make the fire hot enough to melt the metal, so they lined up many Indian workers and had them blow hard through pipes into the fire. Knives made of metal have been found among Inca ruins.

THE CLOTHES OF THE INCAS WERE HAND-WOVEN AND HAND-MADE

The clothes of the Inca ruler were made especially for him. He wore coats of feather cloth made by tying the quills of beautiful colored feathers to strings and sewing the strings onto coarse cloth. His poncho or shawl was of finest wool from an animal called the vicuña (vee-coon'yah), and he wore a golden sun ornament on his chest, and large golden ear plugs. His breeches were of specially woven cloth with designs of birds or fish worked into the wool. The distinctive badge of the Inca ruler and his nobles was a headdress called llautu (yow'too). This was a narrow braid wound several times round the head with a fringe hanging down to the eyebrows. On special occasions upright feathers were attached to it. The women of the Incas wore a mantle pinned to the shoulders and hanging loose. Their sandals were of llama hide or braided hempen fiber. They liked to wear ornamental brooches and earrings, beads and combs.

THE INCAS PRACTICED SURGERY

The Incas were far ahead of any other people of their time in the practice of surgery. We know this to be true because many skulls have been found which show that operations have been performed on them. Holes have been cut out of the skull and silver plates inserted, which is considered a difficult operation today. It is not known, however, whether the ancient priests performed surgery to cure head injuries or for some religious ceremony. The operation was evidently done with a sharp flint or a knife made of a hard volcanic glass called obsidian.

THE INCAS MADE A START IN THE ARTS OF MUSIC, DANCING, AND POETRY

It is difficult to imagine the music and dancing of a forgotten people who left no written records. The Indians of Peru today play strange music on flutes, as their ancestors probably did before them. We know the Incas had flutes, and that they played on drums, bells, and rattles to make rhythm for dancing. They also used whistles and trumpets made of conch shells. Pictures on the pottery show people dancing with a hop, skip, and jump to a flute accompaniment. Spanish writers have mentioned ceremonial dances and dramas given during the feasts of the sun. Any plays, songs, or poetry used by the Incas would have to be memorized and passed on from one generation to the other. Some of the poems and religious songs sung in the temples were written down by the Spaniards. Here is a prayer which shows a great resemblance to a Christian prayer.[1]

> Oh, Lord of Divination,
> Where art thou?
> Thou mayest be above,
> Thou mayest be below,
> Or perhaps around
> Thy splendid throne and scepter.
> Oh hear me!
> From the sky above,
> In which thou mayest be,
> Creator of the world,
> Maker of all men,
> Lord of all Lords.
> My eyes fail me
> For longing to see thee.

THE ROOTS OF THE PRESENT ARE DEEP IN THE PAST

This is the civilization which the Spaniards who conquered Peru so ruthlessly destroyed. One old Spaniard was so impressed by the Incas that he wrote back to his king, "We have destroyed by our evil example the people who had such a government as was enjoyed by these natives." The people were so well

[1] From Philip A. Means, *Ancient Civilizations of the Andes.* Scribners.

governed, he said, that there was not a thief among them. They never let war interfere with their agriculture or their trade. "They were so free from committal of crimes that the Indian who had 100,000 pesos' worth of gold and silver in his house left it open, merely placing a small stick at the door as a sign that its master was out.... When they found that we had thieves among us they despised us!" [2]

There are still many descendants of the Incas living in the Andes. They are called Quechuas and make their living today much as their ancestors did, tending llama herds and making cloth of their wool. The agricultural land is still parceled out to the heads of families and the herds and pastures belong to the village in common. We leave the Incas and their empire for the present. But let us keep in mind that modern Peru, Ecuador, and Bolivia are built upon the foundation of these ancient people and their splendid civilization.

[2] From Clements Markam, *The Incas of Peru.* Dutton.

Are You a Careful Reader ?   Test Yourself !

I. Supply the correct word for each blank:

1. The early Peruvian tribes who lived on the coast raised .... and sold it to the ... .

2. The Inca empire was at its height in the ..... .

3. Inca subjects were not required to work after the age of ..... .

4. One method by which the Inca united his people was to require all conquered people to learn the ....

5. The success of the Inca empire depended upon the .... of every subject.

II. Match these words and statements:

1. Tiahuanaco   a. language spoken by Incas and their descendants
2. Cuzco   b. knotted cord used for counting
3. Machu Picchu   c. capital of Inca empire and present-day city of Peru
4. obsidian   d. fortified city on a mountain peak
5. Quito   e. ancient city near Lake Titicaca once inhabited by the Collas

6. Quechua   *f.* a hard stone used in performing surgical operations
7. ear plugs   *g.* name of an Incan flute still used in Andean villages
8. vicuña   *h.* official symbol of maturity in an Inca youth
9. quipu   *i.* worn by the high priest at the altar
10. unity   *j.* an animal whose fine wool was reserved for the nobility
                              k. the cornerstone of the Inca empire
                              l. northern capital of the Inca empire

Food for Thought and Discussion

1. Do you think the Incas were like the Nazis in their treatment of conquered people? Why or why not?
2. What do you consider the greatest achievements of the Incas?
3. Why were the common people contented under the Inca rule?
4. Does our government furnish as much security for the aged as the Inca government did?

Chapter 6

Central America Becomes the Home of Mayan Civilization

COLUMBUS, on his fourth voyage to America in 1502, saw a large canopied canoe close to the coast of Central America. It was rowed by Indian slaves and under the canopy sat a merchant, richly clad in white cotton embroidered with colors. In the canoe were bales of bright cotton goods and stacks of pottery. Columbus thought the merchant was a subject of the Emperor of China, and, confident that he would meet many others, he merely hailed the canoe in passing and sailed on. But Columbus had not seen a Chinese merchant; he had seen a Mayan Indian from one of the Yucatan cities on his way to trade along the coast of Central America.

THE MAYANS ARE A MYSTERY PEOPLE

The Mayans were civilized Indians living in Central America long before Columbus came. Much of their history is buried with them, but archeologists have pieced together part of their story from the art and the architecture that they left behind in

MAYAN DATE STONES like this one found in the jungle of Guatemala tell the story of a vanished civilization. The carved symbols framed in ovals are Mayan dates.

their ancient cities. Stories told to the Spaniards by a few intelligent natives who still lived in the cities of Yucatan, and a few books of Mayan picture writing, have helped fill in their history.

We do not yet know where the Mayans lived before they came to Central America. We do know that they must have lived somewhere else while they were learning the steps of civilization, for they built great cities in the jungle where not even little towns had been before. The story of the Indians in Peru is fairly clear because they lived in the same region from the time they first learned to plant corn until they built their empire. But there is no trace of an earlier Mayan civilization in Central America. Who were these people whose cities suddenly sprang from the jungle? Perhaps archeologists working now in the southern part of Mexico may be able to answer these questions and solve the mystery of the Mayans.

THE MAYANS BUILD CITIES IN CENTRAL AMERICA AND THEN MOVE TO YUCATAN

Stone date markers found in Mayan ruins tell us that the Mayans settled in the Central American coast region about the first century A.D. This means that they were well settled here long before the Incas fortified themselves at Machu Picchu. They built large cities and their civilization flourished until about A.D. 600. Traces of one of these cities can still be seen by tourists who go to Guatemala City. Three miles from the train-stop in the middle of a banana plantation are five huge stone date markers and elaborately carved altars which remind us that a great people once lived and worked here.

For some reason we do not know, the Mayans left their beautiful cities about A.D. 600 or 700 and moved in a body to the Yucatan peninsula. Here they settled themselves and built new cities. We know this to be true, because when the Spaniards came in the 1500's they did not find a single inhabitant in the Mayan cities on the coasts of Central America. These cities had already been claimed by the jungle and were in the same ruined condition which we see today. Many Mayans, however, continued to live in the highlands of Guatemala.

The Mayans were in the habit of marking the date when a building or a temple was erected, and also setting up a carved marker at the end of every five years, but there are no stone markers recording dates after about A.D. 600. In Yucatan, however, no markers were found with dates earlier than A.D. 650 or later than A.D. 1350. When the Spaniards arrived, people were still living in Yucatan cities and farmers were coming in to worship at the temples.

Why did the Mayans move away? The old cities in Central America must have been pleasant places in which to live. They were surrounded by fertile farms growing all kinds of tropical foods, and the trade winds brought abundant rainfall then as they do today. Yucatan, on the other hand, does not seem to be a good country in which to settle. It is difficult to grow food there or to raise cotton. As you remember, the ground is of limestone, and the northern part of the peninsula is very dry. Farther south, the water from the heavy rains runs down through the limestone into underground rivers. The Mayans could reach the water only by digging pits in the limestone and cutting stairs in the steep sides so the water could be carried up. This water supply was certain the year round.

It is possible that the Mayans left their homes in Central America because of an unfavorable change in the climate. Or it may be that epidemics appeared year after year until the people thought the land was not favorable to the gods. The most likely explanation is that the soil became exhausted.

The Mayan farmers who lived outside the cities were not kind to the land. When they first cleared the jungle, it gave them fine crops, but in the second year the land did not produce so much. In the third year, only about half as much could be grown. So the Mayan farmers cleared land every two years and let the old fields go back to the jungle. After ten years they would burn the jungle off and start all over again. But every time they burned it off the land produced less, partly because the heavy tropical rains washed away the soil into the rivers. Perhaps the time came when the land could no longer feed the hungry cities.

At any rate, the Mayans took what possessions they could carry and moved. It was as if all the population of the eastern United States should pick up and move beyond the Mississippi River, leaving New York and Boston deserted! Mayan colonists had founded settlements in Yucatan long before the great moving day, but the people of the great cities must have considered them mere frontier towns.

The Mayans took some time to get settled in their new homes. But by the year 1000 their capital city of Chichén Itzá (chee-chen' eet-sah') was perhaps the greatest city in America. About the time that the Vikings were visiting the Atlantic coast of North America, Chichén Itzá joined with two other new cities in a league. This league of peace and friendship with the Mayan cities of Uxmal (oosh-mahl') and Mayapán (mah-yah-pahn') lasted 200 years.

CIVIL WAR DESTROYS THE MAYAN CIVILIZATION

The Mayans were not bound by a strong ruler as were the Incas. In 1195 the ruler of Chichén Itzá and the ruler of Mayapán had a quarrel. Then, as now, war seemed to be the easiest way to settle a difficulty. To help him defeat Chichén Itzá, the Mayapán ruler imported Toltecs from the Valley of Mexico, a thousand miles away. These were professional soldiers and hardy fighters who believed in a god who was a feathered serpent, as well as in human sacrifice. The Itzá people were conquered and the Toltecs took over the city. They set up many new stone buildings and carved feathered serpents, the symbol of their god, in the stone. We do not know whether the Toltecs all remained in Chichén Itzá, but we know they left a bloody mark upon it, as we shall find later.

After the battles with the Toltecs, the city grew strong again and sought revenge on Mayapán. This time Mayapán was defeated, and then began years of civil wars between the cities. A whole generation would be wiped out. The survivors would rebuild the cities, store up crops, and in twenty-five years or so, the civil war would break out again with a new generation of young men to do the fighting. This tale of ancient warfare sounds much like the story of Europe in the twentieth century!

Finally the people of Chichén Itzá completely destroyed Mayapán. But this victory was the end of Yucatan. Farming had been neglected and victors and vanquished succumbed to famine and disease. The Uxmal people moved their capital to a new site, which they called Mani, meaning "It is finished." Some of the common people stayed on in the cities, but they came less and less to the temples. Building and progress ceased. Others went to live in jungle villages. When the Spaniards came in 1540, there were not enough people in the cities to stop their conquest.

Thus can bitter warfare destroy a people. Perhaps there is a lesson we can learn from these ancient Indians. About 1200, a Mayan poet sang an unhappy prophecy for his people, which the Spaniards wrote down. Here are a few lines of it: [1]

Eat, eat, while there is bread;
Drink, drink, while there is water.
A day comes ... when a blight shall wither the land ...
When ruin shall fall upon all things, ...
When eyes shall be closed in death, ...
Father, son and grandson hanging dead on the same tree, ...
When ruin shall fall upon all things and the people be scattered abroad in the forest.

CHICHÉN ITZÁ REVEALS MAYAN LIFE BEFORE AND AFTER THE TOLTECS

Let us go back to the time of Mayan greatness to see how people lived and discover why their cities were considered the centers of art and learning. It is possible to visit Chichén Itzá today. Although it is a ghost city now, we can imagine it as it was in the days of its glory.

The ruins are reached by going from Mérida (may'ree-dah), the capital of Yucatan, and traveling past thatched Indian villages deep into jungles of Yucatan for about one hundred miles. Suddenly after a turn in the road the great pyramid of Chichén Itzá looms ahead. This pyramid, like all pyramids built by the Mayans, is topped by a temple.

[1] From Gregory Mason, *Columbus Came Late*. Appleton-Century.

Gendreau

THE PYRAMID OF CHICHÉN ITZÁ looks like this today. Parts of it have crumbled through the years, but the steps on the right ramp have been restored and you can climb to the temple at the top.

Visitors can climb the steep stone steps leading to the summit and stand by the great carved columns. These are beautifully carved to represent feathered serpents, so we know that the temple was built after the Toltecs came.

The pyramid faces a plaza in the center of the city where all the principal buildings of Chichén Itzá stood. It overlooks the remains of a city that once covered several square miles, but today it is possible to see only about twenty buildings that have been recovered from the growth of the jungle. If you have seen the highly colored buildings of any of the recent world fairs, you can imagine something of what Chichén Itzá may have

looked like. The buildings, even with the jungle creeping in, seem as fantastic in shape as those of a modern world's fair, and they were once as brilliantly decorated. The only street is the Sacred Way leading from the steps of the pyramid down a half-mile to the sacred well. It is doubtful whether this well was ever used for water, because there are no steps leading to the water level. The rain god was supposed to dwell in the waters of the well. There is a gruesome story about the sacred well which you will read soon.

The deep well which actually supplied water to the city lies behind the pyramid, a half-mile into the jungle. Chichén Itzá means "mouth of the

Sawders

ON THE BEAUTIFUL "HOUSE OF NUNS" weeds are growing, but you can still see the bold carving and the god who stands above the square doorway.

wells where the tribe of Itzá people live." The city was built in this particular spot because of the two wells of pure water which were fed by the underground streams of Yucatan.

Beyond the pyramid are large buildings which must have been here before the Toltecs came, for no feathered serpents adorn their walls. We are particularly interested in the "House of Nuns," which is covered with elaborate carving in geometric designs. In the center of the stone facing is the figure of a god. It is the most beautiful example of Mayan art remaining today. This building was not a nunnery but a chieftain's palace. The Spaniards gave it that name because they saw the many tiny rooms and thought they must be the cells of a convent. You see, the Mayans did not know how to con-

struct an arch with a keystone as the Europeans did, so they had to use overlapping slabs which met in the center of the arch. The most important buildings had tiny rooms because of the thick walls which were necessary to support the great stone slabs which made the roof. The exteriors of the buildings were faced with stone and were beautifully carved around the doors and along the steep stairways.

THE TOLTECS BUILT OVER OLD MAYAN TEMPLES

Across the plaza from our pyramid we look at the most famous building put up after the Toltecs came, the Temple of Warriors, which stands five stories high. The entrance columns of this temple are carved snakes. At the foot of the pyramid on which it stands is a row of columns which once held up an arcade or covered walk. These continue to form a large hollow square which must have enclosed the market place. On all four sides the columns are carved with sculptures of the warriors from whom the temple got its name. They are in full costume and are evidently real portraits of Toltec warriors. Dates and picture writings which have not been deciphered appear on the columns and probably tell the story.

When archeologists were working to replace all the fallen stones of the pyramid, they found a smaller pyramid inside. Stairs led to a temple at the top which was brilliantly painted with pictures of Mayan life. It was apparent that the Toltecs used this early Mayan temple as a foundation for their larger one by piling rocks and cement around it and facing it with cut stone.

THE MAYANS PLAYED A GAME LIKE BASKETBALL

To the north of the pyramid is the most interesting building in Chichén Itzá. It is called the "Ball Court" and has been completely restored by the Mexican government. Here the Mayans once played a game like basketball. The goal posts were large stone rings set in the walls of the court. The floor and sides of the court were paved so that the ball would bounce back to the players. Teams of seven men used a solid rubber ball that weighed eight or ten pounds. Imagine how difficult it must have been to get the ball through the ring eighteen feet above the player's head!

It is pleasant to imagine that during the peaceful days of the league, the teams came from Uxmal to play the home team at Chichén, with as much excitement as at a modern football game. It is easy to imagine the game in full swing, the walls lined with gaily dressed and cheering spectators and the ruler of Chichén Itzá sitting in the specially reserved gallery at the end. In the beautiful temple overlooking the court, perhaps the priests asked the gods for a victory for the Chichén team!

CARVINGS AND PAINTINGS SHOW THE LIFE OF THE MAYANS

Most of the beautiful carving on the temples and important buildings had to do with the gods or religious festivals or war. The war scenes on the carved columns of the Temple of Warriors show fighters carrying dart-

THIS MAYAN GOD has a hollow in his middle to hold sacrifices. Behind him two feathered serpents guard the Temple of Warriors. Their open mouths expose great fangs and the columns which form their bodies are carved in feathers.

Gendreau

throwers and bows and arrows. They wear cotton-padded armor and carry shields. There are scenes showing hand-to-hand conflict between the people of Chichén Itzá and Mayapán. We know that any enemies captured in war were sacrificed or held as slaves.

The bright paintings of the earlier temples tell the life of the people. Not all Mayans lived in the stone houses in the cities. The common people lived in round thatched huts like those of the Mayan Indians in Yucatan today. The women are shown grinding corn on stones just as the Mexican Indians do today. In all the pictures the women are clothed in long white blouses with heavy embroidery around the neck and the bottom. This is still the costume of the modern Mayans as seen in the market place at Mérida.

The men were the dandies in ancient Yucatan. Those of the ruling class appeared in high feathered hats and leopard skins or gorgeous feathered mantles. They had nose and ear decorations of jade and tattooing on their faces.

Young people were married at twenty to mates their parents chose for them. The groom went to live in the bride's home and worked for her parents for five years. Then he could establish a home of his own. Evidently he always liked the bride his parents chose for him, because there was no divorce or desertion among the Mayans. He and his wife had to be ready always to feed all friends and strangers, as there was a real spirit of hospitality. If a man died before he had returned all his invitations to feasts, the son had to carry on and give all the banquets his father owed his friends. It was a debt of honor which could not be overlooked.

When the Spaniards came, they marveled at the cleanliness of the Mayans who always bathed at least once a day. This was unheard of in Europe where even the nobility took few baths.

THE MAYAN MERCHANTS TRADED BY LAND AND SEA

Columbus saw a Mayan trader traveling by sea to exchange goods with other cities of the coast. Archeologists know that Mayans were traders, because objects from all over Mexico and Central America have been found in Mayan graves and in the sacred wells. There are turquoise beads, made by no other Indians than those of New Mexico; there are articles of gold from Costa Rica and pottery from north of Mexico City. There are even pearls and emeralds from Colombia, but no articles to show that the Mayans ever had any trade with the Incas. The merchants traveled on stone roads thirty or more feet wide, remains of which we find between some of the cities of Yucatan. When they went north to Mexico or south to Central America, they probably traveled by sea like the trader whom Columbus saw.

THE MAYANS DEVELOP PICTURE WRITING

The Mayans had a system of picture writing which used symbols to represent certain things or ideas. They left books of hemp fiber with symbols somewhat like the hieroglyphics of the Egyptians. As we noted before, this writing dealt mainly with the calendar and the religious ceremonies, and was known only by the priests. Archeologists have figured out some of the stone date markers found in the temples, but as yet they cannot read the other writing.

THE MAYAN PRIESTS WERE A POWERFUL GROUP

The priests were not only the leaders of the Mayan religion, but they were often the heads of the government as well. All the learning, too, seems to have developed among them. They had studied the heavens and knew a great deal about astronomy. They had worked out an accurate calendar with their own system of counting. Even today there are villages in the highlands of Guatemala where native priests still count the days with grains of red corn by an ancient calendar.

The Mayan belief centered on the sun and the stars. The seasons and the months were closely related to their religion just as they were to the religion of the Incas. The priests must have watched certain pillars in the temple to determine by their shadows when the longest and shortest days of the year were to come. They watched the moon as well as the sun, and could tell the time of the full moon a thousand years ahead. They knew how the planets moved and where they would be found in the heavens each night. There was an observatory in Chichén Itzá for the study of astronomy with windows placed in such a way that Venus and Jupiter could be seen on certain religious days. In Europe, over a century later, the great astronomer, Galileo, was threatened with imprisonment for trying to find out facts about the heavens which the Mayans had already discovered!

There must have been a great gulf between the powerful, educated priests and the ignorant common people in their thatched houses. But we must remember that it was the artists and the craftsmen from among the people who made the temples and buildings beautiful. What remains of their art today shows that the Mayans not only loved beauty but could create it.

THE TOLTEC RELIGION TAUGHT HUMAN SACRIFICE

The Incas worshiped chiefly the sun as a god who was good and kind. The Mayans had many gods, some good, some evil. When the Toltecs came to Chichén Itzá, the Mayans apparently accepted their god, and their horrible practice of human sacrifice.

The Toltec god was Quetzalcoatl (ket-zahl-kwah'tal), who had been a king with a fairer skin than the other Toltecs. Their legend says that he went away to a distant land with many warriors. Whether he returned or not, we do not know, but the Toltecs believed that he became a god in the form of a feathered serpent.

Many feathered serpents to represent Quetzalcoatl were carved on the buildings of Chichén Itzá. Altars for human sacrifice were built and hundreds of people were killed every year. The victims were usually slaves or captives who believed that by giving their lives they would go to heaven. Those who disobeyed the gods went to a hell, which to these tropic people meant not a hot, but a cold place!

THE SACRED WELL REVEALS HUMAN BONES

One of the most famous places for human sacrifice was the sacred well at Chichén Itzá. When the rainy season was delayed, the Mayans believed the rain god was angry, so they sought to please him by casting into the sacred well a young girl to be his bride. A girl was chosen from an important family, decked out in fine clothes, and led by chanting priests to the well. There, with much ceremony, she was hurled into the water seventy-five feet below to join the rain god. If she sank, the god was pleased and sent rain. If she floated, the priests would lower a rope and pull her out, hoping for a message from the gods.

The Spaniards were told this story by the Mayans. It also appears in the legends which have been handed down to the present Mayan Indians by their ancestors. When the sacred well was dredged by archeologists some time ago, the skeletons of ninety young girls were found at the bottom! So the story of the sacred well has turned out to be true.

It seems strange that people who put so much beauty into their religious buildings could take part in these cruel ceremonies. But we cannot judge them by our standards, for human life was not valued by semi-civilized people.

Are You a Careful Reader? Test Yourself!

I. Are the following statements true or false?
1. The picture writing of the Mayans was known only to the priests.
2. The Sacred Well was used for drinking water.
3. The fair god Quetzalcoatl was represented by feathered serpents carved in stone.
4. The Toltecs were warriors from South America.
5. The original home of the Mayans was in Yucatan.
6. A Mayan poet foresaw the doom of Mayan civilization.
7. The Mayans had discovered how to construct the arch.
8. The Mayans did not believe in human sacrifice.
9. The ruins of the ancient city, Chichén Itzá, have recently been uncovered.
10. The Temple of Warriors can be seen in Chichén Itzá today.

II. Can you choose the best answer?
1. Most of our knowledge of the Mayans comes from: (*a*) archeological discoveries in buried cities; (*b*) ancient Mayan books now in European museums; (*c*) stories told by the natives of the cities to the Spaniards.
2. The best solution to the mystery of why the Mayans moved their cities seems to be: (*a*) epidemics wiped them out; (*b*) the soil became exhausted; (*c*) the Toltecs came and conquered them.
3. The Mayan cities in Yucatan were almost entirely destroyed because: (*a*) the Spaniards tore down the buildings; (*b*) the people moved back to Guatemala; (*c*) a long civil war killed off the people.
4. We know that the Mayans traded with New Mexico because: (*a*) turquoise found only in New Mexico has been dug from Mayan graves; (*b*) fine roads were built for the traders between the two places; (*c*) the feathered serpent is used as a carved design by both peoples.
5. The Mayan priests used the pillars in their temples: (*a*) to determine by their shadows the long and short days of the year; (*b*) as altars for human sacrifice; (*c*) as permanent markers to record the births of kings.

Food for Thought and Discussion

1. Why is civil war often more destructive than war with an outside enemy? Can you give an example?

2. Why do you suppose the Mayans never traded with the Incas?

3. Would you say the Mayans enjoyed freedom of speech and worship? Why?

Chapter 7

The Aztecs Build an Empire in Mexico

VISITORS TO MEXICO see many reminders of the Aztecs whose civilization flourished before the white men came. They notice the flag of Mexico with its strange emblem, an eagle perched on a cactus holding a serpent in his beak. This is an ancient symbol of the Aztecs which the Mexicans adopted when the country became an independent republic. Visitors see Aztec designs decorating modern buildings and statues of Aztec rulers along the beautiful boulevards of Mexico City. There are still Indian people in the hill villages who speak only the Aztec language. Women croon ancient lullabies and crush their corn on stone grinders used by their Aztec ancestors.

Who were these people whose civilization has left such a rich heritage to modern Mexico? Let us turn back to the centuries before the white man came, when Indian tribes lived in Mexico.

CIVILIZED TRIBES LIVED IN MEXICO BEFORE THE AZTECS CAME

We know that Indians had lived in the high Valley of Mexico for hundreds of years before Columbus. They had learned to spin, weave, make pottery, and to trade with each other. With their plows modern Mexicans often turn up crude objects which were made by these early inhabitants of the valley. One of the tribes that migrated into the valley was the Toltecs, of whom you have already heard. As they grew more powerful, they began to conquer neighboring tribes in the valley. Gradually, the Toltecs established an empire and ruled the Indians of that region.

The Toltecs built great pyramids to the sun and the moon and a temple to their god, Quetzalcoatl, in their capital city of Teotihuacán (tay-oh-tee-whah-cahn'). Travelers can still see the magnificent ruins of these

Sawders

QUETZALCOATL, THE FEATHERED SERPENT, was originally a Toltec god. The priests of his temple at Teotihuacán had to climb the steep narrow steps past these fierce serpent heads to reach the temple at the top.

buildings not far from Mexico City. The Toltecs were a warlike people and, as you know, sent an army to Yucatan to help conquer Chichén Itzá in the 1200's.

THE AZTECS MIGRATE TO MEXICO AND LEARN CIVILIZATION

Some time in the 1200's, a primitive Indian tribe wandered into the Valley of Mexico from what is now the United States. These people called themselves Aztecs. There is an Aztec legend which tells how the priest-leader of this wandering tribe had foretold that there would be a sign from the gods showing them where to settle. When they came to Lake Texcoco (tes-ko′ko) at the southern end of the Mexican plateau, they saw the sign — an eagle standing on a cactus plant in the middle of the lake devouring a serpent. The legend says they founded a city here as soon as they saw the eagle. It is more likely that they built grass-hut villages around the large lake which then covered much of the southern end of the valley. The Aztecs did not need to acquire civilization step by step, because they could learn from the Toltecs.

THE AZTECS BUILD A POWERFUL EMPIRE

From the time that the Aztecs first came to the valley they were brave and clever fighters. As they grew stronger, the Toltecs and other tribal groups in the Valley of Mexico were glad to make peace and pay tribute to them. Thus the Aztecs built up a strong league with their own ruler at the head. By the early 1500's, tribes within a radius of 300 miles sent taxes every year to the Aztecs. These taxes were paid in feathers or blankets, corn and other grains, animal skins, or clay and metal objects. If the other tribal groups resisted the payment of tribute, they would find themselves at war again with the efficient Aztec army, and their young soldiers would be carried off to be sacrificed. It is interesting to know that some of these members of the Aztec confederation so disliked their overlords, the Aztecs, that they were willing to help the Spaniards in defeating and destroying the great Indian civilization.

THE AZTECS BUILD A BEAUTIFUL CAPITAL CITY

When the Aztecs became powerful, they began to build the city of Tenochtitlán (ten-otch-teet-lahn') in place of their grass and cactus villages. They built on islands in the middle of Lake Texcoco, because this location could easily be defended from their enemies. When they settled on the islands, they had to grow crops somewhere, so they covered rafts with soil from the bottom of the lake and planted their corn. These rafts gradually settled in the shallow lake and roots growing downward anchored them firmly so that they formed more islands. As time passed, there was room for a large city on the land in the lake. Because of the many small islands, the main streets of Tenochtitlán were canals, and gay-colored canoes made their way from one island to another. Engineers built four raised highways from the island city to the mainland. The water from the lake was swamp water, so drinking water was piped from near-by springs by means of an earthenware aqueduct.

We know how the city of Tenochtitlán looked at the height of its power, for the Spaniards saw it in 1520 and wrote letters and stories back to Spain describing it. One of the men, called Bernal Díaz (dee'ahs), wrote a long description of the beautiful city. Its white towers and temples shone in the sun and immense pyramids reared toward the heavens. The houses of the people were made of adobe somewhat like the pueblo houses of our own Southwest. They were painted red and white, with colored decorations. Thousands of workers were kept busy cleaning the streets and scrubbing the buildings until they shone. There were many trees and gardens in the city. The ruler lived in a palace surrounded by parks. He kept birds of all kinds to grow plumage for the cloaks of the nobility. So many eagles were kept in captivity that it was said five hundred tame turkeys had to be slaughtered every day to feed them. What a colorful city this must have been with its gay houses, its many canals sparkling in the sun, and its walks crowded with people in bright costumes!

THE MARKET AT TENOCHTITLÁN REVEALS THE LIFE OF THE AZTECS

The heart of the city was the great stone-paved market place. Throngs of people came and went continually, for this was the shopping center of the Aztecs. Bernal Díaz's description of the market has been translated from the Spanish, so that we have an eye-witness view of what it looked like.

Díaz marveled at the elegant clothing of the men, the fine embroideries, the fur and feather mantles. He speaks of the women whose "raven tresses floated luxuriantly over their shoulders, revealing features which, although of a ... cinnamon hue, were not unfrequently pleasing."

The square itself was three times as large as a famous square in Spain. Traders and craftsmen from all over Mexico were gathered here, and each had a booth to display his wares. There were goldsmiths who had golden ornaments for sale, also "curious toys ... made in imitation of birds and fishes, with scales and feathers of gold and silver, and with moveable heads and bodies." [1]

There were booths of the weavers where cotton materials dyed in bright colors and tapestries trimmed with pure gold could be bought. Elaborately carved vases of wood stood near pottery of all shapes and designs. There were mirrors and swords of the hard volcanic glass called obsidian. Druggists carried all sorts of medicines, and barbers waited to shave customers with sharp glass razors. Beautiful flowers from the floating gardens were offered for sale by florists.

THE AZTEC ARMY WAS NEEDED TO MAINTAIN THE EMPIRE

The army was considered very important by the people of Ten-

[1] William H. Prescott. *The Conquest of Mexico*, George Allen and Unwin, Ltd.

OPEN AIR MARKETS like those seen by the Spaniards four hundred years ago are still common in Mexico today. This Mexican hat market has no shelves or counters; most of its wares seem to be on the ground.

Black Star

ochtitlán. Every young man had to serve his time in the army. Instead of captains, lieutenants, and sergeants, the Aztec army had "tiger men" dressed in tiger costumes, "eagle men" dressed in feathers, and a group called "wandering arrows." A young man could be promoted from a common warrior to a "wandering arrow" by bringing in captives. The principal weapons were bows and arrows and swords edged with volcanic glass. The Aztecs protected themselves from enemy arrows by wearing armor made of quilted cotton, stiffened by soaking in salt water.

War was almost a ceremony. An appointment was made between the Aztecs and their enemies to meet in a certain place. If one side got there first, they waited for the others. At nightfall all fighting stopped. The Aztecs were great traders, and many wars started when merchant caravans were attacked in foreign territory. Aztec runners were trained to take news of all such troubles back to the capital. They could carry messages two hundred miles in a day and did not need to learn the words, for the Aztecs could write.

THE AZTECS USED PICTURE WRITING

The Aztecs kept records of taxes and of religious festivals in a picture writing which is easier to read than that of the Mayans. The name of the town of Mazatlán (mah-saht-lahn'), for example, sounds like the Aztec words for "deer" and "teeth," so the Aztecs represented the town by drawing a deer head and some teeth. After this symbol, they might make a picture of blankets or pottery and follow that by a number sign. This writing would mean that the people of Mazat-

lán owed the Aztecs a tribute of so many hundred blankets and pieces of pottery. Most of their books were records of some such tribute.

The books were painted on long strips of paper. This paper was made from fibers of the agave or century plant, which you remember grows in Mexico. The long paper was folded up like a fan. If you want to read an Aztec book, you unfold it and begin at the top, reading from left to right, just as you do in this book.

THE AZTEC CHILDREN WERE WELL BROUGHT UP

Aztec parents were anxious that their children should grow up to be fine men and women according to their standards. To judge by their own words, their standards were not much different from ours today. Here is a speech by an Aztec father to his son, who is starting out to make his way in the world: [1]

Console the poor and unfortunate with kind words. Do not talk too much and never interrupt others. Eat not too fast and show no dislike if a dish displeases thee.... Live by thy work, for thou shalt be the happier therefore. Never lie. When thou tellest anyone what has been told thee, tell the simple truth and add nothing thereto. Be silent in regard to the faults thou seest in others.

The girls who read this book may be interested in the advice an Aztec mother gave to her daughter: [2]

My beloved daughter... take care that your garments are... de-

[1] From Compton's *Pictured Encyclopedia*, F. E. Compton and Company.
[2] From William H. Prescott, *Conquest of Mexico*.

cent and proper, and observe that you do not adorn yourself with much finery, since this is a mark of vanity and folly... neither mince when you speak... nor speak through your nose, but let your... voice be gentle. Walk through the street quietly and with propriety.... See likewise, my daughter, that you never paint your face, or stain it or your lips with colors, in order to appear well.... My dear daughter, whom I tenderly love, see that you live in the world in peace, tranquillity, and contentment, all the days that you shall live.

Both girls and boys were trained in schools set up by the government. They did not learn from books as we do. Boys learned the rules of war and the care of crops, and the girls learned how to do household tasks.

TENOCHTITLÁN WAS GOVERNED WISELY

The ruler of the Aztecs was chosen by the principal chiefs from the grown men of the reigning family, usually a brother or a nephew of the former king. This gave them a chance to select the man best fitted to rule, instead of having to accept the oldest son of the king, as was the custom in Europe. Montezuma was the ruler when the Spaniards arrived. He was assisted by a council of lesser chiefs and by a great number of officials who led his armies and collected taxes from the subject peoples. The council met in a great ceremonial building in the center of Tenochtitlán.

There was a court of justice which tried people who were accused of breaking the law. All crimes were severely punished, and there was equal justice for all. The son of a noble or a poor slave received the same sentence of death if convicted of murder. If a young man spent his father's money wastefully or was found guilty of continual drunkenness, he was put to death.

THE AZTEC CALENDAR MARKED BLOODY RELIGIOUS CEREMONIES

So far we have read only about the fine things in Aztec life. In spite of their civilization, they lived under the influence of a horrible religion. The Toltec idea of sacrificing people to the gods was practiced on even a larger scale by the Aztecs. In the center of Tenochtitlán was a great pyramid. On top of this pyramid were two temples, one dedicated to the Aztec war god, the other to the god of rain. Before the temples was an altar on which the war captives were killed as sacrifices. The victims were led up the long steep stairs of the pyramid and thrown down upon the altar. There a priest using a knife of volcanic glass cut out their hearts. At the height of the Aztec power, tens of thousands of captives were sacrificed every year in these ceremonies.

All the sacrifices were made on certain festival days marked on the Aztec calendar. A large stone called the Calendar Stone was dug up from the swampy lake in 1790, and is now in the museum in Mexico City. The symbols are carved on a twenty-four-ton block of stone. In the center is the figure of the sun, and around it are four squares representing earth, air, fire, and water. The two rows of signs around the outside are symbols of the days and years.

QUETZALCOATL INSPIRED THE AZTEC CRAFTSMEN

Like the Toltecs and the Mayans, the Aztecs also believed in the god

Black Star

THE CALENDAR STONE of the Aztecs is being inspected here by modern Mexicans. Perhaps you recognize the design on the stone, for it has been reproduced on many articles made in Mexico and sold to tourists.

called Quetzalcoatl whose symbol was the feathered serpent. They thought of him as a great teacher and leader who had once really existed as a man. They believed that he had shown the Aztecs how to build temples and make beautiful objects of stone and metal. When the Spaniards came, the Aztecs were still singing the "Hymn to Quetzalcoatl." It describes the pyramid which had been raised in his honor: [1]

There in grandeur reared his temple,
Reared aloft its mighty ramparts
Reaching upward to the heavens;
Wondrous stout and tall the walls were,
High the skyward climbing stairway,
With its steps so long and narrow . . .
That there scarce was room for stepping. . . .

[1] From John H. Corynyn, *The Song of Quetzalcoatl*. Antioch College Press.

Anyone who has tried to climb the pyramid of the sun at Teotihuacán or the great pyramid in Chichén Itzá knows how narrow and steep the steps up to these temples are. The poem goes on about the subjects of Quetzalcoatl:

As master workmen worked they,
Fashioned they the sacred emeralds,
Smelted they both gold and silver.
Other trades and arts they mastered. . . .
And in Quetzalcoatl all these
Arts and crafts had their beginning;
He, the master workman, taught them
All their trades and artifices.

We shall never know how much finer a civilization the Indians would have developed if America had not been discovered when it was. Perhaps they might have worked out a better writing, the use of the wheel, and better tools. After the Spaniards came, all chance for native improvement was ended.

To appreciate and understand our Latin American neighbors of today, we must keep in mind the interesting story of the Indians. One reason that Latin America is different from Spain is that the Indian civilizations were here when the Spaniards came. No modern Latin American nation which is built over an Indian civilization has quite forgotten it.

Are You a Careful Reader? Test Yourself!

I. Complete each of these statements correctly:

1. The Toltecs had learned civilized ways when the primitive .... wandered into the .... of .....

2. The Aztecs built the city of .... on .... in Lake Texcoco.

3. Aztec runners did not need to carry knotted cords because the Aztecs had developed .....

4. Aztec boys and girls went to schools run by the .... ; the boys learned .... and .... , while the girls learned how to .....

5. The war captives of the Aztecs were .... by the .... in a religious ceremony.

II. Match these words and statements:

1. Tenochtitlán
2. obsidian
3. Texcoco
4. Pyramid of the Sun
5. Mazatlán
6. Montezuma
7. Bernal Díaz
8. Calendar Stone
9. wandering arrow
10. Quetzalcoatl

a. leader of the Toltecs
b. lake where Aztec city was built
c. town whose name was written as "deer's teeth"
d. ruler of the Aztecs when the Spaniards arrived in Mexico
e. Spaniard who wrote a description of Tenochtitlán
f. the fair god
g. arrow edged with obsidian
h. volcanic glass
i. capital city of the Aztecs
j. built by the Toltecs at Teotihuacán
k. now found in museum in Mexico City
l. military rank in the Aztec army

Food for Thought and Discussion

1. Which of the Indian governments had the most complete dictatorship? Why?

2. Using your knowledge of the Aztec and Inca governments, can you explain why subjects of the Aztecs were willing to aid Spanish conquerors while subjects of the Incas did not?

3. Read again the advice given to the Aztec boy and girl by their parents. What part would be good advice for the boy and girl of today? Why? What suggestions sound out-of-date for young people of your generation? Why?

Looking Backward

Turn back to the questions given in the preview on page 43. With the information you now have about the great Indian civilizations of the Americas you should not find these questions difficult. Use them in class discussion or for written work.

Interesting Things to Do

1. Read and report on the work of one of the following famous archeologists: Herbert Spinden, Hiram Bingham, Adolf Bandelier, Sylvanus Morley, Manuel Gamio.

2. Look up and tell the class about Dr. Julio Tello, Peruvian archeologist, who is a full-blooded Indian.

3. Report on one of the Indian tribes of our own Southwest: the Pueblo Indians, the Cliff Dwellers, the Basket Makers, the Zuñi, the Hopi, the Navajos.

4. Read and tell the class about one of the *National Geographic* expeditions to such ancient cities as: Pachacamac, Tiahuanaco, Machu Picchu, or Mitla.

5. Explain to the class the Inca or Mayan calendar system.

6. Make a clay model of the Aztec Calendar Stone, a Chimu water jug, or other ancient pottery. Make a sketch of the Calendar Stone for the cover of your notebook.

7. Write a story about one of the following: the rain god's bride, a Chimu boy living under the Incas, an Aztec girl or boy.

8. Lead an informal debate on the question: Could the Aztecs and Incas ever have achieved a higher degree of civilization without the wheel or without domesticated animals (except the llama)?

9. Give an illustrated talk to the class on Mayan, Aztec, or Inca art and architecture. Show as many pictures as you can find. (Use the *National Geographic*.)

10. Find and play for the class phonograph records of the music of the Pueblo, Navajo, or Hopi Indians.

Interesting Books to Read

For Further Information

Brown, F. Martin, *America's Yesterday*. Lippincott. Interesting; many illustrations.

Embree, Edwin Roger, *Indians of the Americas*. Houghton Mifflin. Information on all Indian groups.

Mason, Gregory, *Columbus Came Late*. Appleton-Century. Description of how the ancients lived and worked.

The National Geographic Magazine. Issues containing the best archeological accounts: March 1913, April 1913, June 1914, February 1915, May 1916, February 1922, August 1923, January 1925, September 1925, February 1927, July 1931, October 1932, January 1933, November 1935, November 1936, June 1937, August 1939, May 1940, September 1940.

For Pleasure

Malkus, Alida, *The Dark Star of Itzá*. Harcourt, Brace. Also other fast-reading stories by the same author, telling about boys and girls of ancient America.

Morris, Ann Axtell, *Digging in Yucatan*. Junior Literary Guild. Adventures of an archeologist's wife.

Niles, Blair, *Day of Immense Sun*. Bobbs Merrill. An historical novel of the Incas.

Verrill, A. Hyatt, *Before the Conquerors*. Dodd Mead. A seventeen-year-old boy's part in an archeological expedition.

Part Three · THE SPANIARDS COME TO

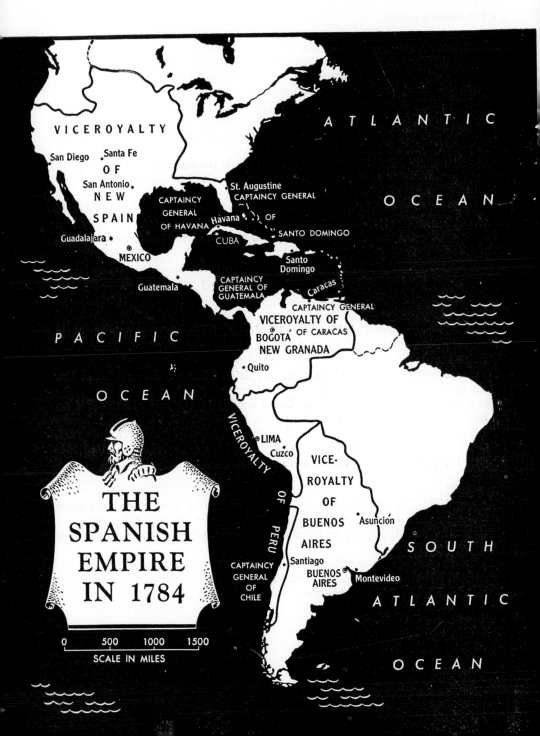

VICEROYALTY
OF
NEW
SPAIN

San Diego
Santa Fe
San Antonio
Guadalajara
MEXICO

CAPTAINCY
GENERAL
OF HAVANA

Havana
CUBA

St. Augustine
CAPTAINCY GENERAL
OF
SANTO DOMINGO
Santo
Domingo

Guatemala

CAPTAINCY
GENERAL OF
GUATEMALA

Caracas

CAPTAINCY GENERAL
OF CARACAS

VICEROYALTY OF
BOGOTÁ
NEW GRANADA

Quito

ATLANTIC

OCEAN

PACIFIC

OCEAN

VICEROYALTY OF PERU

LIMA
Cuzco

VICE-
ROYALTY
OF
BUENOS
AIRES

Asunción

CAPTAINCY
GENERAL
OF
CHILE

Santiago
BUENOS
AIRES

Montevideo

SOUTH

ATLANTIC

OCEAN

THE
SPANISH
EMPIRE
IN 1784

| 0 | 500 | 1000 | 1500 |

SCALE IN MILES

THE NEW WORLD TO STAY

WHY WAS OCTOBER 12, 1492, an unlucky day for the Indians of the Americas? It was on this day that the copper-skinned natives of a tiny island in what is now the West Indies saw three ships anchor off their coast. Little did they guess that the strange white men who set foot upon their shore would seal the fate of all the dusky inhabitants of the Western Hemisphere! They could not know that these men were the forerunners of thousands who would force the proud Indian empires to bow to the might of Spain.

In this part of our book we shall watch the story of three hundred years roll by in the great New World discovered by Columbus. We shall see Spanish soldiers and priests building a huge Catholic empire on top of the Indian civilizations. We shall see this huge empire lost by Spain, and the independent republics of Latin America emerge from its ruins. We shall see great men carrying high the banner of freedom through indescribable hardship and suffering.

The map opposite shows the enormous territory owned and governed by Spain. First find the northern and southern limits of the empire. Does it include the former territory of the Aztecs, the Incas, and the Mayans? Can you name the four viceroyalties or governmental divisions and tell what present countries they included? What were the important cities in each of the viceroyalties?

As you read Part III, it will help you if you keep in mind the following questions:

1. How did the early explorers change the map of the world?
2. How large was Spain's colonial empire and how was it governed?
3. How did life in the Spanish colonies differ from life in the English colonies in America?
4. Why did the Spanish colonists revolt from the mother country?

Chapter 8

Early Explorers Make a Large Round World Out of a Small Flat One

YEARS AGO there were Indian people and Indian civilizations south of the Rio Grande; today the blood of the Spanish conqueror mingles with that of the Indian, and the ancient civilizations have vanished. The language of Spain is spoken by the men who live in the land of the Incas and the Aztecs. No longer do Indian priests salute the rising sun; Catholic cathedrals stand where formerly great pyramids stood. The imprint of Spain is almost everywhere in Latin America.

In 1492, no one in Europe knew that the American continent existed. Yet in a short half-century, amazing things occurred. The Americas were discovered; a handful of Spaniards conquered many thousands of Indians; a Spanish civilization was taking root in the New World.

What brought the Spaniards to American shores? How could they conquer a population five times as large as that of Spain? Why did they completely destroy the Indian civilization? To find the answers to these questions we must turn to Europe, for the fate of the Indians is linked with the story of Spain. This is a story of adventure and heroism, of religious enthusiasm, as well as of conquest and destruction.

SPAIN OUSTS THE MOORS AND FOUNDS A CHRISTIAN KINGDOM

From your study of European history, you may remember that Spain was a part of the great Roman Empire until the barbarians destroyed Rome. Before Spain could settle down as an independent nation, she was invaded by the Moors who came up from North Africa. The Spaniards were too weak to oppose the Moors and the rulers of Spain were driven into the northern mountains.

The Moors controlled most of Spain for 500 years. They encouraged skilled craftsmen, merchants, and scholars to settle there, and soon southern Spain became the most prosperous and civilized country in Europe. Although the Moors allowed the Spaniards to keep their Catholic faith, the people lived for the day when they could throw out the hated Moors. For the Moors were not Christians but followers of the Mohammedan religion, and were considered infidels by the Catholic Spaniards.

There were two little Christian kingdoms, Castile and Aragon, in the north, which had slowly become strong during the years that the Moors controlled southern Spain. By 1252,

Castile and Aragon had conquered all of the peninsula except the little kingdom of Granada in the far south. In 1479, after Ferdinand, ruler of one kingdom, had married Isabella, ruler of the other, they united forces to drive out the last of the Moors. This took many years, but finally in 1492, just before Columbus discovered America, they were successful. Spain was at peace for the first time in many years and anxious to become a powerful nation.

In those days, Christians behaved with great cruelty to those who did not believe as they did. Since Isabella was very religious she determined to stamp out all other religions in Spain. She gave the Jews, and later the Moors, remaining in Spain, the choice of being baptized as Christians or of leaving Spain altogether. Those who did neither were bitterly persecuted. Thus, the Spaniards began to imprison, torture, and even kill their fellow subjects in the name of the Christian religion. This is important to remember because it will help you to understand the Spaniards' treatment of the Indians in America.

IT WAS A SMALL WORLD IN THE YEAR 1200

In the centuries before Columbus, the people knew very little of the world in which they lived. They thought that Europe, southern Asia, and the northern part of Africa were all the land there was. It was the firm belief of most people that anyone venturing beyond these lands would meet mountains of ice to the north and great barriers of fire to the south. To the east and west, the earth simply dropped off into space, and woe betide the luckless mariner who sailed too far in either direction!

People knew that there were such countries as India and China or Cathay, as it was called. They knew of the Spice Islands, which clustered to the southeast of the mainland of Asia. Goods had been trickling into Europe by camel train from the East for many centuries. The Roman women had worn silks and perfumes from China and India. The soldiers of Europe, who went to Jerusalem in the 1000's and 1100's, brought home silks, spices, and perfumes from the Far East. Europeans were becoming more eager to get the wonderful products which only the East could supply: the spices for flavoring their food, the "notemege to put in ale," and the "cloths of silk and gold."

By 1200, merchants were sending ships from Genoa or Venice in Italy to ports in Palestine or Syria. Here they connected with the camel caravans which arrived in these cities with Eastern goods. Ships also went to Alexandria in Egypt to meet traders who had come by boat from India, up the Red Sea, and across the Isthmus of Suez by land. Farther than these ports the traders dared not go because they feared the Mohammedans who controlled all the land routes to the East. Of course, articles brought to Europe this way cost many times their actual value.

The people of Europe had heard vague stories about the countries from which the silks and spices came. Daring men, who wished to see for themselves what these lands were like, began to venture inland along the caravan routes. The most celebrated of these was a young Venetian named Marco Polo, who after many years spent in China brought back wonderful tales which were spread far and wide by travelers, merchants, and priests.

EUROPEANS CHANGE THEIR IDEAS OF THE WORLD AND TURN THEIR EYES TOWARD INDIA

The desire for cheaper eastern goods and the tales of crusaders and travelers roused an interest in a water route to India and Cathay. Scholars began to turn back to study ancient writings which had been gathering dust for years. They discovered that the famous Greek, Aristotle, had known of Cathay. He had even wondered whether the "Ocean Sea" which bordered Cathay might not be the same as the "Sea of Darkness" which lay west of Europe. If this were true, then the earth would have to be round, not flat as they had believed.

Italian geographers began to draw maps using information given by the travelers and seamen. A map of Europe drawn in 1351 showed the Atlantic on the west and the Indian Ocean to the east finally joined together, suggesting a round world instead of a flat one. Although the African continent was drawn much smaller than its actual size, this map showed clearly that India could be reached by sailing around Africa. It was believed that the trip would be only about 1000 miles. Actually it is more nearly ten times that far.

The interest in a water route to the East became greater in the 1400's. The Mohammedans in Asia Minor, whom the Europeans called the Turks, had been moving farther and farther westward toward Europe. The crusaders had gone to stop them, but had failed. In 1453, Constantinople, at the very gateway of Europe, fell to the Turkish army. Europe gave up the idea of forcing back the Turks. They still wanted to trade with the Far East, but to pass through the territory of the feared and hated Turks or to pay them taxes on caravans was very humiliating. A water route would allow them to have their silks, perfumes, and spices and at the same time avoid the Turks.

PRINCE HENRY OF PORTUGAL ENCOURAGES EXPLORATION, AND DREAMS OF REACHING INDIA BY WATER

The actual trip to India by sea was the result of the dreams of a great man. Before Spain had finished driving out the Moors, a prince of Portugal

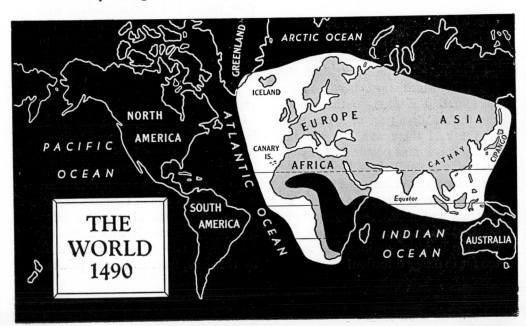

had become interested in exploration. Little Portugal had long been an independent kingdom tucked in on the Atlantic coast to the west of Spain. Prince Henry the Navigator, a son of the ruling family, spent his life and his fortune in finding out more about the world. Sea captains hired by Henry ventured out into the Atlantic near Portugal and found the Madeira Islands off the coast of Africa, the Azores far to the westward, and even the Cape Verde Islands many miles to the south. These were claimed by Portugal and given to nobles of the court as personal property. They became profitable to their owners as plantations for sugar cane and grapes.

It was Prince Henry's greatest ambition that the Portuguese should find a route around Africa to the East. During his lifetime the Portuguese had explored the unknown coast of Africa almost as far as the Equator. One daring navigator, Bartholomew Díaz (dee'ahs), later found the southern end of Africa at the Cape of Good Hope. He was followed by Vasco da Gama (vah'scoh dah gah'mah), who actually reached India in 1498.

COLUMBUS BELIEVES A WESTWARD VOYAGE TO THE INDIES POSSIBLE

By now the time was ripe for someone to attempt a trip to the Indies by sailing westward. Everyone knows something about the story of Christopher Columbus. At the age of fourteen this son of a wool comber in Genoa had become a sailor and later a trader and map-maker. When he settled in Portugal, he spent most of his time poring over old and new maps and talking to sea captains about what land lay to the west. Columbus decided that the route the Portuguese were trying to find was actually the

longer route to the Indies and that, if the world were round, the Indies might be as readily found by sailing west, following the sun in his daily journey.

It now became Columbus's ambition to reach the Indies by sailing west and to discover any new land that might exist. In those days, kings were the only ones rich enough to furnish boats and supplies for exploration. Columbus applied first to the king of Portugal, who refused him help. He was next refused aid by the king and queen of Spain, who felt the trip was not practical. When Columbus applied a second time for aid, Ferdinand and Isabella had almost completed their conquest of the Moors and they were eager to build a powerful nation in Spain. Spain was very poor after years of war and the prospect of finding new lands and gold in the Indies must have been very tempting. So they gave permission for Columbus "to discover and acquire certain islands and mainlands in the western ocean," to keep for himself one tenth of all revenues obtainable there, and to be "Admiral and Viceroy and Governor" of any lands he found.

COLUMBUS DISCOVERS WHAT HE BELIEVES TO BE THE EAST INDIES

We all know how Columbus set out in 1492 with his three sailing ships, the *Niña*, the *Pinta*, and the *Santa Maria*, to face the unknown waters of the Atlantic. They sailed past the Canaries and kept on to the west. It was not a long nor a hard voyage compared to that of other mariners in later years, but it did require courage to sail out into the unknown. Columbus was scarcely surprised to reach the island which they later named San Salvador (sahn sahl'vah-dohr), for he

Brown Brothers

COLUMBUS left no known portrait of himself. This is one of several that appeared some years after his death.

had expected to reach the islands of the Indies. He put on a red robe worn by the admirals of Spain and went ashore to kiss the earth which he had discovered. Naked Carib Indians who lived on the islands clustered about to look at the "white-winged" ships and the strange men. They were especially interested in the Spaniards' beards, for no hair grew on their own faces. Although the island was actually one of the Bahamas, Columbus took for granted that it belonged to the East Indies, so he called the savages Indians. That mistaken name is still used for native Americans today.

On this first voyage, Columbus sailed farther through the Caribbean and found the islands of Cuba and Hispaniola. He greatly admired their jungle scenery and told of the flocks of parrots "so dense as to conceal the sun," but he found no cities of Cathay nor any king to whom he might present the letters of introduction from Ferdinand and Isabella. So Columbus built a fort on the island of Hispaniola, left 44 men there to hold the land for Spain, and returned home.

Ferdinand and Isabella were delighted with the forty gorgeous parrots and the Carib Indians which Columbus brought as proof that he had really found new lands far to the west. So impressed were they by his discoveries that they not only asked him to sit at their feet, but gave him the grand title, "The Admiral of the Ocean Sea and Viceroy and Governor of the Islands discovered in the Indies!" You can imagine how the king of Portugal felt when he heard of Columbus's success, for he might have had all this honor and glory instead of Spain.

COLUMBUS FINDS THE MAINLAND OF SOUTH AMERICA

Now Columbus had only to ask, to get anything he needed for further exploration. He returned to the islands in 1493 with more ships and 1500 men. He founded a larger colony on the island of Hispaniola and made his brother the governor. Young Spanish nobles and other adventurers came out to make their fortune in the new colony. On a third trip he came upon the coast of South America where the Orinoco flows into the ocean. When Columbus saw the huge mud flats cut by many rivers which mark the mouth of the Orinoco, he realized that such a huge river could mean only one thing, that he had found the mainland of a continent. But Columbus, of course, thought the continent was Asia.

Meanwhile, there was trouble in the colony of Hispaniola. The soldiers and other colonists had expected to find easy wealth. They did not want to labor on plantations to make a living. Consequently, there was discontent and quarreling in the colony. Ferdinand and Isabella sent a new

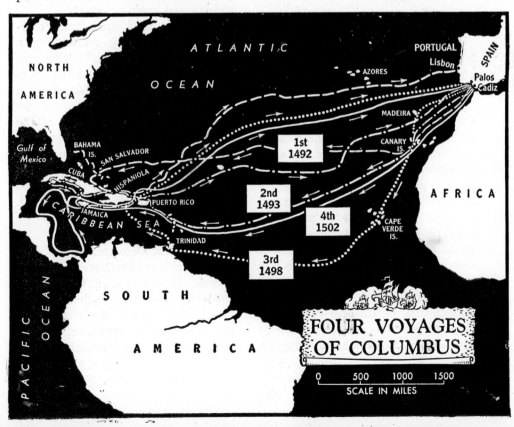

FOUR VOYAGES OF COLUMBUS

governor to Hispaniola who returned Columbus and his brother to Spain in chains. But the colony continued to grow as more Spanish adventurers came out to seek their fortune.

Columbus, who had been immediately set free on his return to Spain, made one last voyage in 1502. It was on this trip that he saw the Mayan trader who he thought was a Chinese from the mainland. When he returned to Spain two years later, after his last trip, he found that he was no longer a popular hero. While he had been seeking China, the Portuguese had reached the Indies by the eastern route and were bringing back spices and jewels. They were glad to point out to Spain that Columbus had not found the Indies at all, but possibly a land separated from Asia by a strait, perhaps even an ocean. Columbus died without knowing what an immense new world he had discovered.

AMERICA GETS ITS NAME

Even in 1506, the year of Columbus's death, not a great deal was known about the newly found territory. New maps were made showing the islands of Cuba, Hispaniola, Puerto Rico, and Jamaica. The Spaniards knew a little about the coast of Central and South America as far as the Orinoco. Descriptions of the new lands began to be written. Among these writers was an Italian named Amerigo Vespucci (ah-mer'ee-go vespoot'chee) who had accompanied one of the early explorers in the wake of Columbus. He was the first man to state in writing that these lands were not part of Cathay, but new regions "which may be called a new world, since our ancestors have no knowledge of them." A German geographer, who believed that Vespucci himself had discovered these lands, printed a book about them and drew them in on a map. He called the territory America, after the supposed discoverer. That is how the name, America, came to be attached to the New World.

THE POPE DIVIDES THE NEW LANDS BETWEEN SPAIN AND PORTUGAL

In claiming new territory for themselves, Spain and Portugal apparently believed that finding is keeping. Spain was afraid that Portugal would try to get a share in the new lands. After Columbus returned in 1492, Ferdinand and Isabella wrote to the Catholic Pope, asking that Spain be granted "all lands to be discovered in the western ocean." As we know, Portugal had already colonized many islands which were certainly in the western ocean. Naturally the Portuguese king protested after the Pope had granted Spain's request.

Finally, in 1493, Spain and Portugal signed a treaty establishing a "Line of Demarcation." This was an imaginary line drawn 370 leagues west of the Cape Verde Islands. (A league is about three miles.) All new lands discovered to the east of the line were to belong to Portugal and all lands west of the line to Spain. This arrangement gave Portugal a free hand along the route to India and in the islands she already had settled.

PORTUGAL CLAIMS BRAZIL

The Line of Demarcation also gave the Portuguese a foothold in the New World. If you look at the map on page 104, you can see that the line cuts through South America at the mouth of the Amazon River. All the land east of the line belonged to

Portugal. The year after da Gama established a trade route around Africa to India, Portuguese merchants fitted out a fleet of thirteen ships to trade with a city in India called Calicut. The captain, Pedro Cabral (cah-brahl'), followed da Gama's charts. He either sailed too far west into the Atlantic before he turned south, or was blown off his course. At any rate, after several days he sighted land which he thought to be an island, but which turned out to be the coast of Brazil. He landed, and claimed the land as lying within the jurisdiction of Portugal. This explains why Brazil has a different story from the other countries of South America, and why the Brazilians speak Portuguese instead of Spanish.

BALBOA FOUNDS A COLONY IN PANAMA AND DISCOVERS THE PACIFIC

Sooner or later someone was bound to find that there was another ocean west of the new lands. The first man to see the Pacific was a Spaniard named Vasco Nuñez de Balboa (vah'-scoh noon'yez day bahl-boh'ah). Balboa was a very ambitious man who had gone to Hispaniola to make a fortune and instead had run into debt. When he heard that a ship was being sent to the coast of what is now Colombia to rescue some Spaniards who had gone to establish a colony there, he stowed away on the boat. When Balboa arrived there, he helped the leader, Francisco Pizarro (frahn-sees'-coh pee-sah'roh), to move the colony to the east coast of Panama. He must have felt that his fortunes were improving when he was made leader of the new settlement.

Balboa was not cruel to the Indians as were many other explorers. He

Keystone

BALBOA appears here in the heavy armor and plumed helmet worn by Spanish soldiers of noble birth.

made friends with the natives and got food for his colony. It was from these Indians that he learned about the great ocean across the isthmus, and about the Indians of the western coast who had much gold. The chief of a friendly tribe had told him that this western coast extended southward without end. Far down the coast, he said, lived people who built great cities and used long-necked animals to carry their burdens. He even made a model of a llama out of clay to show the Spaniards. The people to the south were, of course, the Incas.

Balboa was determined to look upon this other sea, so he set out in 1513 across the jungles of Panama with several hundred Indian bearers, and about 200 men, including Francisco Pizarro. The short distance of 45 miles took the Spaniards 18 days. They hacked their way through dense jungle and swam or waded across tropical streams. At last Balboa climbed a hill and stood alone looking out over the blue ocean. As the Isthmus of Panama extends from west to east, he was actually looking to the south. So he named this sea the South Sea, and so it was called by Spaniards for many years. But little did Balboa himself dream what a vast ocean he had discovered.

Before Balboa's story of the Pacific finally reached the king, he sent a new governor named Pedrarias Dávila (pay-drah'ree-as dah'vee-lah) and 1500 adventure-loving Spaniards to help him in further exploration. But the governor was jealous of Balboa, and his followers were not prepared for expeditions into the jungle. Instead of the gold and pearls which

MAGELLAN was only forty-one years old when he was killed in the Philippines on his trip around the world.

Brown Brothers

they had hoped to find in Panama, the disappointed men found only mosquitoes and malaria. Half of them died. When Balboa began to build boats for the exploration of the west coast, the jealous Pedrarias accused him of planning to set up an independent government. He was arrested and beheaded for treason. It was left to Pizarro to embark seven years later on the adventure of finding Peru.

MAGELLAN SAILS WESTWARD AROUND THE WORLD AND PROVES THAT AMERICA IS A NEW CONTINENT

In spite of the discovery of the Pacific Ocean, most Europeans could not grasp the idea of a much larger world, and still believed that Asia lay close to America. It was a Portuguese named Ferdinand Magellan who discovered that a huge ocean separated the two continents. He was sure that he could find a short cut to the East Indies by sailing westward. Spain furnished him five vessels for a two-year voyage.

In 1519, Magellan started on a voyage that was to make the voyage of Columbus a mere pleasure trip in comparison. After many days of searching along the east coast of South America, he and his men finally found the straits that bear his name and made their way through to the Pacific. Three months of starvation and suffering followed before the ships at last reached the Philippine Islands. When Magellan met traders there from the mainland of Asia, he realized that he had sailed around the great unknown part of the world. Although he himself was killed by natives, one of his ships made its way around Africa to Spain in 1522.

Thus was completed the first trip

around the world. Europeans now realized that the world was much larger than anyone had imagined. They knew that a huge continent and a boundless ocean lay to the west between Europe and the Indies. Spain was content to give up plans to conquer the Indies and turned to exploring and colonizing the great New World.

Are You a Careful Reader? Test Yourself!

I. Choose the best answer:

1. For the first time in centuries the rulers of Spain were free to become a powerful nation because: (*a*) they were no longer at war with England; (*b*) they had driven out the Moors and now controlled their own country; (*c*) they had trained many fine navigators and were interested in trading with India.

2. There was a greater interest in water routes to the Far East after 1453 because: (*a*) the land routes were practically closed to Europeans; (*b*) it had been proved that Africa could be encircled by ship; (*c*) books written by travelers and explorers had been translated into European languages.

3. After 1522 a westward route to the Indies was no longer sought because: (*a*) the world had been proved to be round; (*b*) no strait had been found through America; (*c*) Magellan had proved that the Pacific was a vast ocean.

4. Descendants of America's earliest inhabitants are called Indians today because: (*a*) Europeans considered all dark-skinned people to be natives of the Indies; (*b*) Columbus believed that the natives he found were inhabitants of the East Indies; (*c*) the Mayans, Aztecs, and Incas were descendants of nomadic Indian tribes.

5. Columbus knew he had reached a large continent on a later voyage because: (*a*) he could not find a passage through to the Indies; (*b*) the natives told him of civilized tribes living far inland; (*c*) the Orinoco River seemed so large that he knew it must drain a huge area.

II. Match these words and statements:

1. Moors	*a.* governor of a Spanish colony in Colombia
2. da Gama	*b.* Portuguese leader in the science of navigation
3. Columbus	*c.* Mohammedan conquerors of Spain
4. Prince Henry	*d.* reached India by sailing around Africa
5. Cathay	*e.* "Admiral of the Ocean Sea"
6. Vespucci	*f.* first land of the New World to be seen by a white man
7. Line of Demarcation	*g.* governor of Panama
8. Pedrarias Dávila	*h.* given credit for the discovery of the New World through error
9. Balboa	*i.* early name given to China
10. San Salvador	*j.* city in Spain from which the Moors were driven
	k. divided the New World between Spain and Portugal
	l. he stood on a peak gazing upon a great ocean

Food for Thought and Discussion

1. Using the globe, explain why Columbus discovered the New World by accident.

2. Who do you think was of greater service to humanity — Columbus, Balboa, Prince Henry, or Magellan? Why?

3. Explain the meaning of the name of this chapter.

Chapter 9

The Spaniards Conquer, Colonize, and Convert

IN SPITE of her disappointment at not finding a westward route to the Indies, Spain saw that the discovery of new lands was a great opportunity for her. Thousands of daring soldiers were eager for the adventure and the possible gold which the new lands offered. As if that were not enough, here was a chance for a deeply religious country to spread Christianity among the natives of these heathen lands. Spain made the most of her opportunity. Across the seas they went, daring soldiers and devout priests, to gain gold and souls for the glory of Spain.

THE SPANIARDS FIGHT THE INDIANS

Everywhere the conquerors, or *conquistadores* (kohn-kees-tah-doh'rays), as they were called, fought the Indians and took their treasure. With the exception of a few leaders like Balboa and some of the priests, they treated the Indians with great harshness. It is said that within fifty years or a few generations after the Spaniards came to Cuba and Hispaniola there were almost no Indians left on the islands. Those who were not killed in battle, or worked to death in the mines and on the plantations, died of diseases which the Spaniards brought with them.

Contradictory as it may seem, one of the principal objects of the religiously-minded Spaniards was also to civilize and Christianize the Indians. And if many of the *conquistadores* were interested chiefly in finding gold and silver, many others tried to protect the natives from oppression. They built schools and hospitals for them, and tried to reduce them to an ordered village life.

Too often, however, the early conquerors left death and destruction behind them. On the monument to the last of the Aztec rulers in Mexico City is a scene of torture carved in stone. Two Aztec chiefs are writhing in agony as Spaniards apply fire to the soles of their feet. Probably they are trying to make them reveal hidden gold.

The Spaniards have been called cruel, and cruel they were. But we must remember that their cruelty was only a reflection of the manners of their time and that most Europeans in the 1500's were less sensitive to human suffering than we are today.

CORTEZ LEADS AN EXPEDITION TO MEXICO

The story of the conquest of Mexico and Peru is the story of two daring *conquistadores*. One of them, Francisco Pizarro, conqueror of Peru, we have already met; the other is Hernando Cortez (air-nahn'doh cor-tes'), who conquered Mexico and Central America.

For some years after 1492, the only colonies in the New World were those in the West Indies and Panama. But the magic word, gold, led the governor of Cuba to send an expedition into Mexico. Reports had come to the Spaniards of a rich Mexican empire where civilized Indians lived under a king. It was said that they had quantities of gold. You remember that so far the Spaniards had found only uncivilized Indians on the islands of the West Indies and in Panama. Therefore, news of a rich kingdom must have been very welcome to them.

Hernando Cortez, a popular colonist on the island of Cuba, was chosen as leader. Cortez was a soldier of noble birth who had decided to try his fortune in the New World. He was ordered by the governor to spy out the land, baptize the Indians, and return to Cuba in a short time. One member of his expedition was Bernal Díaz, the historian whose writing we quoted in the story of the Aztecs.

Cortez and his fleet landed on the east coast of Mexico near where the city of Veracruz is today. Runners had already carried word to Montezuma in Tenochtitlán of the strange white men who appeared in ships with wings like birds. Montezuma feared that Cortez might be the fair-skinned god Quetzalcoatl, who the Aztecs believed might some day return. He dared not offend him, so he sent messengers to the coast with gifts of fine embroidered cloths, gold and silver ornaments, and headdresses of feathers and precious stones. Cortez es-

pecially liked the two plates, one of silver and one of gold, which measured three feet across. These are estimated to have been worth $300,000 in our money. Some of the gifts of Montezuma which were sent by Cortez to the king of Spain are still to be seen in museums in Europe.

CORTEZ JOINS THE ENEMIES OF MONTEZUMA

Cortez was more anxious than ever to conquer a king who had plates of solid gold, but his forces were too few to risk against Montezuma's many warriors. Then Cortez learned that Indian tribes on the coast who hated Montezuma's rule were willing to join the Spaniards in attacking him. When he heard this, Cortez made a bold decision. He decided to break with his former friend, the governor of Cuba,

THE BOLD CORTEZ looks more like a scholar in this picture than like the adventurous *conquistador* who conquered Mexico.

Guillumette

UNITED STATES
DE SOTO 1539-'42
ATLANTIC OCEAN
Colorado R.
Arkansas R.
R.
Mississippi
Zuñi
CORONADO 1540-'42
Rio Grande
GULF OF MEXICO
CABEZA DE VACA 1528-'36
Havana
CUBA
Santiago
CORTEZ 1519-'21
Compostela
MEXICO
Veracruz
CARIBBEAN SEA
CORTEZ 1524-'25
PACIFIC OCEAN
ALVARADO 1523-'24
Guatemala
CENTRAL AMERICA
BALBOA 1513
SPANISH EXPLORATIONS IN NORTH AMERICA
0
500
1000
SCALE IN MILES

and go ahead on his own responsibility. He declared the group of men at Veracruz to be a new colony directly responsible to the king of Spain, and had himself elected governor of the colony. To make the break final and to prevent anyone from weakening and returning to Cuba, Cortez burned all the ships. In August of the year 1519, he set out with his Indian allies on the difficult journey up to the Valley of Mexico.

It was not until November, after several battles with Indians on the way, that the Spaniards stood on the causeway (a raised highway) leading to Tenochtitlán and looked at the dazzling city. They were delighted with the lake, the gardens, and the houses. Montezuma decided to make the Spaniards honored guests and to let them live in one of the royal residences on the great square. He probably thought that if these fair-skinned men were not gods, they would make fine sacrifices on the great pyramid. Although it was dangerous, Cortez and his men entered the city and lived for months in splendor.

Spaniards left on the coast suddenly sent up messengers to tell Cortez that the governor of Cuba had sent an expedition against him. Cortez returned to the coast, captured the leader of the expedition, and won the other Spanish soldiers to his side.

Now he had plenty of men to seize the city. Meanwhile, in Tenochtitlán, a terrible tragedy had occurred. Alvarado (ahl-vah-rah'doh), a young lieutenant whom Cortez had left in charge, feared the Aztec chieftains were plotting against the Spaniards. He foolishly decided to act first. He and his soldiers turned on their hosts in the midst of a religious festival and slaughtered hundreds of them.

But the Aztecs had also killed some Spaniards and they now knew that these men were not gods. Nor were the godlike dragons, their horses, immortal. The Indians in fury drove the Spaniards back to their quarters, and tried to starve them into submission. When Cortez heard this news, he hurried up from the coast with hundreds of new Spaniards and re-entered what was now a sullen, hostile city. A real war had begun.

THE SPANIARDS FIGHT THEIR WAY OUT OF TENOCHTITLÁN

It was in June, 1520, that the Aztec warriors closed in around the Spaniards, fighting hand to hand and outnumbering them hundreds to one. Montezuma tried to intervene and was killed by a stone thrown at his forehead. Finally the Spaniards, after six days of street fighting, decided to force their way out of the city. They gained the causeway in the middle of the night. Bridges along the raised highways across Lake Texcoco had been destroyed and the Spaniards, with their horses and the gold and jewels which they had hoped to save, were plunged into the lake.

Cortez and Alvarado were fortunate enough to get across. Of the 1250 Spanish troops which Cortez had at the beginning of the war, 450 were killed that night. This night is known in Mexican history as "La Noche Triste" (noh'chay trees'tay), the sad night. You can still see the large old tree on the outskirts of Mexico City under which it is said Cortez sat and wept over the loss of his men.

TENOCHTITLÁN FINALLY FALLS TO THE SPANIARDS

Cortez had gambled everything on a conquest of Mexico. He could never return to Cuba unless he wished to be hanged for treason, and he certainly could not go back to Spain unless he had gold and lands to offer the king. There was only one course for him to take. That was to conquer Tenochtitlán and the Aztec warriors. Cortez spent months winning over more Indian allies, planning his campaign, and letting his men rest.

The Aztecs had been preparing, also. Montezuma had been killed, but they chose a young king named Guátemoc (gwah'tay-mok) to lead them. Cortez had to attack the city again and again. Eight months of fighting passed before Guátemoc was forced to surrender himself and his city. In spite of their numbers, the Aztecs were no match for the cannon and the superior weapons of the Spaniards.

The brave young Aztec king, who had led the long fight, became a hero of Mexico. There is a large statue of him in Mexico City today. But nowhere in Mexico is there a statue of Hernando Cortez. Many Mexicans dislike him, for with his coming began the enslavement of the Indians.

THE SPANIARDS BUILD MEXICO CITY ON THE RUINS OF TENOCHTITLÁN

After the surrender of the city in

1521, the Spaniards proceeded to re-build and rename it. Perhaps Tenoch-titlán was too difficult for Spanish tongues. At any rate, they changed the name to Mexico (we call it Mexico City) after the Valley of Mexico in which it lies. They tore down every temple and the half-ruined buildings of the Aztecs. Many of the beauti-fully carved stones they threw into the lake to fill the canals and make streets for a new Spanish city. On the great square or Zócalo (so'cah-lo), where the big pyramid stood, the priests who came with Cortez started to build a Catholic church. The cathedral which later replaced the church still stands on the Zócalo in Mexico City today.

Many Spaniards remained in the city to settle down and become col-onists of the New World. Land was parceled out to them, and the Indians

THE DASHING ALVARADO on the *Noche Triste* made a leap which saved his life. He escaped by planting his spear in the mud of the shallow canal and vaulting across a gap in the causeway!

Culver

were forced not only to work on the land, but to be baptized in the Chris-tian religion. What a hard fate for the former inhabitants of beautiful Tenochtitlán to have their city torn down over their heads and to become slaves of the conqueror!

CORTEZ SENDS MEN TO EXPLORE NORTHERN MEXICO

In the meantime, Cortez sent ex-peditions against the neighboring In-dians until all the civilized tribes be-longing to the Aztec empire had been subdued. This took his men as far west as the region where the city of Guadalajara (gwah-dah-lah-hah'rah) stands today. Beyond was still more territory to explore. Most of north-ern Mexico was semi-desert inhabited by wild tribes who had never belonged to the Aztec empire. The Spaniards later attempted to make them Chris-tians and to force them to work in the silver mines of northern Mexico. They were not very successful, al-though they carried on wars for years with these Indians.

CORTEZ AND HIS LIEUTENANTS GO SOUTH INTO THE MAYAN COUNTRY

After the conquest of Mexico, Cortez turned his attention to the lands to the south. He sent expedi-tions to explore and settle what is now Central America.

Alvarado headed an expedition to conquer Guatemala, which was said to be a very rich country. Guatemala was the home of a branch of the Mayans who had lost much of the civilization of their ancient ancestors. To conquer these people, Alvarado used the same methods that Cortez used against the Aztecs, but he acted with greater cruelty. Finding that the two principal tribes were frequently at war, he allied himself with one against the other. Even with his Indian allies, it took Alvarado two years to destroy their chief city and conquer the various tribes. Meanwhile, in Guatemala the Spaniards built a new Spanish capital which was soon moved to the site of the present city of Antigua (ahn-tee'gwah). As we shall see, this city became a center of government for all of Central America.

In Honduras, one of Cortez's captains rebelled, just as Cortez himself had rebelled against the governor of Cuba. Taking Guátemoc, the Aztec ruler, as hostage, Cortez began a long march from Mexico across the base of the Yucatan peninsula to subdue the captain. The Spaniards may have passed by many of the ruined cities of the Mayans which the archeologists are only now beginning to uncover. In one Indian town, they left a lame horse. The people thought it was a god and fed it only on flowers. When it died, they carved a stone horse, and were still worshiping this idol when other Spaniards visited the town a hundred years later!

On this expedition Cortez executed Guátemoc because he suspected him of plotting with other Indian chiefs against the Spaniards. When Cortez had restored peace and order, he hastened with his men back to Mexico City, where the Spaniards who had been left behind were already quarreling among themselves.

THE LAST OF MAYAN CIVILIZATION IN YUCATAN IS WIPED OUT

You remember that after the civil wars in the thirteenth and fourteenth centuries the civilization of the Mayans had decayed. Only a fraction of the former inhabitants still lived in their neglected cities. Francisco Montejo (mohn-tay'ho) was sent in 1527 by Cortez and the king of Spain to conquer these people. But among them, as a chieftain, lived a Spaniard who had been shipwrecked on the coast of Yucatan many years before. He taught them how to fight the Spaniards. He told them not to form lines so that the cannon of the enemy could mow them down. They attacked the Spaniards and forced them after a few years to give up the attempt to conquer Yucatan.

Twenty years later, Montejo's son came again with a Spanish army to conquer the Mayans. He used the Spanish trick of setting one group of Indians against another. The people of Uxmal still hated the people of Chichén Itzá enough to help the Spaniards defeat them. As soon as Chichén Itzá was conquered, the Spaniards turned on Uxmal and subdued that city also.

The Spaniards forced all the remaining Mayans to build a new city, Mérida (may'ree-dah), which is now the capital of Yucatan. The Indians were driven to this labor and few were allowed to work in the corn and yam fields. What little food grew, the Spaniards ate. Thousands of miserable Mayans died of hard labor and starvation. Thus was written the final chapter in the history of the ancient Mayans. Their once marvelous civilization, which had already decayed after the civil wars, was now entirely blotted out by the conquerors.

CORTEZ BECOMES CAPTAIN-GENERAL OF NEW SPAIN

The Spanish conquest of Mexico and Central America was finished. It had been a mighty undertaking. Tremendous stores of gold wrested from the Indians had been sent to Spain. Mines were discovered which produced still more gold and silver. Millions of Indians had been enslaved and vast territories explored and colonized.

Cortez, who had staked everything on the conquest of Mexico, became very popular in Spain. When he went back for a visit he was greeted as a national hero. Had he not gained rich lands for his country and as proof of their wealth sent yellow gold back to Spain? He returned to America as "Captain-General of New Spain" (Mexico). As further reward he was given hundreds of square miles of Mexico as his personal estate. The king, however, afraid of leaving the government in the hands of so powerful a subject, delivered it over to a court of judges called an *audiencia* (ow-dee-en'see-ah), whose duty it was to check on the captain-general. Later this court was replaced by a great Spanish nobleman with the title of viceroy.

SPANIARDS BRING TALES OF CITIES MADE OF SILVER

While Cortez was busy in Mexico, other expeditions were sent out from the islands of Hispaniola and Cuba. Ponce de León (pohn'say day lay-ohn') had discovered Florida in 1512. Spaniards had sailed up the coast beyond Florida as far as the Carolinas. They even tried to settle a colony among the wild tribes of Florida.

There is an interesting story about one expedition along the west coast of Florida. The men on land lost contact with their ships and were forced to build small boats from the hides of their horses. One by one these vessels were lost until the last one was wrecked on an island off the coast of Texas. Cabeza de Vaca (cah-bay'-sah day vah'cah) and some companions were enslaved as medicine men by primitive Indians in Texas. After five years among the Indians, Cabeza de Vaca was able to escape and travel on foot as a great medicine man westward as far as the gulf of California, and eventually back to Mexico City. He brought stirring tales of rich lands far inland. He had seen settled communities and had heard stories of the Pueblo Indians, whose towns were called the "Seven Cities of Cíbola" (see'boh-lah), and said to be made of silver. These tales caused great excitement both in Spain and in Mexico.

EXPLORERS PENETRATE INTO THE SOUTHWEST AND THE SOUTHEAST

In 1540, the viceroy sent an expedition, headed by Francisco de Coronado (coh-roh-nah'doh), north from Mexico to seek out the silver cities. As the Spaniards advanced north of the Rio Grande, they were told in every village that the Cities of Cíbola lay farther on. For two years the trusting Spaniards kept searching over desert and mountain and plain, going as far as the center of the present state of Kansas, but they never found the Seven Cities. The Indians had indeed sent them on a wild-goose chase.

Coronado was bitterly disappointed, for he had seen himself as the discoverer of great riches. Some good came of the difficult trip, however, for a great deal of what is now the southwestern part of the United States had been explored. Coronado and his

Sawders

AMBITIOUS PIZARRO, a swineherd in his youth, persuades Charles V of Spain to help him in the conquest of Peru. The agreement drawn up between them calls for kind treatment of the Indians.

men had discovered the Rio Grande and the Colorado rivers; they had found the Pueblo Indians of New Mexico and even the Grand Canyon of the Colorado.

At the same time that Coronado was penetrating the Southwest, a Spaniard named Hernando de Soto (air-nahn′doh day soh′toh) was exploring in the Southeast. He set out from Cuba in 1539 with over 600 men. They spent three years exploring the region about the Gulf of Mexico, suffering terrible hardships. De Soto discovered the Mississippi River, but, worn out by his labors, he died soon after and was buried in the great river by his companions. The remaining

men built rude boats and made their way down the river and along the shore to Mexico.

PIZARRO FULFILLS BALBOA'S DREAM OF FINDING PERU

Let us turn now to Francisco Pizarro, the conqueror of Peru. You remember that he accompanied Balboa in 1513 on his trip across Panama to find the Pacific. Since the death of Balboa, he had remained in Panama, exploring with his soldiers. Once an Indian chieftain saw the men of Pizarro and Balboa fighting over a few golden trinkets. The chief was disgusted and said, "What is this, Christians? Is it for such a little thing that you quarrel? If this is what you prize, I can tell you of a land where they eat and drink out of golden vessels, and where gold is as cheap as iron is with you." Then he added, "It is necessary that you be more in number than you are now, for you will have to fight your way with great kings." [1]

Pizarro was determined to find this land where Indians drank from golden vessels. He had been only a swine-herd in Spain and had run away to join an expedition to the newly discovered islands. He could not even read or write, but he had qualities which counted for more than education and family in this new world. Pizarro could work hard, he could endure hardships, and he could keep going when things went wrong.

Pizarro's first attempts to reach the Inca empire took him as far as northern Peru. Finely clothed Inca subjects allowed him to land and see the town. They told him of the great cities of Quito, Caxamarca (kah-hah-mar'kah), and Cuzco far up in the highlands. They gave him many gifts, and among them was a golden vessel to drink from, such as the Indian chief had described.

Pizarro was determined to find the rich cities of the Incas. Armed with his gifts and stories of what he had seen with his own eyes, Pizarro went directly to Charles V, now king of Spain. The king was greatly impressed and gave him permission to collect men, horses, and ships for the expedition. Pizarro persuaded two of his brothers to go with him. When

[1] Elsie Spicer Eells, *South America's Story*, copyright, 1931, by Elsie Spicer Eells. Reprinted by permission. Dodd Mead and Company, Inc.

he landed on the coast of Peru in 1531, Pizarro had about 300 men.

He set out immediately to meet the Inca emperor in Caxamarca, starting his troops up the steep western range of the Andes. Never had the Spaniards seen such mountain trails as these. The hardy Spanish horses had to be led over the dangerous Inca roads. When they finally reached Caxamarca, they found the town empty. In the open valley was the ruler, Atahualpa (ah-tah-whal'pah), waiting to meet them with his Inca warriors.

The Incas had no legend of a fair-skinned god to put fear in their hearts. They knew the horses were not gods because some horses had been killed on the journey. Pizarro and his men could not hope to defeat Atahualpa's army, so they tried a trick. Atahualpa consented to meet Pizarro in the main square of Caxamarca. Pizarro had hidden his soldiers in the side streets and empty buildings, and had put two cannons in the square. When Atahualpa entered at the head of a great procession, he found only a priest and a young Inca interpreter who had been seized on the first trip.

The interpreter was instructed to tell Atahualpa the story of the Christian God and the sacred writings of the Bible. The priest showed the Inca a copy of the Bible, but, of course, the Indian leader was unfamiliar with any kind of writing. He looked through the leaves and threw it to the ground. This gave the Spaniards a good excuse for capturing the leader. The Spanish soldiers rushed into the square, slaughtered thousands of unsuspecting Incas, and took Atahualpa prisoner.

Atahualpa feared that his half-brother, from whom he had recently seized the empire, would rouse the people against him while he was prisoner. He noticed how hungry the Spaniards were for gold, so he offered to fill a room with the yellow metal in two months' time if they would set him free. Each day messengers went out to all parts of the empire. They returned with many types of gold and silver objects — vases and goblets from the temples, hammered golden sheets, golden models of birds and animals, even small golden trees and plants complete with leaves, flowers, and fruit.

Meanwhile, Atahualpa was held as the personal prisoner of one of the Spanish leaders, who taught him to play cards and chess, while each learned the other's language. After two months, $15,000,000 worth of gold had been collected. Pizarro, like Aladdin, had rubbed the magic lamp. The king of Spain received one fifth of this money, but even the foot-soldiers who came with Pizarro got over $50,000 each. Meanwhile Atahualpa, still believing that his brother was conspiring against him, secretly ordered him to be murdered. The Spaniards became afraid of the undivided loyalty of the Indians to Atahualpa. They held a trial for Atahualpa on the ground of murdering his brother and condemned him to death.

PIZARRO CONQUERS THE LEADERLESS INCAS

The Incas were now almost helpless with Atahualpa and his brother gone. They were so used to a powerful leader that they could not think for themselves. Within a year the triumphant Spaniards conquered Cuzco, the great Inca capital. At about the same time, one of Pizarro's lieutenants marched north and captured the city of Quito. Pizarro had not only found the gold of the Incas, but he had taken an empire from them.

Just as the followers of Cortez explored north and south of Mexico City, so did Pizarro's men search for more rich lands up and down the Andes. An expedition was sent south beyond Lake Titicaca in search of more golden kingdoms. But they found only wild Indians and barren country. Chile was explored, but the Spaniards reported that the land was all mountains and desert and that the Indians there were very good fighters. The story was told that when one Spaniard asked repeatedly for gold, the Indians captured him and tied him with his mouth propped open. They melted up their supply of gold and killed him by pouring the molten gold down his throat. Thus did one goldhungry Spaniard get his fill of gold!

CHILE, COLOMBIA, AND VENEZUELA ARE COLONIZED

An ambitious lieutenant of Pizarro, named Valdivia (vahl-dee'vee-ah), determined, however, to make Chile into a Spanish colony. In 1540, he took 150 Spaniards, 1000 Indians, and a great deal of livestock and crossed the deserts of northern Chile into the fertile land beyond. He discovered the beautiful harbor of Valparaiso and founded the city of Santiago in an inland valley. He planned the streets, the plaza, the sites for the church and the town hall of the present beautiful city of Santiago, capital of Chile.

Venezuela was first settled by an expedition sent out by a group of German bankers. The king of Spain, who owed the bankers a large sum of money, had granted them permission

CARIBBEAN SEA

CENTRAL AMERICA

PANAMA

A T L A N T I C

CARACAS

Orinoco R.

PIZARRO 1531-1533

BOGOTÁ

QUESADA 1536-1538

O C E A N

QUITO

Amazon R.

Caxamarca

ORELLANA 1541-1542

CABRAL 1500

LIMA

Cuzco

P A C I F I C

O C E A N

ASUNCIÓN

Paraná R.

MAGELLAN 1519-1522

VALDIVIA 1540-1541

SANTIAGO

MENDOZA 1535-1537

BUENOS AIRES

Río de la Plata

Line of Demarcation

EXPLORATIONS IN SOUTH AMERICA

0 — 500 — 1000

SCALE IN MILES

to found a colony in payment. They believed that they could find gold and capture slaves to be sold at good prices. The king later canceled the concession he had given to the Germans and their great plans came to nothing. After they had retired from the colony, many Spaniards came to Venezuela and later built the city of Caracas.

You will remember that a civilized people called the Chibchas lived on the high plateau of Colombia where Bogotá is situated today. It is still a long journey to the plateau of Bogotá, except by air, and the Spanish expedition sent to conquer these people in 1536 had a difficult time. Their leader, Jiménez de Quesada (hee-may'-nays day kay-sah'dah), finally arrived on the plateau, quickly subdued the Chibchas, and founded the present city of Bogotá. Many stories of the gold which the Chibchas possessed had reached the Spaniards in the New World. Their king was supposed to be clothed in gold dust and called *El Dorado*, or "The Gilded One." While Quesada himself was in Bogotá, two other expeditions came through the Andes to the plateau, trying to find the gilded king. No one believed that the Chibchas were the people of the legend, so many Spanish expeditions continued to wear themselves out searching for *El Dorado*.

ORELLANA SAILS DOWN THE AMAZON TO THE ATLANTIC OCEAN

The *El Dorado* tale was responsible for a great discovery. A brother of Pizarro, named Gonzalo (gon-sah'loh), had set out from Quito across the Andes in search of *El Dorado*, but bad weather and the dense wilderness east of the mountains had forced his expedition to return. Some of the men, under a leader named Orellana (oh-ray-yah'nah), deserted Gonzalo Pizarro, built a boat and started down one of the rivers in the foothills of the Andes. Orellana soon found that the small river on which he started had become part of a great river. His determination to find out where this river went led to the first trip down the Amazon.

After weeks of living on herbs, Orellana managed to get food from friendly Indians along the shore. They were often attacked by wild Indians. In one place, women came down to the river's edge and fought with bows and arrows. Do you remember the Greek legend about the warlike maidens called the Amazons? Orellana decided to name the river Amazon, after the fierce women who attacked him and his men along its shores.

At last, the Spaniards reached the wide mouth of the river. Even then, it was some time before Orellana knew they had reached the ocean, for the fresh water of the Amazon continues far out to sea. Finally they reached the island of Trinidad, where there was a Spanish colony. In spite of Orellana's efforts, the Amazon country was claimed and settled by the Portuguese, who had already discovered Brazil.

THE SPANIARDS SETTLE IN THE PLATA RIVER BASIN

You remember that Magellan sailed into the Plata River while looking for a strait through South America. The territory in this region was not particularly attractive to the *conquistadores*. There were no Indian civilizations to conquer nor any gold to plunder, but there were thousands of acres of fertile land which later attracted settlers. An expedition of 1200 colonists came to the Plata in 1536 under Pedro de Mendoza, but in one year hostile Indians had killed all but 700 of them. Most of these went up the Paraná River, which flows into the Plata, to found a colony among more friendly Indians. The colony was called Asunción (ah-soon-see-own') and is today the capital of Paraguay.

Over forty years later, a group of 60 Spaniards accompanied by 200 Indian families came down from Asunción with cows, sheep, tools, and seeds to try another settlement on the banks of the Plata. This new town was located on the same spot where the Spaniards had landed in 1536, and was called Buenos Aires. It was not considered an important colony by the Spanish rulers. There were no precious metals to be sent back to Spain and no civilized Indians to be made to work for the Spaniards. Although Argentina is one of the most important countries today, for 200 years it remained one of the poorest and most backward parts of the Spanish empire in America.

Brazil, another important nation in South America, was explored and settled by the Portuguese. This is an entirely separate story and has made the history of Brazil quite different from that of the Spanish American countries. You will read the story of the founding of Brazil in Chapter 35.

SPANISH COLONIES STRETCH FROM BUENOS AIRES TO THE RIO GRANDE

In 1492, no one knew of the great new lands to the west. By 1600, the Spanish colonies covered most of the territory between the Rio Grande and the Plata River in South America. In the century between, the Spaniards had explored a new world, conquered millions of Indians, converted many of them to Christianity, planted colonies, and founded cities. We shall read in the next chapter how the Spaniards ruled their new possessions.

Are You a Careful Reader?   Test Yourself!

I. Complete these statements correctly:

1. The Spanish name for conquerors is . . . . .
2. Cortez was able to defeat the . . . . because he had better . . . . .
3. The name given to Mexico and the southwestern part of the present United States was . . . .
4. Pizarro was able to conquer the Incas after . . . . had been killed because they were powerless to act without a . . . . .
5. After Peru was conquered, settlements were made by the Spaniards in . . . . , ... , and . . . . .

II. Are the following statements true or false?

1. Orellana sailed down the Amazon from the foothills of the Andes.
2. Valdivia established the first settlement in what is now Colombia.
3. Guátemoc was defeated and finally executed by Cortez.
4. Alvarado accompanied Pizarro in his conquest of Peru.
5. Atahualpa was the leader of the Aztecs against Cortez.
6. Coronado led the expedition looking for the Seven Cities of Cíbola in New Mexico.
7. Quesada conquered the Chibchas in what is now Colombia, and founded Bogotá.
8. The Gilded One was a legendary king of the fierce Indians of Chile.
9. De Soto was buried in the great river which he discovered.
10. Francisco Montejo failed to conquer the Mayans because they had been taught how to fight by a shipwrecked Spaniard.

Food for Thought and Discussion

1. Does the fate of the Incas show a weakness in their type of government? Why?
2. Do you think the Spaniards were any more cruel than other Europeans of that time? How did English colonists treat the Indians? How were women suspected of witchcraft treated in England and the American colonies?
3. What advantages did the Spaniards have over the Indians at the time of conquest? What advantages did the Indians have over the Spaniards?

Chapter 10

Spanish America Lives for Three Centuries Under the Flag of Spain

IF WE COULD TURN time back to the year 1500 and watch the next three centuries come and go in the New World, what should we see? There would be a vast colonial empire, dotted with cities and towns, stretching from Buenos Aires in the south to California in the north. Great numbers of Indians, no longer owners of their native soil, would be laboring hopelessly on the land and in the mines. We should see the Christian cross carried by brave Catholic priests into every corner of the land. Huge and topheavy galleons laden with treasure would be sailing home to Spain, while pirates lie in wait to seize them. Most important of all, we should see a new race being created in whose veins flowed the blood of conqueror and conquered, destined to become the leading race in many parts of Latin America. Let us look closer at Spain's colonies in the New World.

SPANISH BLOOD WAS IMPORTANT IN THE NEW WORLD

There were hundreds of Indians for every Spaniard in Spanish America, but it was not hard for the Spaniards to keep the upper hand. They saw to it that they controlled the Church, owned most of the land, operated the government, and kept an army. It was a Spanish world, run by and for Spaniards. The Indians were looked upon as a source of wealth, just as were the mines and the land.

The Spaniards had transplanted their language and customs alongside an Indian civilization. As the colonies grew, four or five distinct classes developed. At the top were the Spaniards from old Spain, who held all the important positions in the government and in the Church. They were called *gachupines* (gah-choo-peen'ays), which means "man on horseback wearing spurs." They considered themselves far above the pure-blooded Spaniards born in America, who were called *criollos* (kree-o'yohs) or creoles to distinguish them from the native Spaniards. The creoles were allowed to hold only unimportant offices in the government, but they became wealthy landowners, merchants, and mineowners in the colonies. They were just as arrogant as the *gachupines* and both classes considered themselves far too fine to do any manual labor.

Gachupines and creoles both looked down upon the *mestizos* (mes-tee'sohs), who were part Spanish and part Indian. Not many Spanish women came to the colonies at first, so most of the men took Indian wives. There was no feeling against the Indians because their skin was dark, perhaps because the Spaniards were used to the dark-skinned Moors who had lived in Spain for so many centuries. The *mestizos* became the largest group in the colonies and worked as small farmers, or as laborers and craftsmen in the cities. Many of them were miserably poor, but they were no worse off than most of the people of Europe at that time. The *mestizos* are important because they make up a large percentage of the Latin Americans today.

A still lower class were the humble Indians who worked long hours in the fields and in the mines to produce wealth for the conquerors. There are still millions of pure-blooded Indians living in Mexico, Central America, and the highlands of the Andes today. They live in little farm villages and speak the native tongue of their fathers.

The lowest class in the colonies was the Negroes who had been brought over from Africa as slaves. The Spaniards found that they were sturdier than the Indians and better able to endure hard work in the tropical heat. Many Negroes labored in the cotton and sugar plantations of the New World. Most of them were found in the islands of the West Indies and the coastlands of the Caribbean. That is why Negro people form a large part of the population of these regions today.

SPAIN TRIES TO PROTECT THE INDIANS

Every Spanish leader who established a colony in the New World was allowed to keep a huge estate for himself and divide the rest of the land among his followers. In this way the good land was soon taken up by large estates, which were worked by the Indians. To civilize the Indians and protect them from overwork, the Spanish government devised a clever plan. The Indians were distributed in lots of fifty or a hundred or more to Spanish colonists of good reputation, who were to look after their welfare and see that they were provided with a priest, a school, and plots of land to cultivate. In return the Indians were expected to work on the estates or in the mines of the Spaniards, but for wages like any free workman. These allotments of Indians were called *encomiendas* (en-coh-mee-en′dahs), and the Spaniards who received them *encomenderos* (en-coh-men-dair′ohs).

The plan for the welfare of the Indians did not work out as the Spanish government intended. Most of the colonists were not interested in the Indians except as a source of cheap labor. They had come to the New World to get rich and they paid little attention to the laws sent from Spain to protect the Indians. Instead they abused the natives shamefully, overworking and almost starving them. Millions of Indians who had worked their village lands for centuries found themselves forced to work the fields for the Spanish owners.

A Spanish priest, Father Las Casas (lahs cah′sahs), tried to help the unfortunate Indians. He went to Spain to protest against the cruel treatment of the natives. Because of his pleas, new laws were passed, which forbade the *encomenderos* to demand work from the Indians. They might accept only tribute in the form of produce or money. But these rules were also difficult to enforce, and millions of Indians continued to be grievously exploited by the Spaniards. This system lasted for centuries, and even today poor Indian and *mestizo* farmers live and work on great landholdings in many countries of Latin America.

THE GOVERNMENT OF THE NEW WORLD IS CONTROLLED FROM SPAIN

Pizarro and Cortez and other early conquerors had held great power in the lands they conquered. Later on, as the colonies grew larger, the king of Spain decided to send his own personal representatives to Mexico and Peru. These officials were called viceroys, and were required to be Spanish noblemen with no land or families in the colonies. This was to make sure that they always put service to the king first.

A viceroy carried a heavy responsibility. He was expected to be a father to his people, a friend to the missionaries, a protector of the poor. Seventy different laws had been issued to list his duties and govern his conduct! You can imagine that he had a difficult time being fair to everyone. If a viceroy wanted better treatment of the Indians, the rich landowners opposed him. It was often an easier course to accept bribes than to try to enforce the laws, and many viceroys were dishonest and corrupt. Though there were some good viceroys, most of them cared little about the Indians and were interested chiefly in making a fortune and returning to Spain.

The arrival of a viceroy was always a great event in the colonies, for he and his party traveled in fine style. His ships were greeted by the booming of guns at the seaport. People thronged the streets to watch his entrance into the capital. One viceroy entered on a prancing white charger

with a canopy of crimson velvet over his head. He was followed by a brilliant procession of soldiers and noblemen mounted on horseback. Beautiful ladies in silks and jewels rode in their coaches or stood in their balconies to watch the parade. In his palace the viceroy lived like a king and kept a court almost as fine as that of Spain.

In the first 200 years, the vast colonial empire was divided into two great viceroyalties, each headed by a viceroy. The viceroyalty of New Spain included Mexico, Central America, the island colonies, and the settlements in our Southwest, with its capital at Mexico City. The viceroyalty of Peru included the colonies in South America and was governed from Lima. It was so huge and unwieldy that in the 1700's two new viceroyalties were formed. The viceroyalty of New

FATHER LAS CASAS, friend of the Indians, labored all his life to make their lot easier. In this picture he may be writing his king to ask for another law to protect his humble people.

Hispanic Foundation, Washington, D.C.

Granada included the present countries of Colombia, Venezuela, Ecuador, and Panama, with the capital at Bogotá. The viceroyalty of Buenos Aires governed the Plata River colonies and Bolivia, and had the city of Buenos Aires for its capital.

Since the viceroys could not possibly look after the affairs in such huge territories, the viceroyalties were divided into districts. Some of these districts were called captaincies-general; others were called presidencies. Each was governed by a special court of judges called an *audiencia*. There were four in New Spain and six in Peru. When you realize what an immense territory the colonies covered, you can see that the government could not be very efficient.

THE CHURCH IS IMPORTANT IN THE NEW WORLD

After the conquests, the Catholic Church was established throughout the colonies. It was really a part of the colonial government. The king of Spain selected all the bishops and other important clergymen, and they joined with the government officials in seeing that the colonists remained loyal to the king and to the Church. Since the Spaniards were exceedingly religious people, the Church became a powerful force in the colonies. It also grew very rich. Besides the usual tithes and fees required of church members, huge gifts of land and of gold and silver were given to the Church by the deeply religious and wealthy Spaniards. Bishops had palaces as fine as those of the nobles. The churches and cathedrals were magnificent, and there were monasteries and convents whose fine buildings and grounds covered many acres.

THE CATHOLIC FAITH IS MAINTAINED BY PARISH PRIESTS IN THE SPANISH TOWNS

Not all the clergy lived in luxury, however. The Spanish kings considered it their duty to convert as many Indians as possible in the new lands. Priests came in great numbers from Spain to spread the Christian faith among the Indians and build churches for them. When Spaniards founded towns and settled down with civilized Indians to work for them, an ordinary parish priest was sent to the town. He held Mass for both Spaniards and Indians. Every Spanish town had at least one church, sometimes two or three. The Indians did the building and the decorating under the direction of the priest. Many of the most beautiful churches in the Spanish colonial towns today are the handiwork of Indian artists.

The priests founded church schools in some of the towns also. Indian children were taught how to read and write Spanish, to draw and paint. They were taught a trade, such as bricklaying, carpentry, or masonry, under the direction of the priests. The Spanish rulers received enthusiastic letters from the priests telling the progress they were making in teaching the Indians and describing their pleasure in the church service and the singing.

Some priests tried to save a part of the Indian culture, realizing that it should not be lost to the world. They learned Indian languages and helped the Indian leaders write their history and the legends of their people, using Spanish letters. But many priests were eager to destroy all traces of the heathen learning and religion. In Yucatan almost every Mayan book or religious scroll was burned. In a

Black Star

THE SPANISH CHURCH followed the *conquistadores* to the New World. There was scarcely a village or town in the colonies that did not have a church like this one. Notice the wall and the graveyard at the rear.

few years, hundreds of temples and thousands of images were destroyed in Mexico alone.

MISSIONARY PRIESTS CONVERT AND CIVILIZE THE INDIANS ON THE FRONTIER

Missionary priests made their way into the frontier territory of both North and South America where the Indians were not civilized. These priests were members of religious orders in the Catholic Church, and devoted their lives to spreading Christianity among the Indians. The courageous priests often walked miles through hot desert or over mountains to reach a native settlement. They would go into an Indian district, build a little thatched chapel, and preach to the Indians through an interpreter. In this way they won many Indians to the Catholic faith. Later, as they gained more converts, they built large mission churches with schools

and living quarters for the Indians.

The mission became an Indian community, directed by the priests. Land was cleared and planted to corn, wheat, and orchards. The Indians were taught by the hard-working priests to weave and to work with leather and iron. The women learned housework and cooking. Soldiers were sent from among the Spanish troops to protect the mission from hostile Indians. These soldiers often brought their families and settled down outside the mission. In this way towns often grew up on the frontier where the mission settlements were.

SPAIN LEAVES ITS MARK ON MANY TOWNS IN THE UNITED STATES

Many towns in the United States can trace their ancestry back to Spanish colonial days. All through the Southwest old Spanish missions remind us of the days when the missionary priest worked and lived with the Indians. There were twenty-one missions founded in California, and many of these are still used as churches by people of the Catholic faith. San Diego, Santa Barbara, San Francisco were all mission towns named after saints. Santa Fé in New Mexico and El Paso in Texas started as Spanish settlements. St. Augustine, Florida, the very first town in the United States, was founded by the Spaniards in 1565 as a frontier fort.

Wherever the Spaniards went in the Southwest, they left their imprint. Rivers, towns, and streets still have Spanish names. Many Spanish words have crept into the vocabulary of the people who live in the Southwest, words from the old Spanish ranch days, such as lasso, corral, plaza, adobe, rodeo. Americans often call a quarter of a dollar "two bits," because it took two of the Spanish silver pieces used in colonial days to make twenty-five cents.

MISSIONS ARE ESTABLISHED IN PARAGUAY

In South America the brave missionary fathers labored among the Indians on the plains of the Orinoco River and in the wilderness east of the Andes. Their most famous mission villages were established among the Indians of the Paraná River region. Under their direction the communities became prosperous. The Indians worked the fertile land, planting wheat, corn, and rice and raising cattle; they learned to build boats and traded with the towns down the river. The white colonists of Paraguay did not like the missions because they prevented them from getting Indian labor. When the missionary priests

were ordered out of the colonies by the king of Spain, the Indians went back to their former primitive life. Today a few ruined churches are the only reminders of the thriving Indian communities.

THE SPANISH TOWNS WERE PLEASANT PLACES IN WHICH TO LIVE

Let us suppose you are a soldier fighting under Cortez, helping him to capture Tenochtitlán and other Indian cities. After the conquest is over, you would like to settle down and make your living peacefully in the New World. Cortez is now a great landowner, and you know that you, too, are entitled to some of the land you helped to conquer. Every founder of a colony is required by law to build three towns on land not a part of his estate, and you decide to live with some of your comrades in one of these new Spanish towns. You are given land enough to pasture 20 cows and 1000 sheep outside the town, so you buy the livestock and start in on your little hacienda (ah-see-en'dah) or ranch. There is an Indian village on the outskirts of the town and the Indians work for you, building the adobe house and caring for your livestock.

That is the way the colonial towns were started. Foot-soldiers and young noblemen from Spain who hoped to make their fortune in the New World took up small landholdings. The towns were required by law to be built around a central square, and to have at least one church, a town hall, and a prison. The well-to-do people had houses on the plaza. Like all Spanish homes, they were built around a central patio or courtyard where figs, oranges, and flowers grew. The grilled

Galloway

SANTA BARBARA, CALIFORNIA, is proud of its Spanish background. Most of its downtown buildings and many of its homes are built in Spanish style. This hotel with its red-tiled roof is an example of modern Spanish architecture.

street windows and tiled roofs made them seem like their homes in Spain.

THE GOVERNMENT WAS NOT DEMOCRATIC

In every Spanish town there was a council which in some cases was elected by the householders. There were also one or two magistrates, and other town officials. Only those citizens who owned land could hold a seat on the council. Sometimes the council held an open meeting to which the prominent citizens were invited to come and discuss important questions. However, they were not like the town meetings of the colonists of New England, who met and carried on their town's business. There was no such self-government in the colonies of Spain. That is probably one reason why today there is less real demo-

cratic government in Latin republics than in the United States. The Spanish colonies lived under viceroys for 300 years before they had any opportunity to try democratic government.

WEALTHY SPANIARDS LIVED LIVES OF EASE

Shut off almost entirely from the outside world, the Spanish upper classes lived in idle luxury waited upon by Indian servants. They built fine homes like those of the nobility in Spain and sent to Spain for fine tapestries, heavy carved furniture, and other luxuries. We should probably consider their life rather dull, for bullfights, religious celebrations, and entertainments at the court of the viceroys were their chief amusements. The upper-class women must have

Sawders

ELABORATE HAND–CARVED DOORS for the homes of wealthy Spaniards were often made by Indian craftsmen. As in all Spanish houses this door opens from the street into a patio garden, giving privacy to the inhabitants.

had uninteresting lives. Like the women in Spain, they were expected to stay at home. They had little to amuse them except glimpses of life on the streets below, seen from their latticed balconies. When they went to church or for the afternoon airing in the plaza, they had to wrap themselves in black *mantones* (shawls) so that little of them could be seen.

If we could see one of the colonial cities, we should find it very dirty, like all cities of that time. Garbage was thrown out into the streets, and pigs and dogs roamed about eating it. Although the nobility dressed in fine clothes and rode about in painted coaches, they seldom took a bath! Plagues and diseases often attacked the people, for they knew nothing of sanitation.

SPANISH AMERICAN CITIES WERE CENTERS OF CULTURE AND LEARNING

In 1574, over thirty years before the first English colony was founded, Mexico City had a population of 15,000 Spanish families besides many Indians. It was a city of impressive buildings, but was subject to periodical floods. Filling the old canals with building stones to make streets had not worked very well, for heavy storms caused the lake to overflow into the streets, and at one time the city was partly abandoned for several years. Later a drainage system for the whole valley was begun, but this was not completed until after 1900.

In Mexico City the Spaniards kept the old square, or Zócalo, as the center of the new city. The great cathedral which stands in the Zócalo today took 200 years to finish, and is the largest, and one of the oldest and most beautiful churches in America. There are many other handsome churches as well. Some of the old houses of the 1600's can be seen in the slums of the city today. They are built of stone around a patio and have Spanish iron balconies at the windows. There are also many fine houses of the 1700's to be seen in Mexico City. They are of red stone and decorated with carvings or Spanish tiles. One famous colonial house was made entirely of white and blue tiles.

Mexico was the center for Spanish culture in North America. The University of Mexico was graduating students of law and religion long before any of the thirteen colonies were founded. There was a printing press in Mexico City as early as 1536, and hundreds of books were published: religious works, poetry, and books on geography and the Indian languages. People could enjoy Spanish plays in their theater and they could listen to an orchestra which played the best music of Europe. The capital city of Mexico was by no means a pioneer town.

Lima, the capital of the viceroyalty in Peru, must have seemed like home to the viceroy from Spain. It was

THIS BEAUTIFUL MONASTERY in Quito is a fine example of Spanish colonial architecture. Notice the graceful arches of the cloister, also the formal garden and fountain in the foreground.

Galloway

an entirely new city built by Pizarro after the pattern of Spanish towns with houses of colored stucco and patios filled with flowers. Lima, too, had a beautiful cathedral built on a central plaza, and a palace for the viceroy on one side. The noblemen in Lima lived in great mansions with balconies built out over the streets and patios floored with Spanish tile. They dressed in the latest fashion and rode about in fine coaches driven by slaves in livery. The Spaniards of Lima "turned their backs on the Andes" and considered the rest of Peru a "strange, barbarous country." Cuzco, up in the highland region, was almost as difficult to reach in those days as Spain itself.

Lima was full of beautiful churches built by the pious people and their priests. There were great monasteries and convents where the friars and nuns lived, and hospitals built near the church so that the sick might be cared for. The city had a daily newspaper about the time of the American Revolution. The University of San Marcos, founded in the same year as the one in Mexico City, remains today the oldest university in all America. Large shipments of books came from Spain, which were inspected before they could be sold. Residents of Lima were able to read novels, history, and adventure stories.

Bogotá, capital of the viceroyalty of New Granada, was a cultured and aristocratic city. Although its location on a high plateau prevented contacts with the outside world, its people were interested in books and in learning. Quito was another proud city of churches and beautiful buildings. Buenos Aires, now the largest city in South America, was, until the 1700's,

no more important to the colonial empire of Spain than the pioneer town of Santa Fé in New Mexico. At the time Lima was a thriving city, Buenos Aires was only a small town on the Plata River with no harbor and no trade. We shall find out the reason for its slow growth later in this chapter.

We must remember that all the education and culture in the cities was transferred from Spain for the Spanish people only. The great mass of Indians and *mestizos* lived lives of poverty with little or no education. They were ignorant and superstitious. Most of them had never heard of a play or a newspaper or an orchestra, to say nothing of a university.

SPANISH AMERICANS MADE A LIVING BY FARMING AND HANDICRAFT

The *conquistadores* encouraged farming in the colonies. On his second voyage, Columbus brought to Hispaniola "mares, sheep, heifers, goats, pigs, and chickens." Pizarro brought the first cow from Spain and sold it for $10,000. Within two years there were so many more that they were worth only $1000 apiece! Cortez introduced a fine breed of sheep into Mexico, as well as the mulberry tree and the silkworm. He ruled that every Spaniard who had 100 Indians working for him on his estate must set out 1000 grapevines or other useful plants. Orange, lemon, fig, and olive trees were brought from Spain and planted in the orchards. The first grains of wheat in Peru are said to have been found by a lady of Lima in a barrel of rice from Spain. She carefully planted the seed, collected the new wheat, and replanted it until she had enough wheat to give her friends. Crude Spanish plows were sent to

Sawders

CRUDE WOODEN PLOWS like those introduced into the colonies from Spain are still used by Indian farmers in many parts of Latin America. Spaniards also brought over the cattle to help the farmer with his work.

the colonies to take the place of the sticks used by the Indians. There is a story told about some Indians of Peru who first saw a plow drawn by oxen. They murmured among themselves about the laziness of the Spaniards who let animals do their work for them! Cotton and wool were produced on the farms to clothe the colonists and enough was left over to export to Spain. The people in the frontier regions made their living by cattle-raising or by mining.

In the cities, master craftsmen had come over from Spain and started guilds which were something like labor unions of today. They trained a few men to be silversmiths, saddle-makers, weavers, and potters. Unfortunately they did not allow the Indians to belong; membership in the guilds was for Spaniards only.

SPAIN KEPT STRICT CONTROL OF COLONIAL TRADE

Spain, like England, believed that the colonies were founded to make the mother country rich. You may remember that one of the grievances of the thirteen colonies was that England would not let them trade with other countries or build their own ships. Spain was very much more strict with her colonies than England was. The colonies were not allowed to grow or produce anything made in Spain. Cortez, as we learned, had started several Indian communities growing silkworms. Many mulberry trees had been planted for the worms to feed on and the industry would have grown rapidly. But the silk-growers of Spain protested because they wanted to sell silk to the colonies at high prices, so the mulberry trees were uprooted and the silkworms were killed. Much the same thing happened to the wine industry in Peru. Spanish winemakers were selling wine in Peru at 300 per cent profit and they objected to grapes being grown there.

No goods could be brought to the colonies in Mexico except in Spanish ships to Veracruz, and merchants were charged an enormous price by the Spanish firms. The trade laws were particularly hard on South America because of the difficulty of transportation. All goods for South America came into the port of Puerto Bello (pwer'toh beh'yoh) on the Atlantic coast of Panama. The goods were unloaded there and carried by mules forty miles across the Isthmus to Panama City. There they were loaded on ships which had been built in Panama's shipyards, and sent to Lima on the Pacific coast. But if the goods were meant for the colonies in the Plata region, there was still another trip. They were packed on mules and sent over the Andes through the interior of what are now Bolivia and Argentina to Buenos Aires and other towns.

In spite of the fact that Buenos Aires was a port town and could send and receive goods directly from Spain, no trade was allowed except through Puerto Bello. For this reason Buenos Aires remained a small town with an empty harbor during most of the colonial period. Goods from Spain were extremely scarce and prices were very high. It is no wonder, therefore, that Dutch and English smuggling ships were welcomed. They brought goods direct from Europe and sailed into the mouth of the Plata River, right to Buenos Aires.

The strict trade laws of Spain made it impossible for France, England, and Holland to trade with the Spanish colonies. Bold buccaneers from these countries began to prey on the commerce of Spain, often with the consent of their governments. To protect Spanish ships from these marauders, Spain, in the 1500's, forced all vessels to sail in two great fleets each year. These fleets were convoyed by armed galleons. One fleet sailed in the spring to the Mexican port of Veracruz, bringing merchandise from Spain. The other fleet sailed in the summer to Cartagena (car-tah-hay'-nah) in New Granada and then to Puerto Bello on the Isthmus. Here a great trade fair was held each year and colonial merchants from as far away as Buenos Aires bought the luxuries and manufactured articles from Spain. Early in the following year the fleets sailed for Havana, and from there returned to Spain laden with the king's share of the gold and silver and the products of the colonies.

The chief purpose of the colonies had been to make money for the Spanish government. In spite of the millions of dollars in gold and silver that had gone to Spain from the colonies, the royal treasury was empty by 1700. Stupid kings and long wars with other countries had used up the gold doubloons and silver pieces faster than they had come from the mines.

The policy of Spain had kept the colonies from developing a prosperity of their own. Although this policy was relaxed in later years, the colonists were growing more and more dissatisfied with the trade regulations. They also resented the fact that they had no share in the government. The time was ripe for something to happen. We shall see what did happen in our next chapter.

Are You a Careful Reader?   Test Yourself!

I. Supply the correct word for each blank:

   1. The lowest social classes in Spanish America were the . . . . and . . . . .
   2. The viceroy of New Spain lived in . . . . ; the viceroy of Peru lived in . . . . .
   3. The two oldest universities in the Western Hemisphere are in . . . . and . . . . .
   4. Spanish goods reached Mexico through the port of . . . .
   5. Missions to convert and civilize the Indians were built in the frontier regions by . . . .

II. Match the following words and statements:

1. gachupín	*a.*	Catholic priest who befriended the Indians
2. New Granada	*b.*	a city in Peru
3. creole	*c.*	the viceroyalty located in northern South America
4. St. Augustine	*d.*	a court which governed certain districts of the viceroyalty
5. mestizo	*e.*	the oldest city in the United States
6. Las Casas	*f.*	the system of allotting Indians to Spanish landowners
7. encomienda	*g.*	personal representative of the king
8. viceroy	*h.*	ships used to carry gold back to Spain
9. galleons	*i.*	pure-blooded Spaniard born in Spain
10. audiencia	*j.*	pure-blooded Spaniard born in America
	k.	a person of mixed Spanish and Indian blood
	l.	Spanish port on the Isthmus of Panama

Food for Thought and Discussion

   1. In what ways do you think the strict class system of Spanish America discouraged democracy?
   2. Why were the Spanish colonists not ready for self-government?
   3. Using a map, point out the long trip taken by Spanish goods destined for Buenos Aires. Show also the short water route possible between Spain and the La Plata colony.

Chapter 11

The Colonies of Spanish America Win Their Independence from Spain

---

"Viva la Independencia!" (Long live independence!) This is the cry of the crowds on Independence Day in Mexico City. They stand in the Zócalo on the fifteenth of September and watch the president of Mexico come out on the balcony of the National Palace. He strikes a bell and all the people shout. This is called the "Cry of Dolores," because on this day in the year 1810 a priest from the town of Dolores (doh-loh'rays) rang his church bell and gave the cry for Mexican independence.

THE SPANISH AND ENGLISH COLONIES IN AMERICA HAVE THE SAME STORY OF INDEPENDENCE

All of you know the story of how our thirteen colonies proclaimed their independence and fought a war to free themselves from England. But how many of you know that almost the same story was repeated thirty-five or forty years later in the American colonies belonging to Spain? Both English and Spanish colonies had grievances against the mother country because of the taxes and the trade regulations imposed on them. People in both colonies held meetings to air their grievances and set up local governments independent of the king.

In both colonies, a war was fought before their independence was recognized.

But in the case of Spanish America the winning of independence was a much more difficult undertaking. The thirteen colonies had only a narrow strip of land along the seacoast, but the territory of the Spanish colonies stretched across one whole continent and part of another. Settlements were far apart and any communication between them was difficult. The very land itself discouraged military operations because of its great mountain ranges.

The character of the people themselves made independence harder to win in the Spanish colonies, for these people were as different from the English colonists as the *conquistadores* were different from the Pilgrim fathers. The English came to the New World in a spirit of independence and set up governments in which they themselves took part. But the Spanish colonists brought no such ideas of freedom or self-government. The king's rule was imposed on them in America as in Spain. The winning of independence by the Spanish colonists in the face of all these difficulties was a glorious achievement.

THE SPANISH COLONISTS HAD MANY GRIEVANCES AGAINST SPAIN

We have mentioned the trade regulations imposed on the colonies by Spain. As time went on, those who wanted to make money in the New World grew more and more bitter against these restrictions.

Besides restrictions on trade, the most serious grievance of the colonists was that the important public offices were nearly always given to Spaniards, both in the government and in the Church. The governors and judges and bishops were men from Europe who had little sympathy with the Spanish Americans over whom they were placed, and whom they were inclined to despise as mere "colonials." Naturally this attitude offended the pride of the creoles.

There were other grievances also. The colonists not only wanted to have a share of the public offices; many of them wanted a more modern form of government in which the people had a vote. But Spain tried to prevent the spread of such ideas. The colonists could not buy any books that had not been approved by the Spanish authorities. No information about the North American Revolution could be circulated, nor could any colonist visit in the United States without the permission of the king's officials. The Spanish government did not want the people to get any ideas of independence from North America.

THE AMERICAN AND FRENCH REVOLUTIONS INFLUENCE THE SPANISH COLONIES

In spite of the fact that little news from North America was allowed to filter into the Spanish colonies, the people of Mexico and South America knew that the English colonies had gained their independence. No laws could keep out news of the French Revolution ten years later, in which the people rose up against the king and nobles who had mistreated them. The salt fish and cheese which came to the colonies from Europe were often wrapped in English and French newspapers, which the censor missed. These wrappings were eagerly read and the views they contained were passed on.

The American and French Revolutions had a tremendous effect on the colonies of Spain. Our Declaration of Independence, with its inspiring statement that every man has the right to "life, liberty, and the pursuit of happiness," was translated into Spanish and circulated freely. Young creoles who had been sent to European universities returned home enthusiastic about independence for the colonies. Secret societies were organized to promote revolution.

THE DESIRE FOR INDEPENDENCE WAS INCREASED BY CONDITIONS IN EUROPE

As you may remember, Napoleon in the early 1800's was trying to get Europe under his control. He had driven the Spanish king off his throne and made his own brother king of Spain. Imagine the effect this had on the colonies! They all proclaimed their loyalty to Ferdinand, popular son of their former king. They refused to obey any orders which came from Napoleon's brother in Spain. Their defiance of authority gave them a feeling of independence, which they did not lose even when the Spanish king was later restored.

This feeling grew stronger when they believed that England was willing to help them secretly in a fight for independence. England would not come out openly in their favor because she was engaged with Spain in opposing Napoleon in Europe. But England saw that if the colonies were free, she would profit by trading with them.

THE SPANISH KING CRUELLY CRUSHES THE FIRST ATTEMPTS AT INDEPENDENCE

In 1810, patriots believed that the time had come to demand what they thought were their rights. The movement was strongest in the provinces which had the weakest connection with the mother country. Venezuela had never been very close to Spain. In 1811, she announced her independence, and in 1813, the frontier country of Paraguay did likewise. In 1810, the parish priest at Dolores started the revolution in Mexico. In Buenos Aires, Chile, and Colombia

FATHER HIDALGO was sixty years old when he rang the little church bell which is now Mexico's Liberty Bell. Today there are monuments to this humble priest throughout Mexico.

Pan American Union

the colonists did not renounce their allegiance to the king, but they did expel the Spanish officials and set up governments of their own.

Four years later, in 1814, Napoleon was defeated by his enemies and the Spanish King Ferdinand regained his throne. At the same time the Spanish authorities in America had recovered control everywhere except in the Plata River colonies. Ferdinand, if he had been wise, could easily have made terms with the remaining rebels in America. He might have offered them freer trade and a share in the government of the colonies. Instead he restored all the old regulations and sent a large army to South America which tried to stamp out rebellion in the northern provinces. Of course, by such actions the flame of liberty was fanned, instead of being put out. The Spanish colonists were determined now to keep on fighting for their freedom. Leaders began to appear who were willing to carry on the struggle. The story of Spanish American independence is really the story of the great men who led the people in their struggle for liberty.

A PRIEST AWAKENS THE MEXICAN PEOPLE

The "Cry of Dolores" that started the long struggle for independence in Mexico was given by Miguel Hidalgo (mee-ghel' ee-dahl'goh). He was the parish priest of a small village. He had felt great sympathy for the Indians ever since his boyhood, when he had seen Spanish soldiers carrying aloft on their pikes the heads of a few Indians who had taken part in a revolt. He devoted his life to teaching these downtrodden people to make a living on the land. Indians for hundreds of miles around Dolores looked upon him as their friend.

It was natural that Hidalgo should work for the independence which would mean so much to his Indian friends. When his secret plans for revolt were discovered by the Spaniards, he brought the movement into the open by ringing the church bell and shouting " *Viva la Independencia!* " The creoles had no sympathy for Hidalgo and his Indian movement, for they wished to keep the power in their own hands. Hidalgo worked hard to train and arm his growing band of Indians. At first he was successful and captured many important towns. But both sides in the struggle indulged in horrible cruelties, and finally Hidalgo was defeated and captured. A firing squad ended his life, but not before he had inspired others to carry on his work.

MORELOS CARRIES ON THE MOVEMENT FOR INDEPENDENCE

One of Hidalgo's leaders was a priest named José Morelos (hoh-say' moh-ray'los). He himself was part Indian and had been a mule driver carrying loads of goods between Mexico City and the interior. After he was educated for the priesthood, he determined to better conditions for the common people in Mexico. He joined the forces of Hidalgo and took over the leadership of one division of the rebel army. When Hidalgo was captured, Morelos fled to the mountains, where thousands of Indians flocked to him. He tried to set up a government independent of Spain. From his mountain headquarters small groups of Mexican fighters carried on what is called guerrilla warfare, attacking towns in small bands and then retreating. In 1815, the viceroy's army was able to capture Morelos and to

disband the congress which his new government had called. He himself was taken to Mexico City, where he was tried and executed. Morelos did not die in vain, because under him the spirit of revolution had increased and many more people knew about the struggle which was going on.

AN AMBITIOUS ARMY OFFICER GAINS INDEPENDENCE FOR MEXICO

Hidalgo and Morelos had given their lives so that the common people and the Indians of Mexico could have the rights to which they were entitled as human beings. They wanted more than independence for Mexico, for they knew that the lot of the people would not be improved if the government merely passed from the king of Spain to the hands of the Spanish upper class in Mexico. It is sad to think that when Mexico finally became independent, that is just what happened. The cause of the common people for which Hidalgo and Morelos died was forgotten for many years.

One of Morelos's lieutenants named Vicente Guerrero (vee-sehn'tay gay-ray'ro) carried on the revolution after his death, but the cause looked hopeless. Guerrero was much of the time a fugitive in the mountains, and his poorly trained and equipped followers were hardly a match for the troops of the viceroy.

Meanwhile, all over Spanish America people were protesting against the despotic rule of Ferdinand and his representatives. The movement for revolution was fast becoming a great tide which could not be stopped. In Spain itself the liberals rose against the king and forced him to accept a constitution. But this constitution was too liberal for the ruling class in

Mexico, which feared the loss of its property and its power. The people of the upper class decided that the safest thing to do was to side with the revolutionists, gain independence for Mexico, and then take over the government. In this way they would keep the land system and all the rights of government for themselves.

Guerrero was suspicious when a young creole officer named Agustín de Jturbide (ah-goos-teen' day ee-tur-bee'day), who had been fighting against him, suddenly offered to join forces with him. He finally agreed to accept Iturbide's help, entirely unaware, until too late, of the trick the upper classes were playing on him. When Mexico City was taken in 1821, by the joint forces of Iturbide and Guerrero, the old revolutionists were soon ousted from control. Shortly after that, Iturbide and his soldiers declared the independence of Mexico. They also took over the government by proclaiming Iturbide Emperor of Mexico. Although he stayed in power only one year, the cause of democracy was set back many years. In spite of their independence, the common people found themselves little better off than they had been under Spain.

VENEZUELA PROCLAIMS HER INDEPENDENCE

Now let us turn to South America to see what had been going on there while Mexico was struggling for her freedom. We have already mentioned that Venezuela had declared her independence in 1811, but that the patriots were not at first successful. There is a great deal more to that story. Let us go back to 1811, when the people of Caracas in Venezuela wildly cheered a white-haired old man who rode at the head of their revolutionary army. Francisco Miranda (frahn-sees'coh mee-rahn'dah) was a native of Venezuela who had been in Europe most of his life working for the cause of freedom in South America. He spent years trying to interest European governments in giving aid to the independence movement. He founded patriotic societies for young creoles who had gone to Europe to be educated. Among those who listened to his fiery speeches for independence were many young men who were to become leaders of the revolutionary movement in South America.

Miranda was an old man when he heard that the creoles had set up a government of their own in Venezuela, but he returned there to give his aid. With him came another Venezuelan, young Simón Bolívar (see-mohn' boh-lee'var). Under Miranda's influence a declaration of independence from Spain was proclaimed. He had at last achieved his great ambition, to help free his own country from Spanish oppression.

But as we know, the young republic was destined to have a short life. When an earthquake destroyed Caracas in 1812, the priests told the frightened and superstitious people that God had sent the earthquake to punish them for breaking with Spain. Other tremors followed day after day as though in warning, and 600 of Miranda's soldiers were crushed in their barracks. Absolutely terrified, the soldiers deserted and Miranda was powerless to stop them. Many of the fickle people turned to the support of the royalists. It was at this time that Miranda did something which is hard to explain. He asked for peace and signed a treaty recognizing Venezuela as a royal colony again.

Bolívar and other revolutionary leaders felt that Miranda had betrayed their cause. When he went down to the seacoast from Caracas to board an English ship, they took him prisoner and turned him over to the Spanish governor. The unfortunate Miranda was sent to prison in Spain, where he lived until his death four years later. We do not know why he gave up the fight so quickly, but we do know that his enthusiasm inspired many younger men under whose leadership South America gained her freedom.

BOLÍVAR BECOMES THE REVOLUTIONARY LEADER

The revolutionists did not give up their cause. The position of leader of the revolutionary army was taken over by young Simón Bolívar. The memory of this man still lives in the hearts of South Americans. He is more than a hero to them; he has become the symbol of the liberty for which they fought. School-children are thrilled by stories of his marvelous exploits.

Bolívar was the son of one of the wealthiest and most aristocratic creole families in Caracas. As a child he spent some time on the cattle ranch of his family in the *llanos* of Venezuela, where he learned many feats of riding from the tough *llaneros* (yahnay′ros), or cowboys. Little did he know that some day these men would aid him in liberating Venezuela! One of his tutors was an unusual man who believed strongly in free government and the rights of the people. His

SIMÓN BOLÍVAR was a proud and sensitive man with remarkable powers of leadership. Although he was deeply patriotic, he also loved honor and position for himself.

Pan American Union

talks with Bolívar left a deep impression on the youth.

Bolívar went to Europe for education and travel like many young creoles of that day. He was a slight, handsome youth with flashing black eyes and a charming and fiery nature. When he was nineteen, he married a beautiful Spanish heiress of sixteen, whom he brought back to his family estate in Venezuela. His happiness was short, for his wife died of yellow fever not long afterward. The grief-stricken Bolívar returned to Europe, where he heard much talk of revolution among his South American friends. In London he joined Miranda's revolutionary club for young patriots and heard the old patriot's impressive speeches for the liberation of his homeland. Aroused to action by these talks and by a reunion with his old tutor, the ardent young man dedicated the rest of his life to liberating his beloved country. This was the man who became the leader of the revolutionists in Venezuela.

BOLÍVAR CONTINUES THE STRUGGLE FOR INDEPENDENCE

After the fall of the "earthquake republic," Bolívar reappeared in the neighboring region of New Granada (Colombia). Here he joined the revolutionists and devoted his time to organizing a strong enough force to attack the Spaniards again in Venezuela. The magnetism of his personality and the eloquence of his speeches inspired many patriotic young men to join his army. Within a year he had built up a large force. He marched on Caracas, overcame the Spanish soldiers, and was welcomed with tears of joy by the people. Twelve beautiful girls pulled him through the streets in a chariot. Bolívar must have enjoyed all this attention, for he liked honor and glory.

Unfortunately for Bolívar, the Spaniards were able once more to defeat the revolutionists and he was forced to withdraw again to New Granada. When a large army arrived from Spain, Bolívar retreated to the British island of Jamaica. What a bitter day that must have been for this man who had poured out his strength and his fortune for the revolutionary cause! But he refused to acknowledge defeat. His fertile mind made new plans, and he looked ahead to the day when the free nations of South America would be joined in a great peaceful federation.

Bolívar returned to make another attempt to win independence for Venezuela. Eventually he made his headquarters in the valley of the Orinoco River, where he was joined by other patriot leaders. There he called together a congress and drew up a democratic government for the new republic. Bolívar now conceived a daring plan. Caracas was too strongly fortified to attack, but across the Andes in New Granada the Spanish forces were weak. Why not surprise them?

BOLÍVAR WINS INDEPENDENCE FOR COLOMBIA AND VENEZUELA

Bolívar had collected a new army of 2100 men. Some were the tough *llaneros* of the plains under their *llanero* leader José Páez (pah'es). British soldiers of fortune and mestizo troops made up the rest. Bolívar led these men on an almost impossible march over the mighty Andes into Colombia. The men dragged cannon and munitions up the headwaters of the Orinoco and over the "freezing, barren, trackless Andean heights." All of the horses and hundreds of men died from cold and hunger, but they kept on, urged to new heights of courage by their leader. The daring plan succeeded. After only a few days' rest, Bolívar's worn and ragged men met a surprised Spanish army of 3000 men at Boyacá (boy-yah-cah') and defeated them on August 7, 1819. This is one of the great independence days in South America.

Bolívar was now in a position to conquer the Venezuelan forces and unite Colombia and Venezuela into one republic. In 1821, he gathered together all the patriot forces into one army and attacked the Spaniards at Carabobo in western Venezuela. The Spanish army was defeated and put to flight in this decisive battle, and independence for northern South America was achieved. In the same year a new congress drew up a constitution for the Republic of Great Colombia and elected Bolívar the first president. Bolívar was honored throughout the republic as a great liberator, and the grateful people gave him all the glory and praise that were his due. But he knew that his work was not yet done. He knew that South America could not be independent until the last Spanish fort was taken and the last Spanish soldier driven out. The next step was to conquer the strong viceroyalty at Lima. In this venture Bolívar had the help of another great revolutionary leader from the South.

THE PLATA RIVER SETTLEMENTS GAIN THEIR INDEPENDENCE

While Bolívar was liberating northern South America, the provinces in the south had become independent.

Buenos Aires and the settlements on the Paraná River were not considered important by Spain until the last half of the 1700's, when Buenos Aires was made a viceroyalty. The spirit of independence there was strong, and the people of Buenos Aires in 1810 dismissed the viceroy and set up a government of their own. Several years later they issued a declaration of complete separation from Spain. The people of Paraguay did the same. Spain never regained her power in these countries in spite of the fall of Napoleon and the restoration of Ferdinand. But the people of the United Provinces of the Río de la Plata, as they called the new republic, realized that their independence was not very safe as long as Spain controlled Peru.

SAN MARTÍN CROSSES THE ANDES AND FREES CHILE

The man who was to aid Bolívar in his great struggle to free South America from Spain was José de San Martín (hoh-say' day sahn mahr-teen'). He was born in Argentina, the son of a Spanish captain. He had been educated in Spain and had spent twenty years in the Spanish army. Although he had not been in South America since he was a boy, he loved his native land. He had known Miranda and other patriots in Europe. When he heard of the movement for independence in Buenos Aires, he gave up his career in Spain and sailed for home in 1812 to offer his services to his countrymen. They needed his military training and his experience in warfare.

San Martín, like Bolívar, conceived a daring plan. The republican troops had been defeated when they tried to attack Peru by land. Why not, then, cross the Andes to Chile, free that country, and go by sea to attack the last stronghold of Spain in Peru? To carry out this plan, San Martín asked to be made governor of the mountain province at the foot of the Andes. Then he set about preparations for the campaign. The women in the province made uniforms and prepared bandages and medicines. Money and food were contributed, and women gave their jewels to help the cause. Horses and mules by the hundreds were imported into his province and were trained in climbing up to elevations of 12,000 feet. Careful measurements were made so that they could tell just how heavy a load a man or a horse could carry in high altitudes.

Meanwhile, San Martín was joined by Chilean patriots lead by Bernardo O'Higgins, who had fled from Chile

SAN MARTÍN had black eyes, a Roman nose, and a firm chin. Although, like Bolívar, he fought for his country's freedom, he cared little for personal glory.

Pan American Union

after a defeat by Spanish forces. O'Higgins was the son of an Irishman who had settled in Chile and had later become viceroy of Peru. He also had been inspired by Miranda and was one of the revolutionary leaders in Chile.

San Martín worked hard to get the co-operation of his countrymen for his cause. Part of his plan was to mislead the enemy. Into Chile and Peru he sent carefully prepared stories to make the Spaniards think he was weak and foolish. At last, after three years of preparation, his Army of the Andes was ready to set out. Do you remember Uspallata Pass from our air-view of South America? That is where San Martín's army crossed over into Chile. Can you imagine an army, with cannon and equipment, making its way over those enormous heights? Yet that is what San Martín's army actually did. Carrying sleds to move their cannon through the snow of the Andes, portable bridges to cross mountain rivers, and extra shoes for the mules, they toiled up through the pass single file and down again into Chile. This march over the Andes is said to be one of the greatest military feats in history.

The Spanish army in Chile did not know which pass through the mountains San Martín would take. They were busily guarding all the possible passes, and so were unable to concentrate their forces. San Martín successfully surprised and defeated the Spanish army at Chacabuco (chah-cah-boo′coh) in February, 1817. The following year, San Martín again defeated the Spaniards and brought King Ferdinand's rule to an end in Chile. The grateful Chilean people gave him 10,000 ounces of gold, but

he would not accept it, asking only
that a library be built with the money
in the city of Santiago. Bernardo
O'Higgins was appointed head of the
new republican government in Chile.

SAN MARTÍN'S ARMY SAILS UP THE COAST AND ENTERS LIMA

The strong Spanish armies in Peru
had yet to be defeated. In 1820, with
the help of the Chilean fleet under a
former British admiral, San Martín
was able to cut off supplies from Lima
and capture the Spanish ships which
lay in the ports of Peru. He finally
landed his army on the coast north
of Lima, and waited for the people of
the capital to invite him to come to
the city. He was not sure that the
people here in this seat of viceroyal
power really wanted independence.
The viceroy feared the revolutionary
troops who waited outside the city
and withdrew farther inland.

The republicans invited San Martín
and his troops into Lima, where he
was greeted with wild acclaim. The
people shouted *"Viva nuestro general!"*
(Long live our general!) "No, do not
say that," said San Martín. "Instead join with me in crying out,
'*Viva la independencia del Peru!*'"
(Long live the independence of Peru!)
At a town meeting, the people voted
for independence from Spain. San
Martín proclaimed the independence
of Peru before a great crowd in the
central plaza. He did not wish any
office, but finally took the title, "Protector," agreeing to stay in command
only until all the Spanish forces were
gone. San Martín was not interested
in personal glory.

Peru was not yet liberated from
Spain. The Spaniards remained thor-
oughly entrenched in the Peruvian

Weimer

SAN MARTÍN'S FAMOUS MARCH over the Andes
is commemorated by this magnificent monument at
Mendoza, Argentina. Liberty stands high above the
fearless leader and his men.

highlands and San Martín did not
think his forces were strong enough
to oust them.

SAN MARTÍN RESIGNS HIS LEADERSHIP IN FAVOR OF BOLÍVAR

Bolívar, now in Quito with his own
victorious army, believed that the
two armies should be united to free
Peru. When San Martín wrote saying that he was coming to meet him
at the port of Guayaquil, Bolívar was
delighted. He expressed his eagerness to greet San Martín as the best
friend of himself and his country.

On July 26, 1822, occurred one of
the most important meetings in South
American history, more eventful than
the meeting of Pizarro and Atahualpa.
San Martín alighted from a ship in

the harbor of Guayaquil and walked into the main square of the town between long lines of cheering soldiers. Bolívar came out of the government house on the square and advanced to meet San Martín. The two generals embraced as is the custom between Latin American gentlemen. Then they went into a secret meeting, with no one else present.

No one has ever been quite sure what was said in this interview. Some historians think that Bolívar did not wish to lessen his power by sharing his command with San Martín; that he refused even to command San Martín's troops as long as San Martín himself remained in Peru. Some believe that the two men disagreed because San Martín sincerely believed that the liberated colonies should become independent monarchies. Bolívar, on the other hand, believed just as sincerely that the new territories should be republics united under one ruler — himself.

San Martín was ill, and weary of jealousies among his own followers. At any rate, he decided to withdraw from Peru and to leave his army to fight under Bolívar. He must have been disappointed in Bolívar, for he afterward told a friend that the Liberator was not the man they took him to be. However, in spite of his personal ambition, Bolívar was a sincere patriot.

San Martín left without even waiting for thanks from the people. He accepted from the Chilean government a small pension large enough to educate his beloved only daughter. At the age of forty-six he and his daughter sailed to Europe, where he lived a quiet life. He was a man who helped to free three countries, but who wished no honors. Especially in Argentina and Chile his memory is deeply revered. He was one of the most unselfish and patriotic leaders in the story of South American independence.

SPAIN IS DRIVEN OUT OF SOUTH AMERICA

A year after the momentous interview at Guayaquil, Bolívar entered Lima in triumph. In 1824, a great battle was fought between the Spanish troops and the united forces of Bolívar and San Martín at Ayacucho (ah-yah-coo'choh) in the Andes of southern Peru. The revolutionary forces were led by Bolívar's ablest general, Antonio José de Sucre (soo'-kray). The last Spanish viceroy was defeated and captured in this battle, which has been called the Waterloo of South American history. Peru's independence was an accomplished fact. At last South America was entirely free, and the dreams of Miranda, Bolívar, San Martín, and all the thousands of other patriots had come true.

Spain did not recognize the independence of the republics in the New World until many years later. Their path was to be a difficult one. The story of these new republics is the story of the modern nations of Latin America, which will be covered in the remainder of this book.

UNITED
STATES
OF
MEXICO

ATLANTIC

OCEAN

REPUBLIC
OF HAITI

UNITED
PROVINCES
OF
CENTRAL AMERICA

GREAT COLOMBIA

PACIFIC

PERU

EMPIRE OF

BRAZIL

OCEAN

BOLIVIA

PARAGUAY

CHILE

ARGENTINE
CONFEDERATION

URUGUAY

LATIN AMERICA AFTER THE WARS FOR INDEPENDENCE ABOUT 1828

0   500   1000   1500
SCALE IN MILES

Are You a Careful Reader?   Test Yourself!

I. Supply the correct word for each blank:

1. One grievance of the Spanish colonists was that the important offices were al-ways given to . . . .

2. The colonists were greatly influenced by the . . . . and . . . . Revolutions.

3. . . . . won her independence, but became an . . . . under Iturbide.

4. . . . . was the first country in South America to declare herself an independent republic.

5. The two greatest independence heroes of South America were . . . . and . . . . .

II. Match correctly the following words and statements:

1. Ayacucho	*a.*	date of South American independence
2. Miranda	*b.*	venerated independence leader who inspired young Venezuelans
3. 1824	*c.*	date of Mexican independence
4. 1821	*d.*	Mexican revolutionary leader tricked by Iturbide
5. Hidalgo	*e.*	emperor of independent Mexico
6. O'Higgins	*f.*	king of Spain after the defeat of Napoleon
7. Guerrero	*g.*	lieutenant of Bolívar who helped liberate Peru
8. Iturbide	*h.*	Chile's independence hero
9. Ferdinand	*i.*	military leader who freed Buenos Aires
10. Sucre	*j.*	famous battle which ended Spain's power in South America
	k.	Mexican priest who gave the cry of independence

Food for Thought and Discussion

1. In what ways did the revolution in Mexico differ from that in South America?

2. How do you think independence affected each of the four classes of society listed in Chapter 9?

3. In what ways did Bolívar and San Martín differ? Give examples to prove your points.

4. How did the movements for independence in the United States and in Latin America differ? How were they alike?

Looking Backward

Now that you have read the story of how the Spaniards colonized the New World and how these colonies won their independence, turn back to the beginning of Part III and answer the questions given on page 83. If there are any you cannot answer, study again the pages which you need to know better.

Interesting Things to Do

1. Make a map showing the routes taken by the explorers mentioned in Chapter 8.

2. Show on a map the routes taken by the Spaniards who explored in what is now the United States. See Chapter 9.

3. Enjoy history written by the men who helped to make it. Read translations

of the following: Bernal Díaz's own story of the conquest of the Aztecs; Cortez's let-ters to the king of Spain; Garcelaso de Vega's description of the Incas.

4. See if you can find additional interesting information on any of the conquerors or explorers you read about in Chapters 8 and 9.

5. Get better acquainted with some of the Latin American heroes of independence mentioned in the text.

6. Find out about the missionary priest, Father Junípero Serra, and his work; report to the class on life in a Spanish mission.

7. Select one of these topics on life in the Spanish colonies and prepare a report for the class: colonial dress, colonial homes and furniture, life among upper or lower classes, food of the colonists, education, architecture.

8. Make drawings to illustrate some of the topics in number 7 or on some subject of your own choosing.

9. Write a play describing the arrival of Cortez in Mexico or the meeting of Pizarro and Atahualpa; write the imaginary conversation between Bolívar and San Martín at Guayaquil.

10. Prepare a radio play telling the story of Latin American independence.

11. Read to the class Joaquin Miller's poem, "Columbus," or John Keats's poem called, "On First Looking into Chapman's Homer." What mistake in history was made by Keats?

Interesting Books to Read

For Further Information

Eells, Elsie, *South America's Story*. Dodd Mead. Interesting sidelights on ro-mantic history.

Lansing, Marion, *Liberators and Heroes of Mexico and Central America*, and *Lib-erators and Heroes of South America*. L. C. Page. Two books of biography of independence leaders.

Peck, Anne Merriman, *The Pageant of South American History*. Harpers. History told in story form.

Webster, Hutton, and Hussey, Roland, *History of Latin America*. Heath. A good high-school reference history.

For Pleasure

Craine, Edith Janice, *Conquistador*. Dodd Mead. A boy's adventure, translated from an old Spanish manuscript.

Hodges, Walter C., *Columbus Sails*. Coward McCann. Account of a sailor on the *Santa Maria*.

Kingsley, Charles, *Westward Ho!* Grosset Dunlap. Famous novel of the Spanish Main.

Niles, Blair, *Maria Paluna*. Longmans. Novel of the conquest of Guatemala by Alvarado.

UNITED

STATES

LOWER CALIFORNIA

GULF OF CALIFORNIA

Nogales

El Paso

Rio

Grande

Cattle

Laredo

Monterrey

Mazatlan

Cattle

San Luis Potosí

Guadalajara   Silver

Chapala

L. Chapala

Oil   Tampico

L. Pátzcuaro

Toluca   MEXICO

Cuernavaca   Puebla   Veracruz

Taxco

Coffee

Oil

Oaxaca

Mitla   Bananas

GULF

OF

MEXICO

Mérida

YUCATAN

Henequin

Chicle

British Honduras

GUATEMALA

HONDURAS

PACIFIC

OCEAN

MEXICO

0   200   400

SCALE IN MILES

EL SALVADOR

NICARAGUA

NATION INTERESTED

INDIAN PEOPLE

WE ARE NOW READY to make a longer and more intimate visit to our southern neighbors. We have already viewed them from the air; we know the story of their founding and their independence. Let us now visit each of the twenty republics of Latin America as neighbors who would like to get better acquainted.

Our first visit will be "south of the border, down Mexico way." First, we shall tour this fascinating land, exploring her highways and byways and her interesting towns and cities. Next, we shall turn back to the year when Mexico gained her independence and trace the fortunes of the new republic from that time to the present. We shall see how often and how unfortunately the threads of her history have tangled with our own. We shall get acquainted with some of the great Mexicans who have made history and are making it today. Finally, we shall meet her charming people and learn some of their customs which differ so greatly from our own.

Before we start on our trip, suppose we get our bearings from the map. On the opposite page is our neighbor, Mexico. What country is Mexico's neighbor to the south? Can you find Mexico City, the capital, and also the ports of Veracruz and Tampico? Locate the Yucatan Peninsula. Do you remember what famous Indians once lived here? Whose descendants would you expect to find living in the Valley of Mexico? Where are the cities of Guadalajara and Oaxaca?

While you are studying Mexico, try to find the answers to these important questions:

1. Why were dictators once able to seize and control the government of Mexico?

2. Why have Mexicans in the past had reasons to be suspicious of the motives of our government?

3. How is modern Mexico solving the problem of land and education for her Indian people?

Chapter 12

We Take a Tour of Modern Mexico

MEXICO, of all the Latin American nations, is perhaps the least understood. Many adult Americans still think it is dangerous to travel in Mexico because of bandits. Many of us are inclined to think of all Mexican people in terms of some we have seen working on the ranches in the southwestern part of the United States. We forget that thousands of Mexicans in our southwestern states were brought there by American companies who wanted only cheap labor. We forget how little opportunity has been given to these people in the United States. We forget how musical and artistic the Mexican people are, and what contributions they have made, not only to the culture of Mexico, but also to the life and characteristics of the towns of our Southwest.

Americans often misjudge the land of Mexico, as well as the people. They think they have seen Mexico if they have crossed the Rio Grande and looked at the border towns on the other side. Tourists to California have visited desert resort towns in Lower California and have come back with souvenirs and stories of bullfights and racetracks. All Mexico is no more like these northern desert towns than all the United States is like Hollywood. The farther south one goes in Mexico, the more beautiful and picturesque is the land.

ALL ROADS LEAD TO MEXICO CITY

After an air-view of Mexico, we know something of what the land is like with its tropical coasts, its mountains, and its plateaus. Suppose we now come down to earth in Mexico and get acquainted with the towns and the people. To reach Mexico City, the goal of all visitors, we have a choice of several routes, in addition to the route by air. We may take one of three different railroads or we may go by automobile down the east coast of Mexico. If we go by car, we shall follow the new Pan-American Highway from Laredo (lah-ray'do), Texas, which will take us along 750 miles of paved road to the capital city. If you trace the road on the map on page 428, you will notice that it goes through Monterrey (mohn-teh-ray'), which is a modern factory town often called the "Little Pittsburgh" of Mexico. The trip takes about three days of easy driving through beautiful scenery. Since we have seen the east coast of Mexico from the air, let us choose the train route down the west coast.

WE TRAVEL INTO THE TORRID ZONE

We take the train at the border town of Nogales, part of which is in Mexico and part in Arizona. First we change our United States money into *pesos* (pay'sos), getting eight or

Black Star

THIS MEXICAN LANDSCAPE shows the rolling hills in the Valley of Mexico. The old Spanish water tower and the aqueduct were once part of the water supply system of the nearby town. Do you know the plant in the foreground?

nine *pesos* for every dollar in an average year. We feel very rich, clinking so many silver pieces in our pockets. We get on the train, cross the border, and travel through the uninteresting desert land of northwestern Mexico. At the tiny village stations along the way, Mexican Indians meet the train and sell *sarapes* (sah-rah′pays) or native wool blankets and bright Indian baskets to the tourists through the train windows. Many Indians get on the cheaper second-class car. They are loaded down with vegetables and fruits which they plan to sell at the nearest market town a few kilometers farther on. (We must think of distance now by the kilometer, which is five eighths of a mile.)

When the train pulls into Mazatlán on the coast, we are glad to buy fresh pineapples or bananas from the train window. Mazatlán is a hot town just below the Tropic of Cancer, and we are not sorry to leave it. Now comes a very rough stretch of mountain country on the way to Guadalajara. This region is part of the Sierra Madre Occidental, which you will remember runs along the west coast of Mexico.

GUADALAJARA IS FAMOUS FOR ITS GLASS

Guadalajara is a quiet city without the bustle and noise of our cities in the United States. It is hard to believe that there are 280,000 people living here. Like all old Spanish colonial cities, it has a central plaza or square and a cathedral. The

PÁTZCUARO INDIANS use these picturesque nets to dip up the *pescado blanco* or white fish which they sell in the village market. In the foreground other nets are drying on a rack.

cathedral was begun in 1571, fifty years before the Pilgrims built their log church at Plymouth.

Here we see for the first time a Latin American outdoor market. At open booths along the street are corn, beans, and squash brought by the farmers from their little villages in the mountains. The native farmers sit on the ground selling their produce. We cannot leave the markets of Guadalajara without buying some of the Mexican pottery with its hand-painted designs, or some blue hand-blown glass from the famous Guadalajara glass blowers. We forget, in our urge to buy all these beautiful things, how difficult it is to carry pottery and glass around in our suitcases all summer or to ship it safely back to the United States!

PÁTZCUARO IS AN INTERESTING LAKE REGION

From Guadalajara to Mexico City it is one night's ride on the train. But let us go by bus a longer way around to see a beautiful lake in a more primitive region. Around Lake Pátzcuaro (pahtz′cwah-roh) in ancient times lived the Tarascan Indians, a proud people who never admitted the superiority of the Aztecs. Today Indian people live in tiny towns on islands in the beautiful highland lake, and around the shores. Towns are called Cuca Chucha, Tzin Tzun Tzan, Jaracara, and other fantastic-sounding names. The Indians come by canoe across the lake to trade their hand-made straw hats and reed mats in the cobbled streets of the market town of Pátzcuaro.

They fish in the lake with large nets, often shaped like butterflies. In the town of Pátzcuaro, we stay at native inns, rent canoes, and go paddling across to visit the Indian towns. Here we find beautiful lacquer work for sale, painted in brilliant flower designs.

TOLUCA IS HIGH IN THE MOUNTAINS OF CENTRAL MEXICO

From the Pátzcuaro Lake country, the bus goes up, up into heavily wooded mountains at 10,000 feet above sea level, through beautiful scenery which looks much like the Canadian Rockies. In the valley of Toluca (toh-loo'cah), the bus passengers can stop for lunch at booths on the Toluca plaza, the highest large plaza in Mexico. It is cold in Toluca,

and it is easy to forget that this high mountain country is in the tropics. For lunch there are corn pancakes called *tortillas* (tor-tee'yas) wrapped around meat and cheese and fried crisp, and delightful large flat cookies made of nuts and caramelized sugar for which Toluca is famous. These are sold through the bus window by little Indian boys in the Toluca market. Their mothers are busily selling embroideries and hand-weaving in booths close by. All along the road to Toluca, in the high mountain passes, we see burros trotting along loaded with produce to sell in this market, or with sticks of charcoal for the housewives' fires.

MEXICO CITY IS A SURPRISE

From Toluca we come down a

THE GREAT CATHEDRAL OF MEXICO with its twin towers required seven generations of Mexican workers to complete. The beautiful altar inside the Cathedral is supported by huge marble columns.

thousand feet into the Valley of Mexico, where Mexico City is situated. After our bus ride through the country villages, where all the houses are adobe and the people are in native costume, Mexico City is a great surprise. Except for signs in Spanish, the native people on the streets, and the old colonial houses and churches, it is easy to imagine oneself in any modern American city. The streets are lined with hotels, theaters, and shops. But nowhere in the United States can beautiful hand-made articles be purchased so cheaply as in the tourist shops in Mexico City. Later on, you will learn more about the pottery and silver-work, the glassware, and the colorful *sarapes*.

Now let us visit the famous square or Zócalo in the center of the city where the streetcars and buses meet. This, you remember, was once the great plaza in front of the Aztec pyramid in the ancient city of Tenochtitlán. You can go under the street to see the old passages which have been dug out, the walls carved with the feathered serpents of the Aztecs. Today, in place of the pyramid is the Cathedral, the oldest and largest in the Americas. The National Palace, where the president has his offices, is on the square, too.

A block away from the Zócalo is the National Museum, where relics of the civilization of the Aztecs may be seen. The streets leading from the Zócalo are named for the national heroes and the holidays of Mexico. There is even a street named for Queen Isabella!

While in Mexico City, almost all tourists go to see the pyramids at Teotihuacán, those ruins of the Toltec city which we described in an earlier chapter. A reminder of the Aztecs can still be seen in a trip from Mexico City to the floating gardens of Xochimilco (so-chee-meel'co). You remember that the Aztecs planted gardens on rafts covered with mud, and floated them in the lake at Tenochtitlán. These floating gardens took root and today are flower-covered islands. Mexican families go there on Sunday afternoons, hire flower-bedecked boats, and paddle up and down among the islands singing to the guitar and calling to their friends who pass in other boats. Around about them are the canals and the cypress trees, and in the distance, across the Valley of Mexico, are the two famous snow-covered volcanoes, Popocatepetl and Ixtaccihuatl, guarding the valley.

AUTOMOBILE ROADS LEAD TO BOTH COASTS

As you know, Mexico City is on the high central plateau of Mexico. You can now drive in an automobile down to the *tierra caliente* on either the Atlantic or the Pacific coast. On the road to the Pacific is the interesting town of Cuernavaca (cwair-nah-vah'-cah). It is below the colder mountain valleys, and everywhere one finds semi-tropical flowers. Here Cortez built himself a palace of red stone which still faces on the cobbled street in the center of the hilly town. On its walls Diego Rivera (ree-vay'rah), Mexico's modern artist, has painted a scene of the coming of Cortez and his cruelty to the Indians.

The road from Mexico City to the eastern coast on the Gulf of Mexico leads through even more beautiful country. The majestic mountain peak of Orizaba looms above the road.

Sawders

AT XOCHIMILCO Indian women dart about in tiny canoes selling flowers. The little excursion boats are named for girls — Carmen, Consuelo, or Angelita — and young men rent boats named for their best girls.

In the semi-tropical towns gardenias grow everywhere, and one can buy for a very few Mexican pennies a split section of banana tree, packed with wet moss and filled with twenty or more white gardenias. Far below the road is the blue Gulf of Mexico. Sometimes the road goes through wooded stretches where wild orchids grow in the trees. Tropical foods like mangos, fried plantain bananas, and avocados are sold at the bus or train stops.

The road ends at Veracruz (vay-rah-croos'), the oldest Spanish town in Mexico, founded by Cortez before he climbed up the mountains to Tenochtitlán. In Veracruz there is a big modern harbor, the main entrance port for Mexico. Veracruz also has its old plaza and its cathedral. The poorer people live in little wooden houses painted bright blue and pink and yellow, snuggled among the palm trees. The water of the Gulf of Mexico, which is turquoise blue along the beaches, is almost too warm for swimming; although in Veracruz people often come down to swim in the cool of the evening.

OAXACA AND TEHUÁNTEPEC ARE WORTH A VISIT

If you wanted to continue the route which the Pan-American Highway is taking, you would go south from Mexico City to the old colonial town of Puebla (poo-ay'blah). You would pass under the shadow of Popocatepetl and Ixtaccihuatl. Puebla is today a large modern city, but its ancient churches are the most beauti-

141

ful in Mexico. Perhaps this is because of the colored glazed tiles used in their decoration and made in Puebla, which were famous even in Spain. The mountain pass south from Puebla to the Valley of Oaxaca (wah-hah'cah) is one of the most difficult regions in Mexico in which to build a highway. The train, however, runs down in twenty-four hours, and any tourist who goes to Oaxaca is glad to have made the trip. Here is one of the most interesting Indian markets in all Mexico, in the square near the old colonial plaza.

The city of Oaxaca with about 30,000 inhabitants seems to be in a different country than Mexico City. To the plaza come Indian people wearing peaked hats made of felt. The women are dressed in long blouses of unbleached muslin with bright magenta-colored sashes, or in embroidered blouses gathered in at the waist, and very full skirts. These Indians whom we see in the Oaxaca markets come from the hills which surround the Oaxaca Valley. They are descendants of the Zápotecs who built the city of Mitla, which you can drive out to see. Today the weavers of Oaxaca still use the same designs which the Zápotecs employed hundreds of years ago.

From the Valley of Oaxaca, the Pan-American Highway now goes across another divide and down into more tropical country. The narrowest

THIS PRETTY TEHUÁNTEPEC GIRL is dressed in her very best *huipil* of red silk embroidered in flowers. Her headdress is of pleated lace and she carries a decorated gourd to use in a dance.

Lanks

point in Mexico is called the Isthmus of Tehuántepec; there is also an interesting tropical town of the same name. The Indian women who live there are called *tehuanas* (tay-whah'-nahs). They are supposed to be the most beautiful in all Mexico, and wear a colorful embroidered costume.

So this is Mexico! We have traveled her highways and byways, we have seen the charm of her towns and of her light-hearted people. Now we are ready to learn what has been happening in Mexico since she first became independent.

Are You a Careful Reader? Test Yourself!

I. Supply the correct word for each blank:

1. Monterrey, Mexico, is a factory town often called the . . . . of Mexico.
2. Toluca is a cold town because of its . . . . .
3. The Pan-American Highway in Mexico will run from the border town of . . . . , Texas, to the Isthmus of . . . . .
4. Wool blankets, woven by the Mexican Indians, are called . . . . .
5. The natives of Oaxaca are descendants of the . . . . ; the Indians of the Valley of Mexico are descendants of the . . . . .

II. Match these words and statements:

1. peso	a. central plaza of Mexico City
2. Nogales	b. capital of the state of Yucatan
3. Guadalajara	c. costume worn by Indian women of Tehuántepec
4. Pátzcuaro	d. corn pancakes
5. Zócalo	e. Mexican silver piece
6. Veracruz	f. border town between Arizona and Mexico
7. Xochimilco	g. large port city on east coast of Mexico
8. Mazatlán	h. city famed for its blue glassware
9. tortilla	i. lake with floating gardens near Mexico City
10. tehuana	j. tropical town on Pacific coast of Mexico
	k. Mexican candy
	l. lake where Indians fish with butterfly nets

Food for Thought and Discussion

1. Is it unfair to judge a country by its citizens who have migrated to the United States? Why?
2. When we are traveling in another country ought we to make comparisons with the United States? Why?
3. If you visited Mexico, what would you expect to admire in that country?
4. Tourists from the United States visiting other countries have often been the cause for dislike of all Americans. How does it happen that this is true?

Chapter 13

The Republic of Mexico Wins Democracy After a Century of Strife

INDEPENDENCE DOES NOT BRING PEACE TO MEXICO

IF FATHER HIDALGO had known that his movement to help the peons (peasants) was to be thrown aside when Mexico became independent, he might never have rung his church bell on that night of September 15. No sooner had the Republic of Mexico been launched than it embarked upon a stormy sea. It was to know emperors and cruel dictators; it was to fight a foreign war and lose half its land; civil wars and finally revolution were to drench the land with blood before there was peace.

We left the story of Mexican independence at the point where Iturbide seized control of the government after the republicans had helped him to gain Mexico's freedom from Spain. Shortly after Mexican independence was declared, Iturbide, still at the head of the army, had himself crowned emperor. Many of the patriotic Mexicans who had joined Iturbide did not like the idea of an emperor. In 1824, Iturbide was executed and the Republic of Mexico was at last established. A constitution was drawn up providing for a president and a congress somewhat like that of the United States. A tricolored flag was also adopted for Mexico, with red for unity of all races, green for independence, and white for religious purity. In the center was the coat of arms of Mexico, the Aztec symbol of the eagle sitting on a cactus, devouring a snake.

For the next twenty years Mexico was to know only war and political strife. No one in Mexico knew how to run a republic now that they had one. They had no experience in voting for members of congress or in obeying the laws made by congress. The leaders for independence who had been tricked into helping Iturbide distrusted the creole landholders. The creoles, or Spanish people, did not want a real democracy, but were interested chiefly in keeping their immense estates and in running the government for their own benefit. Political parties were backed by armed soldiers ready to fight for the leader they wanted. The military leader with the strongest forces behind him was the man who became president. For many years not one president was elected according to the constitution and not one served a full term of four years. Of course, all this political confusion helped the Indians and the *mestizos* not at all. They were no better off under a republic than under the rule of Spain, for they still worked as peons or peasants on the estates.

This confused situation in Mexico was a perfect background for some strong man to step in and make himself dictator. That is exactly what happened. A leader of Spanish blood named Antonio Santa Anna (sahn'-tah ah'nah) finally gained control of the government in 1833. Although he was expelled a few years later, he kept coming back into power from time to time until 1855. During the years when Santa Anna was in power, Mexico lost half her territory in a war with the United States.

AMERICANS SETTLE TEXAS AND WIN THEIR INDEPENDENCE FROM MEXICO

The new Republic of México claimed all the land that the Spaniards had colonized as far north as the last California mission. You remember that this territory extended over the whole southwestern part of North America. By this time the people of the United States had long outgrown the thirteen original colonies on the Atlantic seaboard and had been expanding farther and farther to the west and southwest. In 1820, an American named Moses Austin had asked the government in Mexico for permission to start an American colony where the present state of Texas is located. He promised that the colonists would belong to the Catholic faith and become Mexican citizens. At that time, the territory north of the Rio Grande was thinly settled and the idea of increasing the population pleased the Mexicans.

Colonists thronged into Texas during the period of the Mexican revolution and by 1835, 30,000 Americans

THE ÁLAMO has become a monument to the memory of those brave Texans who gave their lives defending it. Today this old mission is surrounded by skyscrapers in the city of San Antonio, Texas.

Monkmeyer

had taken up land in Texas. But they did not keep their agreement with Mexico. Few of them had any intention of becoming Mexican citizens. They brought Negro slaves in spite of a law against them. There was much quarreling with the Mexican government, and finally, when Santa Anna became dictator, the Texans declared their independence. This aroused the Mexicans and Santa Anna led troops into Texas. One of the great stories of the war is the defense by 180 Texans of a mission called the Álamo (ah'lah-moh) at San Antonio against an army of 4000 Mexicans. Although they held out for eleven days, all but six were finally killed. "Remember the Álamo!" became the war cry of the Texans. After the defeat of Santa Anna two months later, the Mexicans were forced to withdraw across the Rio Grande and Texas became an independent country in 1836.

TEXAS IS ADMITTED TO THE UNITED STATES AND THE MEXICAN WAR FOLLOWS

The loss of Texas marked the beginning of the end of Mexico's vast territory north of the Rio Grande. After Texas had been independent for ten years, she applied for admission to the United States. It is not hard to see why this angered the Mexicans greatly. They felt that it had been Austin's purpose from the beginning to win Texas for the United States. The government of Mexico had never recognized the independence of Texas. Santa Anna told the government of the United States that if Texas were admitted to the Union, it would mean war. To add to the difficulty, Texas claimed the Rio Grande for the boundary line be-

tween her territory and that of Mexico, while Mexico claimed a line several hundred miles farther into Texan territory.

Many Americans wanted war. They believed that it was the destiny of the United States to extend from ocean to ocean. They had their eyes on California, which the government of the United States had tried to purchase from Mexico. The fact that Americans did not have much respect for the confused politics and the frequent revolutions of their weak neighbor made matters worse. The Mexicans, on the other hand, underestimated the strength of the United States.

In 1845, Texas was admitted to the Union. The Mexican ambassador in Washington said, "This is the most unjust act of aggression which can be found in the annals of modern history." The two-year war with Mexico which followed was a one-sided conflict. American forces easily took possession of California and New Mexico. General Winfield Scott landed a force at Veracruz and advanced upon Mexico City. When he reached Chapultepec (chah-pool-tay-pek'), the ancient fort three miles from Mexico City, he found only young cadets in training to defend it. Those boys who died fighting the Americans are among the heroes of Mexico. When American troops entered Mexico City, the war was at an end.

Mexican soldiers had fought bravely in the war, but their army was not well organized and equipped. Mexico lost nearly half of her territory as a result of the war, while the United States was richer by the states of California, New Mexico, Arizona, Utah, Nevada, and part of Colorado.

Galloway

CHAPULTEPEC CASTLE on the heights above Mexico City was once the home of Maximilian and Carlota, and their luxurious rooms can still be seen. The castle contains an interesting historical museum, and is surrounded by a beautiful park.

Mexico had to accept the Rio Grande as her border and received $15,000,000 for the territory she lost. Mexicans have always felt that the United States fought the war in order to gain that territory, and even today many of them are inclined to be suspicious of our motives toward Mexico. There is peace today, however, along the border of the Rio Grande.

THE REFORMS OF JUÁREZ LEAD TO CIVIL WARS IN MEXICO

After the Mexican people had lost this great expanse of territory to the United States and had been defeated in a war, they had a difficult time maintaining an orderly government. In 1853, after a series of revolts, General Santa Anna was brought back into the presidency. He made himself absolute dictator and even gave himself the title of "Most Serene Highness." Liberal-minded leaders opposed Santa Anna and asked for a new constitution. Finally in 1855 Santa Anna was forced to leave the country.

One of the most famous leaders of the group of reformers who were responsible for his downfall was Benito Juárez (bay-nee'toh whah'rehs). This man is often called the Abraham Lincoln of Mexico. He was a full-blooded Indian from a mountain village near Oaxaca in southern Mexico. Until he was twelve years old, he had herded goats near the thatched hut of his uncle, speaking only his native Indian tongue. A parish priest, who became interested in Benito because he was so intelligent, sent him to school to be educated in Spanish and in reading, writing, and arithmetic.

When he was fifteen, he went to a secondary school run by priests, and from there to a college in Oaxaca where he learned to be a lawyer. This may not seem at all unusual to you, but you must remember that there was a strong prejudice against Indians in Mexico. Even the *mestizo* boys in the cities had very little chance for an education, to say nothing of an Indian from the country!

While still a young man, Juárez served as judge and afterward as a deputy to Congress in Mexico City. He was one of the few pure-blooded Indians there. Everywhere he became known for his honesty and his liberalism. Later he was chosen governor of Oaxaca, and succeeded in cleaning up the dishonest politics in

JUÁREZ, THE INDIAN PRESIDENT and "Abraham Lincoln" of Mexico, spent his life working for reforms which would help the downtrodden people of his native land.

Sawders

his native state. When Santa Anna returned to power, he had Juárez put in prison. Juárez was sent to the worst dungeon in Mexico, which was on an island in the Veracruz harbor. Later he was exiled to New Orleans, where he stayed until the revolution against Santa Anna brought him home again.

When his political party came to power after the exile of Santa Anna, Juárez worked to lessen the power and wealth of the Catholic Church. A great deal of the agricultural land in Mexico was owned by the Church, and because it controlled so much of the land, the Church had a very great influence in political affairs. This may be hard for us to understand because neither the Catholic Church nor any other church has any political power in the United States. In Mexico, however, the Catholic Church was officially recognized by the government and had many special privileges. For instance, members of the clergy who violated the laws of the country were tried in special courts.

Under the new liberal government laws were passed which required the Church to sell its agricultural land, and required the clergy to be tried in the regular government courts as were other law violators. These laws were made part of a new liberal constitution for Mexico in 1857. Many people thought that Juárez and the liberals were fighting against religion itself, when his only aim was to rid the Church of its political power; others felt that the government was moving too fast and that Mexico was not yet ready for such changes. So they joined the church leaders in starting a civil war against the liberals and their constitution.

Brown Bros.

HANDSOME MAXIMILIAN AND BEAUTIFUL CARLOTA appear here in all their royal splendor. The unfortunate emperor was shot but Carlota lived until 1927 believing herself still the Empress of Mexico.

THE FRENCH ESTABLISH A PUPPET EMPIRE IN MEXICO

The long civil war between Juárez and the conservative classes brought much trouble to Mexico. Napoleon III, a nephew of the great Napoleon, was Emperor of France at this time. He hoped to build up a strong French empire with powerful friends throughout the world. He believed that if he could place a ruler friendly to the French government at the head of a Latin American nation, the power of his empire would spread to the New World.

During the civil war against Juárez the Mexicans borrowed a great deal of money from European countries. In 1861, Napoleon III gained the support of England and Spain in try-ing to collect these debts by force. It gave him an excuse to intervene in Mexico. He had not dared to attempt any conquest because the United States had adopted a policy called the Monroe Doctrine which warned all European countries to keep hands off in the Western Hemisphere. But from 1861 to 1865 the United States was busy with its own war between the states. So Napoleon III made the most of his opportunity. He sent French forces to Mexico which attacked and ousted Juárez and his government. Napoleon III chose a young archduke of Austria, Maximilian, to be emperor. The people of Spanish blood and the church officials preferred even the French to Juárez.

THE FRENCH EMPIRE IN MEXICO WAS SHORT–LIVED

Maximilian was a handsome, pleasant young man, but was lacking in decision and the ability to judge men. He and his beautiful wife, Carlota, did not know Mexico at all. They were told that the Mexican people were anxious for them to come and establish a strong government backed by French soldiers. They came to Mexico bringing carriages, servants, and furniture to establish a royal court. Nothing in their reception led them to suspect the true state of affairs. They were welcomed in Mexico City by a staged reception in which people in the streets had been trained or bribed to cheer for their coming. The French troops sent over by Napoleon had driven the Mexican patriots out of the capital.

As long as the United States was busy with her Civil War, Maximilian was successful in Mexico. He and his wife held court on the elaborate scale of European kings. But when the war was over, the United States was again able to enforce the Monroe Doctrine. When Napoleon III saw that the United States would be willing to help Juárez against him, he began to call his soldiers back to France.

Although the unfortunate Maximilian was captured by Juárez's soldiers and shot on June 19, 1867, Carlota was not aware of his death. She had returned to Europe, where her troubles had affected her mind and she became insane.

The whole affair of Maximilian and Carlota was just a brief interlude that had little effect on Mexico. But their tragic story has become a part of the history of that country. Tourists may see the gardens where Carlota liked to walk during the summer. In the National Museum their state carriage is preserved for young Mexicans to see. Maximilian's favorite rooms can be seen in Chapultepec Palace.

MEXICO BECOMES A DICTATORSHIP UNDER DÍAZ

Juárez became president of Mexico again after Maximilian's death, but unfortunately his reforms were never completely carried out. He died suddenly of heart failure in 1872 He is still loved by the Mexicans as the Indian boy who became president and worked for the welfare of the common people.

The president who followed Juárez was overthrown in 1877 in a revolution which was led by Porfirio Díaz (por-fee'ree-oh dee'ahs). Díaz was a young *mestizo* of Oaxaca who had studied law under Juárez and served as general in his army during the war against the French. Juárez had considered him a sincere reformer with the good of the people at heart, although he had never allowed him to become president. But Díaz soon showed that he was interested in power for himself rather than in reforms for the peons. The constitution forbade the re-election of the same man to the presidency, but after his first term Díaz had it changed to allow himself to remain in power. He ruled Mexico continuously from 1884 until 1911.

Díaz put an end to revolutions by generals and politicians. No one dared start a revolt while he was in power. Under his rule, Mexico developed rapidly. Railroads were constructed, factories were built, electricity was installed in Mexico City, and streets were paved. After 1900, the oil wells of Mexico began to pour out millions of barrels of oil. But Mexico paid dearly for all this progress. Díaz had allowed foreign companies who wanted to invest money in Mexico to build the railroads and produce the oil. It was not long before almost all of Mexico's resources and industries were controlled by American and English companies.

Under the "reign of Díaz," the condition of the peons became worse. Díaz had no desire to help the peasants and workers. More and more land fell into the hands of the wealthy landowners and foreign companies. The ancient villages where Indians had lived for centuries were seized because they could not show a deed of ownership. Hundreds of thousands of Indians were left homeless. Large landowners closed off village cornfields to use them for growing cotton or henequen, or for grazing cattle. They made themselves wealthy from the beef and hides, while the Indians starved. Never had the landed classes been more powerful; never had the Indians been more miserable.

The Indians who lived on the large estates suffered also. The landholdings in Mexico were called *haciendas* (ah-see-en'dahs) and sometimes contained several Indian villages. The landlord lived in his mansion in the center of the estate, with homes for his foremen and barns for his livestock near-by. The Indians or peons lived at a distance in their miserable huts and worked for a share of the crop or for tiny wages. Most *haciendas* had their own store, their own church, and their own priest. The landlord set the prices at his store and encouraged the peons to buy on credit. The peons were almost always in debt to him no matter how hard they worked. The wealthy landlords themselves often did not live on their estates, but stayed in Mexico City, or even Paris or Madrid, and paid no attention at all to the welfare of the Indians.

THE PEOPLE OF MEXICO REVOLT AGAINST DÍAZ AND THE LANDOWNERS

As Díaz grew older and showed no intention of giving up his powers, the nation began to weary of his rule. Those classes who had fought for a revolution under Hidalgo and Guerrero in 1810 were desperate. For more than a hundred years they had waited for reforms in the unjust land system of Mexico. In 1910, rebellion broke out when Díaz was elected again. The story of the next ten years in Mexican history is the story of the peons' fight to get back the land. This is the real revolution of Mexico. When any modern Mexican refers to the "Revolution," he means the fight of the people to reform the government of Mexico and recover the land for themselves.

During most of these years between 1910 and 1920, all Mexico was a bloody battlefield. The men left the villages to join the forces of one leader or another. The women and children tried to harvest the corn by themselves. Thousands of women and children starved. Few schools were open. Matters became so serious that the United States at one time threatened to intervene.

Many revolutionary bands formed from the scattered rebel groups under their neighborhood leaders. The Revolution was not a well-planned movement with one man at the head. There were many leaders and they did not always agree. But they were held together one and all by hatred of the kind of rule Díaz had given them, and by dreams of what Mexico would be after the Revolution. Although the whole story of the Revolution which swept Mexico like a great flood is too long to tell here, let us learn about some of the brave men who led the people in their fight.

THE LEADERS OF THE REVOLUTION ARE HEROES OF MEXICO TODAY

Francisco Madero (frahn-sees'coh mah-day'roh) was the first leader to succeed against the forces of Díaz, and he brought about the exile of the old dictator. Madero had been educated in the United States. He knew that Mexico needed a more democratic government, but he did not understand the land problem or the Indians' desire for the land. When he was elected president, he allowed many of Díaz's followers to remain in power. They turned upon Madero and murdered him. After the murder of Madero, the Revolution flamed up again, and the people followed other leaders who promised to help them.

One of the leaders of the revolutionary armies has become a hero to the Indians of southern Mexico. Emiliano Zapata (ay-mee-lee-ah'no sah-pah'tah) was a pure-blooded Indian from a little village in southern Mexico. During Díaz's reign, the village land had been seized and the Indians were forced to go elsewhere. Zapata went to Mexico City as a stable-boy. We can imagine how he felt to find the horses of the wealthy Mexicans

living in marble stables, with more to eat than the poor Indians of his own village. Zapata's purpose in joining the Revolution was to get lands for all the peasants immediately. Although he could not read or write, he became a general, and great numbers of the peons from his own state joined the revolutionary army under his leadership. His men were so loyal that even after he was killed, his guerrilla bands kept up the fight for Indian rights.

Pancho Villa (pahn'cho vee'yah) has become almost a legend with the Mexican people. He was a sort of rough Robin Hood and champion of the underdog. He led the forces of northern Mexico in the Revolution. After a quarrel with another leader named Carranza, Villa stopped fighting for the people and became a bandit. He and his men would make daring raids, striking terror into towns and villages, and then retreat into the hills. He even crossed the border and raided a town in New Mexico, killing several Americans. President Wilson in 1916 sent soldiers under General Pershing into Mexico after him, but Villa escaped into the hills. He has become the bogy man of Mexico, and even today mothers say to their children, "Be good, or Pancho Villa will get you!"

Venustiano Carranza (vay-noos-tee-ah'noh cah-rahn'sah) is important because during the years when he was in power a new constitution was adopted. This Constitution of 1917 shows clearly what the people were fighting for. It provides that the president shall serve for a term of six years, but may not be re-elected for the following term. That, of course, was intended to prevent a dictator

Paul Guillumette

REVOLUTIONARY HEROES are portrayed in murals by Diego Rivera on the walls of Chapultepec Castle. Madero sits his horse with hand upraised; the banner to the right carries the slogan, "Land for All."

from seizing power. The members of the Mexican Congress, and other officials, are chosen by a vote of the people. The constitution also states that the oil and mineral lands, which were then in the hands of foreign companies, belong to the nation and cannot become the property of private concerns. The rights of the town laborers were given special protection, and the government received the power to divide the huge estates among the people.

When Carranza tried to retain his control of the government by forcing the election of a man he wanted, there was another revolt which drove him from the presidency. Its leader, Alvaro Obregón (ahl-vah′roh o-bray-gohn′), was then elected president in 1920, and the fighting was about over. This first election under the new constitution was fair and peaceful, which was unusual in Mexico. The people had finally accepted the constitution as the goal for which they had been fighting. To the peasants, who had probably dreamed of living in plenty, with land and fat cattle, a mere constitution must have seemed an empty victory. But the presidents who have carried out the provisions of that constitution have brought to the peons of Mexico more than they dreamed of — land of their own, better food, and schools.

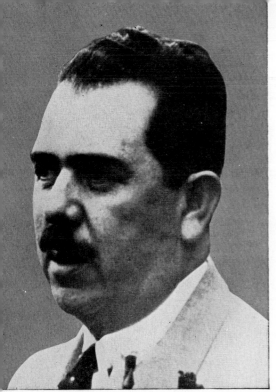

Three Lions

LAZARO CARDENAS will long be remembered as the man who did the most to lift the Mexican Indians from the misery that had been their lot for four hundred years.

CÁRDENAS OF MEXICO ROSE FROM PEON TO PRESIDENT

The man who was president of Mexico from 1934 to 1940 did more for the peons than any previous president. Lázaro Cárdenas (lah'sar-roh cahr'day-nahs) was born a poor *mestizo* boy in a village near Lake Pátzcuaro. When he was thirteen, he was supporting his mother and seven brothers and sisters. By the time he was eighteen, he had become the village jailer. When the armies of the Revolution came through the town, he released his one prisoner and they both joined the army. In two more years he was a lieutenant under Obregón.

After the Revolution, Cárdenas became governor of the state where he was born. It must have surprised the people to see that a poor "Indian" boy had returned as governor. He set to work immediately to break up the large estates and distribute the land to the Indians, as was provided for in the new constitution. About a quarter of a million acres were given to 181 villages in his state. He built roads, started irrigation systems for the land, and founded schools in every tiny village. His fine record in his own state brought him to the attention of the president, and he was asked to serve in his cabinet in Mexico City. The people in the capital scorned his low birth. They said, "He smells of *petate*" (pay-tah'tay), which is the straw mat on which Indian people sleep. Over half of Mexico's population sleeps on *petates*, so this made him more popular than ever with the poor people. It was as though a president of the United States fifty years ago had been accused of being born in a log cabin!

In 1934, Cárdenas was elected to the highest office in the land, the presidency of Mexico. At last he was in a position to help all of Mexico. He traveled on horseback from village to village checking up on the local government, the water supply, or the crop failures. Mexican presidents before him had always visited a town at the head of a military delegation and accompanied by an armed bodyguard. The people felt that this simple man who rode along among them was their friend and they welcomed his help.

When Cárdenas's term was over, he did not try to name his successor or to change the constitution so that he could serve a second term. He had no desire for power or glory for its own sake. He had not used the presidency to build for himself a personal fortune as had some presidents before him; instead he was known as a man of great honesty. He was recognized, even by those who did not approve his program, as a man who sincerely wished to help the common people.

In 1940 Manuel Ávila Camacho (mah-noo-el' ah'vee-lah cah-mah'cho) was elected president. Under his leadership Mexico's relations with the United States were friendly and co-operative. He was succeeded in 1946 by Miguel Alemán (mee-ghel' ah-lay-man'), after one of the fairest and most peaceful elections in Mexico's history. Alemán's program for Mexico was to increase the farm production and develop the country's industry. President Truman was the first president of the United States to visit Mexico City. His trip to the Mexican capital, and President Alemán's return visit to Washington, D.C., showed that these two neighboring countries were now good friends.

Are You a Careful Reader?   Test Yourself!

I. Can you match these words and statements?

1. Santa Anna
2. Cárdenas
3. Juárez
4. Alemán
5. Maximilian
6. Álamo
7. Zapata
8. Villa
9. Carranza
10. Díaz

   a. Indian leader in the Revolution who fought for Indian rights
   b. president under whom the new constitution was made in 1917
   c. American general who fought in the Mexican War
   d. harsh dictator whose long "reign" was overthrown by the Revolution of 1910
   e. military dictator and general who was defeated in the war with Texas
   f. recent Mexican president who carried out a program to aid the Indian people
   g. Indian president whose reforms were interrupted by Maximilian
   h. revolutionary leader who became a bandit in northern Mexico
   i. a town in Texas
   j. mission at San Antonio defended by a few Texans against an army of Mexicans
   k. president of Mexico elected in 1946
   l. former emperor of Mexico

II. Can you choose the best answer?

1. Independence for Mexico did not aid the common people as Hidalgo had hoped because: (*a*) they were not allowed to vote; (*b*) the constitution of the republic did not call for reforms; (*c*) the government merely shifted from rule by Spain to rule by ambitious creole landholders.

2. From the Mexican point of view, the war with the United States occurred because: (*a*) California and New Mexico wished to revolt from the mother country; (*b*) the United States annexed Texas which had once been part of Mexico; (*c*) cadets in the Chapultepec Castle in Mexico City were killed by United States troops.

3. In Juárez's time many Mexican people disapproved of the part played by the Church because: (*a*) the Church founded missions and encouraged the Indian people

to revolt; (b) the Church owned a huge amount of land and held political power in the government; (c) they wanted to abolish all religion.

4. The real cause of the Revolution in 1910 was: (a) the desire of the common people for reforms in the unjust land system of Mexico; (b) Díaz's increasing tyranny as he grew older; (c) the control of Mexico's railroads and oil wells by American concerns.

5. The Mexican Constitution of 1917 is unusual among national constitutions because: (a) it is the third constitution in Mexico since independence; (b) it limits the president to one four-year term; (c) it provides that the oil and mineral lands belong to the nation and cannot become the property of foreign companies.

Food for Thought and Discussion

1. If you were a Mexican school student what reasons would you give for the former unfriendly feeling of your country toward the United States?

2. Read the story of the Mexican War of 1848 in an older American history book. Ought Americans to feel proud of winning the Mexican War in 1848? Why?

3. Why did it take a hundred years before Mexican leaders were able to give definite help to the Indian people?

Chapter 14

Modern Mexico Controls Her Resources, Distributes Her Land, and Educates Her People

"MEXICO FOR THE MEXICANS!" IS THE SLOGAN OF MODERN MEXICO

México para los Mexicanos! expresses the spirit of Mexico today. Mexico in her own way is working out the problems which she has faced since becoming independent. Slowly but surely, the changes for which the peons fought are taking place in Mexico. Millions of acres of land have been given back to the peons; schools by the thousands have been established in the country villages where schools were never known before; the government has regained control of Mexico's great oil resources; Mexican labor is better paid than it has ever been.

Not all the presidents since the Revolution have carried on the reforms called for in the constitution. It is easy to understand why that is

Black Star

MEXICO'S OIL PRODUCTION has begun to prosper again since an agreement was reached with the American companies. Today Mexico holds sixth place in the world's oil production.

true. To get land for the peasants meant that it had to be taken away from the men who owned it. The wealthy estate-owners were naturally not in favor of giving up their estates to the peons even though the constitution did provide for it. Of course, the owner was to be paid, but he had to take government bonds instead of money. It was not a simple matter, either, to oust the foreign companies which had so many millions of dollars invested in Mexican oil, agriculture, and cattle lands. When Cárdenas was elected president of Mexico in 1934, he made up his mind that in spite of objections he would go ahead with the changes Mexico so badly needed.

CÁRDENAS GAINS CONTROL OF THE OIL RESOURCES OF MEXICO

Part of Cárdenas's program was to restore the mines and oil lands of Mexico to the government. You remember that in order to enrich the country, Díaz allowed American and other foreign companies to develop the mines and the oil wells, and to build the railways and other industries of Mexico. Naturally these companies did not want to sell their holdings to the Mexican government.

Mexico's greatest resource was her oil. The story of its discovery is a fascinating one. The oil fields in the Tampico region were discovered in 1900 by two Americans. Later, other fields were found in the state of Tabasco, and in San Luis Potosí, which lies inland from Tampico. Because it was located in the oil region, the city of Tampico grew from a tiny town to one of the most important oil-shipping ports in the world. From a mere 10,000 barrels of oil in 1901, Mexico leaped to a production of 153,000,000 barrels by 1920.

Many stories are told of the famous Tampico oil fields. The *Dos Bocas* or "Two Mouths" well has been called the "greatest single oil well in the world." When it was drilled in 1908, the pipes went down 1800 feet, or about one third of a mile. When oil was reached, there came a great explosion like an earthquake, which cracked open the ground for 250 feet around. With the explosion, the oil in the well caught fire and sent flames 1500 feet up in the air. The whole countryside was lighted up at night for miles around. The fire burned for 58 days and was finally put out by pumping sand into the well. The oil flowed out so rapidly that it could not be caught in barrels. The earth was dug out around the well and a huge lake of oil was formed.

From Mexico's point of view there were many objections to the ownership of the wells by foreign companies. Certainly the resources of a country should be used for the benefit of the people of that country. The profits from the oil were going out of Mexico to the United States and England, and Mexico needed that money. The workers were paid wages which were low in comparison with those of oil-well workers in the United States. The foreign companies which controlled so much of Mexico's industries were not interested in the welfare of Mexico.

When, in 1938, the British and American oil companies felt that they could not meet the higher wages and other demands for the workers made by the government, Cárdenas simply took over the oil properties. Of course, the oil companies objected to this and their governments protested to Mexico, but Cárdenas stood firm. His government offered to pay compensation for these properties, but not until recently has it been able to reach an agreement with the oil companies as to what the price should be. In 1942, representatives from the United States and Mexico reached a settlement which Presidents Roosevelt and Camacho signed. The oil companies received about one sixth as much money as they had originally asked, but the American government urged them to accept this price in order to preserve our friendship with Mexico during wartime.

Americans and Mexicans should feel proud that so serious a problem did not lead to ill feeling between the two governments. The peaceful settlement of this dispute helped to prove that the United States sincerely wishes to be a "Good Neighbor." Today the oil wells are operated by the Mexican government, and Mexico is still an important country in oil production.

MEXICO'S INDUSTRIES AND LANDS ARE BEING RETURNED TO MEXICANS

Foreigners had also gained control over Mexico's cattle industry. You have already read how Díaz had allowed American companies to come in and buy up thousands of acres of grazing land and how they often took over village lands which had belonged

Gendreau

HENEQUEN FIBERS are spread on drying racks on this Yucatan plantation. For every pound of these fibers, twenty pounds of the long, fleshy cactus leaves must be cleaned of pulp by machine.

to the Indians for centuries. One American is said to have owned an area in northern Mexico as large as one of the smaller states in our country. Millions of dollars were made in the cattle industry by Americans. Cárdenas saw to it that these lands were seized and returned to the people. This has been another cause of misunderstanding between Americans and the Mexican government. But a just price was decided upon by special courts, and the Mexican government has begun to make yearly payments to the American owners.

Another industry which has been returned to the peasants of Mexico is that of the great henequen plantations of Yucatan. These plantations were the chief source of wealth in that part of the country. Henequen is a cactus plant whose strong fibers are used to make twine and has grown for centuries in Yucatan. The ancient Mayans twisted henequen fibers into rope which they used to move the huge stones used in their temples. The Spaniards also used it for ship cables as a substitute for the stronger rope made of hemp. In the early 1900's, thousands of acres of jungle were cleared and planted to henequen. It became the leading industry of Yucatan, and over half a million bales of the dried and cleaned fiber were exported. Most of it went to the United States to be used for bags and binder twine. Thousands of peons worked on the plantations, and large profits went to the people who owned the land, while the Indian workers received pitifully small wages.

Today the peons are gradually learning to run the plantations as community property.

Anyone who has been to Mexico City has seen the thousands of acres of *maguey* (mah'gay) plants growing on the plateau about the city. This plant is a type of cactus whose juice is used to make the favorite national drink called *pulque* (pull'kay). Mexican workers suck into gourds the juice which collects at the base of the leaves, and allow it to ferment. There are as many *pulque* shops in Mexico as there are soda fountains in our country. The *pulque* plantations have now been divided up among Indian families who work the plantations as a community undertaking.

MEXICAN LABOR WORKS UNDER IMPROVED CONDITIONS

The presidents who followed the Revolution also became interested in the problems of the Mexican factory workers. Although Mexico is not an industrial nation, there are many thousands of workers in Mexican factories. The village people of Mexico use a great deal of cotton cloth for their clothing, especially their native costumes. For this reason, Mexico has many textile factories. The workers are now organized into strong unions and receive a much higher wage and shorter hours than they ever had before.

We must not forget that the standard of living in Mexico is not so high as that in the United States. Mexican workers do not live so well as American workers. They do not have as much to eat or wear, nor do they live in houses with running water. A worker is paid perhaps nine pesos a day, which in our money is one dollar.

MEXICO IS NOT A RICH COUNTRY

Mexico is often described as a horn of plenty, but actually it is a rather poor and undeveloped country today. Except for the oil, the silver, and other metals, Mexico has few other resources which bring in wealth. Seventy per cent of its 25,000,000 people depend for a living on the crops they raise, and they must work hard to get barely enough to eat. All the corn raised in Mexico is only about one sixth of Iowa's corn crop.

Outside of the rich central plateau, there is not a great deal of good land. Only seven per cent of Mexico's land can be farmed. The rest is too dry or too mountainous. There are no more new lands to be developed because all the farming land is already cultivated. The only way that more food can be raised in Mexico is to teach the peons more modern methods of farming, so that their crops will be larger.

CÁRDENAS REDISTRIBUTES MEXICAN LANDS TO MEXICANS

If you were to ask an Indian of Mexico what Cárdenas had done for him, he wouldn't mention the oil wells or even the labor laws. He would probably say, "He gave us back our land." Cárdenas was part Indian and he knew the intense love of his people for the land. Do you remember the *hacienda* villages, whose inhabitants were part of the estate, bound in debt to the landowners? Do you remember also the free villages which lost their land under Díaz? The government has been following a plan of settling these people on the land again in a way that will seem natural to them. The Mexican Indian was never an independent farmer who owned his own plot of land with a fence around it. The Aztecs and the Mayan peasants lived together in community villages, owned their land in common, and shared equally in the work and the crops.

Co-operative villages, called *ejidos* (ay-hee'dohs), have been established where the people can work together as they have always done. Families who have no land form a group and apply to the land commissioner for a tract of land. The government buys a large estate from the owner and turns over a part of it to these families for a village. Each family may draw lots for its plot of land, or the group may decide to own and work all the land in common. As long as the land is cultivated, the villagers may keep it and pass it on to their children. If it is not cultivated, it must be re-turned to the government. Each village has its own mayor and council, who decide the village problems.

Fifty-seven million acres of land have already been distributed in this way to over one and a half million families, two thirds of it in the time of President Cárdenas. This means that half of the good crop land of Mexico is in the hands of about one third of its population. There are still many *hacienda* villages on the estates, but the peons are better off today than they have ever been before.

MEXICO ESTABLISHES A RURAL SCHOOL SYSTEM

Since Mexico is an agricultural land and raises barely enough food for its people, it is very important that the *ejido* villages raise more food than

A MODERN THRESHING MACHINE is being used on this *ejido*. A co-operative village can often afford modern machinery which no individual peon could possibly own. Not many *ejidos* are as modern as this one, however.

Black Star

Black Star

NOT ALL MEXICAN SCHOOLS are primitive rural schools and not all pupils are barefoot peons. In this boys' school in Mexico City the pupils have many advantages not enjoyed by their humble countrymen. How would you know that this is not a schoolroom in the United States?

was produced under the old land system. The leaders of Mexico realize that its peons must be educated. We are so used to our free public schools, even in rural districts, that it is hard for us to imagine a country without public schools. Until after the Revolution, schools for the common people in Mexico were very few, even including some church schools run by the Catholic Church. There were no school buildings and no teachers except in the larger towns and cities. In more than one third of the villages the people did not even speak Spanish, but a form of the Aztec or the Mayan language. So, you see, the people interested in ed-

ucating the Indians had plenty of problems to solve.

The Department of Education wanted to establish schools that would meet the needs of the people. They worked out an entirely new plan of education. They gathered groups of enthusiastic young people who knew the Indian language and who could teach simple rules of sanitary living and first aid. They found young men who could construct water systems and others who could show the farmers how to raise better livestock and crops. Fine potters, weavers, and artists from larger towns were found who could teach the Indians how to make the baskets or

162

pottery for which their region had once been famous. These teacher groups were called "Cultural Missions." By truck and on the backs of mules and burros, they were sent into the villages, where they were welcomed by the people. They stayed long enough in each village to start a school and to give some training to young Indians in the community who might serve as teachers. Then they moved on to another village.

Meanwhile, normal schools were started in the Mexican states so that teachers might be trained near their home communities. The Cultural Missions visit the schools every year to help the teachers with new ideas and materials. When a new school is completed, there is a town *fiesta* or celebration. In one town the Cultural Missions had helped to pipe water into the center of the town.

A *fiesta* is still held every year to celebrate the event.

In some regions the Indians are still quite uncivilized. The people speak Aztec, Zapotecan, or some other Indian language. To train these people and to teach the Spanish language, a few schools have been set up in a central location where the children may come to board. The young people learn civilized ways and the older people begin to understand that the school is intended to help them. Then, as soon as they wish, they may have a school in their own villages.

Let us visit the typical Indian village of Santa Cruz Etla (sahn'tah croos et'lah). You can then see for yourselves what the new school program has done for the humble Indian people who live in little villages scattered throughout Mexico.

MANY MEXICAN VILLAGE SCHOOLS are like this one. Notice the crude wooden benches used for desks. In the Santa Cruz Etla school, pupils of all ages are taught in one room.

Department of Education, Mexico

Lanks

THIS NATIVE BAKER, at a village in the mountains of southern Mexico, bakes in a beehive-shaped oven like those used by our Pueblo Indians.

SANTA CRUZ ETLA BECOMES A FREE VILLAGE

The little village of Santa Cruz Etla is situated high up in the hills in the state of Oaxaca south of the Valley of Mexico. It belonged for many years to a great *hacienda*. After the Revolution, the government notified the fifty families who lived in the village that they were to be made a free village and that they could choose the way they wanted their land distributed to them. It is hard for us to understand the joy which this news brought to the hearts of the peons.

Today each family has a five-acre plot of fertile land for crops. In addition, there is forest and pasture land which is owned by all the people in the village. Anyone who wishes to cut a burro-load of wood from the timberland, to sell in the Oaxaca City market, may do so. Likewise, anyone in the village may keep his sheep or goats in the community pasture land.

The village has a mayor and a council who look after the village interests. The simple people of Santa Cruz Etla have the dignity of men who own their land and share in the government of their town. They address each other as Don Pablo or Don Julio (dohn hoo'lee-oh), or Doña Sofía (dohn'yah soh-fee'ah), because *Don* and *Doña* are the titles of superior people. Of course, when they go to the market at Oaxaca with their burros loaded with firewood or beans, they are looked upon by the townspeople as poor peons and are never called Don or Doña. But when they get back to Santa Cruz at the end of the day, they become once more Don Pablo or Doña Sofía. They bow to no one, for are they not a free village?

THE PEOPLE OF SANTA CRUZ ETLA RAISE THEIR OWN FOOD

Every plot of land in Santa Cruz Etla is planted in corn and beans. Farming is hard labor for the men, for they have only the most primitive tools. The corn is hulled, boiled in lye water, and then ground on a stone corn grinder called a *metate* (may-tah'tay). From the corn meal the women make the flat corn cakes called *tortillas*, which are the principal food of Mexico. In every little yard about the adobe houses are gardens growing squash, chile peppers, avocados, oranges, and limes. There are chickens and pigs and turkeys around the doorstep, and in the community pasture land are young lambs and goats for special occasions.

THE VILLAGERS CONVERT FIREWOOD INTO CASH

The people of this village cannot supply all their own needs. They raise money by cutting and selling firewood from their timberland. Other villages which have no wood to sell make money by weaving blankets or making pottery. The money of the villagers goes for many things. It buys the white cotton cloth for the men's pajama-like work clothes and for the women's full skirts and gathered blouses. It is used to buy *rebosos* (ray-boh'sohs), the heavy dark-blue shawls that Indian women wear throughout Mexico, and which they use for so many things — to cover their heads against the sun, to carry their babies slung over their shoulders, to tie up a purchase when bags are scarce. Money is often needed to buy leather sandals or *huaraches* (whah-rah'chays) from a sandal-making town. Sometimes, when they cannot use firewood in trade, the villagers must have money to purchase from a mat-weaving town the reed mats or *petates* on which most Indians sleep.

Sometimes they want extra money for rockets to set off at a *fiesta*, or special refreshments to serve at a funeral. Sometimes they buy figures of saints to put up on the walls of their thatched huts or candles to burn in the chapel three miles away.

A RURAL SCHOOL CHANGES LIFE IN SANTA CRUZ ETLA

One year, a wonderful thing happened that changed the lives of everyone in Santa Cruz Etla. The fifty families of the village had had a brief visit from a Cultural Mission and they wanted a school. There had never been one in the whole hill region. Only two of the men in Santa Cruz Etla could read and write, and none of the women and children. Plans for building a school were sent from Mexico City to the village council. All the people worked together to make adobe bricks. Timbers were brought by ox-cart to make the rafters. Tiles were made for the floor. The school became the only big central building in the town. A fine young *mestizo* teacher from the Oaxaca teacher-training institution came to start the school. The children in the first classes, about sixty altogether, were considered the most fortunate children who had ever lived in Santa Cruz Etla.

Soon, another teacher was sent from Oaxaca City who planted a garden near the school. In the garden were other vegetables besides the corn and beans which the Indians always

A VILLAGE BASKET MAKER in the state of Puebla fashions baskets to sell in the nearest market town. Baskets are much in use in rural Mexico for purposes of storage and transportation.

Lanks

plant, and the ground was enriched by fertilizer. The men of the town watched the garden and saw the fine crops that grew there. They began to try the same methods on their own plots of ground. One of the teachers formed a mothers' club and got the mothers to come to the school every day for training in first aid and child care. When anyone is hurt or seriously sick today, he is brought immediately through the corn fields to the school for the teacher to examine.

The young teachers were asked to teach the adults at night. The town purchased a gasoline pressure lamp, which is still a source of great delight to all the people. First the young men of the village who were too old for the day school, and finally the old men, came to learn to read and write by the light of this lamp. The teacher at first had very few books and could only teach the older people from the childish primary readers. The old men knew more of the Zapotecan language than they did Spanish. They sweated over the primers, in the light of the gasoline lantern, try-ing to write "*Mi mama me ama*" (My mother loves me).

The school has been the finest thing that ever happened to Santa Cruz Etla. There are still problems for the villagers to solve. One is the bad water supply, which comes from the brook where the oxen ford the stream. Another is the primitive methods of plowing and harvesting the steep hillside corn fields. But Santa Cruz Etla has come a long way since the school was built.

In the last few years the education program of Mexico has reached farther than the Indian villages like Santa Cruz Etla. The government started a program to teach every illiterate grown person to read and write. This plan is called "each one teach one," and has been so successful that it has aroused interest all over the world. Under this plan, each person who knows how to read and write must teach one person who does not. A simple primer has been distributed by the government to make the task easier, and the plan has been copied in other parts of Latin America.

Are You a Careful Reader? Test Yourself!

I. Can you supply the correct word for each blank?
1. Mexico's oil wells are no longer owned by . . . . , but by the . . . .
2. Millions of acres of land have been distributed to the peons in the form of . . . .
3. Since almost three fourths of the Mexican people depend on . . . . for a living, the peons must be taught how to . . . . their crops.
4. Traveling schools to introduce rural education in the villages are called . . . .
5. Today almost every town and village in Mexico boasts a . . . . .

II. Can you match these words and statements?
1. peons   *a.* stone on which corn is ground
2. huaraches   *b.* a free village which owns its own land
3. Don   *c.* title of respect in Mexico

4. Tampico
5. petate
6. henequen
7. maguey
8. pulque
9. ejido
10. hacienda

d. straw mat on which peons sleep
e. port from which oil is shipped
f. shawl worn by women
g. sandals worn by peons
h. Indian peasants who work on the land
i. type of cactus used to manufacture twine
j. type of cactus from which juice is collected
k. plantation or ranch in Mexico
l. national drink of Mexico

Food for Thought and Discussion

1. It has been said that Mexico is going through a peaceful revolution far more important than any military revolution. Can you explain this statement?

2. Reading and writing are not the most important subjects in a Mexican village school. Can you name others more important and tell why?

3. The death rate is very high in Mexican villages, especially among babies and children. Why is a sanitary water supply necessary? How could the people be taught the importance of sanitation and child care? How are smallpox and typhoid fever carried?

4. Do you believe that under the present program of education more leaders will develop among the Indian people? Give some good reasons for your answer.

Chapter 15

The Customs and Culture of Mexico Reveal a Colorful and Artistic People

Tropic land, why did you fill
My hands so full of color?
Everything I touch is turned to gold.[1]

IN THESE short lines, a Mexican poet expresses his feeling about his colorful native land. There is color everywhere in Mexico, in the brilliant hues of the gardens and the tropical countryside, in the vivid embroideries and gay skirts of the native costumes.

[1] From Carlos Pellicer's *Deseos*, Crown Publishers.

There is color in the romantic songs and lively dances and in the rich paintings of Mexican artists. The Mexicans themselves have colorful personalities, for the romance and fire of the *conquistadores* are in their blood.

THE CITY LIFE OF MEXICO REFLECTS THE CUSTOMS OF SPAIN

To the American visitor, Mexico City appears at first like any large modern city. But he soon begins to notice manners and customs which set it apart from any city in the United States. In most parts of Mexico, as in Spain, everyone takes a *siesta* (see-es'tah) or nap in the afternoon. Except in up-to-date Mexico City, banks and business houses close at one o'clock for the *siesta*. Stores open again at three-thirty and remain open until after seven o'clock. Mexicans eat a very light supper at nine o'clock, with chocolate, small *tacos* (tah'cohs) ("sandwiches" made of *tortillas*), and sweet cakes, or perhaps merely beans and coffee.

Another feature of Mexican life which seems odd to the American visitor is the lack of freedom of the women. Women in Mexican cities or towns cannot go about as American women are accustomed to do, because they are still bound by Spanish ideas of what is proper for women. In the large Mexican cities, the modern girl is much like an American girl, but in other towns a girl does not go out with a boy at all. Even today courtships are carried on with the young woman sitting on the balcony, or behind barred windows, and the young man below in the street playing on a guitar. This is called "playing the bear." Often the young man seems very comical coming night after night to sing in front of his sweetheart's window.

On Sunday evenings, he can see her in the plaza, but all the girls walk in one direction and the men and boys in the other. The town band plays in the plaza center and the mothers and fathers sit on the park benches watching the boys and girls go by. That is the nearest the young people from good families in Mexico come to having a "date." At *fiestas*, young girls stay very close to their mothers, or to their chaperons or *dueñas* (doo-ayn'yahs), even though they may be dressed in the gayest of costumes. Young men are accustomed to being very courteous to the girls and their *dueñas*. This may be one reason why Mexicans and other Latin Americans are considered to be the most courteous people in the world.

MEXICANS WEAR THEIR NATIONAL COSTUMES FOR HOLIDAYS

On Independence Day, September 16, and on May 5, the anniversary of a battle against the French, Mexicans like to wear their national costumes. On these holidays and on Sundays the men of the better class like to parade on handsome horses along the bridle paths of Mexico City, dressed in the gay *charro* (chah'roh) costume of the Spanish *caballero* (cah-bah-yeh'ro) or horseman. They make a dashing sight with their wide, silver-trimmed sombreros, fancy leather jackets, and snug-fitting trousers embroidered and buttoned down the side of each leg. The women and children like to join the parade, dressed in the national costume for holidays and *fiestas*. This is a full, red skirt covered with gold spangles and a full, gathered blouse, gaily embroidered. It is called the *china poblana* (chee'nah poh-blah'nah) dress. Somewhere on the blouse or skirt must appear the coat of arms of Mexico, the eagle and the serpent and the cactus. Every girl in Mexico takes great pride in her *fiesta* costume and saves her money so that she can have a lovely one.

MEXICANS LOVE A FIESTA

Mexico is a land of *fiestas* and Mexicans love to dress up for one. Many

Black Star

FIESTA COSTUMES are worn by these gay Mexicans. The girls are wearing elaborate *china poblana* dresses, while the man is in *charro* costume. Note the national emblem on the skirt at the left.

towns are named after a Catholic saint, and hold a *fiesta* on that saint's holy day. Some towns celebrate other religious holidays which they combine with ancient Indian festivals. An interesting *fiesta* is held every year in Oaxaca City called "Monday on the Hill." On this day the ancient Indian people used to hold a religious ceremony on the top of a certain hill in Oaxaca Valley to ask the goddess of corn to bring them a good crop. When the Spaniards came, they turned this "Monday on the Hill" into a ceremony in honor of the Virgin. Down in the church on the

square, the statue of the Virgin is still honored with special ceremonies.

But on top of the hill, a throne for an ancient goddess has been erected by the school-children. The most beautiful girl of pure Zapotecan Indian blood from the Oaxaca School for Training Rural Teachers is chosen to be the goddess. All the young people of the town, dressed in costumes like the ancient Zapotecans, follow her in a procession up the hill. At the end of the procession come four young men dressed in masks and costumes to resemble a jaguar or mountain lion, an eagle, a crow, and

169

Lanks

TORTILLAS are the staff of life in Mexico. This Tehuana girl is cooking tortillas on a clay griddle over an open wood fire. No grease is used and the tortillas are turned by hand when browned on one side.

a wolf. Do you remember the Aztec soldiers and their animal emblems? The young Zapotecans give group dances offering flowers and fruits to these animals. The animals are supposed to plead with the goddess for them, asking that she bring a good crop.

Grown men who have come on foot to the Oaxaca *fiesta* from distant villages do their own village *fiesta* dances. One of these requires that the dancers wear a plumed headdress of dyed chicken feathers which stretches three feet across. Headdresses for this dance were sent as a part of the Mexican exhibit to the World's Fairs in the United States.

THE FOOD OF MEXICO HAS A CHARACTER OF ITS OWN

All over Mexico the traveler can hear the pat-pat of the women as they flatten between their palms the *tortilla* which takes the place of bread. Even in the restaurants of Mexico City, you are asked whether you wish bread or *tortillas*. *Tortillas* have probably been eaten in Mexico ever since the first natives settled down by their corn fields. Cortez and his men took to eating them, because they found them nourishing on their long marches. To the visitor, they seem rather tough and flat-tasting, especially when cold.

The method of making *tortillas* has not changed much in the last few centuries. In the cities, even, they are made much as they are made in Santa Cruz Etla. The corn is ground on the stone slab or *metate* with a rough stone shaped something like a rolling pin. The doughy meal is then patted into flat cakes and fried on a griddle. In most of the homes of

170

Mexico, the *tortilla* griddle is of clay; in the better homes iron griddles are placed over a charcoal fire in a brick stove.

We think of all Mexican food as highly seasoned. It is true that Mexicans love the hot chile peppers and other spices which almost blister our tongues, but they are usually put in a sauce which is poured over the food. So anyone wishing to avoid the peppery taste may omit the sauce. We could not talk about Mexican food without mentioning the ever-present *frijoles* (free-hoh'lays) or reddish bean which, with the *tortillas*, forms the main diet of four fifths of the people.

The delicious, cinnamon-flavored hot chocolate which is served in Mexico is a real native drink. The Aztecs prepared a similar product of the cacao bean, which they called *chocolatl*. The chocolate is beaten to a froth with a wooden stick twirled between the palms.

When you ask for coffee in a Mexican inn, you get a cup of hot milk, to which you can add coffee from a bottle of coffee extract on the table. The Mexicans roast the whole coffee beans until they are almost burned, grind them on stone, and make a concentrated solution from them.

MEXICANS STILL GO TO BULLFIGHTS

Many a Mexican boy has an ambition to become a bullfighter. For Mexicans, like many other Latin Americans, consider bullfighting a great sport. Football and baseball are becoming popular in Mexico, but bullfights on Sunday afternoons are still well attended. In Mexico City and other cities there are great bull rings built like our football stadiums, where rich and poor alike go to watch the skill of the *matador* (mah-tah-dohr'). The bulls are a special vicious breed reserved for bullfighting.

The Sunday afternoon show opens with a gala procession. There are loud cheers as the fighters appear in their lace-trimmed and spangled costumes and their three-cornered hats. There are *picadores* (pee-cah-doh'-rays) or horsemen, the *banderilleros* (bahn-der-ee-yer'ohs), who tease the bull with darts and lances, and the *matador*, who finally kills the bull with a sword. No matter how fierce the bull is, he always loses, although he sometimes succeeds first in goring a horse or even a man. Some of the best bullfighters are as famous in Mexico City as the popular movie stars are in our country.

THE COLORFUL MEXICAN HANDICRAFT SHOWS THE SKILL AND ARTISTRY OF THE INDIAN

The visitor to Mexico is generally fascinated by the variety of beautiful hand-made things for sale. Mexico has been called the land of handicrafts, for the Mexican Indian has always created beautiful things by the work of his hands. Every village used to have a special handicraft by which it was known and which was passed along from one generation to the next. The government today is reviving the native arts which had almost died out in some places.

Mexicans make pottery of all kinds, from crude clay water jars and *tortilla* griddles to beautifully decorated and glazed bowls. In a little village near Guadalajara, for instance, they make a tan pottery with quaint Indian scenes painted on the side. There is no pottery factory. The potters simply work in a big patio where flowers and banana trees grow. Some press the clay into molds, others paint on the design freehand; still others watch the kiln or oven, fanning the charcoal fire to keep it hot. There is no rush; everyone seems to be happy and contented. Each worker is a craftsman who has learned to create an artistic thing and enjoys doing it. The charm of the Mexican handicraft is that no two pieces are ever quite alike.

The little old colonial town of Taxco (tahss'coh), in the silver-mining region, has become famous through the work of its silversmiths. Ornaments and other articles were made from Mexican silver by the Aztecs centuries ago. The silver handicraft also flourished when Mex-ico was a Spanish colony. The guild of the silversmiths became one of the strongest in Mexico City. This industry was revived in Taxco when Mr. William Sprattling, an American, became interested in Taxco and its silversmiths. He set up a shop where the smiths could work and teach young Indians their ancient craft. Today the lovely hand-worked silver pins, bracelets, and necklaces of the Taxco craftsmen are known all over the United States, and fortunate indeed is the person who has a piece of Taxco jewelry!

There are many other handicrafts, such as basket-making, lacquer-painting, leather-work, brilliant feather-work, and *sarape*-weaving. Perhaps some day you will go to Mexico and see these things being made.

IN TAXCO you can imagine yourself back in the days of the viceroys. The great church in the background is decorated with bright-colored glazed tile.

Gendreau

Sawders

Mexican Tourist Association

Left: **LACQUER WORK** in brilliant colors is popular in Mexico. Here a design is being completed on a large wooden tray. *Right:* **MEXICO IS FAMOUS** for its handicrafts. In this picture the worker is carving peasant figures on wooden plaques to sell to tourists.

MODERN PAINTERS PORTRAY THE SPIRIT OF MEXICO IN MURALS

In their joy over the new world promised by the Revolution, the painters of Mexico began to paint the story of Mexico and its humble people. They cast aside all traditional ideas of painting. Most of their work was not done on canvas, but in huge murals on the walls of public buildings. This fresco painting, as it is called, had to be done on freshly plastered walls while the artists stood on scaffolds. The artists showed the Mexican as a squatty, brown-skinned peon, and they painted his life as it often was, sordid and sad. At first the critics were astounded and indignant at these unusual pictures, but the art of modern Mexico today is considered the most powerful ever produced in America.

The greatest of these mural painters is Diego Rivera, a Mexican who is part Indian. He was already a well-known painter when he was commissioned to paint murals on the walls of some of the public buildings in Mexico City. His murals on the Department of Education building are perhaps the most famous. The entire four walls of the three-story building facing the great interior patio are covered with a story of Mexican life. When a visitor sees the picture of the peon working in the fields under the lash of the overseer, he, too, feels the anger and sorrow that Rivera must have felt as he painted. The neighboring picture shows the peasants crowding in to get their promised land and the hope of the painter that a new day has dawned for these humble people. All

Black Star

THIS RIVERA MURAL, on the wall of the public market in Mexico City, shows peons harvesting grain. In the foreground real peons are offering bananas for sale.

of Mexico is spread out in these pictures, the *fiestas* and gay costumes, the potter with his clay, the weaver at his loom, the leaders of the Revolution — all painted in the rich earth colors and the square figures of the Aztec and Mayan art.

MEXICAN MUSIC IS A COLORFUL MIXTURE OF SPANISH AND INDIAN

Mexican people love music. They sing their colorful and romantic folksongs in the plaza to the tune of guitars. The young man strums his guitar as he serenades a pretty señorita. In the towns and cities, street musicians wander about with guitars slung over their shoulders, ready to play and sing for the few coins they may get from passers-by. Perhaps you know some of the commoner Mexican tunes, such as *La Paloma* (the Dove), *La Golondrina* (the Swallow), *Amapola* (the Poppy), and *Estrellita* (Little Star). If you have studied Spanish, perhaps you have sung the Spanish words in your class, for most of these sentimental songs have been inherited from Spain.

There is a serious side to Mexican music also. Carlos Chávez (chah'-vays) is a well-known composer and orchestra conductor who has led the best symphony orchestras in America as guest conductor. He is devoting his life to a study of primitive Indian tunes and rhythms. He has lived among non-Spanish-speaking tribes, and has made recordings of folk-tunes, and of the music of Indian instruments, which have never been written down. His recordings are being studied by students of music in Mexico City. Who knows but that Mexico may produce a modern music as she has a modern art?

Are You a Careful Reader? Test Yourself!

I. Supply the correct word for each blank:

1. Stores and banks in Mexico City close from .... to .... o'clock for .... .
2. Women and girls in Mexico are still bound by .... customs, and girls must be accompanied in public by .... .
3. On national holidays men can be seen dressed in the dashing .... costume, while women and girls wear the .... dress.
4. A majority of Mexicans live on .... or corn pancakes, and .... or red beans.
5. On Sunday afternoons many Mexicans go to the .... to watch the skillful .... kill the bull.
6. The beautiful handicraft for which Mexico is famous is made by the .... who have been skilled with their hands for generations.
7. The town of Taxco is noted for the beautiful handmade articles made of .... .
8. A famous mural painter of Mexico is ....
9. .... is a Mexican composer interested in Indian music.
10. An ancient Zapotecan Indian festival is held every year in .... .

II. Are these statements true or false?

1. The town of Taxco is noted for beautiful handmade leather articles.
2. Diego Rivera is a famous painter of Mexico.
3. Mexicans love to sing to the music of the marimba.
4. Carlos Chávez is one of Mexico's modern composers.
5. The modern painters of Mexico depict the life of the Spanish upper classes.

Lanks

STREET MUSICIANS of Mexico are playing for passers-by. Can you name the instruments which they use? Notice the wide sombreros.

Food for Thought and Discussion

1. Can you explain why Spanish customs still persist in Mexico after 400 years?
2. Why do Indian skills and customs also persist in the Mexico of today?
3. Are modern music and art a true reflection of the spirit of the Mexican people? Why?

Looking Backward

You have read the four chapters about our next-door neighbor, Mexico, and have tested yourself on these chapters. You have also discussed several important questions about Mexico in your class. You are now ready to turn back to the questions in the preview on page 135 to see if you can answer them orally or in writing. If you cannot, this means that you need more study.

Interesting Things to Do

1. Plan a tour of Mexico. Write to the Southern Pacific Railway, the Pan American Airways, or a local travel bureau asking for illustrated travel folders on Mexico. Plan what route you will take, a time schedule for the trip, and what it will cost. Describe what you will see in the cities on your route.
2. Get better acquainted with one or more of the men who made Mexican history. Select someone who interests you in Chapter 13 and read more about him.
3. Give a talk on Diego Rivera, showing copies of some of his work to the class.
4. Collect articles for an exhibit of Mexican handicraft, such as leatherwork, *sarapes*, baskets, *huaraches*, glass, tiles, pottery, etc.

5. Give a debate on the subject, "Resolved: That Mexico was justified in taking over her oil wells from foreign companies."

6. Write one of the following: an imaginary diary of a teacher in a typical rural school like that of Santa Cruz Etla; a letter a Mexican teacher might write back to her children if she were visiting in an elementary school in the United States; a scenario for a motion picture on the story of Maximilian and Carlota; a poem on your own impressions of colorful Mexico.

7. Get acquainted with the music of Mexico. Listen to records or sing some of the Mexican songs mentioned on page 175.

8. Has any member of the class been corresponding with a pen-pal from Mexico? If so, he should read his letters to the class.

9. Choose a member of the class to take charge of a quiz on Spanish words and their meanings.

10. Draw cartoons which might have been made by a Mexican after the Mexican War; when foreign companies began to develop Mexico's oil; during the Revolution.

Interesting Books to Read

For Further Information

Beals, Carleton, *Mexican Maze.* Lippincott. Geography and history combined for older students.

Chase, Stuart, *Mexico, a Study of Two Americas.* Macmillan. History and present conditions, with drawings by Rivera.

Brenner, Anita, *Your Mexican Holiday.* Willett. A guidebook for tourists.

Redfield, Robert, *Tepotzlán.* University of Chicago Press. Detailed, scientific study of life in a remote village.

For Pleasure

Baretto, Larry, *Bright Mexico.* Farrar and Rinehart. Personal story of out-of-the-way places.

Franck, Harry, and Lancks, Herbert, *The Pan-American Highway from the Rio Grande to the Canal Zone.* Appleton-Century. Travel story with beautiful photographs.

Peck, Anne Merriman, *Young Mexico.* McBride. Stories of different regions.

Smith, Susan, *Made in Mexico.* Knopf. Descriptions of beautiful handicraft work.

THE OLD SPANISH MAIN
BECOMES THE
CARIBBEAN OF TODAY

0	200	400	600

SCALE IN MILES

HOME OF NINE SMALL REPUBLICS

OUR NEXT TRIP takes us south of Mexico to the Caribbean region where we shall visit nine of the twenty republics of Latin America. First, we shall learn something about this region where Mother Nature causes the earth to shake and great tempests to rock land and sea. Then we shall travel back to the days when Spanish galleons rode the seas and the Caribbean was the crossroads of the New World. We shall learn why most of the Caribbean countries were unable to use the freedom which they won from Spain. We shall look at the United States through the eyes of these little republics and see how, in the past, they considered us a great octopus reaching out for its prey.

Next, we shall travel through each of the colorful little republics to get acquainted with their governments and their people. We shall see pure-blooded Indians who speak only an ancient Mayan tongue and live in highland villages unchanged since the days of Cortez. We shall see Negro people who speak a strange dialect, half French, half African, and believe in the "evil eye." This trip will take us over all of Central America as well as two islands of the West Indies.

On the left-hand page is a map of the Caribbean region. Can you find the nine small republics of this region? What name is given to the six countries in the southernmost tip of the North American continent? What two republics are located on the island of Hispaniola? Where is the Panama Canal? In what direction does it run? Can you tell from its location why it is such an important waterway?

As you read these chapters on our interesting neighbors in the Caribbean, look for the answers to these questions:

1. On what grounds did the United States interfere in Caribbean affairs?

2. How do we happen to own Puerto Rico? to rent the Canal Zone?

3. Why is the Caribbean such an important region today?

Chapter 16

The Old Spanish Main Becomes the Caribbean of Today

Fifteen men on the dead man's chest —
Yo-ho-ho and a bottle of rum!
Drink and the devil had done for the rest —
Yo-ho-ho and a bottle of rum![1]

PIRATES! Buried treasure! Pieces of eight! This pirate song takes us back to the days when bold buccaneers sailed along the Spanish Main, when Drake, Morgan, or de Grammont swooped down upon the treasure ships of Spain. Small, fast boats crowded to the gunwales would lie in wait for these lumbering, topheavy galleons laden with gold and silver for the King of Spain. Often the daring buccaneers would pounce down upon the port cities and strike terror into the hearts of the inhabitants.

Today luxurious passenger liners and merchant ships sail the waters where once the pirates defied the flag of Spain. Tourists from the United States go on winter cruises to warm Caribbean lands. Oil tankers from Venezuela, banana boats from Central America, freight ships from all over the world ply back and forth on this historic sea. The Panama Canal now connects the two great oceans where the old Cruces Trail used to cross the Isthmus; soldiers and sailors guard the strip of land where mule trains once carried the silver of Peru.

[1] From Robert Louis Stevenson, *Treasure Island.*

The Spanish flag no longer waves over the Caribbean; in its place are the flags of eleven Latin American nations. The Caribbean has become one of the most important regions in the world today because of its nearness to the Panama Canal. Every inch of Caribbean soil is vital to the defense of the American republics, and their friendship is very important to us. Caribbean trade is also important. We depend on these tropical neighbors for products which we cannot raise and they in turn depend on us for manufactured articles. In this part of the book you will get acquainted with the Caribbean region and the republics of Latin America which lie along its shores.

WHAT IS THE CARIBBEAN REGION?

When we use the term "Caribbean," we usually mean more than the sea or the islands in the sea. We refer to all the lands that lie near or touch the Caribbean Sea. If you will turn to the map on page 178, you will see that the Caribbean lands form a "middle America" lying between North and South America. Let us examine them more closely.

Find the island of Cuba just off the tip of Florida and trace with your finger along Cuba, Hispaniola, Puerto

Keystone

THIS PEACEFUL SCENE might be almost anywhere on the Caribbean islands or mainland coasts. Life is easy for these Negro natives; the climate is hot and no one works very hard.

Rico, and the curve of the Lesser Antilles to the island of Trinidad off the coast of Venezuela. Now follow the northern shore of South America to the Isthmus of Panama (note the Panama Canal), then along the coast of Central America and the Yucatan peninsula and back to Cuba. This is the Caribbean region. The Bahamas north of Cuba are also consid-ered part of the Caribbean region. Notice that they guard the entrance to the Caribbean between Florida and Cuba, and that the Lesser Antilles guard the eastern gateway. You can understand why this is called a land-locked sea.

In tracing the boundaries of the Caribbean you have covered an actual distance of over 5000 miles, which is equal to the distance from New York to San Francisco and halfway back again. You have covered an area larger than all the states east of the Mississippi River.

FLAGS OF MANY NATIONS WAVE OVER THE CARIBBEAN

The visitor to the Caribbean may salute the flags of many nations. There are the three independent island republics of Cuba, Haiti, and the Dominican Republic; there are the six Central American republics of Guatemala, El Salvador, Nicaragua, Honduras, Costa Rica, and Panama; and there are the two large South American nations of Colombia and Venezuela. Colombia and Venezuela are Caribbean countries because they face that sea. But since they are also part of South America, their stories are told in this book with those of other South American nations. The following chapters will deal with the nine small independent republics of the Caribbean area.

However, we cannot get a fair picture of the Caribbean region unless we give a little attention to the many islands which are not independent. The Stars and Stripes wave over Puerto Rico and the three Virgin Islands. Great Britain owns the largest number, for the Union Jack claims the Bahamas, Jamaica, most of the Lesser Antilles, and even a slice of the Yucatan peninsula called British Honduras. The tricolor of France covers two of the Lesser Antilles, while the Dutch flag flies over six small islands in the eastern Caribbean.

These foreign-owned islands are not important except for their position near the Panama Canal. The Canal must be protected so that our Navy can move freely to defend either Atlantic or Pacific shores. In time of war it would be exceedingly dangerous if an unfriendly power gained a foothold in the Caribbean.

HURRICANES AND EARTHQUAKES ROCK CARIBBEAN LANDS

The traveler who first sees the sparkling blue of this tropical sea and the velvet green of its shores may think that here is a region where Mother Nature always smiles. But the people who live in these lands know that Nature can be cruel as well as kind. They are often rocked by violent earthquakes and endangered by erupting volcanoes. Their cities have been destroyed and rebuilt, not once, but many times. The mountains which form a background for the beautiful Caribbean landscape are responsible for this violence. They are part of the backbone range of the Americas.

A traveler might easily miss an earthquake or a volcanic eruption, but if he were in the Caribbean between August and November he would probably see a hurricane. Violent storms are not new in this region. The early Indians had a god named "Huracán" whose "frown disturbed the sky and troubled the sea." Many of the explorers were shipwrecked or blown off their course by the fierce hurricanes of the Caribbean. Columbus wrote to Ferdinand and Isabella about a terrible storm which drove him about on his fourth voyage. "There was rain and thunder and lightning continuously, so that it seemed as though it were the end of the world."

The inhabitants of the Caribbean know only too well when a hurricane is approaching. Dark and torn clouds travel rapidly across the sky; the sea begins to rise and all the world is still as death. Suddenly with the speed of a bomber comes the hurricane wind and the earth is deluged with rain. Boats are tossed about on the sea, trees are uprooted, crops are ruined and houses are demolished on land. The amount of damage depends on the speed of the wind and size of the storm's path.

WEALTH COMES FROM THE GOOD EARTH

The tropical climate of the Caribbean produces more than a crop of winter tourists. From the fertile soil of this region come two thirds of all the bananas, one third of all the sugar, and one third of all the coffee that go into the world's commerce. It produces also quantities of cacao, tobacco, cotton, coconuts, and fine woods.

Caribbean countries are agricultural countries and do almost no manufacturing themselves. They depend on the sale of sugar, coffee, bananas, and other crops for their supply of manufactured articles. Radios, furniture, trucks and tractors, automobiles, ready-made clothing, tools and hardware must all be purchased from manufacturing countries. It is not wise for countries to depend on one or two crops for an income, as we shall see.

THE CARIBBEAN IS A MELTING–POT OF RACES

The United States has been called a melting-pot of nations, and in a much smaller way this is true of the Caribbean. In addition to the Indian and Spanish races, the blood of a third race appears. The descendants of former slaves have populated the islands and the coasts of the mainland with Negro people. Several racial mixtures are found in the Caribbean. In addition to the *mestizo*, who is part Spanish and part Indian, you will see the mulatto, who has both white and Negro blood, and the *zambo*, who is Negro and Indian.

Some of the islands are almost entirely Negro and mulatto, while others, like Cuba, still have many Spanish people. *Mestizos* and *zambos* are scarce on the islands because the Indians had almost died out before many Spaniards or Negroes came. Generally speaking, there are many Negroes on the hot mainland coasts of Central America, but *mestizos* make up the largest proportion of the total population. In all the Central American countries, of course, there are still many Spanish and native Indian people.

"PATCH AND THATCH" LIVING IS TYPICAL OF THE CARIBBEAN

Although there are many cities in the Caribbean region, by far the greatest number of people are poor natives living on tiny plots of land in the country. Because of the hot climate, the fertile soil, and the abundant rainfall, a way of living has developed which is about the same in all the tropical regions. This is called "patch and thatch," because the native makes his home in a thatched hut and grows his food from a patch of ground.

Whether he is a *mestizo* in Honduras or a Negro in Haiti, the "patch and thatch" farmer has a simple and easy life. He has one tool which he could not do without. This is his *machete* (mah-chay′tay), a heavy long-bladed

Lanks

THE THATCHED ROOF of this hut will be of grass instead of palm leaves. Notice the bamboo poles running the length of the hut to which the layers of dried grass are being tied.

knife which he uses for everything from hacking out tough jungle growth to plowing the ground. He cuts bamboo with his *machete* to make the walls of his hut and thatches the roof with palm leaves. He makes holes with it in the fertile soil and plants bananas, sugar cane, and cacao. Close to the house he usually has a garden of corn, beans, yams, and other vegetables, and tobacco for his own use. His clothes are washed in the river. A frying-pan to cook his food is the only other tool he uses besides the *machete*. When he needs money for his scanty clothing, he sells some of his extra crops at the market in the nearest town, or works a few days on the coffee or sugar plantations. This is the life of millions of natives who live in the Caribbean tropics.

THE CARIBBEAN WAS COLUMBUS'S SEA

In spite of the great number of people of Negro blood living in the Caribbean republics, the background of all these nations except **Haiti** is Spanish. Spanish language, customs, and even architecture prove that the "roots of the present are deep in the past." Let us review the European beginnings of this "middle America." The Caribbean itself might well have been named after Columbus. He and his sailors were the first Europeans to sail into its sparkling waters and explore its beautiful shores. He was the first to name an island in that sea, calling it *La Isla Española* (lah ees′lah es-pahn-yoh′lah) or Spanish Island, because it reminded him of southern Spain. This island today is known as Hispaniola.

The story goes that when Columbus asked the natives of one of the smaller islands in this sea what they were called, they answered "Carib." Thus the sea was named after those fierce and warlike tribes who lived on the small islands of the Lesser Antilles, and not after the man who discovered it.

THE CARIBBEAN WAS THE CRADLE OF SPANISH CIVILIZATION IN THE NEW WORLD

The first colonies of Spain were established on the islands of the West Indies and on the Isthmus of Panama. You remember that Santo Domingo on the island of Española was the first city to be founded in the New World. From here in the early 1500's colonists crossed to near-by Puerto Rico and Jamaica. Later, others went to Cuba, where they settled Santiago and in a few years, Havana. At the same time Spaniards were establishing themselves on the northern shore of the Isthmus of Panama.

From these settlements the *conquistadores* assembled their fleets and men and set out to conquer the mainland. You remember that Cortez was sent from Cuba to conquer Mexico; Balboa's life as an explorer began when he left Española; Pizarro and Balboa both used Panama as their headquarters. Every expedition had to sail through the Caribbean to reach Mexico or Central America. The route to South America lay across the sea and over the Isthmus to the Pacific.

Just as all roads used to lead to Rome, so did all roads lead to the Caribbean in colonial days. It was the center of trade between the colonies and the mother country. Colonists and supplies passed through it

bound for Mexico or South America. Treasure galleons waited to receive the silver of Peru at the Caribbean end of the Cruces (croo'says) Trail crossing the Isthmus. Puerto Bello and Panama became important trading cities in the colonial period because of their location at each end of this trade route across Panama. On the mainland of South America, called the Spanish Main, the cities of Santa Marta, Cartagena, and Caracas were thriving settlements.

SPAIN LOSES HER POWER IN THE CARIBBEAN

Spain's great empire was never safe from raids and invasions of other powers. The Pope's division of the New World between Spain and Portugal meant nothing to England and France. They were determined to get

THE MACHETE is held in both hands as this worker slashes notches in a *zapote* tree. Sap from this tree is used to make chewing gum.

Galloway

Sawders

THE OLD CITY OF PANAMA built by the Spaniards was destroyed by Morgan and his pirates in 1671, but its ruins are still standing near the present Panama City. Here is a tower of the former cathedral.

a share of these rich lands by fair means or foul. The whole Caribbean coast became infested with freebooters and pirates. Sir Francis Drake and Henry Morgan captured and held for ransom many of the rich coast cities of the old Spanish Main; buccaneers of England and France seized ships bound for Spain. The governments of these countries winked at these unlawful attacks by their citizens upon Spanish possessions.

Later on, foreign powers became bolder and began to seize the small islands of the Lesser Antilles which were not strongly occupied by Spain. One by one they fell into the hands of France, England, and Holland. Denmark claimed the Virgin Islands near Puerto Rico and the English succeeded

in taking the island of Jamaica. English log-cutters invaded and claimed a part of the east coast of Yucatan which is today British Honduras. Even the mainland of South America was nibbled at by these powers, with the result that the three Guianas belong to England, France, and Holland. France gained control of the western end of Española, which had been occupied by buccaneers of French blood. Unlucky Spain managed to keep the rest of her Caribbean lands until the urge for independence reached them. After the Spanish colonies gained their independence, danger from foreign invasion became less because the United States did not welcome European powers in the Western Hemisphere.

NO TWO OF THE CARIBBEAN REPUBLICS
ARE ALIKE

In the 1800's the Caribbean colonies broke away from the mother country and went their separate ways. They had the same background of Spanish language and civilization and the same geographical region in which to live.

Yet each one of these modern republics has a character of its own, and each one has a story just a little different from that of its neighbor. They are like several children in a family who have the same parents and the same home, yet grow up to be entirely different individuals.

Are You a Careful Reader?   Test Yourself!

I. Can you supply the correct word for each blank?

1. The Caribbean region contains .... of the republics of Latin America as well as possessions of .... , ... , ... , and .... .
2. The Caribbean is one of the most important regions in the world today because of the ....
3. Among the products of the Caribbean are .... , ... , and .... .
4. The type of living of the Caribbean natives is called .... and .... .
5. Although there are many Negroes on the hot coastlands, the majority of the people are .... .

II. Can you match these words and statements correctly?

1. Puerto Bello	*a.* small islands bordering the Caribbean on the east
2. Puerto Rico	*b.* islands north of Cuba belonging to England
3. Bahamas	*c.* Indian god of bad weather
4. Huracán	*d.* island belonging to the United States
5. Lesser Antilles	*e.* knife used by the natives of the Caribbean
6. machete	*f.* the mainland of South America bordering on the Caribbean
7. Spanish Main	*g.* important Spanish port on the Caribbean coast of Panama
8. mulatto	*h.* person of white and Indian blood
9. Caribs	*i.* person of Negro and Indian blood
10. *zambo*	*j.* person of Negro and white blood
	k. Indians who inhabited the Caribbean islands
	l. city in Cuba

Food for Thought and Discussion

1. The Caribbean has been called the "crossroads of civilization" in the days of the Spanish colonial empire. Can you explain why?
2. Today the Caribbean is considered one of the most important regions in the world from a military point of view. Can you explain why?
3. Why is the United States a natural market for Caribbean products?

Chapter 17

Our Central American Neighbors Progress from Spanish Colonies to Independent Republics

How MANY of the Central American countries can you name? Most Americans know very little about these six tiny republics which nestle in the tapering end of North America like peas in a pod. If all six of them were placed on the state of Texas, a piece of land the size of North Dakota would be left over! Small as they are, these neighbors are well worth knowing, as some Americans have discovered. Central America is a fascinating place where bananas and coffee grow, where Indians unchanged since the days of Cortez play the marimba, and where airplanes carry butter and eggs to isolated mining camps. The map on page 178 shows them all: colorful Guatemala, crowded El Salvador, banana-raising Honduras, Americanized Nicaragua, democratic Costa Rica, and Panama, home of the Canal.

CENTRAL AMERICA IS LIKE A MINIATURE MEXICO

Geographically, Central America is a small edition of Mexico. The wide Caribbean coast is covered with hot, rain-soaked jungle, while the Pacific coast is narrower and not quite so hot and wet. As in Mexico, the mountains rise abruptly from the Pacific coast and are crowned by a chain of volcanoes. Although there is no large central plateau like that of Mexico, there are many smaller plateaus and valleys. The climate ranges from tropical heat on the coast to springtime on the mountain slopes, and in some places to the extreme cold of high altitudes. As you would expect, most of the people live in the highland regions above the heat of the coast.

The soil, as in parts of Mexico, has been made rich from the lava thrown out by many volcanoes. Central Americans make their living almost entirely from the land. Coffee from the highlands and bananas from the lowlands are their most important exports. Their fertile ground supplies them with all manner of fruits and vegetables, with cotton, cacao, and sugar. No one need starve in Central America if he will take time to plant a garden!

THE COUNTRIES OF CENTRAL AMERICA ATTEMPT UNION AND FAIL

As you look at the small area of Central America, you may wonder why six separate nations exist there today. Nicaragua, the largest of the republics, is no larger than Florida, while Costa Rica and El Salvador are so small that there is barely room to print their names on the map. It would seem the sensible thing for them to unite into one strong republic. That is just what they did a little over a century ago.

In colonial days Central America was part of the viceroyalty of New Spain. It was governed as the captaincy-general of Guatemala, with its capital at Guatemala City. Except for the large Spanish population in the capital, there were few Spaniards in the rest of the region compared to the large numbers of Indians and *mestizos*. When Iturbide proclaimed himself emperor of independent Mexico, he sent troops to Guatemala to make sure that this part of New Spain did not slip away. After the fall of Iturbide, the little provinces of the captaincy-general of Guatemala announced their independence of "Spain, Mexico, and any other power." In 1824, they formed the "United Provinces of Central America," with a president and congress which were to meet at Guatemala City.

At first this Central American federation made a fine start on the road to good government. In many towns schools were started to educate the people. Army and government officials often taught reading and writing because there were few teachers to be had. In Central America slaves were freed and the slave trade was stopped by law for the first time in the Americas. Our own country did not prohibit slavery until forty years later! A law was passed guaranteeing freedom of religion.

The outstanding leader during this period of progress was a creole from Honduras named Francisco Morazán (frahn-sees'coh moh-rah-sahn'). He believed in a liberal government and was a strong champion of the Central American union. He was responsible for many of the progressive laws of the federation. But there were many people who did not like the reforms started by the government, particularly the measures against the Church. The aristocratic Spanish landowners and the Catholic clergy wanted to keep the power they enjoyed before independence so that the Church and the upper classes could control the government.

It was not long before trouble began, for the forces pulling the federation apart were stronger than those holding it together. As in Mexico, the people were divided into two opposing groups, the conservative landowners and the Church on one side, and the liberals who wanted to create a more popular government on the other. In addition, the wild and rugged country made roads between the provinces impossible, and quarrels arose which could not be settled. The small provinces were jealous and suspicious of Guatemala because it was the richest and most powerful member and because the federation government met in its capital.

Revolutions against the government became common; the provinces warred among themselves. When a terrible epidemic of cholera broke out, some of the clergy took this opportunity to stir up revolt among the ignorant Indians and *mestizos*. They declared that the epidemic was a punishment from God. The little "united provinces" became less and less united as the strong forces of the conservatives and the Church gained control of the local governments. At last, in spite of Morazán's efforts to save the union, the tottering federation dissolved and the five separate republics of Central America emerged to go their five separate ways.

THE IDEAL OF A CENTRAL AMERICAN UNION STILL EXISTS

The feeling in favor of union, however, never quite died down in Central America. At various times in the 1800's and even in the 1900's it flared up. Morazán planned to reunite the provinces, but was executed by his enemies in 1842. Guatemala, under a liberal president, attempted to restore the union in 1885, but the president was killed in a war and the plan failed. The weaker states of Honduras, Nicaragua, and El Salvador tried unsuccessfully several times to unite. There is still a strong sentiment toward union in Central America. It is an ideal which the people like to think of, but which is not practical at present.

CIVIL WAR AND REVOLUTION GRIP CENTRAL AMERICA

The troubles of the weak little republics did not end with the break-up of the federation. A hundred years of bloodshed and violence lay ahead of them in which little progress toward better living could be made. There was peace only when a strong man gained control of the government and crushed all opposition by force. Such men made themselves rich at the expense of the country. They often borrowed huge sums from European countries which hoped to gain a foothold in Central America. When their rulers became too tyrannical, the people followed some ambitious man in a revolution against the government. Liberals in one state would join with liberals in another to overthrow a dictator supported by their opponents. The politics of Central America became a vicious circle of bad government followed by revolu-

tion. Selfish men had brought their countries to the verge of ruin.

THE UNITED STATES INTERVENES IN CENTRAL AMERICA

At the beginning of the 1900's, conditions had become so bad that several republics had appealed to the United States for aid in straightening out their affairs. European governments were threatening to send warships to collect the money owed them. Revolutions were destroying the lives and property of the United States citizens and of the Europeans who had invested money in Central America. The United States was planning to build an inter-ocean canal, and was very anxious for peace in the countries close to the proposed canal. Under the Monroe Doctrine, we could not allow foreign countries to interfere in Central America. President Theodore Roosevelt decided that if we refused to let European governments collect their debts, we ourselves must step in and help the Caribbean countries to put their houses in order.

The first intervention was in 1906 when the United States and Mexico co-operated to adjust a dispute between Guatemala and El Salvador. Delegates from each country were invited on board a United States cruiser in the Pacific to settle their quarrel. This meeting on a choppy sea in a rolling ship brought a speedy settlement which has been called "The Peace of Seasickness"! In the following year we intervened to stop another war, this time between Honduras and Nicaragua.

Later that year a conference of Central American republics was held in Washington. A court of judges from the five republics was organized to settle disputes by arbitration rather than by bullets. The Central American states went still farther on the road to peaceful settlement of disagreements by signing agreements not to interfere in civil war in neighbor republics. Although these agreements were not always kept, they did a great deal toward keeping peace between the states.

In 1912, when the president of Nicaragua asked for aid from the United States, Marines were sent to maintain a stable government there. The finances of the republic were organized so that foreign debts could be paid off, elections were supervised so that they would be fair, and a police force was trained to keep order. It was twenty years before the government considered that it was safe to withdraw the Marines from Nicaragua. Although our intervention saved several republics of Central America from further bloodshed and from financial ruin, they naturally resented our interference in their affairs. They looked upon us as a huge octopus stretching out its tentacles to seize them. This feeling toward the United States spread over all the countries of Latin America, causing fear and distrust which have been hard to erase.

President Hoover in 1930 began the withdrawal of United States Marines from Nicaragua. When Franklin Roosevelt became President, one of the first things he did as a "good neighbor" was to complete the withdrawal of all United States Marines from the middle American republics. We could hardly expect them to feel friendly toward us while our Marines served as unpleasant reminders of our power! Today we believe that our policy toward these states should be one of friendship and co-operation, while they are beginning to realize the value of our protection without fearing it.

STABLE GOVERNMENTS ARE NEEDED IN CENTRAL AMERICA

For the most part, the Central American states are still governed by dictators. Costa Rica, however, is a real democracy. Although some dictators claim to be democratic and have been chosen by "election," most of them have remained in office far beyond their legal terms. In recent revolutions the people have ousted dictators in Guatemala and El Salvador. Orderly and constitutional government has not yet been achieved in Central America.

Are You a Careful Reader? Test Yourself!

I. Can you supply the correct word for each blank?

1. The first independent government of Central America was a ..... of the provinces.
2. When the federation failed, ... little republics were formed in Central America.
3. Central American republics greatly resented the ..... of the United States in their affairs.
4. The withdrawing of the United States Marines from Nicaragua was begun by ....
5. The feeling of Central American republics toward us today is one of ..... rather than of ......

II. Can you choose the best answer?

1. The union of the Central American countries was not successful because: (*a*) the Indians of Guatemala and the *mestizos* of El Salvador and Nicaragua were not able to agree; (*b*) smaller countries feared the dominance of Mexico; (*c*) jealousy between states and quarrels between liberals and conservatives made union impossible.

2. The United States intervened in Central American politics in order to: (*a*) throw out corrupt dictators; (*b*) keep European governments from sending warships to collect money owed them; (*c*) help the Central American republics unite in a federation.

3. Our intervention in Central American affairs caused fear and distrust of the United States because: (*a*) Central Americans feared that our powerful country would seize their small republics; (*b*) United States Marines created harsh military rule in Nicaragua; (*c*) the Marines trained a police force in Nicaragua.

4. Relations between the United States and Central America are more friendly today because: (*a*) we are buying many tropical products; (*b*) we are planning to build a canal through Nicaragua; (*c*) our present policy is one of friendly co-operation and these countries know they need our protection.

5. Civil war and revolution have been common in Central America because of: (*a*) the intervention of the United States to collect debts; (*b*) the tyranny of strong and ambitious men who seized control by force; (*c*) the failure to establish a federation of states in Central America; (*d*) the control of local governments by the Church

Food for Thought and Discussion

1. Do the Central American republics need the protection of a strong power in the Western Hemisphere? Why?

2. Would a federation of the Central American republics be an advantage? Why?

Chapter 18

Colorful Guatemala and Crowded Little El Salvador Are Neighbors

---

Guatemala

ANCIENT MAYAN CHIEFS used to wear in their headdresses beautiful feathers of iridescent green and purple which were three feet long. They were plucked from the tail of the brilliant quetzal (ket-sahl') bird. Although the quetzal is almost extinct today, it has been made the national emblem for the Republic of Guatemala. It appears on the flag and on the chief coin, called the *quetzal* in honor of the historic bird. Guatemala itself is as beautiful and colorful as the quetzal bird. High in the mountains, volcanoes shrouded in mist stand guard over a lake of deepest blue. On the highway, there are Indians in brightly colored costumes trotting along to market with their goods balanced high above their heads. In the deep jungle, the ruins of ancient Mayan cities can be seen. Wherever the traveler goes, he will be fascinated by Guatemala.

THE GEOGRAPHY OF GUATEMALA IS UP AND DOWN

In a park in Guatemala City is a huge relief map made of concrete which shows the physical features of Guatemala. You can climb a high platform and look down upon a miniature country. First you notice the jagged mountains and the great cones of thirty or more volcanoes. High up among the mountains is Lake Atitlán (ah-teet-lahn'). You can make out plateaus and high valleys reached from the coast by steep mountain passes. To the east the land slopes gradually toward the Caribbean and you see the jungle lowlands that make up one fifth of Guatemala.

Towns, railroads, and highways are also marked on the map. You wonder how roads could be built over this up-and-down land. There is Puerto Barrios (pwehr'toh bah'ree-ohs), the Caribbean seaport of Guatemala, where banana boats stop to load. An inter-ocean railroad runs the 275 miles from the port up to the mile-high capital, Guatemala City, and then down to San José (sahn hon-say'), the Pacific seaport. If you have ever landed at San José, you shudder as you remember being swung through the air in a basket from the ship to a tender. The ocean swell is too great there for boats to land, and ships usually anchor a mile or so offshore. Passengers and goods have to be lifted by a crane into smaller boats or tenders.

GUATEMALA IS PROUD OF HER ROADS

Do you know how you would have to travel if you wished to go by land through most parts of Central America? On the back of a mule over rough mountain trails! Except for completed stretches of the Pan-American Highway, the countries of Central America are not connected by roads. Unless you travel by air, you are likely to take a steamer from one seaport to another, then go by bus or railroad up to the capital. Railroads are only short lines from port cities to capitals or from banana plantations to ports. A trip from Honduras to Nicaragua, for instance, takes only an hour by plane and many days by land and sea. The new Pan-American Highway designed to connect Mexico City and Panama should be a great blessing to these isolated countries.

Guatemala and El Salvador have completed their sections of the Pan-American Highway and buses are running between the countries. Guatemala has a fine road system and you can travel many miles by bus if you do not object to steep grades. The bus climbs up mountain-sides and dips down into valleys in a hair-raising way. Here is a description of the road to Guatemala City from Harry

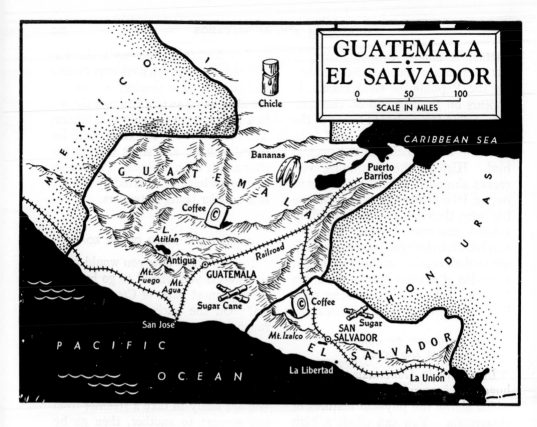

Franck's fascinating book on the Pan-American Highway: [1]

> The highway does not just climb up the mountain-side and have done with it; it grips and claws, slides back, scrambles up again, dips low, then resumes its writhing way upward in sinuous loops, turns back upon itself in breathtaking curves, never resting for any length of time until it tops the last rise and looks down in exhausted silence into the valley....

The roads of Guatemala are made entirely by human labor without road-building machinery of any kind. The law requires that every laborer spend two weeks of each year working on the roads. They are of dirt for the most part, but where the grades are like the road we have just described,

[1] Franck, Harry, and Lanks, Herbert, *The Pan-American Highway*. Appleton-Century.

they are paved with small pieces of stone.

GUATEMALANS MAKE THEIR LIVING FROM THE LAND

You cannot travel anywhere in the highlands without seeing the fragrant white blossoms or the shining red berries of the coffee plants which produce Guatemala's chief crop. The temperate and well-watered mountain valleys with their rich volcanic soil are perfect for coffee-growing. Guatemalan coffee is considered particularly fine in flavor. Most of the coffee is grown on huge plantations or *fincas* (feeng'cahs), which are sometimes thousands of acres in size. They are owned by Spaniards or upper-class *mestizos*, and often by Germans who have settled in Guatemala. Owners of large *fincas* live like wealthy country gentlemen. Although they are often many miles from civilization, electric power makes it possible for them to enjoy such conveniences as radios and electric refrigerators.

A large amount of cheap labor is needed to run the *fincas*. This is furnished by the native Indians, who often live on the plantation. At one time the many Indians of Guatemala were bound to the land by debt, in much the same way as the Indians of Mexico were, under the peonage system. The Indians who were hired to work would buy supplies at the *finca* store and by the end of the season they always owed the owner more than he owed them. This meant that they must remain on the land to work out their debt. A few years ago the government took steps to end this unfair labor system and canceled all debts. However, the Indians are required by law to work 150 days a year, whether they wish to or not, but they are not bound to any one coffee *finca*. Their wages are so small that they would seem like pin-money to us.

There are two other crops which appeal to American appetites. One is the banana, next to coffee in importance. Miles of banana plantations have been planted on the cleared jungle land of the Caribbean coast. Perhaps you have eaten bananas from Guatemala, because the entire crop is sold to the United States. Those of you who are gum-chewers will be interested to know that the raw gum comes from the wild *zapote* (zah-poh'-tay) tree. This tree is found in the jungles of northern Guatemala. When its sap is boiled, it makes a gummy substance called *chicle* (chee'clay).

People cannot live on coffee and

THE PAN–AMERICAN HIGHWAY runs through old towns in Guatemala where cobbled roads laid by the Spaniards are still in use. These Indian women are carrying jugs filled from the town water fountain.

Lanks

Three Lions

THIS MODERN MOVIE THEATER in Guatemala City shows American movies for a fraction of what we pay. The traffic officer blows his whistle regularly whether there is any traffic or not!

chicle, or even on bananas. If there should be no markets abroad for these crops, Guatemala's people would not starve. The government has seen to it that plenty of food crops are grown, especially corn. It is believed that this country may be the original home of the Indian maize or corn which the early Indians learned to cultivate. It is the chief diet of Central Americans as it is of Mexicans.

STRONG GOVERNMENTS HAVE BROUGHT PROGRESS TO GUATEMALA

Guatemala honors as her greatest patriot the man who started her on the road to progress. Justo Rufino Barrios (hoos'toh roo-fee'noh bah'ree-ohs), president of Guatemala from 1873 to 1885, stands head and shoulders above the selfish dictators who ruled Guatemala after independence. He encouraged the building of schools and hospitals, railroads and telegraphs. He passed many laws to improve conditions in his country. Although much of his good work was lost in the unsettled years that followed his rule, Barrios is still remembered by Guatemalans as a great benefactor.

Jorge Ubíco (oo-bee'coh), who was chosen in 1931, ruled with the strong hand of a dictator, but the government was run honestly and efficiently. Laws adopted under Ubíco protected the laborer from peonage and encouraged education, especially in the country regions. In the summer of 1944, after thirteen years of dictatorship, the people finally revolted against Ubíco and forced him to resign. Under more recent presidents, Guatemala has achieved a more democratic government which is trying to improve the lot of the common people.

GUATEMALA HAS HAD MANY CAPITALS

Tourists who visit Guatemala City are surprised to see in this ancient country a little modern city with paved streets, traffic officers, street lights, and air-conditioned movie houses. An earthquake destroyed most of the old buildings in 1917 and this new city rose from the ruins. The people enjoy springtime climate the year round in their highland city a mile above the sea.

Three capitals have been destroyed by earthquake since colonial days. The first one was built by Alvarado, the dashing captain who conquered this region for Cortez. His beautiful wife and several other Spanish ladies came from Spain to live in the new city. Alvarado was crushed to death under a horse while fighting Indians in Mexico and his wife declared herself ruler of Guatemala. How long she could have reigned we shall never know. The city was built close to the volcano Agua (water). After heavy rainstorms and an earthquake, floods from Agua destroyed the city and its woman ruler.

The new capital, which was built some distance away, became a center for Spanish government and culture. It was given the imposing name of "The Most Noble and Most Loyal City of Saint James of the Knights of Guatemala." Beautiful churches were built, a university was founded, a magnificent palace was erected for the captain-general. Spanish ladies and gentlemen dressed in lace and velvet rode through the cobbled streets in fine carriages.

In 1773 there were frequent earth tremors, followed by a terrific quake on July 29. Frightened people rushed into the streets as the earth opened and buildings collapsed. The "Most Noble and Most Loyal City" was abandoned by the Spanish inhabitants who were still alive. They moved with all their possessions to the present site of Guatemala City, twenty miles away. This location did not prove entirely safe, for, as we learned, there was an earthquake in 1917.

HISTORY STOPPED IN ANTIGUA IN 1773

You can visit the old capital today. As you look at the great stone arches and massive pillars of the ruined buildings, the pages of history turn back. You imagine the city in all its grandeur with fountains splashing and the streets thronged with people. In-

THESE INDIANS are dressed in their village costumes — short white pants and hand-woven jackets of red and white wool. Their black hats mark them as important village officials.

Sawders

Gendreau

THIS GUATEMALAN INDIAN GIRL is weaving cloth on a loom which is tied to a post at one end and to her waist at the other. The heavy pattern on her sleeve shows the village to which she belongs.

deed, it is whispered among the Indian people that the inhabitants of former days still haunt the places where they used to live!

After the Spaniards left, Indians from near-by villages moved into the ruins, which they called "Antigua" (ahn-tee'gwah) or "old capital." They lived in the undamaged rooms of great mansions cooking over stoves set on tiled floors. Their goats and chickens roamed about the former lovely patios. Since 1900, the Spanish people have gradually been returning to the homes of their ancestors. Today there are about 8000 inhabitants. The plaza has been repaved and Mass is held every day in a rebuilt church. Buses run back and forth along the highway between Antigua and Guatemala City so that tourists may look back three centuries into the past.

Indians come from miles around to hold their big Saturday market. They gather in the ruined chapel of a former monastery. The roof is gone and the crumbling stairway leads upward into space. The Indians sit on the floor in their bright native costumes and sell their wares as they would in any market.

INDIAN BLOOD PREDOMINATES IN GUATEMALA

We cannot understand Guatemala without knowing something of its Indian people. Sixty-five per cent of all the inhabitants of this republic are pure Quiché (kee-chay') Indians of the Mayan race. Although many of them live on the *fincas* or work as servants in the towns, most of them live proudly and independently in highland villages. They have changed very little since the days when Alvarado conquered them and destroyed their principal city. Let us visit some of these Indian villages.

Along the shore of Lake Atitlán

high up in the mountains are several villages which have never been reached by a wheeled vehicle of any kind. The people own their land in village holdings much like the *ejidos* of Mexico. They raise corn and vegetables for food; they weave their clothes from wool off their own sheep; they make pottery for their dishes; huts of adobe with thatched roofs give them shelter. It matters little to them whether the price of coffee goes up or down, for they live in a world of their own.

Guatemalans can tell the home village of the highland Indians by their clothes. Every village has its own native costume. One village is recognized by the blue skirts or trousers and the white blouses with red and white sleeves, which are worn by its people. In another, the men's trousers are knee-length and embroidered around the bottom by the men themselves, while the women wear a long scarlet skirt with embroidered blouse and a doughnut-shaped ring of red material on their heads.

The most interesting thing about these costumes is that they are woven entirely by hand. The weaving is done by the women on primitive looms with a long stick as a shuttle. Most of them cannot even count, yet they weave the most intricate designs from memory. So beautiful are Guatemalan designs that they are copied by modern textile mills. The woven cloth is very smooth and like fine tapestry.

The Indians from Lake Atitlán walk to market in Guatemala City, 75 miles away. They cross the lake in

THE DANCE OF THE CONQUISTADORES is being performed here by Indians who live on Lake Atitlán. Dressed in imitation of the early Spaniards, these Indians act out the story of their own conquest four hundred years ago.

Guillumette

dugout canoes owned by the village. A little cupboard with shelves to hold corn or pottery or vegetables is slung upon their backs. This is held in place by a strap which fits over their foreheads. The women carry their loads in baskets on their heads. Away up the mountain trails they go, covering about thirty miles a day. Some days later they return, happy if they have made a profit of ten or fifteen cents on the trip!

INDIAN CUSTOMS AND DANCES ARE CENTURIES OLD

Every village has a *fiesta* day and people come from villages miles away to take part. Guatemalan dances, handed down from one generation to another, are performed with fancy costumes and grotesque masks. In the "Dance of the Conquerors," which portrays the coming of Alvarado, they wear velvet costumes and masks which represent the *conquistadores* even to the curled hair! The dancers prance back and forth to the mournful tune of a gourd marimba, keeping the dance going for as long as eight days and nights.

Some of the festivals celebrate ancient religious ceremonies of the Mayans. In one town whole families bring lighted candles to the church on *fiesta* day and stick them on the floor. The father of the family chants in Mayan dialect and swings an incense burner to drive out evil spirits. The religion of the Indians is a strange mixture of Mayan idol worship and Catholic teaching. Between the regular services held by the priest, ceremonies of ancient days, like the one just described, are observed by the Indians.

GUATEMALA IS A LAND OF WORK

At first glance Guatemala may seem to be a land of beauty and color where picturesque Indians live. But when we see the coffee *fincas*, the busy Indian villages, and the miles of road and railroad, we realize that this is also a land where people work. The easygoing spirit of *mañana* is certainly not the spirit of Guatemala. The quiet energy of the Indians whose ancestors once built a great civilization here is still the spirit of this country. Everyone works, from the president down to the humblest Indian.

El Salvador

ALVARADO NAMED EL SALVADOR

When Alvarado and his men struggled out of the difficult mountain country after conquering Guatemala, they saw a rolling green land stretched out before them. Alvarado felt that the Lord was with him and named this country *El Salvador* or "The Savior." The religious Spaniards called several cities after saints, and the capital is San Salvador or "Holy Savior."

Writers often omit the *El* when naming this republic, but the Salvadorans prefer to have us call their country by its proper name, El Salvador. One thing noticed by tourists is that El Salvador is much more crowded with people than Guatemala. There are actually five or six times as many people to the square mile in this tiny country as there are in the rest of Central America.

MOTHER NATURE HELPS AND HINDERS TINY EL SALVADOR

This smallest of all Latin American republics is only about 140 miles long and 60 miles wide. As the map shows you, El Salvador is tucked in between Guatemala, Honduras, and the Pacific. It is the only Central American country without a Caribbean coast. Most of its territory is a pleasant highland region located 2000 or 3000 feet above the Pacific. Volcanoes in long rows watch over the sunny green valleys and plateaus which they have made fertile by their lava.

The geography of the Pacific coastline provides few natural harbors in Central America. El Salvador has the shipping ports of La Unión (oo-nee-ohn') and La Libertad (lee-bair-tad'), but at La Libertad ships cannot come in to dock because of the heavy swells. As at San José, passengers are loaded into launches from the steamer deck and when they reach the dock are hoisted up by a derrick.

Passengers may take a bus along a paved highway from La Libertad to San Salvador, and from there to any town that lies on the new Pan-American Highway. The capital is also connected by railroad with its Pacific ports and with the Guatemalan port, Puerto Barrios, on the Caribbean.

El Salvador has not escaped the earthquakes and volcanic eruptions so common in the Caribbean region. The capital city has been destroyed by earthquake so many times that its inhabitants no longer try to build houses of stone or brick. Most of the buildings are faced with sheets of galvanized iron, cleverly painted to resemble stone.

Nature has done some queer things in El Salvador. Once during an

THIS ORNATE OPERA HOUSE in Santa Ana, El Salvador, is now used for a movie house. Movies are shown probably two or three times a week and are very popular with the townspeople.

Three Lions

earthquake, several little islands in the middle of a lake dropped out of sight. A short time later, one large island rose 150 feet above the water and there it has remained. The lake is called "The Lake of the Miracle." In 1770, the earth suddenly opened in a certain spot in western El Salvador and spouted ashes and lava. In a few weeks a volcanic cone had reared itself to a height of 4000 feet. Today this cone, Mount Izalco (ee-sahl'coh), is the second most active volcano in all of North America, pouring forth smoke and fire every half-hour.[1] Sailors call it "The Lighthouse," for its fires can be seen far out to sea.

SMALL FARMS PREDOMINATE IN EL SALVADOR

As we might expect, El Salvador is a rich agricultural land. Coffee, of course, is the chief crop of the country and makes up 90 per cent of its exports. A hundred million pounds of fine-flavored coffee are sent out of this little state every year. Sugar is becoming more important as a crop, and the growing of tobacco and rubber is being encouraged. Unlike Guatemala, most of the coffee is raised on small farms owned by independent farmers like those in our Middle West. The small landowner also raises his own cows, chickens, fruits, and vegetables so that he is not entirely dependent on his coffee crop.

There are also many large *fincas* owned by wealthy families in El Salvador, but peonage was done away with many years ago. *Finca* owners must hire labor for their coffee fields. After the small farmers and their families finish harvesting their own

[1] Paricutín, the new volcano in Central Mexico, promises to remain the most active.

coffee crops, they often work for wages on neighboring *fincas*.

BALSAM OF PERU COMES FROM EL SALVADOR

Have you ever used balsam of Peru on a cut or sore? It looks a great deal like molasses and is used as a base for medical salves and ointments as well as for an antiseptic. The trees from whose sap balsam is made grow in El Salvador along a stretch of coast north of La Libertad. The balsam is a beautiful tree with a trunk forty inches or more across and with white bark like that of a silver birch. Native workers cut down to the red inner bark of the tree and fasten a yard of cloth below the cut. The sticky sap begins to ooze out and is absorbed by the cloth. Once or twice a week these cloths are collected and boiled in the houses of the natives to remove the sap. The gummy syrup which remains is shipped from La Libertad up the west coast and then to medical-supply factories in the United States.

Perhaps you are wondering why it is called balsam of Peru. In the days of the Spanish colonies, most goods which came through Panama were from Peru. Since balsam was probably sent to Panama to be shipped to Spain, Spanish merchants assumed that it came from Peru.

EL SALVADOR IS A PROGRESSIVE REPUBLIC

The inhabitants of El Salvador are an energetic people. The wealthy Salvadorans are educated and cultured and are interested in the progress of their country. A desire for a more democratic government led Salvadorans to oust their president in 1948. Until 1950 a committee ruled the country; then a free election was held and one of the committee members was elected president.

We can tell a great deal about the progress of a country by looking at its roads and its schools. One hundred years ago El Salvador was almost completely shut off from the outside world except through its Pacific ports. Today, as we have seen, it is well supplied with roads and railroads, which connect it with both oceans and with its neighbor, Guatemala. Its section of the Pan-American Highway is busy with the traffic of automobiles, trucks, oxcarts, and mules.

More schools are being built every year and more teachers are trained. Every child must go to primary school for five years. Those who are able may take a course in secondary school for an additional five years. There are evening schools for adults, and business and normal schools, as well as a university. There is even a Parent-Teacher Association in El Salvador!

Salvadorans are being taught the importance of modern sanitation. American doctors are working with the government to wipe out the hookworm disease which is so common in the tropics. This disease is responsible for the lack of energy in tropical people which has often been considered laziness.

Lanks

A COUNTRY WOMAN OF EL SALVADOR is weighing out grain for sale in the market place. She balances the weight of her corn with a metal cube usually weighing half a kilogram.

Salvadorans enjoy American sports such as basketball, tennis, swimming, and running. Even the girls take part in athletics, which is unusual in Latin America. Almost every town and city has parks and swimming pools where people go for recreation. Horseracing is very popular in El Salvador. Crowds flock to the races instead of to the traditional bullfight.

Are You a Careful Reader? Test Yourself!

I. Can you supply the correct word for each blank?
  1. The national bird of Guatemala is the .... .
  2. The capital of Guatemala is .... ; the capital of El Salvador is ....
  3. Only two Central American countries are connected by road or railroad. These are .... and .... .
  4. The population of Guatemala is .... per cent Indian.
  5. Coffee plantations in Guatemala are known as .... .
  6. El Salvador has more .... farmers than Guatemala.

7. Chewing gum comes from a wild tree called the .... tree.
8. The chief export of both countries is .... .
9. A tropical disease which causes loss of energy is .... .

II. *Can you match these words and statements correctly?*

1. San José
2. Izalco
3. Ubíco
4. Antigua
5. Puerto Barrios
6. Alvarado
7. Agua
8. Atitlán
9. Quiché
10. balsam of Peru

a. sap of a tree in El Salvador used in salves and disinfectants
b. second most active volcano on North American continent
c. banana port on Salvador's Caribbean coast
d. recent president of Guatemala
e. volcano which destroyed early Spanish capital
f. Spanish conqueror of Guatemalan Indians
g. first president of a unified Central America
h. ancient capital of Guatemala destroyed by earthquake
i. Indians of Guatemala descended from the Mayans
j. Guatemala's Pacific port
k. Guatemala's Caribbean port
l. lake in Guatemalan highlands

Food for Thought and Discussion

1. Can you explain why El Salvador is more progressive than Guatemala?
2. What problem has Guatemala which El Salvador does not have?

Chapter 19

We Visit Honduras, Nicaragua, and Democratic Costa Rica

Honduras

HONDURAS, Nicaragua, and Costa Rica are neighbors, but each one is different. They have been called "banana republics," but only Honduras deserves that name. They have been called democracies, but Costa Rica is the only democracy. Let us find out in what ways they are alike and in what ways they are different.

GEOGRAPHY INFLUENCES THE PROGRESS OF HONDURAS

When Columbus was searching for a strait to the Indies, he tried to anchor his ships off the coast of Central America. He found the water so deep that he named the region Honduras (ohn-doo'rahs) from a Spanish word meaning "depths." Today this country named by Columbus has a long way to go before it can be called a modern nation. Its people lead an isolated life in their small communities. They have little contact with each other and with neighboring republics. The geography of Honduras may help to explain why it has been difficult for them to progress.

Honduras is about the same size as its neighbor, Guatemala. It has a long Caribbean coastline, but on the Pacific side there is only a narrow wedge of land along the Gulf of Fonseca (fohn-say'kah). Four fifths of the country is mountainous with great expanses of jungle and forest which man has never conquered. It is still a frontier country waiting to be developed, much like the western part of the United States a hundred years ago.

TRAVEL IS DIFFICULT IN HONDURAS

The only railroads in Honduras are those which carry bananas from plantations to the Caribbean seaport of Puerto Cortez. Unless he travels by air, the simplest way for the tourist to reach the capital city of Honduras is to get off a Pacific steamer at the little island of Tigre (tee'gray) in the Gulf of Fonseca. From here he is carried by launch to the mainland where he rides over a fine modern highway up to Tegucigalpa (tay-goo-see-gahl'pah). If he should land at Puerto Cortez on the Caribbean, he could take a banana train to the little town of Potrerillos (poh-tray-ree'-yohs). From there a road winds up over the mountains to Tegucigalpa.

Much of the countryside looks just as it did when Cortez pushed his conquering way through the jungles of Honduras.

ANCIENT TEGUCIGALPA REFLECTS THE LIFE OF HONDURAS

Long before the Spaniards came Tegucigalpa was an Indian village Today this little town of 40,000 peopl does not look much like a capital city Most of its streets are unpaved and its sidewalks are paths made of stone Oxcarts and mule trains carry freight in and out of town and look much more at home than do the trucks which pass them on the road. Mules and oxen haul goods more slowly, but they also haul more cheaply. Everything from heavy machinery to loads of dynamite can be seen in the plodding oxcarts. Indian people come to town loaded down with produce for the market.

Even in this slow old town without a railroad, modern changes are creeping in. Some of the streets are being paved and a sewer system has been installed. Here and there automobiles and buses appear on the quiet streets.

HONDURAS PROGRESSES FROM OXCART TO AIRPLANE

The last thing a traveler would expect to see in Tegucigalpa is an airport. Yet this little city is a base for an air service which operates all over Honduras and Central America. From a humble beginning of one ancient airplane, an enterprising young man from New Zealand developed the Taca Transport Company. This passenger and freight service, now controlled by Pan American Airways, has over 50 planes and 200 airports in Central

TRANSPORTATION IS DIFFICULT in Honduras. This oxcart is on its way to a silver mine with a load of dynamite. The crude wooden wheels of this cart are made from a circular section of a whole tree trunk.

America. It carries millions of pounds of freight every year.

Every village in Honduras which has enough level land for an airport is served by these planes. Butter, meat, and eggs are carried to mine workers from dairy communities. Mine machinery is transported to out-of-the-way mines by heavy freight planes. Indian people in central Honduras who have never seen a train or an auto, now buy their cotton skirts and shirts from peddlers who come into town by air. Honduras has taken a large step forward now that isolated communities are opened up to new ideas and trade with other sections of the country.

HONDURAS IS A BANANA REPUBLIC

The most important word in Honduras is "bananas." Bananas are the largest crop and the greatest industry of this country. The banana lands, which extend inland 40 to 60 miles from the Caribbean coast are among the finest in the world. Other crops are raised in the rich soil of the plateaus and valleys. There are fields of tobacco and sugar cane; henequen is grown for rope fiber. The leading food crop, supplying food for man and beast, is corn.

MINING IS AN OLD INDUSTRY IN HONDURAS

The Spaniards soon discovered that the mountains of Honduras held rich deposits of gold and silver. Tegucigalpa, whose name means "Hill of Silver," became a mining center. For two hundred years precious metals flowed from the mines of Honduras into the treasury of Spain and into the hands of Spanish gentlemen. Today over a million dollars' worth of gold and silver is still taken from the mines each year.

Along the rivers in the mining

districts, it is interesting to see women working for gold. They patiently sieve out the river sands in search of tiny grains of this precious metal. This is their way of getting a little money to spend.

HONDURAN MAHOGANY IS FAMOUS

Honduras has probably the largest number of mahogany trees of any country in the world. These giants of the tropical forest often grow a hundred feet high, with a crown of branches at the top spreading out 50 feet in diameter. True mahogany is found growing between 10 and 25 degrees north latitude only. If you look at the map you will see that the Caribbean region is the only part of the Western Hemisphere that lies in this zone.

The Spaniards soon discovered that this hard wood was excellent for shipbuilding and began to make the hulls of their ships of mahogany. Sir Walter Raleigh took mahogany wood to England where it became the favorite wood of furniture-makers. It was the desire for this and other woods that gave the English a toe-hold in what today is British Honduras.

There are two reasons why the mahogany industry is not more highly developed. First, the trees do not grow in groves, but here and there in a dense tropical forest. This makes them difficult to find. Second, the trees are so large and heavy that it is very expensive to get them to a seaport. American and English companies which have permission to cut the mahogany send trained spotters into the

jungle in the dry season to locate the best trees. Sometimes these trees average about one to a square mile of forest and since a trail must be hacked to each tree, it is easy to understand why mahogany wood is scarce. Tractors can seldom be used in the jungle, and the cut trees must be dragged out by oxen to the nearest river, where they can be floated to a seaport.

THE GOVERNMENT OF HONDURAS HAS MANY PROBLEMS

Although Hondurans claim Morazán as their national hero, his achievements benefited the Central American federation rather than his own native province. Honduras had its share of revolutions and wars in the stormy days after independence. Today it is the most backward of all the five countries of Central America. Except for the Negroes who work in the banana plantations on the Caribbean coast, the people are largely *mestizo* and Indian. They are very poor and most of them can neither read nor write. According to the constitution, education is free, but there are not enough schools to teach anywhere near all the children. Education for the people is one of the problems facing the government.

Honduras needs more roads and railroads. Road-building is a difficult job in Honduras, but only one road between the Caribbean and the Pacific has been completed. The Pan-American Highway crosses only the narrow wedge of land near the Gulf of Fonseca. Railroads are needed to connect the capital with the seaports, but railroads cost money and Honduras is poor in spite of its great banana industry.

BANANAS ARE A BUSINESS IN CENTRAL AMERICA

We cannot understand the banana-raising countries of Central America without knowing something about the banana industry and the American company which controls it. The story goes back to the 1500's when a priest brought the first plants to the New World from Africa. They spread rapidly and were soon growing wild throughout the tropical regions. In the 1800's, enterprising men from the United States became interested in growing bananas on plantations and shipping them to the United States and Europe. Today banana production is an enormous industry with huge plantations, thousands of workers, miles of railroads, and fleets of ships, all owned by the United Fruit Company.

The Caribbean coast of Central America, with its heavy rainfall, is good banana land. When a new plantation is to be opened, experienced men are sent from the United States to take charge of it. Negro workers are hired from Jamaica and other islands of the West Indies because they can do the heavy work on the plantation in spite of the tropical heat. A little community is built in the jungle with hospitals, stores, and long rows of clean huts for the working-men. The company sees to it that mosquitoes are controlled so that there will be no malaria or yellow fever among the workers.

Next, the jungle is cleared away with *machetes*, and banana roots are set out. In a few months' time trees grow up and flower. A large green bunch forms on each tree with the bananas pointing upward instead of down, as we might expect. Expensive

Galloway

A MULE–DRAWN BANANA CAR runs along a track through this huge banana plantation. Notice the heavy growth of banana trees in the background. Bananas are the major export from Honduras.

spraying systems are installed to protect the plants from diseases which attack bananas. Men work constantly to keep back the jungle which, if allowed to grow, would soon choke the plants. Other workers build railroad tracks from the plantation to the nearest port.

Bananas are not cut until word is received by radio that a banana boat is coming into the port. Then there is a great rush on the plantation, because bananas must be picked green and hurried to refrigerated ships before they ripen in the hot sun. The heavy bunches or "stems" are cut and loaded on mules which are waiting to carry them to the banana cars. The work is so well organized that by the time the ship docks, carloads of bananas are ready for loading. The bunches are put into the canvas pockets of huge conveyors which carry them to the ship. No bruised bunches or ripening bananas can be used. At American ports the bananas leave the chilly hold of the ship and are loaded into refrigerator cars which take them to grocery and fruit stores all over the country.

Nicaragua

NICARAGUA FACES THE PACIFIC

Nicaragua, next door to Honduras, is the largest of all the Central American states. It is shaped like a triangle with two corners on the Caribbean and the third on the Gulf of Fonseca on the Pacific. Notice on the map large Lake Nicaragua and smaller Lake Managua which lie between a mountain range and the Pacific Ocean. Most of the population live in the narrow strip of fertile land in the lake region. Rolling green plains and rich plateaus produce fruits and vegetables of all kinds, as well as grazing land for livestock. The coffee plantations which furnish the chief crop of the country are located here. North of the lakes a range of mountains runs parallel to the coast. Beyond the mountains a great wilderness of forest and jungle covers most of Nicaragua except for the cleared banana lands on the Caribbean coast.

Although Nicaragua is larger than Guatemala, it has about one third as many people. While Guatemala's mountain regions are the home of hundreds of thousands of Indians, the mountains of this country are almost uninhabited. Indian tribes live on the hot eastern lowlands and there are Negroes and a few whites in the banana country. Most of the people, however, are *mestizos* who live in the Pacific region.

NICARAGUA'S CITIES ARE BOTH NEW AND OLD

The capital city of Managua is situated on the lake after which it was named. Like so many capital cities of Central America, it is in a volcano and earthquake region. In 1931, Managua was destroyed by a terrible earthquake. Since then a modern city has grown up with paved streets, an up-to-date movie theater, and a sewer system. It can be very hot in Managua when there is no cooling breeze from the lake.

Northwest of Managua is León (lay-ohn'), an old colonial city which was settled by farmers and laborers from Spain. Its cobbled streets and ancient tiled roofs are a great contrast to modern Managua. The grassy plains about the city feed thousands of cattle and the rich countryside supplies food in abundance. About thirty miles southeast of Managua is the sleepy old city of Granada (grah-nah'dah), once the home of Spanish aristocracy of colonial days. It lies on the shore of Lake Nicaragua in the shadow of two volcanoes. Ancient churches and narrow streets and shady plazas tell the story of its beginnings as a city of colonial Spain.

These three cities can all be reached by a narrow-gauge railroad from the seaport of Corinto (koh-reen'toh) on the Pacific. It takes five or six hours to travel the hundred miles from the coast up to Managua.

RIVAL CITIES KEPT NICARAGUA IN A TURMOIL

Nicaragua has had the stormiest history of all the stormy little countries of Central America. The story of the half-century after independence might be called "A Tale of Two Cities." For forty years the now peaceful cities of León and Granada fought over which one should be the capital of the republic. You remember that the conservative landowners and the Church were opposed to the liberals having power in Central America. This same difference in politics caused the quarrel between the two cities. Granada was the stronghold of the old Spanish aristocratic families, while León represented the more democratic farmers and professional men. They were constantly at war.

When the villain of the story appears in the form of William Walker, an American adventurer and soldier of fortune, Nicaraguan history begins to read like a thrilling adventure. The people of León asked Walker to aid them against Granada. He arrived in León with about fifty daredevils like himself, marched on Granada, and seized it in a surprise attack. In a few months his army had increased because of more recruits from the United States, and Walker made himself dictator of Nicaragua. This was more than León had bargained for. Costa Rica was called on for help and after two years Walker was forced to flee the country. He tried twice to return, but was finally captured in Honduras and shot. Perhaps all this trouble had a quieting effect on the two quarreling cities, but neither one became the capital. That honor was given to the little town of Managua situated halfway between them.

NICARAGUANS WANT AN INTER-OCEAN CANAL

If you should ask a Nicaraguan what his country needs most at the present time, he would probably answer, "An inter-ocean canal." It is the hope of these people that the United States will build a second great canal across their territory. The idea of a Nicaraguan canal goes back to the days of the gold rush, when the forty-niners were eager for a faster route to the California gold fields.

Commodore Vanderbilt, an American, got permission from the Nicaraguan government to start a new route across that country. Boats from New York or New Orleans

ON LAKE NICARAGUA near Granada, oxcarts go out into the shallow water to unload small boats full of produce. These boats bring cocoanuts, bananas, and other products from the villages on the lake shore.

Tanks

landed passengers at Greytown on the Caribbean coast at the mouth of the San Juan (sahn whahn) River. From here they took smaller boats up the river and across the southern end of Lake Nicaragua. Bright blue stagecoaches picked them up and carried them along a hard road the few remaining miles to the Pacific, where a ship was waiting to take them to California. While the gold rush was on, 250,000 people a year traveled by this route at a price of $300 for the trip.

When the United States became seriously interested in a canal between the two oceans, this route across Nicaragua was investigated as well as the Panama route. The lake and river lie in a natural pass through the mountains whose highest point is only 135 feet above sea level. There are fewer mountains to cut through than on the Isthmus of Panama; how-ever, the engineers who studied the two routes recommended that the canal be dug across the Isthmus.

The United States did not lose interest entirely in the Nicaraguan canal. By paying $3,000,000 we secured the right to construct a canal at any time up to the year 2015. Because the present canal is such a vital link in our defense, it might be wise to have a second canal as a safety measure. This would cost more than $750,000,000 and would take several years to build. The chief disadvantage of a Nicaraguan canal is that it would be 173 miles long, which is over three times the length of the one at Panama. Ships passing through a long canal would be in greater danger from the air in time of war. In the meantime, the Nicaraguans are still hoping that the canal will be built, for it will mean prosperity to their country as it has to Panama.

Costa Rica

COSTA RICA HAS THREE CLIMATES

Costa Rica (cohs'tah ree'cah), next to the smallest of all Central American republics, is really a slice off the western end of the Isthmus of Panama. Like Mexico, this little country has hot lowlands on each coast, a high inland plateau, and a mountain region above 6000 feet in altitude. Three fourths of the population live in cities or on small farms on the central plateau, enjoying the beautiful climate of perpetual spring. If the countries of Central America started to advertise the springtime climate of their highland regions, they could put California and Florida to shame without exaggerating the truth at all! Many farmers live in the *tierra fria* above 6000 feet.

There they find fine pasture land for cattle and good soil for crops.

SAN JOSÉ REFLECTS THE LIFE OF COSTA RICA

The capital of Costa Rica is in a high valley 4000 feet above the sea. This modern city of 90,000 people was a tiny village of thatched huts in 1750. It boasts no fine colonial mansions and cathedrals like those of Granada, for San José was not founded by Spanish aristocrats but by simple people. It is a friendly city with wide, shaded streets and many beautiful parks. There are modern shops, movies, schools, street-cars, and electric lights.

The people walk around the plaza

Black Star

THE POST OFFICE BUILDING in San José, Costa Rica, is typical of that modern little capital. The word *correos*, part of which can be seen at the top of the building, is the Spanish word for mail.

in the evenings just as they do in Mexico, the men going in one direction and the ladies in another. Everyone is dressed in modern clothes; there are no Indians in gay native costumes. On Sunday nights there is a band concert in the plaza.

Costa Ricans do not, of course, celebrate *fiestas* with masked Indian dances as they do in Guatemala. They have a beauty contest every year when the "Queen of Central America" is chosen from among the many beautiful girls of the country. The people prefer football to bullfights and their teams are well known in the neighboring republics.

The fine oxen and brightly painted oxcarts which drive through the streets are the pride of the country people. The oxen are matched pairs and a farmer who has a white ox with a brown face will go to great lengths to get another with the same markings. The oxcarts are gaily decorated with geometric designs. In some towns prizes are given each year for the finest team of matched oxen and the most artistic cart. Farmers in Costa Rica all own oxen, which are signs of prosperity in Central America.

COSTA RICA IS A LAND OF FINE COFFEE

American coffee-drinkers are partial to the flavor of Costa Rican coffee. Coffee has been grown in this country ever since 1830, when plants from Cuba were first set out. Since that time coffee production has increased until today there are 37,000,000 trees bearing the little beans that make the fragrant beverage. The fine-flavored coffee from the central plateau of Costa Rica is also a favorite in England and Germany. At present the United States is the best customer for the coffee crop which amounts to three fifths of the exports of this little country. Costa Rican coffee is grown in small fields worked by farmer-owners, not in huge *fincas* as in Guatemala.

THE BANANA INDUSTRY IS CHANGING ITS HOME

Bananas come next on the list of Costa Rican crops, amounting to one fifth of the exports. In recent years the quantity of bananas raised on the Caribbean plantations has been steadily decreasing. This is due to exhaustion of the soil and to a fungous disease which rots the banana roots. New land is now being cleared for plantations on the other side of the Isthmus, and the old fields will be gradually abandoned.

WE LIKE COSTA RICAN CHOCOLATE

As the banana moves out, cacao moves in. Many acres of the former banana plantations are now planted in cacao because the root disease does not affect this tree. The bean which gives us cocoa and chocolate is becoming a more important crop for Costa Rica each year. Our word "cocoa" is an old English misspelling of the name of the tree — "cacao." "Chocolate," you may remember, was the ancient Aztec word for a drink made of the powdered beans. These brown beans are an important item in the North American diet. We eat them as chocolate, we drink them

as beverage, and we flavor cakes, candy, and ice cream with them.

The cacao is a native of the tropical countries of Latin America. It is a beautiful tree with shining green leaves and silver bark. It produces pods which look something like small hubbard squash, and weigh one half to two pounds. When the ripe pod is opened, it contains twenty-five to forty beans about the size and shape of an almond. The beans are allowed to ferment in the sun or in a hot room. This is said to improve their flavor. They are then spread out in the sun to dry and are ready for shipping.

ROADS AND RAILROADS SHOW THE PROGRESS OF COSTA RICA

The first coffee crops were hauled down to the Pacific port of Puntarenas (poon-tah-ray'nahs) in oxcarts along a muddy trail. This was the only road in the country. Today there are miles of highways in the highland region. The recently constructed Pan-American Highway is the first road to run the length of Costa Rica. The southern end is a particularly difficult section because of the steep mountain passes it must follow. The route into Panama is called "The Pass of Death," and the surveyors for the highway found it very hard to follow even on foot. The railroad from Limón (lee-mohn') on the Caribbean up to San José took twenty-five years to build and cost the lives of many men. The new electric line from San José to Puntarenas is owned and run by the government.

COSTA RICA HAS A DEMOCRACY THAT WORKS

The visitor who thinks Costa Rica is just like other Central American countries has a surprise in store for him. If he lands at Puntarenas he travels up to the capital on a railroad run by electric power, which is most unusual in Central America. Once in San José, he begins to notice other differences. The people on the streets are white and appear to have no Indian blood at all. There are no evidences of the rich, aristocratic, landowning class so common in most of Latin America. If the visitor inquires, he will discover some surprising things — that every citizen must vote, that the president is paid only a very small salary, that there are more school-teachers in the country than there are soldiers in the army!

This little country has managed to achieve what only a few other republics in all the Western Hemisphere have achieved — a real democracy.

Let us see if there is anything in the history of Costa Rica which explains why this republic differs from her neighbors.

THE LAND WAS SETTLED BY SPANISH FARMERS

When Columbus landed on the coast of this country, the coast Indians gave him disks of gold which they wore around their necks as ornaments. Columbus, thinking that rich gold mines must be near-by, called this country Costa Rica or Rich Coast. Expeditions inland found no mines, but destroyed most of the roving Indian tribes who tried to defend themselves from the invaders. There was little here to interest the *conquistadores* or fortune-hunting colonists.

The settlers who finally came to Costa Rica were for the most part

THE RAILROAD BETWEEN LIMÓN AND SAN JOSÉ offers a scenic trip which travelers never forget. The train climbs along this beautiful river canyon to reach the highlands where the capital is located.

Black Star

hard-working, sturdy peasants who wanted to work their small farms in peace. There were few grants of huge estates requiring the labor of Indian peons or Negro slaves. Since there were few Indians left, a *mestizo* class did not develop. Spanish peasants married daughters of other Spanish peasants. When Costa Rica was freed from Spain, they became an independent and self-respecting people. Their fertile land produced a good living for them and when they learned that there was a market for coffee and cacao, they planted these crops on the sunny slopes and valleys.

COSTA RICANS HAVE ACHIEVED A STABLE GOVERNMENT

The national hero **of** the Costa

THIS COSTA RICAN SCHOOLBOY is looking at a leaflet about the diseases carried by the fly. He is learning health rules at school as well as the three "R's."

Black Star

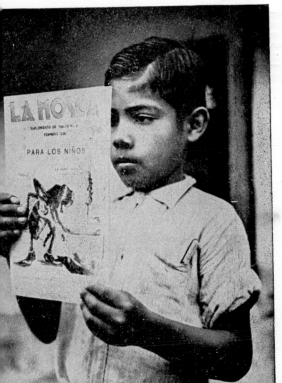

Ricans is their former president, Juan Rafael Mora (whahn rah-fah-el' moh'-rah). He is noted as the man who saved Central American independence by defeating the adventurous William Walker in Nicaragua. Mora did a great deal to develop the coffee industry in Costa Rica. He also established many schools and made primary education compulsory.

Although there were some revolutions in the 1800's, Costa Rica established an orderly government long before her neighbors were able to do so. People who have their own land to till and few grievances against the government are not much interested in revolutions. For well over half a century presidents have been elected according to the constitution, have served their terms and retired. Few countries of Latin America can claim an equal degree of stability. The president of Costa Rica is elected for four years only and cannot be re-elected. This law is never changed to keep a strong man in power as sometimes happens in neighboring republics.

LANDOWNERSHIP AND EDUCATION AID DEMOCRACY

One great step toward democracy is taken when the land is owned by many people rather than a few. Costa Rica has more landowners for its size than any other Latin American country. Four fifths of the land is held in small farms of from one to ten acres. Farms of this size can easily be cultivated by a man and his sons. You remember that in Mexico the peon has struggled for generations to get back to the land. In many countries of Latin America a few wealthy landowners still own most of the good land.

This makes a serious problem which Costa Rica has not had to meet.

Democracy cannot work well in a country whose people do not know how to read and write. Costa Rica established schools soon after becoming a republic. Today she has the best schools in Central America. Years before the children of many of our own states were required by law to attend school, such laws were passed in Costa Rica. In 1864, only about 11 out of every 100 people could read a paper or write their names; today about 85 out of every 100 can do so. To realize what these figures mean, let us compare them with those of other countries. In Mexico today 70 out of 100 can read and write; in Guatemala, only 35; in our own country, 97. This means that little Costa Rica compares favorably in literacy with the United States.

Are You a Careful Reader? Test Yourself!

I. Supply the correct word for each blank:

1. The greatest needs of Honduras are . . . . , ... , and . . . . .

2. Only . . . . can rightly be called a " . . . . republic," while Nicaragua's chief crop is . . . . .

3. Most of the people of Nicaragua live near the . . . . coast.

4. The United States has an option on a canal through Nicaragua until the year . . . . .

5. In . . . . , most of the land is owned by small farmers, not by large landowners.

6. The people of Costa Rica, unlike those of the rest of Central America, are largely . . . . .

7. Costa Rica's chief crops in order of their importance are . . . . , ... , and . . . . .

8. In Costa Rica . . . . out of every 100 people can read and write.

9. The banana industry of Central America is owned and controlled by an American company, the . . . .

II. Match the following words and statements:

1. Vanderbilt
2. San José
3. Puntarenas
4. Tegucigalpa
5. Managua
6. León
7. Taca
8. Fonseca
9. Granada
10. Walker

   a. capital of Costa Rica
   b. founder of Central American airline
   c. American who developed a route across Nicaragua in the gold rush days
   d. engineer who planned Nicaraguan canal route
   e. Costa Rica's Pacific coast port
   f. gulf on the Pacific bordering El Salvador, Nicaragua, and Honduras
   g. capital of Nicaragua
   h. capital of Honduras
   i. aristocratic old Spanish colonial city of Nicaragua
   j. old Nicaraguan city where democratic professional men and farmers lived
   k. American adventurer who became dictator of Nicaragua
   l. name of air service in Central America

Food for Thought and Discussion

1. Can lack of transportation prevent progress? Why? Show that this is true in Central America by giving examples.
2. Is a large, backward native population a drawback to democracy?   Why?
3. How many reasons can you give for the growth of real democracy in Costa Rica?

Chapter 20

The Isthmus of Panama Is the Home of a Canal and a Republic

THERE ARE TWO PANAMAS

To THE PEOPLE of the United States the word "Panama" means the Canal; to the people of the Isthmus it means their native land. The Panama Canal is important because it holds the key to the defense of the Americas, and because it is the channel for trade between the two great oceans. We should not forget that there is also a Republic of Panama which occupies most of the Isthmus. Many people who have traveled through the Canal have seen little of the interesting country which lies beyond.

The crooked finger of land between North and South America has shaped history for four centuries because it is the narrowest place in the great land mass that makes the Western Hemisphere. The jagged heights of the backbone range dwindle to mere hills in eastern Panama.   The volcanoes which dot the landscape of Central America are missing in Panama and earthquakes are few. Nature herself seems to have provided the setting for a canal.

LAND ROUTES FORM THE FIRST LINK BETWEEN THE OCEANS

The route of the present canal has been used for 400 years.   The Spaniards recognized the importance of Panama after Balboa had struggled through the 40 miles of jungle to the Pacific.   The first highway was a mule trail through the jungle over which passed much of the trade and treasure of mighty Spain.   Later a paved road was built across the Isthmus. Panama City on the Pacific and Puerto Bello on the Caribbean became key cities

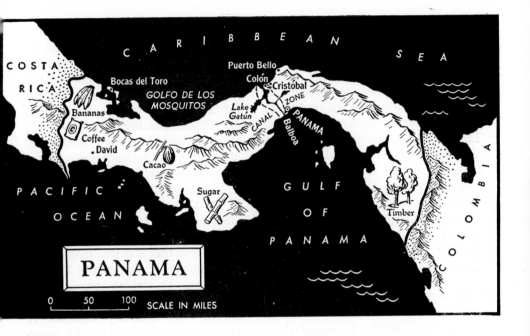

PANAMA

0   50   100   SCALE IN MILES

in the great colonial system, as we learned in Chapter 16.

The next crossing of the Isthmus was by railroad. This is where the United States enters the story. About the time that Vanderbilt was planning his route across Nicaragua for the forty-niners, an American named Aspinwall had a similar plan for a route which would cross the Isthmus by railroad. He obtained permission to build a railroad and in 1855 the first train, with a wood-burning engine, traveled from the Caribbean to the Pacific. Yellow fever and malaria took many lives while men struggled to lay tracks through the jungle, but the road was a success. Thousands of passengers paid $25 to ride 40 miles. They sailed from New York by clipper ship, crossed the Isthmus on the Panama Railroad, and boarded another ship bound for California. When the transcontinental railroad was finished in the United States in 1869, this route became useless. By this time a French company had decided to build a canal across Panama and the railroad was sold to them.

THE FRENCH FAIL IN THEIR ATTEMPT TO BUILD A CANAL

The idea of building a canal across the Isthmus was not a new one. In 1534, the king of Spain ordered a survey to be made, and was informed that it would be impossible to construct such a canal. But the idea persisted. During the 1800's, France, England, and the United States were all interested. While the United States was seriously considering a Nicaraguan canal, a French company was organized to build one in Panama.

Ferdinand de Lesseps, who built the Suez Canal across the desert sands of the Isthmus of Suez, had charge of the construction. Against the advice of engineers, it was decided to build a sea-level canal which meant cutting through the mountain backbone. The project was doomed to failure, for they had reckoned without the dread diseases which lay in wait for white people who tried to live in Panama. Thousands of men died of yellow fever. More workmen would be sent to take their place and they too would die. The Frenchmen kept on until the company went bankrupt and de Lesseps died. The attempt had cost the lives of 40,000 men and $260,000,-000.

Today at the Atlantic end of the Canal tourists can see where the French digging started. Piles of ruined and rusted machinery are ghostly remainders of that tragic failure.

THE UNITED STATES PREPARES TO DIG THE "BIG DITCH"

In 1898, something happened which convinced the United States government that a canal should be built. When we went to war with Spain in that year, it became necessary to send the battleship *Oregon* from the Pacific to help our forces in Cuba. By the time the *Oregon* made the trip around South America and arrived in Cuba, the war was almost over! A treaty was made with England which released the United States from earlier agreements providing for a joint control of any canal between the two oceans. In spite of the French failure, the Panama route was finally judged the best. The next step was to secure the right to build the canal in Panama.

At this time Panama was a province of the Republic of Colombia, but it had always been impatient of control from far-off Bogotá. In fact, Panama had announced her independence from that country several times in the 1800's, yet had always returned. The Colombian government believed, rightly enough, that no digging in Panama should be done without its consent. However, it refused to accept the treaty that had been arranged with the United States. The people in Panama were very anxious for the canal to be built and the idea of independence began to grow. In 1903, a revolt broke out in the city of Panama and the leaders proclaimed independence from Colombia.

Theodore Roosevelt, then President of the United States, has been criticized for secretly prompting the revolt. Although there is no evidence that he did this, it is true that American warships off the coast of Panama prevented Colombian troops from crossing the Isthmus to put down the revolt. We certainly hastened to profit from Colombia's loss by recognizing the new Republic of Panama. The whole affair put us in a bad light with other nations of Latin America, who felt that we had cheated Colombia out of her chance to profit by the canal. For a down payment of $10,000,000 and $250,000 a year, the new republic of Panama leased to the United States a strip of land ten miles wide.

PANAMA CHANGES FROM PEST-HOLE TO HEALTH RESORT

We had learned a lesson from the failure of the French — yellow fever and malaria would have to be conquered before the canal could be built. After the Spanish-American War, American doctors in Cuba had discovered that these diseases are transmitted by the bites of two varieties of mosquitoes. Colonel William Gorgas, who had stamped out yellow fever in Havana, was sent to take charge in Panama. In the ten-mile strip called the Canal Zone, he proceeded to build ditches to drain swamps and ponds where mosquitoes might breed. If the swamps and ponds could not be drained, he covered them with oil so that the larvae would die. Every house was screened. When the Zone was free of mosquitoes, American health engineers set to work on the rest of Panama. Today it is one of the most healthful countries in the tropics, and deaths from yellow fever or malaria are rare. Thus did science conquer disease and make possible the Panama Canal.

THE PANAMA CANAL IS THE GREATEST ENGINEERING FEAT KNOWN TO MAN

Instead of the sea-level canal planned by the French, American engineers decided to leave the long center section 85 feet above sea level and to build locks or stairsteps to raise and lower the boats at each end. The swift Chagres (chah'grays) River was to be dammed to make a huge artificial lake in the higher interior. To keep the canal at a level of 85 feet, a channel, which was sometimes 300 feet deep, had to be blasted through the mountains. Colonel George Goethals, an army engineer, was put in charge of this stupendous undertaking.

For seven years, thousands of men dug and blasted and dredged and built with the aid of powerful machinery. Sun and rain beat down upon them, landslides covered up the work they had already done, an earthquake threatened destruction. At last the day came when President Wilson in far-off Washington pushed a button which released the dammed-up waters and filled the great Canal. The dream of centuries was at last accomplished!

TWENTY-FIVE YEARS OF SERVICE PROVE THE VALUE OF THE CANAL

In 1915, the Canal was formally opened and the first ship passed from one ocean to the other through the gigantic shipway. In 1940 a check was made on its first 25 years of life. It was found that 100,000 ships of 34 nations had used the Canal in 25 years, and 500,000,000 tons of cargo had been carried. All vessels had paid equally at the rate of $1.20 for each ton of their weight. In this way the Canal had paid for its upkeep and the $250,000 a year due to the Republic of Panama. In fact, at the request of that government, the United States had agreed in 1939 to increase the yearly payment to $450,000.

The Canal has served its purpose of bringing closer together the great ports of the world. New York and San Francisco are over 7000 miles closer by water than before; the once isolated ports of the Pacific coast of South America are now nearer to New York and to Europe by several thousand miles; San Francisco and Liverpool, England, are closer by almost 6000 miles.

THE CANAL AIDS IN THE DEFENSE OF THE AMERICAS

During the Second World War, the Canal was one of the most important links in the defense of the Western Hemisphere. It is safe to say that the fate of this hemisphere and perhaps of the whole world depended on our keeping control of the Panama Canal. Without it, our Navy could have been made almost useless, because it could not have moved speedily from one ocean to the other.

In 1941 work was begun on a

second set of locks to be built parallel
to the present ones. They were to be
140 feet wide so that large aircraft
carriers and new battleships such as
the *Iowa* could pass through. The
original locks are only 110 feet wide
and cannot accommodate even the
largest passenger ships such as the
Queen Mary and the *Queen Elizabeth*.
The appearance of the atom bomb,
however, changed the situation, for
the new locks could be as easily
bombed as the present ones. Work
was stopped on the new locks. It may
be that a sea level canal without locks
may be the best answer to the problem. This would cost about a billion
dollars and might have to be built in
a less mountainous region than the
present Canal.

THE CANAL TRIP IS A THRILLING EXPERIENCE

Before we leave the Canal to get
acquainted with the rest of Panama,
let us see what a trip through it is like.
Suppose you are on a boat approaching the Pacific entrance in Panama
Bay. Notice on the map (page 219)

that this Pacific approach is not the
western end of the Canal as you might
suppose, but the southern end. Since
the Isthmus of Panama runs east and
west, the Canal slices through it in a
north-to-south direction. A launch
steams out to meet our boat, bringing
an American pilot and a Negro crew
to take the ship through the Canal.

We pass Panama City and the
American city of Balboa as the ship
enters the channel. We are soon
at the Miraflores (mee-rah-flo'rays)
Locks ready to be lifted up to the
higher level of the Canal. Our boat
noses into a huge concrete compart-
ment, great gates close behind us, and
we begin to move slowly upward as
water is turned into the lock. Suddenly we find ourselves at the top.
Another gate opens and we are pulled
by little electric engines or "mules"
into the next lock. Although we are
at the same water level, our boat is
again at the bottom with steel and
concrete walls towering above us.
Once more our ship rises and we climb
another 20 or 30 feet. The mules pull
us through the lock into Miraflores

HOW LOCKS WORK: Gates A open, ship enters lock B, gates A close.
Water pours in from pipes at the bottom, raising ship to waterline C.
Ship is now level with lock E. Can you explain now how ship reaches
canal K?

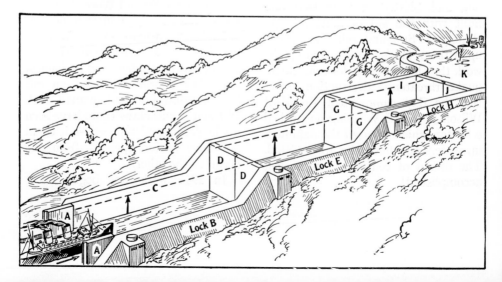

Gendreau

MIRAFLORES LOCKS, like other locks of the Canal, are double so that two ships may go through at one time. This picture shows the double locks and the "mules" which move the ships. Note also the double gates between the locks.

Lake, 55 feet above the level of Panama Bay.

After crossing the lake and going through another set of locks, the boat reaches the highest channel. Although the Canal now seems like a quiet river flowing through the mountains, this was the most difficult part of the project. For a distance of eight or nine miles mountains were blasted away. The man who accomplished this enormous task died before he could see the final results of his labors, but the Gaillard Cut was named in his honor. The channel widens out and we are in Gatún (gah-toon') Lake for a 24-mile run. A great dam across the Chagres River formed this lake in what was once swamp and jungle. Dead trees rear their ghostly branches above the lake, and hilltops have become islands covered with jungle growth.

At the end of the lake are the Gatún Locks which lower our boat the 85 feet to the level of the Caribbean. This time the process is reversed, so that, when the water is let out of the lock, the ship sinks to a lower level. At last we pass the Atlantic port of Cristóbal and its twin city Colón, just outside the Zone, and head for the open sea. It has taken us seven or eight hours to make the 40-mile trip through the Canal.

THE CANAL ZONE IS A MODEL COMMUNITY RUN BY THE UNITED STATES

The United States does not actually own the strip of territory 10 miles wide and about 40 miles long which is called the Canal Zone. We merely rent it to the end of time from the Republic of Panama. Of the 50,000 people who live in the Zone today, about 22,000 work for the Canal in one way or another. Half of them are natives of Panama or Jamaica Negroes who perform the labor necessary to keep the Canal running. The other half are American engineers, pilots, office workers, and of course, the members of the Army and Navy.

The cities of Panama are like two sets of twins. At the Caribbean end of the Canal is the modern and sanitary town of Cristóbal, which is in the Zone. Outside of the Zone, but with only a street between, is the interesting city of Colón, where tourists love to shop for goods from all over the world. Cristóbal Colón is the Spanish name for Christopher Columbus, who searched in vain for the passage to the Indies now cut through by man. At the southern end of the Canal are the twin cities of Balboa within the Zone and Panama City, capital of the republic, just outside.

Most of the Americans employed by the government live in Balboa, which the United States has made into a model town. The government-owned houses are clean and modern with screened porches and tropical gardens. The rents are low and residents may buy food and supplies at government stores or commissaries at much lower prices than elsewhere. There are American schools, clubs, libraries, and movies. In fact, the whole Zone is like a streamlined bit of the United States set down in the jungles of Panama.

OUTSIDE THE CANAL ZONE IS ANOTHER PANAMA

The traveler who steps outside Uncle Sam's ten-mile slice of land soon finds himself in green and riotous jungle! Huge bright blue butterflies flit about the underbrush, rare and lovely orchids may be picked in bunches. Brilliant macaws and parrots and great snowy egrets make their homes not far from the civilized Zone. Iguanas, the long brown lizards which Panamanians eat as we eat chicken, scamper along the rivers. In the jungle, Indians from another age hunt and fish for their food. East of the Canal toward the Colombian border are hostile Indian tribes who have never been conquered.

SEVERAL CROPS GROW IN PANAMA

Many people live on farms and in simple villages, making their living by planting and fishing and cattle-raising. In some of the villages of western Panama, life goes on much as it did in Spanish colonial days. Although only a small fraction of Panama's fertile acres has been cleared of jungle, some important tropical crops are grown. The town of David (dah-veed') in western Panama is the center of an agricultural region where rice, sugar, cacao, and corn are raised. Farther up in the highlands are many coffee plantations. Across the Isthmus from David but not connected by road is the new banana port of Bocas del Toro (boh'cahs del toh'roh). The United Fruit Company has huge plantations here. Panama is the original home of the banana, for it was here that the Spanish priest planted the first trees in the New World.

The Caribbean coastlands produce coconuts from thousands of acres of coconut palms. Most of the groves have been wild, but commercial plantations are being started. Although we may think of coconut cake in connection with this fruit, its oil is much more important. Coconut oil is produced from copra or dried coconut meat. Many of our soaps contain the oil and so do several brands of oleo-margarine, the substitute for butter.

Pearl fishing is an old industry of Panama. For centuries the natives of the Panama Bay region have dived for pearls. Balboa reported that pearls were so plentiful in Panama that the Indians used them to decorate their oars! They are not so plentiful today, but pearl fishing still continues. The chief income of the divers, however, is from the mother-of-pearl shells which are used for buttons and souvenirs.

PANAMA CITY RETAINS ITS SPANISH BACKGROUND

On the other side of Fourth-of-July Avenue in the American town of Balboa is gay and colorful Panama City, capital of the republic. Located at one end of the old Spanish trail across the Isthmus, this historic town has seen men from many nations come and go. Conquistadores of Spain, daring buccaneers of England, forty-niners on their way to the gold fields of California, engineers and workmen from the United States to build the "Big Ditch," tourists on their way through the Canal — all have passed through Panama City. On its busy main streets Negroes from the West Indies mingle with North Americans, Europeans, and native Panamanians. Shops run by Chinese, Japanese, and Hindu tradesmen offer the traveler beautiful silks and embroideries, ivory, jade, and countless other goods from the Orient. After seeing the medley of races that lives in Panama

City, it is a surprise to hear English and Spanish spoken and to read shop signs in these languages.

This city has not entirely lost its Spanish flavor. In old parts of the town are narrow streets and balconied houses which have survived from early days. Panama's dollar, the *balboa*, is a reminder of the great Spaniard who lived and died there. There are promenades about the plaza in the evening and bullfights on Sunday. At the *fiesta* or carnival the women wear the *pollera* (poh-yeh′rah), which is a glamorous version of the native costume. Yards of lace and exquisite embroideries go into the *polleras*, and the costume is topped by dozens of brilliant hair ornaments in the form of flowers and butterflies.

THE REMAINS OF OLD PANAMA CAN BE SEEN TODAY

In 1671, the pirate, Henry Morgan, crossed the Isthmus and took the town of Panama by surprise. After he had looted the town, he set fire to the buildings and returned to Puerto Bello and his ship. The present city of Panama was founded in the next year. Parts of the old town and the Cruces road can still be seen a few miles away. The buildings are crumbled and covered with vines, and the former highway is only a jungle trail. At the Caribbean end of the old road, ancient cannon and crumbling stones mark the fort at Puerto Bello. In a Negro village on the shore, you can see the marble steps of a former mansion, and some of the cottages boast floors of old Spanish tile!

THE CANAL HAS BENEFITED PANAMA

Because of the Canal, Panama is more directly associated with the

THE GLAMOROUS POLLERA COSTUME is worn by this girl as she does Panama's national dance. Notice the lovely lace and embroidery on her dress and the ornaments in her hair.

United States than any other Latin American country. She does not maintain an army or navy because the United States is bound by treaty to protect the Isthmus as well as the Canal. American health officers inspect the jungles for mosquitoes and enforce the law against allowing open water where they may breed. They supervise the native food market in the city and do not allow meat to be kept overnight without refrigeration. The dollar, as well as the *balboa*, is accepted in Panama City. The yearly rent of $450,000 paid by the United States for the Canal Zone supports the government of Panama so that citizens do not have to pay taxes.

Are You a Careful Reader?   Test Yourself!

I. Can you supply the correct word for the following blanks?

1. The first attempt to build a canal across Panama was made by the . . . . under . . . . ; the attempt failed because so many workmen died of . . . . and . . . .

2. Before the United States attempted to build the Canal, Colonel . . . . freed the Canal Zone of disease by stamping out . . . . .

3. The strip of land . . . . miles wide and . . . . miles long is called the . . . . , and is leased from the Republic of . . . . for . . . . dollars a year.

4. The Canal was built under Colonel .... and is .... feet above sea level. It takes a boat about .... hours to travel the .... miles from one end of the Canal to the other. Ships are raised and lowered in the Panama Canal by means of a series of ..

5. The direction of the Canal is not east and west, but more nearly .... and ..... .

II. Can you choose the best answer?

1. The United States may decide to build a sea-level canal in Central America because: (a) the present locks are not wide enough for the largest ships; (b) the present locks are wearing out; (c) a sea-level canal would be safer in case of another war.

2. The revolt of Panama from Colombia added to the fear and distrust felt by Latin Americans toward the United States because: (*a*) the American government had not yet paid Colombia a final price for the canal rights; (*b*) they felt that we had cheated Colombia out of her chance to profit by the Canal; (*c*) we took Panama's finances under military control.

3. The Panama Canal has served its main purpose which was: (*a*) to pay for itself in 25 years; (*b*) to provide an American defense base for the Caribbean area; (*c*) to shorten the sailing distances between the great ports of the world.

4. The Canal has benefited Panama because: (*a*) it allowed her to be independent of Colombia; (*b*) since the opening of the Canal thousands of tourists have bought quantities of goods in Panama; (*c*) the rent on the Canal supports the Panamanian government.

5. An important agricultural experiment being carried on in Panama is: (*a*) the new sugar plantations near the town of David; (*b*) the plantations of Brazilian rubber trees started by the Goodyear Rubber Company; (*c*) the United Fruit Company's banana plantations at Bocas del Toro.

Food for Thought and Discussion

1. What would the results be if the Panama Canal were out of commission in time of peace?

2. Why would this be a much greater calamity in time of war?

3. Do you think our government was right in preventing Colombian troops from quelling the Panamanian revolt?

Chapter 21

Hispaniola Is the Island Home of Two Republics

HISPANIOLA IS AN ISLAND OF MANY NAMES

BETWEEN Cuba and Puerto Rico is an island which Columbus loved so much that he asked to be buried there. *La Isla Española*, as Columbus fondly called it, has had many names. When your parents studied geography they may have called the island Haiti, which is the original Indian name meaning "high country." It has also been called Santo Domingo after the first city established there. Today authorities have returned to a Latin version of the name Columbus used, or Hispaniola. This is the name which will be used in this book.

When Queen Isabella asked Columbus what his "charming paradise of an island" looked like, he crumpled up a piece of parchment paper to show her. The sharp peaks and deep ravines of crumpled paper give a good idea of what the land is like. The center of the island is covered with steep mountain ranges and heavy pine forests. There are other mountains to the north and west. Between the ranges are valleys and plains so fertile that anything will grow there. Today almost every spot fit for cultivation in this garden island is planted. Coffee grows on the hills and sugar cane, cacao, and cotton flourish under the tropic sun.

Hispaniola is the second largest island of the West Indies. It is the home of two republics of Latin America — Haiti and the Dominican Republic. The 3,500,000 French-speak-

ing Negro people of Haiti are crowded into the western third of the island. In the Dominican Republic, which covers the rest of the island, are 2,000,000 Spanish-speaking whites, mulattoes, and Negroes. You would look in vain for an Indian or a *mestizo* in Hispaniola.

Let us now turn back to the colonial period so that we may discover why there are two small republics on one small island.

Haiti

HAITI BECOMES A FRENCH COLONY

The history of modern Haiti began when the buccaneers took over the western end of Hispaniola in the 1600's. French, Dutch, and English adventurers were living there, smoking the beef of the wild cattle they hunted and looting Spanish commerce. France had been watching with a jealous eye the great colonial empire which Spain had created in the New World. When she learned that many Frenchmen were living on one end of a Spanish island, she made the most of her opportunity. The men were encouraged to leave the sea and become farmers. New settlers arrived and two boatloads of girls from France were sent over to become wives of the buccaneers. The region was given the name of Saint Domingue (san doh-maing'), which is French for Santo Domingo, and a governor-general was sent from France. By 1697, Spain was forced to recognize this group as a French colony.

In the 1700's, more French colonists came over to settle on large grants of land given them by the government. To work the land they brought in slaves from Africa or bought them from the Spaniards next door. They planted coffee, cotton, sugar, and other crops until most of the good land was under cultivation. The colony became the richest and most prosperous in the West Indies through the sale of its tropical crops to Europe. A wealthy planter class grew up with thousands of slaves to work for them. As the colony grew, the capital city was founded and named Port-au-Prince (port-oh-prance') or Prince's Harbor in honor of a prince of France.

In spite of the fine crops and prosperity, the colonists were not contented. Frenchmen had married Negro women and a large mulatto class was taking its place in the colony. According to law, these people were free and had the same rights as Frenchmen. This caused jealousy between the two classes. The number of Negro slaves had increased until there were ten slaves for every free man. To keep so many slaves under control, the French were often exceedingly cruel. It was natural that the slaves became discontented.

A NEGRO SLAVE LEADS THE REVOLT FOR FREEDOM IN SAINT DOMINGUE

The Haitian slaves were of a finer type than those in other Caribbean colonies. The French paid high prices to get the strongest and most intelligent Negroes possible because they could do more and better work. Many French slaves had been leading men in their African villages and that fact may help to explain what happened later on.

In the middle of the 1700's, a slave was born on a plantation in Haiti who was to change the course of history in that island. This slave was called Toussaint (too-san'). His grandfather had been the king of a powerful African tribe and he himself was so intelligent that his master became interested in him and taught him to read, write, and figure. With the help of a priest he studied history and French literature, and read the writings of some of the leading thinkers of the day. He was interested in the French Revolution and the belief that everyone is born free and equal. Young Haitians of mixed blood who had been sent to France for an education came back with ideas and literature about freedom. Slaves aided by mulattoes began to revolt against their masters and to declare themselves free.

By 1791, the revolution had broken out in earnest. The beautiful plantations were destroyed by the slaves and the whites began to flee from the colony. Both sides were guilty of terrible cruelties. Toussaint, now a man of fifty, decided to lead his people in their fight for freedom. He became known as Toussaint L'Ouverture (too-san' loo-ver-toor'). By 1801, he had conquered not only Haiti but the Spanish end of the island as well. He declared the slaves free and drew up a constitution giving the island self-government.

By this time Napoleon had become ruler of France, and he had no intention of allowing this colony to govern itself. He sent his brother-in-law Le Clerc and a large army to conquer this bold slave. The French regained control of much of the island and Toussaint agreed to retire to his plantation and fight no more. Le Clerc promised that he would be safe, but

later had him seized and sent to France as a prisoner. Napoleon refused to see this great leader of the colored people and ordered him put into a dungeon high in the Alps. Toussaint, used to the heat of his tropical island, soon died. This man who was born a slave had shown fine qualities as a military and political leader. To the French he was a dangerous man because he had shown the Negroes how powerful they could be.

A FORMER SLAVE BECOMES THE RULER OF INDEPENDENT HAITI

The fight for freedom was carried on by a ferocious Negro who had been one of Toussaint's generals. Dessalines (dess-ah-lean'), however, did not have the power to hold back the ignorant Negro soldiers. They ran riot, plundering the plantations and killing the landowners. It was yellow fever and not the Negroes which finally defeated the French. The French soldiers were dying by the hundreds and Le Clerc himself fell a victim to it. The remaining soldiers were driven to their ships. Dessalines stood upon a rock with the red, white, and blue flag of France in his hands. He tore out the white section of the flag and trampled upon it as a symbol of the end of French rule in the colony. Thus, in 1804, before any other colony of Latin America became independent, the Negro Republic of Haiti was launched.

A STRONG LEADER ESTABLISHES ORDER

Dessalines tried to establish order, but was killed after two years. He was followed by another former slave who had also been a general under Toussaint. Henri Christophe (ahn-ree' crees-tof') could not read or write,

Black Star

THE PRESIDENTIAL PALACE at Port-au-Prince, Haiti, faces a square named for Toussaint L'Ouverture. A statue of this famous Negro by a Haitian sculptor stands in the square.

but he was an intelligent man. Like his hero, Toussaint, he had great plans for his people. He was faced with a situation which would have discouraged most men. Ninety per cent of his people were ignorant ex-slaves and many of them had been born in the African jungles. The plantations had been destroyed; the white people either had been killed or had fled during the revolution. Many Negroes had returned to the savagery of their native Africa and were living in little jungle villages.

Christophe set about putting his country in order. He forced everyone to work. Plantations were replanted and schools were started because he knew that his people could not progress without education. Once more Haiti became prosperous.

Christophe himself was a surprising person. He had himself crowned as King Henri I, and built on a hill a beautiful palace, which he called *Sans Souci* (sahn soo-see'), meaning "without care." Here he lived in splendor with a court of Negro lords and ladies about him. On a mountain above the palace he built a great citadel or fort which could defend Haiti against the French, whom he always feared. Both palace and fort can be seen today by travelers to Haiti.

He was never satisfied with the progress of his country and became more and more cruel in his struggle to improve his people. At last the Haitians revolted against him and Christophe killed himself with a silver bullet which he had reserved for that purpose.

THE UNITED STATES GIVES HELP TO HAITI

After the death of Christophe, the capital was moved back to the port town of Port-au-Prince. Lacking a good and strong leader, Haiti slipped

Galloway

THE FAMOUS CITADEL built by Henri Christophe looks down upon the thatched hut of a present-day Haitian. In the foreground a Haitian woman carries her laundry on her head.

backward and matters went from bad to worse. The people grew lazy and the plantations were neglected. Rulers became tyrants, and there was continual civil war and bloodshed. One president after another was murdered. In 1915, the president was actually torn to pieces by a mob. Haiti, like some of the Central American countries, had borrowed money from European governments which now threatened to come over and collect it.

Conditions became so bad that the United States decided to step in and help Haiti straighten out her affairs. Marines were sent over and they remained there for nineteen years. The revolutions came to an end and

finances were put in order so that Haiti could pay off her debts. Under the direction of experts from the United States, the Marines helped to stamp out disease and teach sanitation. They built roads, trained police, and started more schools. The peasants were much better off and the country was benefited by American help. But the people of Haiti resented the presence of foreign soldiers and our intervention there caused fear and distrust in the other Latin American countries. As part of Franklin Roosevelt's pledge to be a good neighbor, the Marines were withdrawn in 1934, leaving Haiti to the Haitians.

The peasants are still very poor and ninety per cent of them can neither read nor write. The government to-day is in the hands of educated mulat-toes who make up about 10 per cent of the population. Haiti is better off now, however, than it has been at any time in the past.

The Dominican Republic

THE DOMINICAN REPUBLIC HAS HAD A STORMY CAREER

Long before the French built up a strong colony in Haiti, neighboring Hispaniola had become one of the poorest and weakest of the Spanish colonies. The discovery of gold and silver mines in Mexico and Peru had caused many of the adventurous settlers to leave Santo Domingo. It soon changed from the center of Spanish civilization to an unimportant colony where cattle-raising and agriculture were carried on by the inhabitants. After the Negro armies of Toussaint invaded it, many white planters moved out of the island. Spain later regained control, only to have Hispaniola declare its independence in 1821. The unfortunate colony did not enjoy its freedom long, for troops from Haiti conquered it the next year. For 22 years the colony suffered under the harsh treatment of the Haitians, until it managed to regain its independence as the Dominican Republic. Fear of the Haitians was so great that the Dominicans returned to the protection of Spain for four years. When this proved a bad move, they asked to be annexed to the United States! The United States Senate rejected the annexation treaty, although a majority of Dominicans voted for it.

The little republic then plunged into a period of confusion. Revolutions and dictators brought it to the edge of ruin. A huge sum was owed to European countries who were insisting on payment. Finally the Dominican authorities asked the United States to take over its financial affairs. An American official was sent to the bankrupt country in 1905 to assume charge of its finances, and things immediately changed for the better. Later the United States sent a force of Marines to take control so that there would be order in the republic. The Dominicans bitterly resented this, although the country was greatly improved under a stable government. The Americans withdrew in 1924, leaving the Dominicans to govern themselves.

THIS MAGNIFICENT SHRINE in the interior of the cathedral at Ciudad Trujillo is the tomb of Columbus. A bronze casket may hold the remains of the great man.

Galloway

Today the Dominican Republic has an orderly government under a strong-handed dictator-president. Although the peasants are very poor and largely uneducated, the country is at peace and fairly well managed. Dominicans are still largely Spanish although most of them have a Negro strain.

COLUMBUS WAS BURIED IN SANTO DOMINGO

The capital of the Dominican Republic is the first city founded in the New World. Known for centuries as Santo Domingo, a recent president named it Ciudad (city) Trujillo (troo-hee'-yoh) after himself. This old city has seen much history in its day. Many of the old buildings of the 1500's are still used. The ancient cathedral may hold the remains of Columbus who wanted his last resting place to be in Santo Domingo.

There is an interesting story about the remains of Columbus. As he had wished, his body was sent from Spain and buried inside the cathedral. When the colony was ceded to France in 1795, Spain moved what was believed to be his casket from Santo Domingo to Havana, then to Seville. When the cathedral at Santo Domingo was being repaired, a lead casket was found marked, "Cristóbal Colón, Primer Almirante" (Christopher Columbus, First Admiral). A large number of witnesses who saw the second casket opened were convinced that it held the remains of the great explorer. If this is true, Christopher Columbus undoubtedly rests where he desired.

Are You a Careful Reader?   Test Yourself!

I. Supply the correct word for each blank:

1. The island of .... contains the two republics of .... and the ... .
2. Haiti was founded as a colony by the .... , but the population was largely ....
because of the many .... on the island.
3. The .... revolted against the French and established a .... in Haiti.
4. The Spanish colony in the .... end of the island was conquered by the .... ,
but finally emerged as the independent ... .
5. Intervention by the ... . in Haiti and the Dominican Republic benefited
these two countries, but aroused fear and distrust.

II. Match the following words and statements:

1. Dominicans	a. brother-in-law of Napoleon who headed the French Army in Haiti
2. Saint Domingue	
3. Sans Souci	b. French name for Haiti when it was a colony
4. Ciudad Trujillo	c. capital of the republic in the eastern part of the island
5. Christophe	d. capital of the republic in the western end of the island
6. Dessalines	e. president of Haiti
7. Santo Domingo	f. Negro leader of a revolt against France
8. Port-au-Prince	g. people who live in the eastern end of the island
9. Toussaint	h. Negro king of Haiti who lived in royal splendor
10. Le Clerc	i. ruler of France
	j. palace built by Henri Christophe
	k. original Spanish name for capital of the Dominican Republic
	l. follower of Toussaint who established the Republic of Haiti

Food for Thought and Discussion

1. Are the qualities that make great men restricted to any one race? What qualities of leadership did Toussaint and Christophe show?

2. Do you believe that intervention of the United States in the affairs of Haiti and the Dominican Republic was necessary? What might have happened if we had not intervened?

Chapter 22

Colonial Cuba Becomes a Free and Prosperous Republic

TRAVELERS from the United States to Cuba can watch the skyline of Havana rise from the sparkling blue waters of the Caribbean. The golden dome of the new capitol building glitters in the tropical sun and the city makes a romantic picture against the low green hills rising beyond it. Many people from the United States take winter cruises to this beautiful isle where they can bask in the warm sun far away from winter's snow and cold. Havana is only about 100 miles from Florida and 1000 miles from New York City.

NATURE HAS BEEN GENEROUS TO CUBA

Cuba is one of the larger islands of the world and would stretch from New York to Chicago if set upon the United States. Much of its land is gently rolling plain, except for hills along the northwestern coast and a much higher range in the eastern end. Cuba has warm winters and hot summers with no frost or snow. Rich soil, tropical climate, and plenty of rainfall combine to make Cuba a perfect place to grow the tobacco and sugar for which it is famous.

Cuba's irregular coastline has given it the name, "island of a hundred harbors." In the days of the buccaneers, the many bays and inlets were fine hiding places for their ships and men. Havana and Santiago are both situated on the shores of deeply indented bays which make fine natural seaports.

HAVANA IS A MODERN CAPITAL WITH A ROMANTIC PAST

Ships bound for Havana sail past the massive fortress, Morro Castle, which guards the bottleneck entrance to the harbor. Its grim, gray walls are a reminder of the days when Havana had to protect herself against attack by English and French rivals. There is a legend that all ships used to bow to the fortress as they came by. That custom was probably due to the rip tide at the harbor entrance which still causes sailing boats to make a polite curtsy as they strike it.

One of the first sights the tourist sees when he lands is the Prado, beautiful main street of Havana, with its shaded center parkway and its fine modern buildings. At the far end is the magnificent new capitol building whose gold dome can be seen for miles around. The modern section of Havana is like any large city of the United States, but old Havana is not far away. In the narrow streets of the old section, houses with grilled windows are built flush with the sidewalk in the Spanish fashion. In the dignified and ancient cathedral can be seen the niche where the supposed remains of Columbus once rested. There was great bitterness between Cuba and Santo Domingo over the question of who actually had the famous man's remains. The casket was removed from the cathedral in Havana and sent to Spain when Cuba became independent.

Havana is more than a tourist center and capital city. It is the most important shipping center in the whole Caribbean. In normal times millions of tons of cargo pass through its busy harbor. Today, the United States is Cuba's best customer.

CUBA HAS MILES OF ROADS

Cuba is one Caribbean country where travelers might be glad to have their own cars with them, for they can travel on good roads over the beautiful countryside. There is a fine new concrete highway running almost the full length of the island, from west of Havana to the city of Santiago at the far eastern end. The Cuban countryside does not have the spectacular beauty of Guatemala, but the rolling land, like one vast garden, has a charm of its own. Great fields of sugar cane stretch like a pale green sea in all directions. Sometimes there are tobacco fields and orange and pineapple groves, as well as vegetable gardens. Everywhere the Cuban landscape is dotted with the tall and stately royal palms which resemble huge feather dusters standing on end.

Santiago has not been modernized like Havana and still has the charm of an old Spanish town. The streets of pink, yellow, and blue stucco houses topped by red tiled roofs delight the visitor. There is an old plaza built by the first governor of Cuba, where people may sit in the shade and listen to band concerts or the music of guitars. Cuba's richest sugar region is in the eastern end of the island where Santiago is located.

CUBA REMAINS A SPANISH COLONY IN THE 1800'S

Let us pick up the story of Cuba where we left it in colonial days. Cuba did not win her independence from Spain with the rest of the Spanish colonies. Of Spain's great empire in the New World, Puerto Rico and Cuba remained loyal to the mother country. One reason is that the islands were isolated from the mainland countries and revolutionary ideas were easier to keep out. Also, the colonists feared the great numbers of Negro slaves on

Sawders

BEAUTIFUL HAVANA is shown here with its famous boulevard, the Prado. In the distance you can see ancient Morro Castle, which guards the bottleneck entrance to the harbor.

the island. They knew of the massacres in Haiti and preferred to continue under the protection of Spain rather than risk revolts of their slaves.

Spain did not learn by the loss of her other colonies. In her attempt to keep control of Cuba, she tightened her rule. The captain-general was given complete power over Cubans and a large army was kept on the island. Spanish officials were dishonest and overbearing; taxes were heavy. The number of slaves increased, although many Cubans wanted to see the end of slavery on the island.

Patriotic Cubans were aroused by Spain's treatment and began to talk in favor of independence. Some wanted to become part of the United States. The spirit of freedom grew in

Cuba in spite of Spain's attempts to crush it. Revolutionary clubs were formed to work for independence, and uprisings became more and more frequent. In 1868, a revolt broke out which lasted for ten years. Spain promised reforms, but except for the abolition of slavery, conditions were no better.

"CUBA LIBRE!" BECOMES THE WATCHWORD

The patriots working for Cuban independence took up the battle cry of "Cuba Libre!" or "Free Cuba!" One of their great leaders was José Martí (ho-say' mar-tee'), who has been called the soul of the Cuban revolution. From the time he was a boy he had spoken and written against the tyranny of Spain. Most of his life was spent in exile because he did not dare return to his native land. He

237

worked unceasingly among other exiled Cubans in the United States and Central America in planning for a revolution. As a newspaperman in New York, he aroused the sympathy of Americans for Cuba's unhappy plight.

In 1895, the revolutionists issued a declaration of independence and Martí landed with his followers in Cuba to aid them. Although he was a bookish man, not a soldier, he rode at the head of the army to inspire them and show his loyalty to the cause. He was shot by the Spaniards and became a martyr to Cuban freedom. The death of Martí aroused the Cuban people as nothing else could have done. The revolt spread, and soon all Cuba was in the grip of a bloody war. The Spanish government became worried for fear it would lose this last large colony in the Caribbean. General Weyler, nicknamed "The Butcher," was sent to subdue the revolt in Cuba. Stories of his cruel treatment of the people filled the newspapers of the United States. Americans were horrified and clamored for our government to free Cuba from Spain. They were joined by owners of sugar plantations on the island whose property was being destroyed by the revolutionists.

AN EXPLOSION TOUCHES OFF THE SPANISH–AMERICAN WAR

Suddenly the whole situation was touched off by the blowing-up of an American battleship, the *Maine*, which was in the harbor at Havana. Two hundred American sailors were killed. What caused the explosion has never been discovered, but the United States blamed Spanish officials. Since the last thing Spain wanted was war with the United States, it is doubtful whether she was responsible. To a nation already angered at the mistreatment of Cuba, the sinking of the *Maine* was the last straw. War was declared against Spain in 1898 with the understanding that Cuba was to be made a free republic. Cuba and the Philippines, which belonged to Spain, were invaded by our forces.

The war ended in a speedy victory for the United States. The strong young country fighting at her own doorstep had an advantage over a weakened Spain fighting from across the Atlantic. Perhaps you have read stories of Theodore Roosevelt and his "Rough Riders" from the West who won the battle of San Juan Hill near Santiago. Admiral Dewey captured the harbor of Manila in the Philippines in a naval victory over the Spanish fleet. In 1899, Spain ratified a peace treaty by which she gave up all claim to Cuba. She also signed over the last of her great colonial empire to the United States — the Philippine Islands in the Pacific and Puerto Rico in the Caribbean.

CUBA BECOMES AN INDEPENDENT REPUBLIC

The United States had pledged Cuba her freedom at the end of the war, but it would have been unkind to have set her adrift alone in 1899. Starvation and disease were killing her people, the land was torn up by war, and the Cubans had had no experience in self-government. For almost three years Cuba remained under American control while order was established on the island. Towns were built and sewer and water systems installed. Schools were started and the peasants were sent back to the homes from which they had fled. For the first time, Cubans lived under

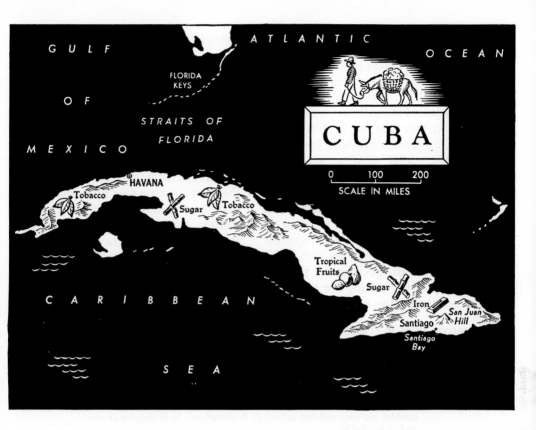

Map labels:
GULF OF MEXICO
ATLANTIC OCEAN
FLORIDA KEYS
STRAITS OF FLORIDA
HAVANA
Tobacco
Sugar
Tobacco
Tropical Fruits
Sugar
Iron
Santiago
San Juan Hill
Santiago Bay
CARIBBEAN SEA

CUBA

0   100   200
SCALE IN MILES

an honest and efficient government. Americans working with Cubans wiped out the dread yellow fever which claimed so many lives each year.

At the end of two and a half years the Republic of Cuba held her first presidential election under the new constitution. An able and educated man, Tomás Estrada Palma (toh-mahs' es-trah'dah pahl'mah), was chosen to be the first president. To the surprise of Europe and the rest of Latin America, American forces withdrew and left Cuba to stand on her own feet. Probably never before in the history of the world has a strong power fought for the territory of a weaker nation, only to let it go free. The United States had an understanding with Cuba that she would protect her from foreign nations, and from uprisings in her own country, which we have done several times.

CUBA IS A PROSPEROUS COUNTRY

Although Cuba was given a better start as a republic than other Latin American states, less than three years of aid were not enough for a country used to centuries of dishonest government. President Estrada Palma had this in mind when he said that Cuba was a republic without citizens. Many politicians were waiting to get government jobs and start the graft and corruption over again. Elections were often dishonest and officials were extravagant.

President Machado (mah-chah'do), who started out well in 1924, turned out to be a dictator of the worst type. He ruled with a hand of iron for nine years. In spite of the world-wide depression and Cuban poverty, his government was extravagant. But in 1933 Machado was overthrown, and after a period of confusion, a new Constitution was adopted in 1940. The new Constitution provides for honest elections, social security, safeguards for labor, and other reforms.

It is safe to say that Cuba has made more progress during her fifty years of independence than she made in all the three hundred years of Spanish rule. Of course, there are still many problems for the government to work out, but the same thing can be said of our own and other countries.

YELLOW FEVER IS CONQUERED IN CUBA

Ever since white men came to the New World, yellow fever had been a dreaded disease of the tropical countries. The British governor of Jamaica figured on losing one man in every five among the soldiers stationed on the island. Puerto Bello on the Isthmus of Panama was known as the worst pest-hole in the colonies. When the French attempted to build a canal they lost so many men by yellow fever that the cemeteries were filled with its victims. In the Spanish-American War more American boys were killed by yellow fever and malaria than by bullets.

After the war, Cubans and Americans were determined to conquer yellow fever. This was before the building of the Panama Canal. No one knew what caused yellow fever nor how it was carried. Some sus-

CUBA'S CAPITOL BUILDING may look familiar to you because it resembles our own national capitol at Washington. It is situated at one end of the Prado.

Roberts

pected that night air was responsible. A Cuban doctor, Carlos Finlay, believed that it was carried by the many mosquitoes which bred in the swamps and the unclean tropical towns, but he was not able to prove it. It remained for two American doctors to prove by experiment on human beings that this theory was right — Colonel William Gorgas, in charge of sanitation in Cuba, and Doctor Walter Reed. The remedy, then, was to wipe out mosquitoes wherever they were found. Havana soon became one of the most healthful cities in Latin America. Other nations began to follow suit and for the first time yellow fever was under control in the civilized parts of the tropics.

CUBA IS THE SUGAR BOWL OF THE WORLD

Men who meet each other on the street in Cuba ask, "What is sugar worth today?" So many millions of tons of sugar are produced in Cuba that it is a part of Cuban life. Upon this huge industry men's jobs depend; railroads and mills are run and ships are loaded because of it. If the crop is large, the children may get new shoes and the government may build more schools. All Cuba prospers when the sugar sells for a good price; when it does not, Cuba suffers.

Sugar has been grown in Cuba since the time when Spanish explorers first brought it from the Canary Islands. The countries of Europe were hungry for the sweet food from her fields, but it was not until the 1700's that the island became important as a sugar producer. Today Cuba can produce more sugar to the acre more cheaply than any other country in the world. Cuba has the capacity to produce 10,000,000 tons of sugar yearly, more

than is used in the entire United States! We are Cuba's best customer, but since we also grow sugar, we use only part of her sugar crop.

The sugar industry, like the banana industry, is well organized and efficiently run. The sugar companies have houses, hospitals, and even schools for the workers on their plantations. Cuttings of cane are planted and grow rapidly in the summer rainy season. During the dry winter season the fields of cane mature and sweeten. At harvest time the laborers strip the long leaves off the stalk and leave them on the ground to rot and fertilize next year's crop. The stalks are cut very close to the ground with long knives, and taken in oxcarts to the railroad. Here they are shipped to the mills so that the sweet juice can be pressed out and sugar made. Some large plantations have their own mills for refining sugar.

Because it was a one-crop country, Cuba suffered when the depression came. She could not sell her sugar for enough to buy food and clothing for the plantation workers. The government encouraged farmers to raise more corn and vegetables so that Cubans would not have to depend on the sugar market for money to buy food. Even the big plantations are growing food for the workers. Certainly Cuba's people need not be hungry in this rich land!

HAVANA'S CIGARS ARE FAMOUS

Cuba is known for her fine tobaccos. Columbus noticed that the natives of this island had a peculiar custom. They rolled the dried leaves of a weed into a cylinder, put one end in their mouths and set fire to the other end. The rolls were called "tabacos."

Galloway

SUGAR is Cuba's chief crop. Here we see Cubans stripping the leaves from the tall sugar cane with their machetes before they cut it. The cane is then tied in bundles like the one shown at the right.

Tobacco is grown in the higher country of Cuba, most of it at the western end of the island. The land and the plants are carefully tended and some of the famous fields produce leaves of such quality that they bring several dollars a pound. Most of the cigar factories are in Havana. Men and women make the cigars by hand, and because it is a monotonous job, a man is often hired to read to them during the day!

THE CUBANS LOVE SPORTS

The Cubans have a national ball game called *jai-alai* (hiy-ah-liy′), which is one of the fastest games in the world. It is similar to handball, but the players catch the ball in long baskets strapped to their wrists. In returning the ball, they hurl it against the wall of the court with terrific speed. *Jai-alai* requires endurance, skill, strong muscles, and fast foot work. Baseball is another favorite sport of the Cubans and they are excellent players.

Bullfighting is no longer allowed in Cuba, but many rural Cubans enjoy cockfighting. Fierce cocks of a fighting strain are bred for this purpose. People pay admission and bet on the outcome just as Americans do at prizefights.

THE CARNIVAL IS CUBA'S NATIONAL FIESTA

Cubans, like other Latin Americans, love a *fiesta*, and the carnival is the big *fiesta* of the year. *Carne vale* means "farewell to meat," and carnival days are the last days of meat-eating and pleasure before the long fast between Lent and Easter which is observed in Catholic countries. The whole island takes part in the celebration. In the little villages the queen of the carnival is given a *fiesta* and all the rural folk dance the rumba in her honor. You may not have known that the rumba with its slow rhythm is the native dance of Cuba. In Havana the carnival, with its king and queen and its masquerade ball and confetti, is an Americanized version of the old Cuban *fiesta*.

Are You a Careful Reader?   Test Yourself!

I. Can you supply the correct word for each blank?

1. .... and .... were the only colonies which remained loyal to Spain.
2. One of the great leaders for Cuban independence was .....
3. The immediate cause of the Spanish-American War was the blowing up of the battleship, ..., in the harbor of .....
4. The Philippines became an American possession after the war because Admiral .... had captured .... in a great naval victory.
5. A Cuban doctor, ..., advanced the theory that malaria and yellow fever were carried by mosquitoes. This was proved by two American doctors, ... and .....

II. Which is the best answer?

1. The movement for independence was delayed in Cuba because: (*a*) Bolívar did not visit the island colonies of Spain; (*b*) landowners were willing to remain under Spanish rule because they feared slave uprisings; (*c*) Spain's rule was weak after the loss of her other colonies.
2. After the rest of Spanish America became independent: (*a*) Spain allowed self-government in Cuba and freed the slaves; (*b*) Spain governed Cuba very efficiently and wisely; (*c*) Spain tightened her rule on Cuba and imposed heavier taxes.
3. The United States went to war to free Cuba because: (*a*) Americans were gen-

JAI-ALAI, claimed to be the fastest game in the world, is played here by two experts from Cuba. The odd-looking things on their hands are the baskets with which they catch and return the ball with lightning speed.

International News

uinely horrified at the cruel treatment of the Cubans and concerned over the destruction of American-owned sugar plantations; (b) Spain was a strong power and was threatening to use Cuba as a base to attack us; (c) the Monroe Doctrine warned European powers not to interfere in the Western Hemisphere.

4. At the end of the war the United States: (a) granted independence to Cuba and Puerto Rico; (b) helped Cuba to prepare for self-government, then granted her independence; (c) kept Cuba and Puerto Rico as colonies to be used as defense bases.

5. One of the problems of sugar-growing Cuba is: (a) to increase the output of sugar; (b) to raise the price of sugar; (c) to develop other crops so that the people will not be entirely dependent on the market for sugar.

Food for Thought and Discussion

1. Do you think Cuba would have made a failure of self-government if the United States had not helped to establish order on the island? Why?

2. Do you think the United States was wrong to reserve the right to intervene in case of revolution in Cuba? Why?

3. What could the Cuban government do to insure food for the cane-workers when the sugar market fails?

Looking Backward

You have now finished the story of the nine small republics of the Caribbean. You can test your understanding of the Caribbean region by answering the questions given in the unit preview on page 179. Your teacher may wish to discuss them in class or may ask you to use them for written work. Can you answer them without looking in Part V?

Interesting Things to Do

1. Can you name the Caribbean republics and their capitals? Make a game called *Latin American Countries and Capitals* and try it out on the class. You can add to it as you study South American countries.

2. Make a chart comparing all Caribbean nations. List in parallel columns important facts of their history, their government, products, type of population (whites, *mestizos*, Indians, etc.).

3. Get better acquainted with one of these men and tell the class about him: Diego Columbus, Toussaint L'Ouverture, Dessalines, Henri Christophe, William Walker, José Martí, Machado, Batista.

4. Find an article on one of the Caribbean countries in the *National Geographic* and report on it to the class.

5. The *machete* of the peon is a knife of many uses. Find out all you can about this knife of the tropics and how it is used.

6. Learn more about the fight against yellow fever and malaria and the men who were responsible for its control, such as Walter Reed and Colonel Gorgas; or report on the hookworm and its effects.

7. If you are interested in the construction of the Panama Canal, study one of these topics and report on it to the class: Colonel Goethals and his work on the Canal; the story of the Gaillard Cut; the lock system at the Canal and how it works.

8. Make a study of Cuban sugar from the plantation to the market, of the great banana industry of Honduras, of the coconut, gum, or vanilla industry.

9. Write one of the following: the diary of a slave freed by the Haitian revolution; the diary of a schoolboy of Cuba during or after the Spanish-American War; a newspaper article announcing the opening of the Panama Canal; a radio play telling the story of the Panama Canal.

10. Plan a debate on the subject, "Resolved: That the United States was justified in her intervention in the domestic affairs of the Caribbean nations."

11. Take the class on a tour through one of these cities: Balboa, Panama City, Havana, Santo Domingo, San José.

12. Read about the Quiché Indians of Guatemala and report to the class, showing pictures if possible.

Interesting Books to Read

For Further Information

Burbank, Addison, *Guatemala Profile*. Coward-McCann. History, geography, and customs combined.

Franck, Harry, *Sky Roaming Above Two Continents*. Stokes. A survey of Caribbean geography.

Gibson, Olive, *Isle of a Hundred Harbors*. Bruce Humphries. History and description of Cuba.

Nicolay, Helen, *Bridge of Water*. Appleton-Century. Panama from the first settlement to the present.

For Pleasure

Beach, Rex, *Jungle Gold*. Farrar. Exciting novel of banana plantations in Honduras.

Newcombe, Covelle, *Black Fire*. Longmans. A story of Haiti and Henri Christophe.

Skinner, Constance Lindsey, *The Tiger Who Walks Alone*. Macmillan. Adventures of a Nicaraguan hero.

Von Hagen, Victor, *Jungle in the Clouds*. Duell, Sloan, and Pearce. A naturalist's story of the search for the quetzal bird.

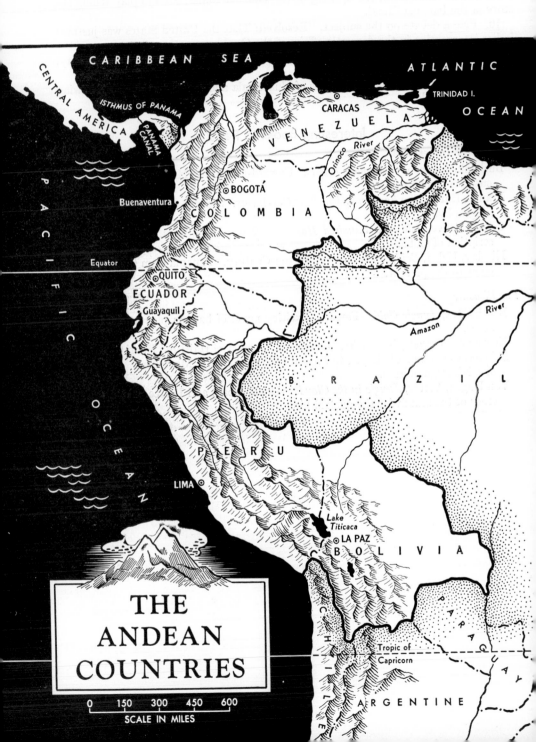

CARIBBEAN SEA

ATLANTIC

CENTRAL AMERICA

ISTHMUS OF PANAMA

PANAMA CANAL

CARACAS

TRINIDAD I.

OCEAN

V E N E Z U E L A

Orinoco River

PACIFIC

Buenaventura

BOGOTÁ

C O L O M B I A

Equator

QUITO

ECUADOR

Guayaquil

Amazon River

B R A Z I L

O C E A N

P E R U

LIMA

Lake Titicaca

LA PAZ

B O L I V I A

PARAGUAY

CHILE

Tropic of Capricorn

ARGENTINE

THE ANDEAN COUNTRIES

| 0 | 150 | 300 | 450 | 600 |

SCALE IN MILES

MODERN NATIONS OF LATIN AMERICA

WHAT WOULD SIMÓN BOLÍVAR see if he should come back today? If the Great Liberator should visit the lands which he freed, he would find five separate republics instead of the strong, united nation of which he had dreamed. He would see that what he had feared had come to pass — that the people, unready to govern themselves, had fallen under the power of one military dictator after another. He would rejoice that Colombia has progressed a long way toward democracy, and that Venezuela, the land of his birth, is becoming a more progressive nation.

He would see the Indians of the Andes living in poverty and ignorance just as in his day, but there would be a gleam of hope for these neglected people. Governments are at last realizing the need to help their native populations. Bolívar would look in amazement at the soaring planes which reach the most isolated places, and at the railroads which scale the Andean heights. He would marvel also at the modern copper and tin smelters in Peru and Bolivia and at the great new docks in the old port cities.

On the whole, we believe that Simón Bolívar would see a promising future for the countries he had freed and would feel that his hardships and sacrifices were not in vain.

On the opposite page is a map of the five republics of Bolívar, often called the Andean countries. Name the five countries of the Torrid Zone through which the Andes pass. Find their capitals. Within this part there is a separate map for each of the countries. Look at the maps on pages 257, 271, 283, 287, and 295. Find the important seaports. Can you locate also the Magdalena, the Cauca, the Orinoco, and Guayas Rivers?

As you read, these questions will help you to keep in mind some of the important points in Part VI:

1. Why is transportation a problem in the Andean nations?

2. Why is democracy as we know it impossible at present in most of these countries?

3. What can be done by the Andean nations to solve the Indian problem?

Chapter 23

The Andean Nations Have a Common Background and Common Problems

---

"HE WHO AIDS a revolution plows the sea." These bitter words were spoken by the Great Liberator after the battle of Ayacucho had ended Spain's rule in South America. They show Bolívar's belief that the revolution to which he had devoted his life had been wasted effort. He had lost his faith in his fellow men. What had happened during these six years to the man who had ridden in triumph through flower-strewn streets and been hailed as Liberator by thousands of grateful people?

You remember how Bolívar freed his native Venezuela and neighboring New Granada from Spanish rule and united them in the Republic of Great Colombia. You recall that when Quito was freed by Bolívar it, too, was added to the new republic. You also know that the troops of Bolívar and those of San Martín defeated the Spaniards in the decisive battle of Ayacucho. But you have not read the rest of Bolívar's story nor what happened in the countries which he freed. In a letter to a friend the Liberator once said, "I fear peace more than war." He knew only too well the difficulties that lay in the path of freedom. Let us turn back to the year 1824 in South America.

BOLIVIA AND PERU RESENT THE AUTHORITY OF BOLÍVAR

Although Ayacucho delivered the great viceroyalty of Peru into the hands of the revolutionists, there were still Spanish troops in possession of Upper Peru. In 1825, General Sucre, hero of Ayacucho, marched his troops on to the high plateau of this mountain province and expelled the royalists from that area as well. Independence was proclaimed, and the new nation was named the Republic of Bolívar. This name was later changed to Bolivia. According to Bolívar's wishes, Sucre was elected president by a grateful congress and the capital was renamed Sucre in honor of that gallant general.

Although Sucre was an able and self-sacrificing leader, there was resentment in Bolivia at being governed by a Venezuelan. There was also fear on the part of Bolivian leaders that Great Colombia had designs on their new republic because Colombian troops were still quartered there. After several years of disorder a rebellion broke out against Sucre. The rulers of Peru also sent an army against him. Sucre resigned the presidency and withdrew from the country with his Colombian troops. Andrés Santa

Black Star

STATUES OF BOLÍVAR are seen everywhere in South America, especially in Venezuela, the land of his birth. This one shows the Great Liberator astride his horse, doffing his hat to admiring throngs.

Cruz (ahn-drays′ sahn′tah croos′), an outstanding political leader, was elected president at Sucre's recommendation.

Meanwhile, Bolívar in Peru was experiencing much the same difficulties as Sucre. He had remained in that country to organize the new government. Because Colombian troops were still in Peru, people began to fear that Bolívar planned to add their country to his republic of Great Colombia, making himself dictator for life. There were some grounds for this fear because it was well known that Bolívar believed in a strong rule for these infant republics. At any rate, when he was called north by trouble in Great Colombia, the Peruvian government ordered Colombian troops to leave the country. A new constitution was adopted and a new government, in which Bolívar had no part, was set up in Lima.

GREAT COLOMBIA BREAKS UP AND BOLÍVAR DIES ON HIS WAY TO EXILE

When Bolívar returned to Bogotá (boh-goh-tah′) in 1826, he found that ambitious political leaders had been stirring up trouble against him. His old comrade, Páez, who had led the *llaneros* against the Spaniards, plotted to separate Venezuela from Great Colombia. In Quito, another old friend, General Flores, led a group who were jealous of the government at Bogotá and wanted independence for their own region. Great Colombia was united in name only; actually it was riddled with jealousy and local intrigues.

Bolívar might have prevented this trouble if he had been able to remain in Great Colombia, but while he was liberating Peru he had left the government in the hands of the vice-president, General Santander. Santander himself was suspicious of Bolívar's ambitions and headed the people who opposed him. There was fear that Bolívar might try to make himself king. So strong was the feeling against him that an attempt was made to assassinate him! In spite of the disloyalty and plotting on the part of his former friends, Bolívar labored until 1830 to hold his republic together. But first Venezuela, led by Páez, declared itself independent. Later, Quito, under the leadership of Flores, followed suit.

Years of hardship in endless campaigns had ruined Bolívar's health. His once great fortune had been spent in financing the revolution. Ill with tuberculosis and discouraged with the failure of his republic, Bolívar gave up the hopeless struggle. He resigned as president of Great Colombia in 1830 and set out to spend the rest of his life in exile. At the seaport of Santa Marta he became too ill to go on and was taken to the home of a friend. But his troubles were not yet over. When word came of the shooting of his loyal comrade Sucre by an enemy, it was the last blow to Bolívar, for he had loved the dashing young general. So the man who had given freedom to five countries spent his last days in a humble cottage, broken in health and spirit. What humiliation his proud spirit must have suffered as he lay there! The people who had lavished upon him the highest honors let him die unhonored and forgotten. Yet his last thoughts were for the harmony and unity of the people for whose liberty he had fought. "If my death should unite them, I shall go to my grave with a calm and contented mind."

We see now why Bolívar died believing that he had merely plowed the waters of the sea. The people to whom he had given liberty had not yet learned how to become nations. This part of our book will tell the stories of the five republics of Latin America which owe their independence to Bolívar and his fellow soldier patriots.

THE ANDEAN COUNTRIES SHARE THE SAME GEOGRAPHICAL PATTERN

The tropical countries of Colombia, Venezuela, Ecuador, Peru, and Bolivia are often called the Andean countries because they are crossed by the great cordillera which forms the mighty backbone of the continent. Even in Venezuela, which is considerably east of the main ranges, a spur of the cordillera curves across to the Caribbean coast and continues eastward in a great ridge for many miles.[1] This rocky barrier is responsible for many similarities in the five countries. Their geography and their products are much alike. In all the countries the mountains have created serious transportation problems and prevented development of agriculture and trade. The mountain regions

[1] To refresh your memory on the geography of the Andean countries, turn to Chapter 2, pages 16 to 25.

have been so isolated from one another and from the coast that people have clung to their local leaders instead of growing into closely united nations.

Writers often speak of three Perus or three Ecuadors when they are describing the Andean countries. They are referring to the regions which we have learned are common to these five countries — the hot, tropical coasts, the cool highlands, and the steaming jungles or grasslands of the interior. The highland or sierra is the heart of the Andean countries. The great ranges of the Andes, crisscrossed by smaller ranges, form a mountain region from 200 to 500 miles wide. In the valleys and plateaus between the mountains live most of the people. With the exception of Lima, Peru, the capital cities of the Andean countries are located in the highlands. It is in these mountain districts that the customs and culture typical of the five countries have developed.

The coastlands are generally hot and wet like the coasts of Central America. The one exception is Peru whose coast, you remember, is cool and dry. Lofty Bolivia has no coast at all. Many important port cities are located on the Caribbean and Pacific coasts of the Andean countries, but few white people live in the unhealthful climate of the tropical coastland. All the Andean countries border on the great Amazonian jungle which covers the interior of South America. One half to three fifths of every country is occupied by the jungle lowlands. In Venezuela and Colombia and also in Bolivia, part of the interior region is grassy prairie instead of jungle. For the most part these regions are undeveloped.

Like the countries of Central America, the Andean nations are chiefly agricultural and depend on foreign trade to give them the manufactured articles they need. In addition to agricultural products, oil, tin, copper, and other minerals are exported in large quantities chiefly to the United States and Great Britain. We have mentioned the coffee grown in the highlands of Colombia and Venezuela, and the bananas produced in Colombia's Caribbean lowlands. Sugar and cotton are also grown in these countries for home use, while in Peru these commodities raised on the coast plantations are that country's most valuable export. The lowlands of Ecuador have long been famous for cacao, and coffee has become more important in recent years.

TRANSPORTATION IS AN IMPORTANT PROBLEM IN ALL ANDEAN COUNTRIES

The mighty Andes appear to defy man to conquer them. Like a great wall they shut off the interior regions from the highland valleys and the seacoast. They make transportation of goods and of people from one region to the other and from one country to the next exceedingly difficult. In Chapter 2 we saw how difficult it is to make a trip between Iquitos in eastern Peru to Lima in western Peru. It is easy to understand why most people in Ecuador or Peru have never seen the great tropical region beyond the mountains.

The mountain barrier is so formidable that only one railroad in all South America crosses its full width, and that is the trans-Andean railroad between Chile and Argentina. The highest railroad in the world is the Central Railroad of Peru which cuts across the Andes at a height of 15,665

Galloway

THIS TRAIN IN THE ANDES between Chile and Argentina is going through one of the snow sheds which are built over the tracks to protect them from heavy snows and snow slides. Some of these sheds extend for miles.

feet. Compare this to the highest railway across the Rockies, which is only 8000 feet above the sea. It is estimated that one of Peru's railways cost $200,000 a mile to build. In most cases it does not pay to operate these mountain roads because of the original construction cost and because of the enormous expense of keeping them running.

The building of roads for wagons or automobiles across the mountains is almost as difficult as the construction of railroads. Peru has an important highway from Lima up over the Andes to the tropical region on the eastern mountain slopes. Venezuela has a road connecting her mountain cities and rich agricultural regions with the capital. Road mileage is slowly increasing in most of the Andean countries, and isolated communities are being connected for the first time.

The commonest form of transportation in all the countries is by llama or mule train. Loaded with goods, these sturdy animals wind over trails made hundreds of years ago as they carry goods to railroad or river boat. The trails are often paths worn out of the rocky mountain-sides. Sometimes an unlucky mule makes a misstep and plunges into the chasm below.

The airplane has done a great deal to stimulate trade and travel in the Andean countries, just as it has done in Central America. Practically every important town is connected with the capital or the coast by airlines. Businessmen in Lima and Bogotá think nothing of flying to New York. Air travel saves weeks of time between mountain and seacoast cities.

THREE RACES MAKE UP THE POPULATION OF THE ANDEAN COUNTRIES

Just as in colonial days, a small group of pure-blooded whites of European descent forms the upper class in the Andean countries. They still hold most of the land, most of the wealth, and most of the political power. Colombia has the largest number of Spanish people. They form about one third of the population, while in the other countries one tenth or less are of unmixed European ancestry. These people own the great estates originally founded in colonial days. They prefer to live in the cities or in Europe on the income from their lands.

We have already mentioned the large Negro and mulatto population on the hot Caribbean coasts. Probably 15 to 20 per cent of the population of Venezuela and Colombia and of the lowlands of Ecuador is made up of Negro people. In fact, the port of Buenaventura (bway-nah-ven-too'-rah) on Colombia's Pacific coast is almost entirely Negro, mulatto, or *zambo*. As laborers and servants, they do work which the white man cannot do in the tropics.

In the high valleys of Peru, Ecuador, and Bolivia live the descendants of the ancient Incas. As in Guatemala, the population of these countries is from one half to two thirds pure-blooded Indian. Like feudal peasants, they till the soil and live together in their own villages, or are bound as peons to the great estates. These millions of brown people speak little or no Spanish, and being unable to read or write, take no part in the political life of the nation. In Colombia and Venezuela pure-blooded Indians are much less numerous.

The *mestizos* make up the largest part of the population in Colombia and Venezuela and the second largest in the other countries. They are the laborers, the miners, the factory workers, the townspeople, and the small businessmen. Their children go to the public schools and are the middle class which every democracy needs if it is to function.

One of the greatest drawbacks to the development of these countries is the small population. Colombia leads with over 11,000,000 people; Peru has a population of 8,000,000; Ecuador has 3,500,000 inhabitants; while huge Bolivia and Venezuela have only about 4,000,000 and 4,500,000 respectively. Few immigrants care to go to the hot coasts where labor is done cheaply by Negroes, or to the highlands where they must compete with the primitive living standards of the Indians.

DEMOCRACY IS DIFFICULT TO ACHIEVE IN THE ANDEAN COUNTRIES

Although each of the five Andean nations has a constitution similar to that of the United States, none of them can truly be called a democracy. That is, if we take democracy to mean government by the people and for the people. When we learn that 50 to 90 per cent of the people cannot read or write, we realize that they are not yet ready for a voice in the government. The land system inherited from Spain has helped to keep the majority of the people little better off than the serfs of the Middle Ages. In the past there have been only two classes of people. There was the small upper class who owned all the land, and there was the large lower class made up of peons who toiled endlessly with no hope of ever owning the land on which they worked. When a large middle class which is neither master nor servant can develop, and when the land is no longer in the hands of a few, there will be hope for democracy in these countries.

Another obstacle to democracy has been the habit of dictatorship. The infant republics of the early 1800's had no experience in governing themselves. The masses of illiterate Indians and *mestizos* were used to strict rule from above. It was easy for strong and ambitious men to gain control of the army and to seize the government by force. Military revolts became a part of the political story of each nation.

Perhaps at one time dictatorship was necessary for these nations-in-the-making. Bolívar and San Martín both knew that strong rule was required for the countries they had freed from Spanish rule. Dictators may have been the only possible stepping-stones from dependence to independence. The best of them aided progress by keeping peace and order and encouraging trade and agriculture; the worst of them involved their countries in bloody wars and squandered their man-power and their wealth. The most progressive of the nations began to throw off the military control of dictators and to elect civilian presidents in orderly fashion. Unfortunately, however, none of the Andean nations has as yet fully emerged from the era of occasional dictatorship.

Hope for democracy in the five countries to which Bolívar gave independence probably lies in the large *mestizo* class. When these people are educated, when they are able to own a fair share of land, then they may take a larger share in the government.

Are You a Careful Reader?   Test Yourself!

I. Supply the correct word for each blank:

1. The first president of Bolivia was ......

2. Remote sections of the Andean countries have been brought closer to civilization by the ......

3. In addition to the Spanish and Indian people, many ..... live in Colombia, Venezuela, and Ecuador.

4. Before democracy can be achieved in the Andean countries there must be a fairer division of the ......

5. A military president often becomes a .... in Latin America.

II. Choose the best answer:

1. The breaking-up of Great Colombia was caused by: (*a*) suspicion of Bolívar's ambitions and petty jealousy; (*b*) its great size which made it hard to govern; (*c*) the disloyalty of Sucre.

2. Bolívar said that he would die happy if: (*a*) Sucre became his successor; (*b*) Bolivia became part of Greater Colombia; (*c*) his death united the Andean countries.

3. It was easy for dictators to gain power in the republics founded by Bolívar because: (*a*) there were many strong generals in Bolívar's army; (*b*) difficulties of transportation made it hard for the people to vote; (*c*) the ignorant masses knew nothing about self-government.

4. There is more democracy in Colombia today than in the other Andean republics because: (*a*) the people are descendants of civilized Indians; (*b*) there is a larger middle class; (*c*) Colombia is a prosperous country.

5. The three regions common to Andean countries are: (*a*) the sierra, the Amazon lowlands, and the tropical coast; (*b*) the coffee, sugar, and banana regions; (*c*) the northern, southern, and central regions.

Food for Thought and Discussion

1. Make a list of all the obstacles to democracy given in Chapter 23. Which are due to geography, which to the colonial system inherited from Spain?
2. Was Bolívar's Great Colombia similar in any way to the Central American federation? Why?
3. Why does the hope for democracy in the Andean republics lie in the *mestizo* middle class rather than in the Spanish upper class or the Indian and Negro lower class?

Chapter 24

We Hail Colombia as a Progressive Nation

A FAMOUS PLACE in the United States received its name because of an episode in Colombia's history! In the early 1700's an English naval squadron under Admiral Vernon besieged the port town of Cartagena. Serving under Vernon was a young lieutenant named Lawrence Washington, who came from the English colony of Virginia in North America. The siege was unsuccessful and Washington later returned to Virginia. He bought a plantation and built on it one of the finest English colonial houses in America. This home he named "Mount Vernon," in honor of the commander

whom he so greatly admired. At his death Lawrence left the estate to his younger half-brother, George Washington.

WE LOOK AT COLOMBIA

The Republic of Colombia, named after the Great Discoverer and given her freedom by the Great Liberator, is today one of the more progressive and enterprising countries in Latin America. In spite of the fact that most Colombians believe the United States to be responsible for the loss of Panama, Colombia is today one of our good neighbors. Her friendship is important to us, not only because she is an American republic, but also because of her trade. Colombia sells us her coffee and other tropical products, and we, in turn, send her manufactured goods. Since Colombia is also nearer to the Panama Canal than any other South American country, we especially need her friendship. You will notice on the map that Colombia is bounded by four South American republics and by two oceans. Note also that it is one of the three countries of the Western Hemisphere which are crossed by the Equator. Colombia is so large that if it were placed upon the southwestern corner of the United States it would cover the states of California, Utah, Nevada, and Arizona. There are over 11,000,000 Colombians. Ninety per cent of them live in the fertile valleys and plateaus of the cordillera.[1]

NEW GRANADA BECOMES AN INDEPENDENT REPUBLIC

When Venezuela and Quito withdrew from the ill-fated Republic of Great Colombia, the middle section was left alone. In 1830, there was formed a new and separate nation of New Granada which also included Panama. Francisco Santander, who had opposed Bolívar's ambitions, became the first president and founder of the infant republic. Santander was not an army general but a lawyer. He was a progressive leader and did a great deal toward encouraging education and opening new schools.

But Santander made many enemies during his administration. In spite of his progressive policies, he was an

[1] Before reading the history of Colombia, turn to pages 18–19 for a review of the geography of this country.

intolerant man who resented all criticism and treated his opponents with great harshness. He was bitterly opposed by the clergy because his government allowed freedom of religion and restricted the powers of the Catholic Church. Although his candidate in the next election was defeated, Santander did not attempt to seize the government, as a dictator might have done.

THE 1840'S MARKED A GOLDEN AGE FOR COLOMBIA

In 1845, an aristocratic and well-educated man who had served in the revolution under Bolívar, was elected president of New Granada. This man was Tomás Cipriano de Mosquera (mohs-kay'rah). He has been compared to Theodore Roosevelt because he had the same qualities of energy, self-confidence, and initiative that made Roosevelt an unusual man. Under Mosquera's capable leadership New Granada made great progress. Industry and education were encouraged and Negro slavery was gradually abolished. Steamboats began to make regular trips on the Magdalena River. Wagon roads were built so that people and goods could move between the interior and the coast.

Toward the end of Mosquera's term, a more liberal party became very strong and in 1849 elected its candidate as the next president. It remained in control of the government most of the time for over thirty years. The period of peace and progress under Mosquera, sometimes called the golden age of New Granada, ended when the Liberals came into power. The republic had until then been governed by a strong central government. The Liberals proceeded to set up in

New Granada a federal system of government somewhat like that of the United States. The republic was divided into a number of partly independent states. The Liberals also carried on a relentless campaign against the Church. In 1853, Church and State were separated. These changes were bitterly opposed by the Conservatives, and many years of warfare between the states and of revolts against the national government followed. New Granada was no longer a nation but a group of quarreling provinces.

NEW GRANADA BECOMES THE REPUBLIC OF COLOMBIA

The man who finally defeated the idea of a federation of states and restored order to the nation was a distinguished writer and lawyer named Rafael Núñez (noo'nyays). After serving for two years as a Liberal president, he began to write many articles in the papers urging the reorganization of the republic, and became the leader of all who wanted a reform in the government. When he was reelected president in 1884, he was faced with a widespread civil war started by the Liberals. It was a year before Núñez succeeded in putting an end to the fighting. In 1886, a new constitution was drawn up under his direction which provided for a strong national government and restored the old authority of the Church, particularly over the schools. This constitution also changed the name of the country to the Republic of Colombia. Núñez then proceeded to develop and strengthen the nation. This intelligent, resourceful man became practically a dictator and controlled the government of Colombia until his death in 1894. Núñez is honored today as one of Colombia's greatest statesmen.

COLOMBIA BECOMES MORE DEMOCRATIC

After an especially bloody Liberal revolt which began in 1899 and lasted three years, Colombians began to realize that thousands of their countrymen had been killed in useless civil wars. The loss of Panama in 1903 was another blow to the country. Wise leaders saw that Colombia must stop her internal strife and work toward becoming a united nation.

Since 1903, Colombia has been comparatively free from revolution and has made great progress. Although there were millions of illiterate people who did not vote, for over forty years Colombia was considered a democratic country because elections were orderly. No dictator seized and held the government by force. Many Colombian presidents were scholars, lawyers, or newspapermen, interested in the welfare of their country. Colombians enjoyed freedom of speech and press and were free to criticize government policies without fear of being clapped into jail. The most active political parties were the Liberals and Conservatives. Their chief disagreement has been over the position of the Catholic Church. Liberals were in control between 1930 and 1948, and during this time Colombia made great progress towards democracy.

There have been several outstanding Liberal presidents in recent years. Enrique Olaya Herrera (oh-la'yah ay-ray'rah), elected in 1930 with the support of many Conservatives, was an able and popular leader, who followed a moderate policy of political and social reform. Alfonso López (loh'pays), elected in 1934, won the enthusiastic support of the common people. It is said that after visiting President Roosevelt in 1934, he became interested in a "new deal" for Colombia. His government did much to aid the workingman, establishing the eight-hour day and workmen's compensation. The constitution was changed to allow religious freedom and make education once more the responsibility of the government rather than of the Church. Under this constitution, the same man cannot be elected twice in succession.

Colombia's record for democracy was broken when a Liberal leader was assassinated in 1948. The Conservative Party was blamed for his death. So many disorders followed that the Liberals refused to vote in the 1950 elections; thus the Conservative president elected did not represent the free choice of a democratic people.

CARTAGENA IS A MODERN PORT AND ANCIENT FORTRESS

A great deal about Colombia and Colombians can be learned from her cities. Travelers sailing into the harbor at Cartagena can see ahead of them the great wall which still surrounds this ancient city. There is a story about this wall. Because Cartagena, like Puerto Bello, was a trading center between Spain and the colonies, it became the prey of buccaneers. Before the siege of Admiral Vernon, this rich city was attacked and looted many times. To fortify it against further attack, the Spaniards had built a wall which was 40 feet high and 50 feet thick! The wall cost $70,000,000 and took 100 years to build. When notice was brought to the king of Spain that it was finally finished, he went to a window and looked out across the Atlantic, saying that he should be able to see such an expensive wall even across the sea! Today you can drive along the top of the old wall and look down upon the weathered churches, tiled roofs, and cobbled plazas of this 400-year-old city.

Cartagena of today is more than an interesting colonial town. It is the port from which much of Colombia's oil is carried to the markets of the world.

A TRIP FROM COAST TO CAPITAL REVEALS COLOMBIA'S ISOLATION

Ocean steamers can sail into the wide mouth of the Magdalena and dock at the tropical port of Barranquilla (bah-rahn-kee'yah), ten miles up the river. Here they pick up the coffee and other products of highland Colombia which have traveled hundreds of miles on barges pushed by river boats. Slow and uncertain as this transportation is, it is still the only route from the highlands to the Caribbean Sea. Even the capital city, Bogotá, is not connected directly with this sea by either road or railroad. Barranquilla is also a port for Pan American planes which fly to and from Miami. From its airfield outside the city planes take off for Bogotá and other inland cities.

The paddle-wheeled river steamers which travel up the river are like the boats which used to ply the Mississippi in the days of Mark Twain. Like the Mississippi, the channel of the Magdalena changes and there is al-

Gendreau

THIS SENTRY BOX on the old wall at Cartagena still stands guard after 400 years. From here sentries used to watch for the buccaneers who preyed on the rich Spanish city.

ways danger of striking a hidden sandbar or a submerged tree. During the dry season navigation is especially difficult because the water in the river is low. When freight boats are stranded, it may be weeks or months before the cargo reaches its destination.

For the first 70 miles or so the river is very wide, then it narrows down so that objects on its banks are easily seen. Negro huts and tiny garden patches appear surrounded by green forest. About 600 miles up the river it is necessary to make a detour around rapids. A narrow-gauge railroad carries passengers and cargo to a point above the rapids. From here a smaller boat continues the journey to the junction of the river and the rail-

Weimer

IN BOGOTÁ a modern building like the one at the left may stand next to an old Spanish building. Notice that the autos run in the center of the street while the trolley cars are at the sides.

road to Bogotá. As you can see by the map, the capital is not on the river, but in the eastern range of the Andes. This last part of the trip is the most exciting, for the train twists and turns and climbs from an altitude of 1500 feet to over 8000 feet in 80 miles!

In colonial days stairsteps were cut out of the rocky flank of the mountain to make a road to the river. You can imagine what a trip this must have been before the days of steam. It is no wonder that two Spanish governors refused to go to Bogotá and stayed throughout their term in Cartagena! Nor is it surprising that goods sent by the route we have just described are doubled in value by the time they reach Bogotá!

BOGOTÁ IS A CITY OF SPANISH PEOPLE AND SPANISH CUSTOMS

Bogotá is built on a high and cool plateau called the Sabana (sah-bah'-nah), where the temperature averages about 58 degrees the year round. The sky is gray and cloudy much of the time. We shiver in the damp air and decide that this is a climate of perpetual autumn rather than one of perpetual spring. The people dress in dark clothes in contrast to the white clothing seen in Barranquilla. In early morning and at night men of the working class wear short woolen ponchos or *ruanas* (roo-ah'nahs) over their shoulders. For three months every fall and three months every spring it rains in Bogotá, making it necessary to carry an umbrella most of the time.

We wonder how this city of 500,000 can exist so far from railroads and ships. Looking at the street-cars and automobiles, we try to picture them coming over the route we have just described. Although there are electric lights, telephones, and modern apartment houses in Bogotá, much of the city has the atmosphere of an old Spanish town. Beautiful churches and old homes tell the story of this city's colonial past.

One of the main streets is named Avenida Jiménez de Quesada after the brave Spaniard who climbed to the plateau in search of El Dorado, and later founded the city. The main Plaza de Bolívar is the center of the city. Here is the old cathedral with its twin towers, and on a corner of the plaza is the national capitol where the congress meets. This is a dignified building with great Grecian columns at the entrance.

On the streets of Bogotá there are no colorful Indians in native costume such as we saw in Guatemala City, nor are there Negro people like those in the coastal ports. What impresses us about the people of the capital city is that, rich or poor, they all appear to be white. We learn that all Bogotanos, from the cultured aristocrat to the humble peon, speak a purer Span-

THE TWIN-TOWERED CATHEDRAL stands on the Plaza de Bolívar in the center of Bogotá. The mountains in the background look down on a modern city whose streetcars and autos do not destroy the charm of an old Spanish town.

Galloway

ish than in most other South American countries. Latin Americans no longer lisp the letters "c" and "z" as they do in Spain, but Bogotá has been so isolated that fewer changes have crept into the original mother tongue.

For the same reason, the social customs of Spain are more strictly followed. Girls are closely chaperoned; women of the upper classes are never seen in cafés and seldom on the streets. On the other hand, the National University on the outskirts of the city has opened its classes to women as well as to men, as is customary elsewhere in South America. This may mean the beginning of more freedom for women in the conservative capital of Colombia.

Men, by contrast, are seen everywhere in Bogotá. It is their custom to gather and talk at cafés, on corners, or in front of newspaper offices where the daily news is written on blackboards. Instead of shaking hands, friends grasp each other by the upper arm as they stand and talk. This custom of the *charla* or chat is a distinctive feature of life in Bogotá. In the late afternoon there are such crowds of men engaged in animated discussion on the main street that all traffic except street-cars is prohibited!

Bogotá has long been known as the Athens of America because of its many writers and poets. It is said that the ability to quote poetry at length was once considered an asset even to a candidate for the presidency! Rafael Nuñez, former president of Colombia, was a poet as well as a politician.

In the mountains near Bogotá are the famous emerald mines of Colombia. They are owned by the government and are the largest deposits in the world. At present they do not add a great deal to the nation's income, because there is not a large demand for emeralds.

MEDELLÍN IS THE SECOND CITY OF COLOMBIA

Medellín (may-day-yeen') is situated northwest of Bogotá on the western slope of the central range above the Cauca River. The valley in which it is situated has a much lower altitude than Bogotá, and the warm semi-tropical climate is very pleasant after the capital's chilly mists. Medellín, a bustling and businesslike town, is the leading manufacturing city of the nation. Cotton and woolen goods, shoes, soap, sugar, and glass are made here.

One of the richest districts of Colombia surrounds the city. Not only is Colombia's finest coffee grown here, but gold is mined in considerable quantities. Most of the gold is obtained by placer mining. It is brought to Medellín, where it is refined and cast into gold bricks. The region about the city is noted for its fine beef cattle, which are white with black ears.

The people of Medellín and the surrounding country are white. Since Spanish settlers found few Indians in this region, the present inhabitants are the original Spanish stock. It is said that many of the early settlers were Jews who had been driven out of Spain. This may explain the energetic qualities of the people, who are more eager to get an education and make a good living than most tropical people. Only a small percentage of the people of Medellín are illiterate. In spite of their businesslike traits, they are typically Spanish in their customs and their devotion to religion.

Weimer

THE PEOPLE OF BOGOTÁ enjoy themselves at the races just as Americans do. Horse racing is a favorite sport in all Latin American countries, and races on Sunday afternoons are a social event.

There is a spirit of rivalry between Bogotá and Medellín. The people of Medellín consider themselves more progressive than the conservative Bogotanos.

CALI AND BUENAVENTURA ARE WESTERN CITIES

The progressive little city of Cali (cah'lee) in the southern or upper end of the beautiful Cauca Valley is connected with Colombia's Pacific port of Buenaventura by both road and railroad. Cali is situated in a region of sugar plantations and cattle ranches, and much of the produce of the upper river valley is sent to Buenaventura by way of this city.

Sugar mills on the plantations make the crude brown sugar called *panela* (pah-nay'lah) which is used throughout Colombia for sweetening.

THE PROBLEM OF TRANSPORTATION IS IMPORTANT IN COLOMBIA

One of Colombia's most pressing problems is that of moving its products to markets. We can understand how the progress of the country is retarded when river freight is delayed for weeks and sometimes months, and injured by exposure to rain and sun. Transportation within Colombia costs more than transportation to New York. For instance, it costs $70 for a ton of wheat to travel from Barranquilla to Bogotá!

More roads and railroads would solve the transportation problem, but both are expensive to build and Colombia is not rich. Construction is difficult, not only because of the high mountain ranges, but because heavy rains bring slides and washouts. It is said that the mountains become moving masses of mud during the rains. Colombia has made some headway in the building of roads. One of the improved automobile roads in Colombia is to be part of the Pan-American Highway. This is the Simón Bolívar Highway, which runs from Caracas in Venezuela to Bogotá, then south to Quito in Ecuador. A road connecting Medellín with the Caribbean near the Panama border is being built through some of the most difficult terrain in South America. As we have learned, there is also a road from Bogotá to Cali which crosses the central cordillera.

Colombia has no such thing as a railroad system. The longest railroad in the country is 350 miles long. Short lines have been built to connect cities with the Magdalena, such as the lines to Medellín and Bogotá. Today there is a railroad connecting Cali and Bogotá except for one difficult stretch over the central cordillera where the automobile road connects the two ends of the railroad. This means that the trip must be made in three sections.

Airplanes have brought Colombia's remote cities in contact with the world. The oldest air system in South America was started in 1918 by an Austrian. His small line developed into the German airlines which were well known in Colombia long before the Pan American planes operated in South America. Today these former German lines are owned by the Colombian government and Pan American Airways. All important cities are connected by air with Barranquilla and Buenaventura and with Cristóbal in the Canal Zone. New York is only one day away by airplane from Medellín or Bogotá.

COLOMBIA'S OIL TRAVELS THROUGH PIPELINES

Colombia's oil means wealth. It means money in royalties and taxes for the fortunate nation which has the black gold beneath her soil; it means jobs for many workers. In Latin America it also means that foreign companies come in to develop the oil

AIR TRAVEL is the easiest way of reaching Medellín. Many business men as well as travelers use this modern little airport.

Weimer

Weimer

THESE BOYS OF COLOMBIA look healthy and happy. They might be a group of schoolboys from almost any city in the United States.

lands, for these countries do not have the money or the machinery or the technical experience needed for this industry. Colombia's oil has been developed by a branch of the Standard Oil Company of the United States. The government gets 10 per cent of all the oil produced and in addition collects an income tax from the company.

The most important oil region lies about halfway up the Magdalena between Barranquilla and Bogotá. Here in the hot and swampy jungle are wells which produce about 25,000,000 barrels a year. The oil company was faced with the problem of how to get the oil to the sea. The Magdalena River was so slow and uncertain that it would not pay to open the wells if transportation must depend on river boats. Finally an 8-inch pipeline, 335 miles long, was built from the oil fields through the swampy jungles of the river lowlands to the port of Cartagena. Food and medicine for the workers and tools and supplies for the job had to be carried up the river on barges while the pipeline was being laid.

THE LAND SYSTEM BRINGS WEALTH TO SOME, POVERTY TO MANY

Colombia has progressed toward democracy, but her land system is not democratic. Most of the land is still divided into large estates as it was in colonial days. This means that the few who own land are very rich and the thousands who work the land are very poor. This is the problem which faces many Latin American nations today. We have learned how Mexico is trying to solve it by breaking up the estates and giving the land to the people. So far nothing has been done in Colombia to change her land system. Perhaps the energetic and intelligent middle class which is growing up in Medellín and other towns will take the first steps when enough of them have political power.

As stated in the last chapter, most Colombians of the laboring class in town and country have a strain of Indian or Negro blood. In the country around Medellín the barefooted peon who works on the land is white, but he fares little better than the peons of other regions. He and his family live in a one-room house with a garden and perhaps a few chickens. As part of his tiny wages he gets a piece of *panela* or brown sugar for his family. He wears short knee-length pants and cotton jacket often full of patches. Like all Latin American peons, he wears a poncho or heavy cloth about his shoulders, slit in the center so that his head will go through. His hat is straight-brimmed with a high round crown. When he goes to market he wears a leather pouch on a strap over his shoulder to take the place of the pockets he does not have. The women wear a large black shawl called a *manta* over head and shoulders. Yet, in spite of their hard lot, the Colombian peons are cheerful and courteous.

The wealthy upper classes of Colombia are charming and cultured people. They have been accustomed to travel in Europe and the United States. They often know many languages and can speak English much better than most educated people from the United States can speak Spanish. They live in beautiful old Spanish colonial mansions furnished with the heavy carved furniture that is typical of Spain. In Medellín and other important cities modern conveniences, such as plumbing and electricity, make these homes more livable.

CORN DISHES AND COFFEE ARE POPULAR IN COLOMBIA

Every country in Latin America has its own particular national dishes. In Colombia there are two dishes made of corn which travelers like. *Arepas* (ah-ray'pahs) are round biscuits made of fine corn meal, salt, and water kneaded together. When these are baked until crisp and eaten with butter, they make very good eating. *Masamorra* (mah-sah-mohr'ah) is made by boiling kernels of fresh corn and serving with *panela*. *Panela* is food for beast as well as man in Colombia. The hard-working mule is often fed a cake of the brown sugar as part of his food. Colombians are fond of coffee and often stop in at cafés several times a day for a cup of strong black coffee sweetened with *panela*. Americans like Colombian coffee in the United States, where it is blended with Brazilian coffee, and they soon acquire a taste for it as it is made in Colombia as well.

Are You a Careful Reader?   Test Yourself!

I. Supply the correct word for each blank:

1. After the breaking-up of Great Colombia, the middle country was first called . . . . , but later became . . . . .

2. The two political parties are called . . . . and . . . . .

3. From 1930 to 1948 Colombia could be called a . . . . because its presidents were not . . . ., but were chosen at orderly . . . . .

4. The capital of Colombia is . . . ., situated on a high plateau called the . . . . .

5. Their crude brown sugar is called . . . . , while the habit of chatting on street corners is known as . . . . .

II. Match the words with the statements:

1. Medellín	*a.* first Spaniard to see the Colombian highlands
2. Cauca	*b.* river of western Colombia in whose valley Cali
3. Cali	and Medellín are located
4. Barranquilla	*c.* famous old walled city and seaport
5. Mosquera	*d.* Colombia's main "highway" from the highlands
6. Nuñez	to the Caribbean coast
7. López	*e.* main street of Bogotá
8. Simón Bolívar Highway	*f.* port of Colombia located on Caribbean
9. Cartagena	*g.* progressive manufacturing city
10. Magdalena	*h.* president who changed country's name to Colombia
	i. the "Theodore Roosevelt of Colombia"
	j. popular "new deal" president
	k. city in Cauca River Valley connected by rail with the Pacific
	l. section of Pan-American Highway from Caracas to Bogotá to Quito

Food for Thought and Discussion

1. Compare the civil wars of Colombia with those of the Mayan cities in Yucatan. What steps did the Colombians take which the Mayans failed to do?

2. What freedoms which we consider essential are always lacking in a dictatorship? Does Colombia enjoy these freedoms today? Would the presence of these freedoms in a country be a good test of democracy in addition to the ones mentioned in the text?

3. Most Latin American countries are not rich. If oil brings new wealth to Colombia, what would you suggest that the government do with some of the money?

Chapter 25

Venezuela, Homeland of Bolívar, Progresses Toward Democracy

VENEZUELA means little Venice! How did this great tropical country happen to be named for the beautiful Italian city of palaces and canals? When the Spaniard Ojeda (oh-hay'dah) led an expedition to explore the shores of South America in 1499, he found Indian villages around Lake Maracaibo. The huts were built on stilts above the swampy shore and the Indians paddled about in canoes. Vespucci, the Italian navigator, was with Ojeda. Probably the scene reminded him of the watery streets and gondolas of Venice, for the region was given the Spanish name of Venezuela.

Much has happened in the years since Venezuela was named. Spanish settlers and soldiers, revolutionary armies, patriot leaders, and harsh dictators have played their part in Venezuela's history. In this chapter you will learn what modern Venezuela is like and how the republic has fared since the days of Bolívar.

THE NEW REPUBLIC TRAVELS A ROCKY ROAD

Venezuela's story as an independent nation began when she withdrew from Great Colombia in 1830 under the leadership of General Páez. This rough, uneducated *llanero* gave Venezuela a good start in national life. He maintained order and encouraged road-building, agriculture, and trade. Under succeeding presidents, Páez remained the real power behind the government. Although there were several revolts by ambitious military leaders, for nearly twenty years the country made considerable progress.

But, as in Colombia, disagreements between Conservatives and Liberals began to upset the government. As quarrels became more bitter, presidents became more dictatorial in their methods, and revolts were frequent. When a new constitution was adopted in 1858 giving more power to local governments, neither party was satisfied and the first civil war broke out. The veteran Páez, who had been in exile in the United States, returned to aid the Conservatives by seizing control of the government and trying to end the war. But the Liberals won several victories and forced him to give up his authority, sending him again into exile. Another constitution, devised by the Liberals in 1864 and providing for a loose federation of states, proved no more satisfactory. Civil war again flared up.

VENEZUELA ENTERS UPON A SERIES OF DICTATORSHIPS

The strife ended when Guzmán Blanco (goos-mahn' blahn'coh), an

Gendreau

HUTS ON STILTS are still used by Indians living on the shore of Lake Maracaibo. We wonder how crude huts like these could have reminded Vespucci of beautiful Venice with its palaces and canals.

ambitious and brilliant soldier-politician, seized the government in 1870. Because of his magnetic personality and his ability he became a favorite of the people. But although leader of the Liberals, he made himself absolute dictator. He worked out a clever scheme which allowed him to control Venezuela for eighteen years. He spent every other term in Europe while a president of his own choosing carried on in Venezuela. Like most dictators, Guzmán Blanco was conceited. He established national essay contests with prizes to be given for the best essays on himself and his achievements! In Caracas, fifteen statues were erected in honor of the "Illustrious American, Guzmán Blanco."

In spite of his vanity, this dictator deserves credit for the progress of his country during his rule. He not only kept peace among the various factions, but he put the finances in shape, mod-

ernized and beautified the principal cities, and built several short railroads. In Caracas, streets were widened and paved, parks laid out, and public buildings erected. But Guzmán Blanco incurred the enmity of the Catholic Church when he greatly reduced its power. In 1888, when his popularity had vanished, he was conveniently in Europe and there he remained.

Disorder again gripped Venezuela. Several presidents ruled in rapid succession; their administrations were punctuated by military revolutions. In 1899, an unscrupulous and greedy tyrant began a dictatorship which lasted for nine years. Cipriano Castro (see-pree-ah'noh cahs'troh) had none of the experience and ability of Guzmán Blanco. He managed to get Venezuela into trouble with several European governments. His rule was extravagant and cruel and there were repeated uprisings against him. In 1908 he wisely left the country and did not return.

GÓMEZ HOLDS VENEZUELA IN AN IRON GRIP

In 1909 began the rule of a man whose name still has power to strike fear into the hearts of many Venezuelans. Juan Vicente Gómez (whahn vee-sen'tay goh'mays) had been elected president after Castro left for Europe. He was an uneducated but shrewd man from the Andes who kept the nation under his tyrant's rule until 1935. To make himself secure, he exiled or imprisoned anyone who opposed him. His spies were everywhere. Young men who dared speak out against him were sent to prison and forced to suffer cruel punishments. It is small wonder that many young men of upper-class families found it more healthful to live in Europe or the United States while Gómez was in power.

Gómez ran Venezuela as though it were a vast estate belonging to him alone. Like many other Latin American dictators, he considered it his right to plunder the treasury of Venezuela for himself and his followers. Rich oil deposits were bringing wealth to the government and many of the oil millions went into the pockets of Gómez and his supporters. He took over great cattle ranches in the *llanos* and sugar and coffee plantations in the highlands. It is estimated that 20 per cent of the cultivated land of Venezuela belonged to Gómez. Gómez disliked aristocratic Caracas, so he built himself a new capital at Maracay (mah-rah-kye'), west of Caracas. Here he and many of his relatives lived protected by a well-trained and equipped army. We can understand why he was called "*El Benemérito,*" or "the deserving one," by his friends, and "*El Brujo,*" or "the witch doctor," by the people who lived in fear of him.

Of course, the government of Gómez was not all bad. He was a fine businessman. It was Gómez who made the shrewd bargain with the foreign oil companies so that large rents and royalties were paid to the government for the right to take out Venezuela's oil. He kept peace and order, encouraged development of the country's resources, and paid off all of Venezuela's foreign debts. He built the concrete road from Caracas to La Guaira (gw-eye'rah) and other roads into the *llanos*. It has been pointed out that most of them ran from Maracay to his own estates and those of his followers.

The common people were certain that "*El Brujo*" would never die. When death came to him at last in 1935, he was 78 years old and had ruled Venezuela for over a quarter of a century. When they became convinced that he was actually dead, the people went wild with joy. They ran through the streets looting the houses of his followers.

MODERN VENEZUELA BEGAN IN 1935

When General López Contreras (loh'pays cohn-tray'rahs), the minister of war under Gómez, was named by the congress as the new president of Venezuela, people began to hope for better government. López Contreras was a frail and mild-mannered gentleman who believed in government by democratic methods instead of armed force. Political prisoners were freed from jail and exiled Venezuelans were

VENEZUELA

0   100   200   300
SCALE IN MILES

invited to return home. People dared once more to speak their opinions in public without fear of arrest. Newspapers were free to support or oppose the government as they wished and cartoonists could poke fun in safety.

Great problems faced the new president. After twenty-six years under Gómez, Venezuela was a backward country. In spite of the millions which had poured into Venezuela from its oil, the people were miserably poor, uneducated, and suffering from tropical diseases. López Contreras realized that democracy cannot succeed if three fourths of the people cannot read or write. Venezuela needed more schools; it needed hospitals and doctors to care for the sick, and scientists to fight disease. It needed clean drinking water and sewer systems for the cities, and roads and railroads to transport its products. Like Cárdenas of Mexico, President López Contreras and his cabinet decided to give his country a "new deal."

VENEZUELA'S OIL IS "PLANTED" IN VENEZUELA

Schools and roads and hospitals cost money, and Venezuela had money. In fact, royalties from oil made Venezuela one of the richest countries in Latin America. Under the new program some of her wealth was to be spent on her people. Patriotic Venezuelans call this "planting the oil."

A Venezuelan who was a graduate of Columbia University in New York was put at the head of the new educational system. Between 1935 and

1940, the number of elementary schools was doubled and the number of pupils was quadrupled! Schools have been established to train much-needed teachers. Those who plan to teach in rural schools are taught agriculture, sewing, and stock-raising, so that they can give the pupils what will help them most. In remote districts where teachers are lacking, radios have been put in the schools and lessons broadcast from Caracas. Movies carried by boat and truck teach the villagers elementary hygiene. Children are learning health rules along with their abc's so that they may know how to wash their teeth and keep themselves and their food clean. In some cities even the parents go to school to learn the care of babies, housekeeping, and sewing.

Water and sewer systems are being installed in some of the cities, while aqueducts and irrigation works are being constructed for the benefit of the farmers. Although Venezuela has money, she has not until lately had the machinery and trained men necessary for construction work. New hospitals are being built and doctors and nurses trained. The Rockefeller Institute has sent scientists and doctors from the United States to help the government fight the tropical diseases.

It is too early to see the results of the new program. Venezuela is greatly handicapped by the scarcity of men able to take charge and by the small population in her rural districts. The country has been so backward that the progress so far is only a drop in the bucket. Much also depends on the government. López Contreras went out of office in 1941. The next two presidents were overthrown by army revolts. After 1948,

Venezuela was governed by a military committee which promised free democratic elections in the near future.

OIL BRINGS MILLIONS TO VENEZUELA

To the world of industry and trade Venezuela means one thing — Oil, with a capital O. Venezuela exports more oil today than does any other country in the world. Venezuela's oil wells, like Mexico's, were developed by foreign money. Today, English, Dutch, and American companies have millions of dollars invested in oil lands. Under a recent law the government of Venezuela receives a royalty of 16⅔ per cent on oil exports, which amount to almost 500,000,000 barrels a year.

The world's greatest oil region is situated in and around bottle-shaped Lake Maracaibo in northwestern Venezuela. In 1922, one of the early wells shot crude black oil sixty feet into the air for nine days before it was capped. There are oil derricks not only on the shores of the lake, but there are hundreds actually in the lake. They are set in long rows like streets and connected by catwalks. Men go about from one section to another in speed-boats. The lake itself is covered with a scum of oil. The city of Maracaibo, situated on the western side of the lake's bottleneck, has become the world's greatest oil port. Ocean tankers can sail directly to its docks and carry away the "black gold."

THE OIL COMPANIES PROVE THE VALUE OF SANITATION

The malaria-infested lowlands about the lake have been made a healthful place for the thousands of oil workers and their families. Swamps have been drained and sanitary villages built for the workers

Weimer

OIL DERRICKS in Lake Maracaibo extend two or three miles out from shore, covering the east coast of the lake for a distance of twenty miles. This is today the world's greatest oil region.

As a matter of good business, free medical care is given to all who are sick. The natives are paid good wages and those who show promise are given special technical training.

The work of the oil companies in health and sanitation has shown that the future of Venezuela depends upon the health of her working people. When the native workers were first hired, they were poorly fed and suffered from hookworm, malaria, and other tropical diseases. They seemed dull, and few could be found to take responsible jobs of any kind. Foreign laborers had to be imported to do the work. Today, thanks to the sanitary living conditions and the medical care, many Venezuelans have become alert and responsible workers. Now, most of the foremen, drillers, and other skilled laborers in the oil fields are natives.

THE HIGHLAND REGION IS THE HEART OF VENEZUELA

Next to oil, Venezuela's wealth lies in the crops grown on her rich highland slopes and valleys. The largest cash crop is coffee. Venezuela's mild-flavored coffee brings a high price in the United States. It is grown for the most part on estates like those in Guatemala, but there are also many small farms where coffee is raised. The next largest crop is cacao, which grows on the lower and warmer slopes throughout the highland region. Venezuela's crude brown sugar called *papelón* (pah-pay-lohn') is interesting, for unlike ours it is molded into rounded cones which look a great deal like bullets. Everybody in Venezuela drinks *guarape* (gwah-rah'pay), a popular drink made from *papelón* and hot water, and tasting like molasses. Cotton is also grown in the highlands,

273

Sawders

THE PORT OF LA GUAIRA is the gateway to Caracas, and all ship and plane passengers bound for the capital city disembark here. The harbor is protected from the sea by a concrete breakwater.

but, like sugar, is used largely in Venezuela and not exported.

There are several cities in the highland region. Caracas, the capital, is the largest city in Venezuela. Valencia is an old colonial town west of Caracas which lies in a rich agricultural district. In the higher ranges toward Colombia are many Andean cities, among them Mérida and San Cristóbal. La Guaira is the seaport for Caracas. Farther west Puerto Cabello (cah-bay'yoh) has the finest harbor in Venezuela.

Transportation of the highland crops has been a problem. The short railroads which connect some of the cities with seaports were built at tremendous cost. The principal line between Caracas and Valencia is only 114 miles long, but it has 219 bridges and viaducts and cost $135,000 a mile to build! Roads are proving cheaper, however. The new road extending westward to Mérida and San Cristóbal connects the western cities for the first time with the ports of Puerto Cabello and La Guaira. (See map on page 271.)

LAND IS PLENTIFUL BUT PEOPLE ARE FEW IN THE LLANOS

The traveler to Venezuela should not miss seeing the vast inland plains of grass which stir in the wind like waves of a rolling green sea. The way to visit the *llanos*, if you cannot swim your horse across the streams as the

274

llaneros do, is to take a steamer to the island of Trinidad off the coast of northeastern Venezuela. From here paddle-wheeled river steamers run along the muddy waters of the lower Orinoco to Ciudad Bolívar (see-oo-dahd' boh-lee'var). From this town go cargoes of cattle and hides from the *llanos*, and gold from the Guiana Highlands. You can sail still farther up the river to San Fernando (sahn fair-nahn'doh) on a branch of the Orinoco. Here in this western end of the *llanos* the grass is heavier. There are enormously large ranches, some extending over thousands of acres of grass and swamp.

The *llanos* are used as a range for the hardy Venezuelan cattle. For half the year, during the rainy season, the Orinoco and its tributaries overflow their banks and flood these lowland plains. Roads and scattered Indian villages near the streams stand deep in water and the natives have to go about in boats. No one attempts to cross the plains in flood time except the *llaneros*, who are among the most skillful riders in the world. Their horses are taught to swim as tirelessly as they run, so that the cattle may be rounded up and driven to higher ground when the floods come. After the floods recede, the plains become a grassy pasture, but all too soon the searing sun dries up the grass. The cattle must keep moving to find food. They are plagued by disease-carrying ticks and flies, while malaria attacks the *llaneros*.

With all the acres of grazing land, not enough meat is raised on the *llanos* to supply the needs of even the native Venezuelans! One reason is the lack of transportation, for there are few good roads and no railroads in this area. The cattle near the Orinoco may be sent out by steamer, but those farther away are driven the long distance to the highlands. They are so thin when they arrive that they must be fattened in near-by pasture land, which few cattle-owners can afford. The other reason for lack of development is the small population of the *llanos*. In the plains area there is an average of fewer than ten persons to the square mile. This vast land clearly needs better roads and more people before the cattle industry can grow.

GOLD IS MINED IN THE GUIANA HIGHLANDS

Very little is known of the jungle wilderness and forest south of the Orinoco. A few dirt roads lead from Ciudad Bolívar to gold mines near the border of British Guiana. Fifty years ago the richest mine in the world was in this region, and the mine is still productive. Today the gold mines are controlled by a British company which depends on planes to deliver the mining machinery and to ship out the gold. Although fortunes are no longer being made, enough gold is taken out to make it third in value of Venezuela's exports. Nuggets about the size of a dime are common and are often of 20-carat gold. Diamonds are also found in the river beds by Indians panning for gold. This wild region is a part of Venezuela whose development lies in the distant future.

CARACAS IS A CHARMING CITY IN A BEAUTIFUL SETTING

We must not leave Venezuela without a glimpse of the capital city. Since the capital has no airport, airliners as well as steamships stop in the tropical port of La Guaira so that passengers

Galloway

THE MUSEUM OF FINE ARTS is located in an important residential section of Caracas. It belongs to the modern Caracas and its classic style is in great contrast to the Spanish architecture of old Caracas.

may make the trip to Caracas. Although the capital is only nine miles inland from the coast, the road climbs and curves along the edge of sheer cliffs for miles before the city is reached. The red tiled roofs and white buildings can be seen below as the highway winds down through a pass in the mountains. Caracas is set in a valley about 3000 feet above the sea, where it is always springtime. Brilliant flowering trees line the streets and the purple blossoms of the bougainvillea cover patio walls.

Although Caracas has become a modern city with new suburbs and a country club, there are still many old Spanish homes built around flower-filled patios. Aristocratic creole families have lived here since colonial days, taking part in the social life and politics of the city. Both Miranda and Bolívar were from Caracas.

It is difficult for a stranger to find his way about the city because of the unusual way of giving addresses. The intersections are named instead of the streets. You might be given an address as number 9, between the Corner of the Church of San Francisco and the Corner of the Congressional Buildings! To the inhabitants, of course, it seems very simple.

Visitors to Caracas never forget the orchids which seem to grow everywhere as freely as dandelions in the United States. They can be bought for a song, and perhaps that is the reason the belles of Caracas seldom wear these exquisite flowers. Large numbers of cut orchids are sent to New York every year, the trip taking less than two days from La Guaira by plane.

The visitor to Caracas is sure to be hailed by men selling lottery tickets who will urge him to try his luck on a number. Lotteries are very popular in Latin America and are found in all the cities from Mexico to Chile. In Caracas people crowd eagerly about on lottery days as the winning numbers are chosen from a wire cage. The lottery is run by the government, and after the prizes are awarded, the money goes to the free clinics and hospitals for the poor. An unexpected sight in this city is the stands where *perros calientes* or hot dogs may be bought.

The open-air markets are full of luscious tropical fruits. But the visitor soon discovers that prices are high in Venezuela, especially on imported foods and other goods. Bread is about 60 cents a loaf in United States money, eggs $1 a dozen. Apples, which are not grown in Venezuela, are about 30 cents apiece and a chocolate bar is the same. An automobile costing about $2500 in the United States costs over $9000 in Venezuela! This is due chiefly to a very high tariff on all foreign goods. Since Venezuela must import most of her food as well as manufactured goods, this high tariff is naturally hard on all but the rich.

CARACAS IS PROUD TO CLAIM BOLÍVAR AS A NATIVE SON

The memory of the Liberator lives on in the city of his birth. In the central square, Plaza Bolívar, the slight, commanding figure of the great

A FRUIT STAND in the Caracas market offers for sale the luscious fruits grown near Valencia, but prices are so high even on home-grown fruit that few can afford them.

Black Star

man sits astride a prancing steed. Below is the inscription: "Simón Bolívar, Liberator of Venezuela, New Granada, Ecuador, and Peru, and founder of Bolivia." The house where he was born is now set aside as a memorial museum in his honor, and his body rests today in a magnificent tomb which visitors may see. Plazas, streets, and cities are named for him, not only in Venezuela, but throughout South America. The coin of the country is called a *bolívar* in his honor. People from the United States are pleased to see a Plaza Washington in Caracas, with a statue of George Washington, whom Bolívar greatly admired.

THE CUSTOMS OF VENEZUELA REVEAL A MIXTURE OF OLD AND NEW

Although the women of Caracas may ride in airplanes and automobiles and go to the movies, they are still bound by ancient Spanish customs regarding women's behavior. If a young man wishes to take his girl out for the evening, her mother or aunt must accompany them as *dueña* or chaperon. Even if the suitor merely comes to call, it is necessary for the mother to be there. Married women seldom go with their husbands to dine and dance in public places. Their place is in the home and most of their entertaining is done among family groups.

There is a custom which seems queer to Americans. When the women and girls promenade in the shopping districts in the afternoon, men like to stand on the corners and make complimentary remarks. This is called "tossing the *piropo*" (pee-roh'poh) and is not resented by the women as it might be in our country.

In Venezuela baseball is *beisbal* and has become a game so popular that

THESE LONG-HORNED CATTLE from the *llanos* are being prodded ahead to a cattle boat in the Orinoco River below Ciudad Bolívar. The crude bridge serves as a gangplank to load them onto the waiting steamer.

Gendreau

cities such as Caracas claim some truly fine teams. Bullfighting is still a favorite sport and stars of the bull ring come from Spain and Mexico to thrill the fans of Caracas. Country people play a game called *bolas* which is something like bowling. It is played on the dirt or gravel roads of the towns. A small ball is tossed ahead of the players, who then try to roll large wooden balls as close as possible. They may knock away an opponent's ball or push their own closer. Sometimes traffic is held up while the winner is decided upon.

JUAN BIMBA IS VENEZUELA'S FORGOTTEN MAN

Everyone in Venezuela knows the little man, Juan Bimba (whahn beem'-bah). He appears in the posters and newspaper cartoons of which Venezuelans are so fond as Mr. Average Citizen. He is one of the millions of poor *mestizos* with bare feet and patches on his pants. Juan Bimba is usually represented either as an *Andino* (ahn-dee'noh) from the highlands or a *llanero* from the plains, and, like most of his countrymen, he lives in a hut and sleeps in a hammock made of rope. Juan uses a five-gallon gasoline can for a stove, if he can get one. With sand in the bottom of the can and a hole cut for a draft, he can build a charcoal fire and fry his corn meal or his cassava bread or a piece of goat cheese.

Even Gómez was not able to suppress Juan Bimba, for he kept secretly appearing in print as a man held under a heavy boot or bowed low beneath the burdens of dictatorship. The cartoons of today show the change slowly taking place in Venezuela. Although Juan Bimba is still barefooted and often sick, he is no longer sad, because he has hope of a better day.

Are You a Careful Reader?   Test Yourself!

I. Can you match these words and statements?

1. Guzmán Blanco
2. Gómez
3. Ciudad Bolívar
4. Páez
5. El Brujo
6. López Contreras
7. Maracaibo
8. Juan Bimba
9. Valencia
10. La Guaira

a. town on the Orinoco
b. dictator who ruled Venezuela 18 years and beautified Caracas
c. recent cruel dictator who ruled Venezuela as his private estate
d. port of Caracas
e. lake in which oil deposits are found
f. principal street in Caracas
g. *llanero* founder of Venezuelan republic
h. nickname for Gómez
i. statue of Bolívar
j. democratic president who followed Gómez
k. old colonial town west of Caracas
l. Venezula's "forgotten man"

II. Are the following statements true or false?

1. Gómez left Venezuela one of the most progressive countries in South America.
2. López Contreras "planted the oil" by spending the oil royalties of Venezuela on a new deal for the people.

3. The rural schools of Venezuela, like those of Mexico, are teaching child care, hygiene, stock-raising, and agriculture.

4. The foreign oil companies found that in spite of sanitary living conditions, good food, and medical care the oil workers remained dull and inefficient.

5. The *llanos* cannot become a large cattle-raising area until the population is increased and transportation is improved.

Food for Thought and Discussion

1. Compare the program of Cárdenas for the peons of Mexico with that of López Contreras for the people of Venezuela. Are they much the same? Why?

2. What does the experience of the oil companies with the Venezuelan workers prove? Do you think the tropics can ever be made healthful for human beings?

3. Does Juan Bimba tell you anything about the Venezuelans themselves? If so, what characteristics does he reveal?

Chapter 26

Beautiful Ecuador, Ancient Peru, and Lofty Bolivia Are Neighbor Republics

Ecuador

ECUADOR is a beautiful and fascinating land. Lush, tropic lowlands stretch from the Pacific to the Andean foothills and in the highlands green valleys nestle at the foot of towering peaks. Cotopaxi, the highest active volcano in the world, rears its magnificent snowy cone high into the clouds. Barefooted highland Indians in bright native costumes walk through the narrow streets of Quito and you hear the soft, sibilant sounds of their ancient Quechua tongue. You see the grue-some dried heads which have come from wild head-hunting tribes beyond the Andes. Shrunken to the size of a man's fist, they still retain the original features and hair! You can visit a cacao plantation in the lowlands to see where a chocolate bar begins, or, if you wish, take a trip to the Equator and stand on the middle of Mother Earth.

Ecuador is one of the three nations of South America which occupy the territory of the former Inca kingdom.

The other two are Peru and Bolivia. The millions of Indians who still live in the lands of their ancestors make these countries quite different from Colombia and Venezuela.[1]

ECUADOR HAS RICH LOWLANDS AND POOR HIGHLANDS

This country, crossed by the Equator and named for it, is a triangular piece of land wedged in between Colombia and Peru. It looks small on the map, but it is at least four times as large as the state of New York.

As you know, Nature has mixed her gifts in Ecuador. The hot lowlands, where people find it difficult to live, produce the only valuable crops, while the cool highlands, where most Ecuadoreans live, can barely support the population. The government of Ecuador is in the highland city of Quito, 9300 feet above the sea, but the wealth of the country is concentrated in the lowland city of Guayaquil in the rich coastal plain. The rivalry which developed between these two Ecuadors has been a serious handicap to the country.

ECUADOR HAS TWO FOUNDERS

Let us pick up the story of Quito back in 1830, when she withdrew from Bolívar's republic and established herself as the independent state of Ecuador. Smallest and the weakest of all the lands which Bolívar had freed, she faced a stormy future.

Ecuador has not one "father of his country," but two! Juan José Flores (floh'rays), the first president, was a military man who believed in a strong central government supported by the

[1] Before you read this chapter, please turn to Chapter 2, pages 19–25, for a review of the geography of Ecuador, Peru, and Bolivia.

Catholic Church. His government was soon challenged by Vicente Rocafuerte (roh-cah-fwair'tay), the leader of a large group of Liberals. The two men made a bargain that they would take turns as president of Ecuador. When it became Rocafuerte's turn, he drew up a new Liberal constitution and gave Ecuador a more progressive government. When Flores returned, he also changed the constitution, making the president's term eight years instead of four. Then he had himself re-elected! The Liberals feared Flores would become a permanent dictator and in 1845 they revolted and sent him into exile.

THE AGE OF GARCÍA MORENO IS A PERIOD OF PEACE

For the next fifteen years Ecuador suffered under frequent revolutions and civil wars. Quito quarreled with Guayaquil where a rival government had been set up. In 1861, a most unusual personality named Gabriel García Moreno (gahr-see'ah moh-ray'noh) succeeded in overthrowing the government at Guayaquil and restoring order to the country. The new dictator was a lawyer and scholar, and a vigorous political writer. What made him unusual was his almost fanatical devotion to religion. He wanted the Church to be the strongest influence in Ecuador, and during his rule it had more power than ever before. He established schools in which boys and girls were taught by the religious orders of the Church.

García Moreno was also an energetic administrator, and did a great deal to improve the country. An honest man, he fought graft wherever he found it. He started a road from Quito to Guayaquil and encouraged ocean trade and agriculture. But García Moreno carried on a reign of terror against all who opposed him, and was finally attacked by his enemies and killed, in 1875.

UNSTABLE GOVERNMENT HAS HINDERED ECUADOR'S PROGRESS

With the strong hand of the dictator removed, Ecuador relapsed into its former state of political turmoil. Conservatives, Liberals, and military adventurers struggled for control. Occasionally there was a period of honest and peaceful government. Then, in 1895, Eloy Alfaro (ahl-fah'-roh) gained control of the state and became one of Ecuador's strongest presidents. He was a Liberal, and for fifteen years the chief political figure in the republic. Under Alfaro, laws were passed to restrict the power of the Church.

One of the outstanding events during Alfaro's presidency was the completion of the famous Guayaquil to Quito railroad. When his daughter drove a golden spike into the last tie, the capital of Ecuador was finally united with the outside world. But Alfaro's end shows the barbarous state of affairs that still existed in Ecuador. Participating in a revolt against the government that succeeded him, he was subsequently imprisoned, assassinated by his captors, and his body mutilated by a mob in the streets. This happened as recently as 1912.

Since Alfaro's time, the Liberals have continued in control. Although Ecuadoreans know that political strife has almost ruined their nation, they have been unable to achieve the stable government so greatly needed. Revolts by the army have been so com-

mon that no president from 1924 to 1948 remained in office his full four-year term. In 1948, Galo Plaza, one of the most progressive leaders in Latin America, was elected president. Under his leadership, Ecuador made progress toward a more stable and democratic government.

ECUADOR HAS SHRUNK IN SIZE SINCE 1830

Civil wars and revolutions were not the only troubles of the little republic of Ecuador. Her more powerful neighbors took advantage of her weakness to encroach upon her territory. She lost thousands of square miles of land in the wild Oriente where boundaries had never been definitely established.

Ecuador's longest and most bitter dispute was with Peru, who claimed 117,000 square miles in that part of the Oriente which Ecuador considered her land. A settlement of the dispute was finally reached by the Pan-American Conference at Rio de Janeiro in 1942. Part of the disputed territory was awarded to Ecuador, while a piece of land larger than the state of Idaho went to Peru. The settlement was welcomed by the American republics because the two countries had been on the verge of war. Probably neither country is entirely satisfied, but at least mapmakers are now able to give Peru and Ecuador definite boundaries!

THE LOSS OF HER CACAO MARKETS HAS BROUGHT POVERTY TO ECUADOR

For many years Ecuador was famous for her fine cacao plantations that lie in the hot coastal plain near the Guayas River and its branches. Transportation by raft and boat to Guayaquil is cheap and easy. But

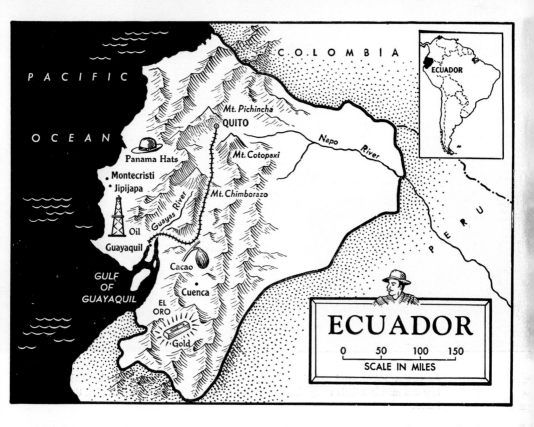

the cacao business is not what it used to be. In 1925, Ecuador was producing more cacao than any other country in the world. Then disease attacked the trees, spreading over miles of the cacao land, and almost overnight her crops decreased until today she produces only three per cent of the world's cacao. Because she depended on that one crop for most of her trade, this has been a serious blow to Ecuador.

Since then cheap African cacao has taken over Ecuador's former markets, and today Africa supplies two thirds of the world's cacao. Yet the situation is not hopeless, because Ecuador can increase her other tropical products. Coffee production, for example, is now being promoted and may some day become as valuable to Ecuador as cacao once was.

PANAMA HATS ARE MADE IN ECUADOR

Ecuadoreans do not like to have Panama get the credit for their beautiful hats! This case of mistaken identity goes back to the fair at Puerto Bello during colonial days when fine hand-woven hats from Ecuador were much in demand in Europe. As you know, products from South America had to go through Panama on their way to Spain. Spanish merchants who bought these hats in the fair at Puerto Bello called them Panama hats, and the name has persisted to this day.

The weaving of hats provides an income for many an Ecuadorean family. Women and children usually do the weaving, and they may spend as much as two or three weeks on a hat of fine straw. It is amazing to watch their fingers fly back and forth

Sawders

PANAMA HATS need finishing touches after the weaving is completed. This boy and man in a little village in Ecuador are blocking the crowns and shaping the brims.

through the many strands of straw. The material for these hats comes from the leaves of the *toquilla* (toh-kee'yah) palm. The long fan-shaped leaves must be cut before they open, and are split into fibers as narrow as a sixteenth of an inch. These are dipped into boiling water several times, then dried and put in the sun to bleach. When ready for weaving, the fibers are like a flat cord and are sometimes as fine as thread.

The weaver does not get much money, though, for her weeks of painstaking work. She may receive only $1 or $2 for the hat that brings in the United States from $10 to $25, or even $150 if it is exceptionally fine. It is said that some are so finely woven that they can be rolled and pulled through a ring! Although hats are made in many parts of Ecuador, the region north of Guayaquil is especially famous. The finest ones carry the names of the towns, such as: *sombrero de Jipijapa* (hee-pee-hah'pah) or *sombrero de Monte Cristi.*

GUAYAQUIL IS ECUADOR'S LARGEST CITY AND CHIEF PORT

One of the most interesting sights in Ecuador is the 35-mile trip up the broad Guayas River to the city of Guayaquil. The water is crowded with picturesque craft of all kinds carrying the tropical products of Ecuador to Guayaquil. There are slender dugouts of balsa logs propelled by a sail; there are rafts of all sizes, small steamers, and launches from the *haciendas* up the river. Whole families travel down the river on rafts loaded with cacao beans and other tropical products. The rafts of balsa logs, with their palm-leaf shelters where the families cook and eat, pass slowly between the river banks where green jungle grows down to the water's edge. Native huts of bamboo stand on stilts above the muddy shore.

At Guayaquil the river is two miles wide. Ocean freighters anchor in deep water offshore and are loaded by means of lighters. The city itself is crowded along the waterfront for two or three miles, while thousands of people live on rafts and boats along the shore. Most of the houses in the town are made of bamboo or wood which are said to be cooler in the sticky heat of this tropical city. The average temperature of Guayaquil is about 83 degrees, and when the rainy season comes, the air is so heavy with

moisture that shoes will mildew overnight!

Guayaquil used to be considered the pest-hole of the Pacific, and ships avoided stopping there because of yellow fever and the dread bubonic plague. By keeping up a constant fight against disease, however, health officers have finally brought these diseases under control, and since 1920 have made the port a fairly healthful place.

Guayaquil is an old and weather-beaten city founded almost four centuries ago by one of Pizarro's lieutenants. Its inhabitants, like those in most port towns of the tropics, are a mixture of Spanish, Indian, and Negro, with Indian predominating. Many are progressive middle-class

AT THE BUSY PORT OF GUAYAQUIL stevedores load bananas from a lighter onto a waiting ship. Notice the conveyor at the right which is used to hoist the produce onto the ship.

Black Star

people and make their living from the trade that moves in and out of the port. Most of Ecuador's old Spanish families, however, live in Quito, not in Guayaquil.

A RAILROAD CONNECTS ECUADOR'S TWO CITIES

Across the river from the port city is the terminal of the spectacular railroad which climbs the Andes to Quito. It took ten years and cost the lives of hundreds of workmen to lay the 280 miles of track, until it was finally completed by an enterprising engineer from the United States. In one place the railroad zigzags up the side of a mountain on a ledge blasted out of solid rock. When the train reaches the highland country and turns north toward Quito, the traveler from Guayaquil finds himself in a different world. Snow-covered mountain peaks are outlined against the horizon. In the valleys and far up the mountain slopes, patches of potatoes, wheat, and barley make a checkered pattern. Indian huts of sun-dried brick take the place of the bamboo huts of the lowlands. The days are cool and the nights are surprisingly cold, considering that Quito is almost directly on the Equator.

QUITO IS THE OLDEST CAPITAL IN THE WESTERN HEMISPHERE

Quito lies at the foot of Mount Pichincha (pee-cheen'chah) in a green valley over 9000 feet above the sea. Named after the Quito Indians, it was an old city when the Incas conquered it. As you know, it became their northern capital, and after the conquest of their empire the Spaniards occupied it. Today Quito has the charm of a Spanish city, with its beautiful churches and colonial homes. Its cobbled streets follow the hillside and are often so narrow that the overhanging balconies of the houses almost meet overhead.

The main square is the Plaza Independencia (een-day-pen-den'see-ah). Here is the big cream-colored cathedral where the body of General Sucre is buried. There are arcades on the plaza with Indian shops selling all sorts of trinkets. Indians in felt hats and striped ponchos shuffle barefooted across the square, and some carry red carnations and white lilies for sale.

One of the special sights of Quito is the street-cleaners. They are a tribe of Indians with long pigtails, wearing short white trousers and red ponchos, who have been especially chosen to clean the streets. Travelers also remember the loud and harsh church bells of Quito, which start ringing at five o'clock in the morning. About a half-hour's ride from the city is the Equator. It is marked by a shaft of pink granite surmounted by a marble globe with a silver line around the center. At the base is inscribed: Latitude 0° 0' 0".

Peru

In the cathedral at Lima in Peru, you can look through the glass sides of a coffin at the mummified body of Francisco Pizarro. You recall the days when this daring and ruthless conquistador scaled the Andes with a handful of men and horses, and snatched an empire for Spain. You remember the proud Inca, Atahualpa, who offered to fill a room with vessels

of gold in return for his freedom, only to be treacherously murdered when he had done so. Pizarro the Spaniard and Atahualpa the Indian are gone; but the civilizations they represented still live side by side. Today Peru is both a modern and an ancient land.

The Republic of Peru is bounded on the west by 1400 miles of ocean, and on the north, east, and south by five countries: Ecuador, Colombia, Brazil, Bolivia, and Chile. Peru shares with Bolivia the highest navigable body of water in the world, Lake Titicaca. Because the recent boundary settlement with Ecuador has increased her size, Peru pushes Colombia from her place as the third largest state of South America. Callao (cah-yah'o), the chief port, and Lima, the capital, are located about halfway down the desert coast.

WAR AND PEACE MARK PERU'S FIRST FIFTY YEARS

We left the story of Peru at the point where Bolívar had departed and a new government had been established. Peru's first years as a republic were full of turmoil. Military leaders who had risen to prominence during the struggle for independence alternated in power, and no other group was able to withstand them. Peru was also involved in wars with most of her neighbors, and for a brief period she joined Bolivia in a confederation formed by the Bolivian president, Santa Cruz. The first strong man to seize the reins of government was Ramón Castilla (rah-mohn' cahs-tee'-yah), who became president in 1844. He was a man of great ability who knew how to get along with his political enemies, and Peru made great progress under his stable government.

A large income had begun to come in from the sale of guano to European countries. Guano, you remember, is the rich fertilizer left by the birds on the coastal islands of Peru. Castilla used this income to pay off Peru's debts and to build railroads, telegraph lines, and schools. Both of Peru's present railroads to the Andes were started by him. In alliance with the Liberals of his time he also freed the Indians from payment of tribute and abolished Negro slavery.

Castilla's rule was followed in 1862 by ten years of extravagance and corruption in the use of the guano income by government officials. During this time Peru became involved in a war with Spain, which had never recognized her independence. Trouble started when Spain sent a fleet to demand damages for property losses during Peru's many revolutions. By seizing some of the guano deposits, she forced Peru to promise to pay a large indemnity. But this interference by the former mother country so enraged the Chileans that they declared war on Spain in 1865, and formed an alliance with Peru, Ecuador, and Bolivia. The war was short, however, for the Spanish fleet, after bombarding Valparaiso and Callao, withdrew to Europe. In a peace treaty of 1879, Spain finally recognized Peru's obvious independence.

PERU LOSES A WAR AND A PROVINCE

In the 1870's political control by the military class began to decline, and Peru was ruled by civilian presidents supported by a new class of wealthy planters and merchants. But unfortunately the republic soon became involved in a war between her neighbors, Chile and Bolivia. Bolivia's coast province of Atacama had rich deposits of nitrate of soda. She had given permission to companies from Chile to mine these nitrates for fertilizer and was making money by taxing the output of the mines. When Bolivia insisted on raising the tax contrary to an agreement, Chile protested, and Bolivia declared war in 1879. When Peru, which had an alliance with Bolivia, tried to mediate, Chile waged war on Peru as well. Neither of the allies was in condition to fight a war against Chile's well-trained army and navy. Chile occupied Bolivia's province of Atacama, and Peru's three southern provinces of Tarapacá, Tacna, and Arica. Troops even invaded the city of Lima and caused much needless destruction.

This one-sided War of the Pacific ended in a treaty of peace which made the Peruvians very angry. Tarapacá was ceded to Chile, and she was also given the right to occupy the provinces of Tacna and Arica for ten years. At the end of this time the treaty called for a vote by the inhabitants to determine to which country they wished to belong. In spite of many attempts, the voting was never carried through because of the feeling between the two countries. When President Hoover offered his services in 1929, the "Question of the Pacific" was finally settled. Chile retained the province of Arica, while Peru received a payment of $6,000,000 and the province of Tacna.

PERU MAKES PROGRESS AFTER 1900

The war was a terrific blow to Peru. She had lost territory and valuable resources; her treasury was empty and she owed an enormous debt. Income from guano had long since declined because of the competition of nitrate of soda and other fertilizers. Peru then settled her debt by turning over to her British creditors the use of her railroads for 66 years and her guano deposits up to 3,000,000 tons.

War had also brought the militarists back into political power, and it was a whole decade before the civilian party was able to gain control of the presidency. When it did, government became more stable and efficient, and Peru recovered more rapidly from the results of the war.

One of Peru's outstanding presidents in the 1900's was Augusto Leguía (ow-goos'toh lay-gee'yah), who was dictator from 1908 to 1912, and from 1919 to 1930. Although his rule was arbitrary and extravagant, Leguía carried out many improvements in Peru. With loans from the United States he built much-needed roads, paved city streets, installed water and sewer systems in over thirty cities. He encouraged foreigners to invest in Peru's cotton, sugar, and mining industries. New schools were built for the children who lived in the towns and cities, for education in Peru does not yet reach out to the millions of Indians in the highlands who have never seen a school. In 1930, Leguía was deposed by a revolution and later died in prison.

A constitution was formed in 1933, but presidents since Leguía have continued the tradition of strong leadership. Unable to read and write, most of the Indians have no share in the government.

EFFORTS TOWARD DEMOCRACY HAVE BEEN MADE IN PERU

For many years there has been a political party in Peru, whose followers believe the Indian people in the highlands should be educated so that they may share in the life of the nation. They would like to see the great estates broken up and the influence of the foreign corporations curbed. They would like to see a democratic Peru rise from the old Peru controlled by the Church, the army, and the landowners. This political party is called Apra. For a time Apra was a powerful force. It helped elect a president in 1945, who later deserted Apra for the property-owning classes. Apra was blamed for a navy revolt in 1948, and its leader was forced to hide. A military dictator took control, and in the election of 1951 Apra did not dare to take part. There was only one candidate, General Odria (oh-dree'-a), who became President of Peru.

NEW ROADS ARE UNITING PERU

One of the finest accomplishments of the government in recent years has been the building of new roads. It is now possible to drive in one day from Lima up over the Andes to Oroya (oh-roy'yah) and down to La Merced in the *montaña*. Fruits and vegetables from tropical valleys in the foothills of the eastern Andes are sent over this trans-Andean road to Lima. Another new road along the coast connects the agricultural valleys of the coastal region which were formerly reached only by sea. Now, for the first time in history, it is possible to drive from Lima to Arequipa (ah-ray-kee'pah), the commercial center of the south, thus connecting the two most important cities of Peru. When the road-building program is finished, the three sections of Peru will no longer be isolated.

DESERT PERU PRODUCES COTTON AND SUGAR

The wealth of many of Peru's families comes from the huge cotton and sugar *haciendas* in the river valleys along the coast. All these valleys are carefully irrigated as they used to be in the time of the Chimus and the Incas. Water from the rivers is controlled and by means of ditches sent through the fields as needed. In many places the old canals of the Indians are used, while in others new and more efficient irrigation works have been built. Yet, even with irrigation, only about one per cent of the coastal lands can be planted. Here is a strange fact: cotton is not planted every year in Peru as it is in the United States. If well fertilized, the same plant will bear from three to five years. The picking goes on all the year round, since there are no seasons in Peru.

It pays to raise sugar in Peru. Fifty dollars profit per acre is usual for sugar cane, many estates having over two thousand acres. The large estates have their own sugar mills to grind the cane, and short railroads to carry it to the nearest port. The workers on the *haciendas* are Indians or *cholos* (*mestizos*, half Indian, half Spanish), who live in adobe huts and cultivate small portions of land for themselves. They are required to work a certain number of days on the estate. Living conditions in the sugar country are very poor, but the Indian has never known better.

The Chiclín sugar estate belonging to a well-known Peruvian family has shown what can be done for Indian workers. The workmen and their families live in cottages with electric light and running water. There is a church, a theater, a playground and schools for the children. The estate makes large profits in spite of the money spent on its workers.

THE SIERRA PRODUCES COPPER, GOLD, AND SILVER

Peru, once famous for its gold and silver, is now best known for its copper. Although gold and silver are still produced to the amount of about $8,000,000 a year, the important mines in the *sierra* are the copper mines. They are located at Cerro de Pasco (say'roh day pahs'coh) in the western Andes, 15,000 feet above the sea. Indian workmen are able to endure hard labor at this altitude, but the white supervisors and engineers find it necessary to return to sea level every few months. A branch line of the Central Railroad goes north from Oroya to the mining region, and carries all the timber, steel, and machinery necessary to develop the mines. The copper is smelted and made into bars at the smelter in Oroya.

LIMA, LIKE PERU, IS BOTH OLD AND NEW

Tourists who visit Lima usually get off a passenger boat at Callao, the chief seaport of the country. Callao is almost directly south of New York City, even though it is on the west coast of South America. This city has one of the few good ports on the Pacific. A spur of rock extending into the sea and a breakwater two miles long form a bay protected from heavy ocean swells where many ships can anchor at the fine new docks and piers.

Sawders

THIS COPPER SMELTER has modern American machinery which is operated by trained highland Indians. The smelter and shops belong to the Cerro de Pasco Company at Oroya, Peru.

There is no difficulty in finding transportation from Callao to Lima, for a railroad, a trolley line, and four highways connect the two cities. A trolley car will take you to the capital in less than half an hour. Lima has no Indian background like Quito. You remember that Pizarro founded this new Spanish city near the coast, with its back turned on the Indian civilization in the highlands. He called it, grandly, "The City of the Kings," but the name was later changed to Lima, the Indian name for the near-by river. It was a proud city, home of the viceroy and of the most aristocratic Spanish society in the New World. The Church had its headquarters in Lima, which added to its importance.

Modern Lima is a city where yes-terday and today live side by side. There are new buildings, wide boulevards, and modern residential districts. The tourist from the United States sees familiar advertisements for American sewing machines and American automobile tires. Stores sell American radios and magazines, and display women's styles from New York and London. In the suburbs are several new government housing projects where the middle class workers live in modern apartment houses. There are also free hospitals in Lima, and fine modern schools.

HISTORIC BUILDINGS LINK LIMA WITH THE PAST

The old Lima can still be seen in the narrow streets built before the days of traffic, in the ancient buildings and the

Sawders

THE PALACE OF THE PRESIDENT at Lima, Peru, is an elaborate modern building with luxuriously furnished rooms. The room shown here is the dining room.

magnificent churches. In the center of the city is the old square called the Plaza de Armas (plah'sah day ar'-mahs). Here Pizarro laid the cornerstone for Lima's first cathedral. Although the original building was destroyed in an earthquake, the cornerstone and the great doors are part of the present cathedral. In this richly decorated church, with its altar of solid silver and its choir stalls of beautifully carved wood, rests the body of Francisco Pizarro. The cathedral is only one of the many splendid churches which remain as a monument to the religious devotion of the Spanish people.

Every visitor should see the stately old University of San Marcos, oldest in all the Americas. Long before any university existed in the United States, young men of the upper classes studied law, religion, language, and

philosophy in the halls and patios of San Marcos. Today, as in any other university, such courses as medicine, science, and engineering have been added.

One of the oldest libraries in America was the National Library of Peru. It had 60,000 rare books and ancient manuscripts. San Martín himself dedicated this library after he had entered Lima. In the year 1821, he spoke from the steps of the building against the ignorance which Spain had allowed to exist in the colonies. In 1943 the old building and its contents were almost completely destroyed by fire.

To visit the Torre Tagle (toh'ray tah'glay) Palace is like stepping back into the 1700's. This beautiful colonial mansion was considered the finest of its day. An elaborate hand-carved balcony of cedar extends across the front of the building. In the floors are exquisite tiles imported from Spain, and beautiful woods from Central America panel the walls. The lives of luxury led by the colonial aristocrats of Lima are revealed by the great stairways and balconies, the elaborate furniture and hangings. Today the palace is used as the Foreign Office, and sometimes renews its former glory when a grand ball is given there on some special occasion.

CUZCO IS AN INDIAN CITY

Lima represents Spanish Peru. The traveler who wishes to see Indian Peru must climb high into the *sierra*. The trip to Cuzco, ancient capital of the Incas, can now be made on the new highway which leaves Lima and climbs in circles up the rocky wall of the Andes to Oroya, crossing a pass 16,000 feet above the sea. As we have seen, the Central Railroad of Peru, highest railroad in the world, also scales the Andean heights to Oroya and the copper mining districts. At Oroya one branch of the road turns south and winds through the high, treeless valleys of the Andes. Here and there are tiny Indian villages of mud huts, and cultivated fields reach far up the mountain-side.

Cuzco itself is like no other city in the world. Here can be seen the two races and two civilizations that met 400 years ago. In its narrow cobbled streets Spanish women with black shawls over their heads walk past silent Indians driving their *llamas*. Ancient Inca walls, once part of the City of the Sun, are still standing.

FAMOUS TORRE TAGLE PALACE dates from the days of the viceroys. Here, at the entrance, you can see the hand-carved balconies of cedar. Notice, too, the iron grills on the street windows.

Galloway

IN THIS CUZCO MONASTERY, built over the Temple of the Sun, much of the original Inca stonework remains. In the foreground are Quechua Indians with their odd-shaped hats and hand-woven ponchos.

They were too solid for the Spaniards to tear down, so they built on top of them. Naturally, the tiled roofs and balconies of Spanish buildings look out of place above the massive Inca stonework.

The large square, Plaza de Armas, surrounded by arcaded sidewalks, is steeped in history. It was here that the palace of the Inca and the dazzling Temple of the Sun once stood. The last Inca prince, who led a revolt against the Spaniards, was executed in this square before his horrified Indian followers. Today, a church and monastery are built over the base of the temple, but one great curved wall of finely fitted stones reveals where the Sun God once dwelt. Also on the plaza is the huge cathedral with its altar of solid silver where today aristocratic Spaniards as well as humble Indians worship. Opposite stands the old university with its cloistered patios, once part of the Church of the Jesuits.

Cuzco is still partly surrounded by its colonial city walls. Except for a new hotel, fortunately built in Spanish colonial style, there is not a modern building in sight. The city seems to have dropped unchanged out of the 1700's, the symbol of an age-long historic past.

Bolivia

Which is the highest civilized country in the world? If you heard this question on a radio quiz, could you answer it? The correct answer is Bolivia. Her cities, mines, and railroads are on a plateau which is 12,000 to 15,000 feet above the sea. The plateau of Tibet is higher, but it could hardly be considered a civilized country. Although trees and grass and flowers are missing on the lofty tableland, there is a grandeur and a dramatic beauty about this bare country that travelers never forget. The thin, clear air makes everything stand out distinctly. Colors seem more intense, buildings are etched sharply against the horizon, and the stark outlines of the mountains pierce the heavens.

BOLIVIA IS AT THE TOP OF THE WORLD

Bolivia is a landlocked country enclosed by Peru, Brazil, Paraguay, Argentina, and Chile. The Andes cross Bolivia at even greater heights than in Peru. Two enormous ranges with peaks of from 19,000 to 21,000 feet rise to towering heights in western Bolivia. To reach the bleak and windy plateau which lies between them, you must climb by train or plane two and one half miles above the sea. Bolivians call this high tableland, on which three fourths of them live, the *altiplano* (ahl-tee-plah'no). This is a level region as large as the state of Ohio, but not nearly so fertile. It is cold and swept by storms in the winter; in summer it is cool except in the sun. The northern half of the *altiplano* has enough rain for crops, but in the south it is like a desert. On the *altiplano* are found Bolivia's chief cities: La Paz, Potosí, and Sucre.

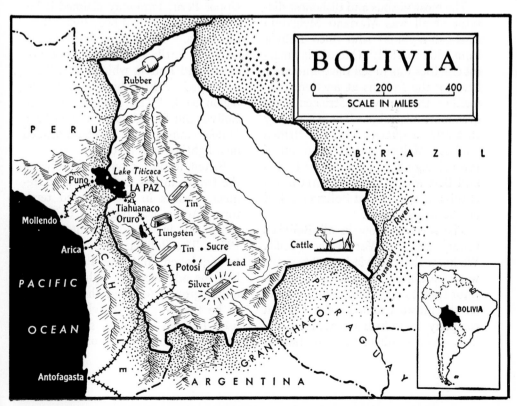

TURMOIL FOLLOWS BOLIVIA'S INDEPENDENCE

Bolivia's history has been the most troubled of all the states of Latin America, Ecuador included. The revolution which caused Sucre to resign was only the first of many that were to come. The new president, Andrés Santa Cruz, got into trouble with Chile and Argentina when in 1836 he attempted to join Peru and Bolivia into a confederation, with himself as "supreme protector." Troops from Chile invaded Peru and defeated Santa Cruz. That was the end of the confederation and, for the time being, of the ambitious ruler, who was forced into exile.

For the next forty years Bolivia's history is the old story of governments made and unmade by force. Dictator followed dictator. Bolivia's record for the 1800's shows 10 constitutions, 60 revolutions, 6 presidents assassinated, and a disastrous war.

The most vicious and dishonest dictator of all was Mariano Melgarejo (mel-gah-ray'hoh) who ruled Bolivia from 1864 to 1871. One of his greatest cruelties was to sell the community lands of the Indians at auction, thus making their poverty-stricken lives even more miserable. There is a story that after a quarrel with the British minister, Melgarejo drove him out of town riding naked on a donkey! It is said that when Queen Victoria heard of this outrage she had Bolivia marked off the British maps.

The severest blow in all Bolivia's history was the War of the Pacific. We know that Bolivia brought on the war with Chile. An unscrupulous dictator tried to collect an additional tax on the nitrates mined by a Chilean company in Bolivia's seacoast province. As a result of the war, Bolivia lost, not only her nitrates, but her Pacific province as well. Some years later, Chile agreed to allow Bolivia the use of the Pacific port of Arica and to build a railroad from that town to La Paz. The railroad was completed in 1913 and is the shortest and most used route to the Pacific.

THE CHACO WAR BRINGS BOLIVIA TO THE VERGE OF RUIN

In 1932, Bolivia became involved in one of the bloodiest and most useless wars in Latin American history. It was fought over the ownership of the Chaco (chah'coh), that huge interior territory between the Paraguay River and the Bolivian foothills. Bolivia, shut off from the sea, wanted a route across the Chaco to the ports on the Paraguay River, so that she could ship goods by boat to Buenos Aires. She claimed the Chaco because in colonial days it had been a part of Upper Peru; Paraguay claimed it because her people had been living there for years. The Chaco itself is not nearly so fertile as many parts of Paraguay and Bolivia which are still undeveloped. A Frenchman visiting the region said, "The struggle between Bolivia and Paraguay over the Chaco jungle reminds me of two bald-headed men fighting over a comb."

Bitter feeling developed between the two countries and there were frequent clashes in the disputed territory. Actual war began in 1932 and continued in bloody earnest until 1935. The Bolivian troops were better equipped, but the Paraguayans had the advantage of fighting on familiar ground for land they believed to be theirs. The Bolivian soldiers, used to high altitudes, suffered terribly in the hot lowlands of the Chaco.

Paraguay was able to occupy most of the disputed area, but could not gain a decisive victory on Bolivian territory. Not until they had lost 100,000 men between them, and were completely exhausted, did the two sides consent to a truce.

As in all wars, the dispute which caused the bloodshed remained to be settled. The neighboring nations joined with the United States in working out a treaty that gave most of the Chaco to Paraguay and an outlet on the upper Paraguay River to Bolivia. However, it will be many years before Bolivia recovers from this costly war.

BOLIVIA NEEDS STABLE GOVERNMENT

The man who did the most to aid Bolivia after 1900 was Ismael Montes (is-my-el' mohn'tays), who served two terms within the period between 1904 and 1917. He is known as *El Gran Presidente* (the great president) because of his achievements. He carried out a program of railroad construction greatly needed in Bolivia. For the first time La Paz was connected directly with the coast. He encouraged agriculture and built many primary schools.

Although Bolivia has made progress in some directions, her government is still unstable. Politics in that country are closely connected with the tin industry. The tin companies often support a president whom the miners dislike and revolutions are frequent.

BOLIVIA FACES MANY PROBLEMS

At present, Bolivia has handicaps which would tax the powers of the most able government. Maintaining her people on a barren plateau is only one of Bolivia's problems. The country is rich in minerals, but they are worthless without machinery and money to mine them, and railroads and highways to take them to markets. The disastrous Chaco War has left the country exhausted of men and money.

Democracy, as we know it, is impossible in Bolivia today, as it is in Ecuador and Peru. Over half of her inhabitants are pure-blooded Indians. They live in poverty on barren land or on the *haciendas*. The Spanish landowners and the better class *cholos* who control the government fear the Indian masses, and are unwilling to educate them or improve their living standards.

TRANSPORTATION IS IMPORTANT TO INLAND BOLIVIA

Railroads and railroad connections are vital to a country whose trade must reach the sea through foreign territory. The railroad-building program started by Montes has added many miles to Bolivia's rails. Today, for example, La Paz is connected with three ports on the Pacific and one on the Atlantic. A traveler can leave La Paz and travel by train to Antofagasta (ahn-toh-fah-gahs'tah) or Arica in Chile, or north via Lake Titicaca to Mollendo, port of Peru. If he wishes to go to Buenos Aires, he can make direct connections from La Paz. Beyond the railroads, however, transportation is primitive. Bolivia has few good roads, because she lacks money and technical skill and the country is large and difficult. Many communities not on the railroad are harder to reach than Buenos Aires, 1500 miles away! Mules and llamas are still the most common and the cheapest method of transportation within Bolivia.

FOOD AND FUEL ARE PROBLEMS IN BOLIVIA

Living is difficult on the *altiplano*. The climate is cold, good land is scarce, and few crops except potatoes and wheat will grow two and one half miles above the sea. Since most of the food and all manufactured goods must make the long, expensive trip from Chilean and Peruvian ports to the *altiplano*, the cost of living is high.

On the *altiplano* there are none of the fuels which we think of in connection with heating. There is neither wood nor coal nor much water power for electricity. The only fuels available are the dried dung of the llamas and a fibrous plant which grows on the rocks. Llama dung is sold in the towns for fuel; imported coal and petroleum are used chiefly in industry.

A NEW BOLIVIA MAY DEVELOP IN THE YUNGAS

On the eastern slopes of the Andes is a region called the *yungas* which is much more pleasant to live in than the bleak and windy *altiplano*. You remember that in the air-view we learned about Bolivia's fertile valleys 5000 to 8000 feet above sea level. Here the climate is excellent and almost any crops will grow. Today, enough food is produced in the *yungas* to make living much easier in the *altiplano*, but it is extremely difficult to transport the crops to La Paz. Only mule trails connect eastern Bolivia with the plateau, but a railway has been started which should help in developing the region. Many Bolivians believe that in time it will become the important area of the republic.

BOLIVIA IS FAMOUS FOR ITS TIN

The outstanding industry in Bolivia today is tin mining. Tin makes up two thirds of her exports and gives her second place in the world's tin production. The two richest mining regions are at Oruro and Potosí (poh-toh-see') in the eastern cordillera. The tin ore is found in veins in the rocky mountain-sides. Some of the veins are five feet across. Because of the lack of coal in Bolivia, the tin is not smelted there, but in the past has been shipped to England where the refining can be done more cheaply. Tin for our tin cans has had to come from a long distance, whether we bought Bolivian tin or that from the Malay States. Since the Japanese occupied the tin-producing areas in the Far East, the United States has constructed a huge smelter in Texas, and now imports its tin directly from Bolivia.

Until the 1900's, Bolivia was famous as a silver-producing country. During the colonial period, a mountain of silver ore at Potosí made vast fortunes for Spanish mine-owners. Potosí became a rich city where the mining aristocracy lived in crude but extravagant splendor. Over a billion dollars' worth of silver was taken from this region alone. At last the silver veins were exhausted, and silver is no longer important in Bolivia. It is interesting to know that the same hill of silver which was honeycombed with tunnels by silver miners is today being mined for tin. The Spaniards found tin when they were searching for silver, but discarded it as worthless.

LAKE TITICACA IS A GATEWAY TO BOLIVIA

Travelers to Bolivia may enter the country by way of Lake Titicaca. The steamship waiting at the pier at

Sawders

SNOW–CROWNED MT. ILLIMANI rises in the background in this view of La Paz, highest city in the world. With a population of over 300,000, La Paz is the actual capital of Bolivia, although the official capital is Sucre.

Puno (pooh'noh), on the Peruvian side of the lake, looks out of place in such a high, remote region. It was built in England, shipped in sections, and put together on the shore of the lake! The boat leaves the barren and treeless shore for a ten-hour trip to the Bolivian side of the water, passing on its course the numerous balsas or reed boats of the Indians, which look much more at home than a steamboat. Because wood is lacking at this altitude, these native lake craft are made of the tall bulrushes which grow along the lake shore. Bundles of the reeds are tied together and turned up at the ends to make the hull of the boat. Mats made of the split reeds serve as sails. When the balsas become waterlogged, they are pulled up on the shore and allowed to dry.

The steamer passes the two sacred islands of the Sun and the Moon where legend says the first Inca and his wife were born. Ruined palaces and temples can be seen on the larger island of the Sun. Near the port on the Bolivian side of the lake are the ruins of Tiahuanaco, that ancient kingdom which flourished long before the Incas. Giant stone idols of men and animals have been dug up from the ruins, but little is known about the men who made them. The Indians are superstitious about these ruins and refuse to work for the archeologists there, without first conducting mysterious ceremonies.

LA PAZ IS THE HIGHEST CITY IN THE WORLD

A new highway which is to be part of the Pan-American Highway runs from the lake to La Paz, forty miles away. The city of La Paz is built in a canyon below the surface of the surrounding plateau, where it is protected from the unpleasant climate above. In its strange canyon, it has streetcars, electric lights and telephones, but little of that colonial architecture which is typically Spanish. Tourists find it difficult to breathe deeply in the rarefied atmosphere of the plateau. Physical exertion causes the heart to pound and the ears to roar. It is even more unpleasant to get the dread *soroche* (soh-roh′chay) or mountainsickness. If you who have been seasick can imagine a headache and lack of breath added to the usual symptoms of seasickness, you will have a good idea of what *soroche* is like.

Most of the market booths are in charge of the *chola* women who buy the goods from the Indians. The *cholas* are a colorful sight in their wide full skirts and shawls of the most brilliant hues — cerise, orange, green, blue, all mixed with a gay disregard of color combinations. Hard derby-like hats are perched on top of their black, braided hair, and many of them wear shoes with the highest heels possible. When the Indians come to town on market days, the streets are full of color from their bright woven ponchos and petticoats.

There are many educated people in La Paz who are deeply interested in literature, painting, and music. As in Bogotá, they gather in cafés for discussion. They are proud of their sky-top republic and of their Spanish-Indian culture.

Are You a Careful Reader?   Test Yourself!

I. Can you supply the correct word for each blank?

1. Three countries occupy the former Inca kingdom, ... , ... , and .... . In all three progress was hindered for a long time by military .... , and by .... war. All three countries have large .... populations.

2. Ecuador has had two rival cities, ... , the highland capital and .... , the port and largest city. These cities are connected by a .... which took .... years to build.

3. Ecuador was once the world's largest producer of .... but she lost her markets to ..... Latitude 0° 0′ 0″ means ..... .

4. Peru's capital is .... and her chief seaport is ..... .

5. Peru fought the .... of the .... with Chile over the .... provinces and lost .... of her provinces to ..... .

6. Peru is building many new .... to connect coastal and highland cities as well as to unite the three regions. .... , ... , and .... are among the chief products of Peru.

7. Bolivia is an .... country without a .... , but her capital, ... , is connected with the Pacific coast by three ..... .

8. Bolivia lost her nitrate province on the .... through her war with ..... Another severe blow to Bolivia was her war with .... over the .... territory.

9. Lack of .... and .... is a great handicap to Bolivia. Bolivia is second in the world's .... production and now exports directly to the ....

II. Can you match these words and statements?

1. Cotopaxi
2. altiplano
3. San Marcos
4. Alfaro
5. Arica
6. Cuzco
7. Leguía
8. Apra
9. Montes
10. Cerro de Pasco

a. Lima's old university
b. copper mine in Peruvian Andes
c. nitrate province of Peru granted to Chile
d. highest active volcano in world
e. ancient Inca capital and modern Peruvian city
f. seaport of Bolivia
g. high plateau where Bolivian cities are located
h. liberal president of Ecuador who completed Quito-Guayaquil Railroad
i. famous colonial palace in Lima
j. dictator of the 1920's under whom Peru made great progress
k. democratic reform party in Peru
l. "The Great President" of Bolivia who built railroads and schools

Food for Thought and Discussion

1. Show by examples what war has done to Peru and Ecuador. Could wise leaders have prevented the disastrous effects of the Chaco War and the War of the Pacific?

2. Do you think the mineral resources and railroads of Peru, Ecuador, and Bolivia should be in the hands of foreign companies? Give reasons.

Chapter 27

The Sons of the Incas Inhabit the Highlands of Ecuador, Peru, and Bolivia

FOUR HUNDRED YEARS ago millions of squat brown men lived in the valleys and plateaus of the Andes. Their cities and villages and farms stretched from Quito in the north to Chile in the south. They spaded the earth with bent sticks and diverted mountain streams to irrigate their crops.

They kept herds of llamas and wove their wool into garments. They worshiped the Sun God, and thought they were ruled by a divine being descended from the Sun. As you know, these were the Quechuas, living in the great empire of the Incas.

Today the sons of the Incas still

Sawders

THIS INDIAN WOMAN of Peru is spinning llama wool just as her Inca ancestors did. She twists the raw wool between her fingers and spins it into yarn on the whirling distaff.

in the Andes. The huts, the dusty streets, and the hills stretching behind the town are all brown. On the two steep streets which clamber up the hill are the windowless mud huts where the inhabitants live. There are a few eucalyptus trees around the huts and in the little plaza; water from a near-by spring pours into a central fountain. There is, of course, a church facing the plaza. Its adobe tower is covered with white stucco and stands a full story higher than the huts. When the bell is rung, the Indian women and children go to Mass and carry on a strange, primitive chanting. But there is no school in Huayao, Peru, as there is in Santa Cruz Etla in Mexico. The Indians cannot read and write, nor can they even speak Spanish. They speak the ancient tongue of the Quechua race to which they belong.

Below the town flows a rushing mountain stream. In the valley of the stream, corn and potatoes are grown by primitive irrigation methods. From the lookout of an Indian herder in the mountains above the town, the valley seems like a live patchwork quilt. There are squares of brown, green, and yellow; some fields newly plowed are brown; some are green with growing corn and potatoes; others are yellow with ripened corn. Each field is surrounded by a hedge of century plants. It seems strange to us that there are no seasons except wet and dry in the highlands near the Equator.

Plowing is unbelievably primitive in Huayao. A traveler in the Andean countries reported that he did not see a single iron plow. Where wheat is grown, the sheaves are trampled on hard earthen floors by oxen as in Bib-

inhabit their ancestral land. Their fine cities no longer exist and the last of the Inca rulers was killed by the Spaniards centuries ago. But the common people work their farms, weave their clothes, and tend their llama flocks much as they did four centuries ago. Although they have become Christians, their religious festivals are still much like the ancient ceremonies in honor of the Sun God. They care little who rules the land if they are left alone to live their lives as did their ancestors before them.

LIFE IS PRIMITIVE IN AN INDIAN VILLAGE

In the high Andes of central Peru is an Indian village which has survived since Inca days. It is typical of the community villages of the Andean Indians. Huayao (whah-yah'oh) is a bare brown town like many others

lical days. Although the Indians work hard and plant every square inch of tillable land, their old-fashioned methods and ignorance of scientific agriculture restrict the size of their crops. Yet they are the farmers of the highlands and upon them depends the food supply of the region.

INDIAN FLOCKS FURNISH WOOL FOR CLOTHING

Flocks of sheep and llamas graze upon the bare mountain-side above Huayao. There are sheep as well as the native llamas. The people are particularly proud of their black sheep whose wool is used for men's clothing and for blankets. The women and children of the village care for the flocks, spin the wool into thread, and weave cloth from it.

The small girl who herds the sheep and llamas on the hillside dangles from her hands a whirling distaff on which her fingers deftly turn the woolen thread. At home in front of the thatched adobe hut, her mother weaves the wool into cloth by means of a hand loom very much like those seen in Guatemala. It is so cold in this high village that heavy woolen clothes are necessary. The women dye the wool of the white sheep with bright red and blue dyes and make for themselves striped skirts and gay shawls or *mantas*. They use the same designs woven by their Inca ancestors. The wool is finer and tighter than that woven by the Mexican *sarape* weavers, so that the cloth will keep out the cold winds of the Andes.

The women do the cooking and prepare the corn beer or *chicha* (chee′chah) which is the common drink for all ages. *Chicha* is a heritage from Inca days when the people were as hearty drinkers as they are today.

PERSONAL HYGIENE IS UNKNOWN IN HUAYAO

Visitors to Huayao would find close contact with the Indians rather unpleasant. The Andean Indian never takes a bath, nor does he wash his clothes. The women's skirts are put on one after another as those underneath fall off in rags. Men, women, and children are usually alive with fleas and vermin. Many of them suffer from diseases which are the result of their unsanitary living conditions.

It is hard for us to imagine a level of living as low as that of the Indians of Huayao and other towns in the high Andes. There are no washbowls in their mud huts, nor any soap. Water may be used for drinking or cooking, but not for washing. All the members of the family sleep with their clothes on to protect themselves from the bitter cold of Andean nights.

THE SILVER STAFF of office is proudly displayed by this Quechua Indian *cacique* or chieftain. Notice, too, the silver cross which he wears.

Black Star

Galloway

ANDEAN INDIANS are threshing the wheat crop which they have grown on their community-owned land. When the wheat is threshed it will be divided among the Indians of the village.

Their bed is a single pallet on the dirt floor.

HUAYAO IS A SELF–GOVERNING TOWN

The people of Huayao have chosen their own chieftain for hundreds of years. They call him a *cacique* (kah-see'kay) and he is distinguished from the other Indians by the silver staff which he carries. Squatting on the dirt in front of the church steps the men of the village hold council meetings. The council decides on the time for plowing, on the care of widows and orphans of the community, or on the celebration of religious festivals. Seldom does the Peruvian government send an official to a free mountain village like Huayao, for the Indians know and trust their own *cacique* and have little to do with the white people in the capital. This attitude is quite different from that of the Indians of Santa Cruz Etla in Mexico, who are proud to have a part in the larger state government.

In Huayao the people own their land in the same communal manner as did their forbears centuries ago. They hold no written deeds to prove their right of ownership, for the land has simply been passed down from generation to generation. Because many community lands have been seized by estate owners or by well-to-do *mestizos*, laws have recently been passed by the government of Peru prohibiting seizure of community-owned lands. Community villages like Huayao are called *ayllus* (eye'yoos) and are like the *ejido* villages in Mexico.

MONEY MEANS LITTLE TO THE PEOPLE OF HUAYAO

The villagers have little use for money, since they grow their own food and make their own clothes. They do not want the luxuries of the white man, and the few things they need which they do not produce on their mountain farms they can usually get at the near-by market town by barter. Sometimes, if he has a particular need for money, the Indian leaves his crops to work in the mines or on the sugar and cotton *haciendas* on the coast. But when the time comes to harvest his crops, he leaves his white employer and returns to his native village. He is happiest when he is alone, working his small plot of land and harvesting his meager crops.

THE FIESTA IS ONE OF THE FEW AMUSEMENTS OF THE INDIANS

The people of Huayao work hard and have few pleasures. One day which they all look forward to is the 28th of July, when they hold their annual celebration in honor of their patron saint. On the church steps they give a play which tells the story of the coming of Pizarro to the court of Atahualpa. Everyone in the village has seen this play every year throughout his lifetime. The parts are all played by men and are mainly in the Quechua language. But the person who carries the part of Pizarro must be able to speak some Spanish because his lines are in that language. Since only a few of the grown men who go away from town to distant markets know any Spanish at all, it does not matter whether Pizarro's part is given in good Spanish or not. The play is not written down, for

THIS RELIGIOUS PROCESSION of Quechua Indians is a queer mixture of ancient Inca customs and the Catholic faith. While the crosses are symbols of the Church, the queer thing in the rear is a saint's statue hidden by green branches!

Black Star

only the priest of the village can read and write; most of the citizens know the play by memory.

As you can imagine, it is a great honor in the village to take one of the two leading parts. Every rehearsal goes on in the village square in front of the same audience which will see the final play — but no one minds. On the afternoon of the *fiesta* day, Indians from surrounding villages come to Huayao and gather in the square. A stage has been erected on the church steps. Women sit on the ground selling *chicha* from large clay jars. The crowd waits and waits. Finally the characters arrive and the story is acted out accompanied by a great deal of Indian dancing and native music. The music, as it is played on a flute and a set of pipes, seems very plaintive and melancholy to us. The songs which are sung at the Huayao *fiesta* have never been written down; but the tunes and the verses, like the parts in the play, are handed down from one generation to the next through the centuries.

The play ends with the death of Atahualpa while the village dancers rush up to the stage and stamp out a dance as a final act. Then the audience files into the little earthen-floored church. The sunset light falls through the open door upon village people kneeling while a procession winds its way to the altar. The Indians have taken off their sandals and hold them in their hands as they kneel. Twelve men form the procession, carrying silver-mounted staffs and wearing red wool hats with high crowns. The priest then blesses the parade and all the characters in the play.

By this time it is dark outside and a cold wind blows through the eucalyptus trees. The Indians pull their ponchos and *mantas* close around them as they go home to their adobe huts. Tomorrow, perhaps, they will sell their extra corn and bright hand-weaving at the market at Huancayo (whahn-cah'yoh) or some closer market town.

LLAMAS ARE THE MOST IMPORTANT ANIMAL IN THE HIGHLANDS

When the Indians of Huayao set out for market on the steep and narrow trail leading out of their valley, they are accompanied by llamas carrying their goods. The Indian's best friend is his dainty, bright-eyed llama who steps along the trail with a haughty and superior air. Indeed the llama is treated almost like a member of the family. When he is full grown, a party is sometimes given for him. His ears are pierced and strands of colored wool are tied in them. He is then ready to work on the trail.

The llama can travel long distances over difficult trails without water, nibbling on the sparse grass by the roadside. He not only carries the burdens, but his wool furnishes clothing to the highland Indians, and his hide gives them leather. The dried dung of the llama furnishes almost the only fuel in the barren sierra, while his meat makes good food.

This animal has a temperament that must be respected. Apparently he remembers that he was once the sacred animal of the Incas. He will not be hurried and he will not be overloaded. He willingly carries a load of about 100 pounds, but if the load is greater, he lies down and refuses to move until it is lightened. No Indian would ever

E. M. Jarrett

THESE LORDLY LLAMAS bow to no man! Loaded with the exact amount which they condescend to carry, they are on their way to market. Notice how daintily they step.

whip a llama, but directs him by whistling. In town the llamas may take a notion to follow worshipers into a church and policemen are powerless to prevent them. But let a small Indian boy step up, whistle, talk to them in Quechua, and they go back to their business.

INDIAN DRESS IS COLORFUL

On the way to market, Indians in bright costumes fill the roads. The gay colors seem a great contrast to their drab lives. In Bolivia women wear scarlet or purple *mantas* and half a dozen full skirts of different colors. Each one carries a load in the *manta* on her back. There may be a baby, two or three live ducks, or both! The men have clothes of black wool embroidered with gay designs. No Indian would be without his poncho, which is often made of llama wool woven in stripes as bright as the skirts of the women.

The straw sombrero of the Mexican is not worn in the Andes. In Peru both men and women wear felt hats made of wool which has been pounded into a damp mass until the fibers cling together. Then it is spread out and dried in order to hold its shape. The hats are often turned up all around so that the wind will not blow them away. Under the hat the men often wear a red cap with earlaps, for it gets very cold two and a half miles above the sea. Even when it is coldest, the Indians seldom wear shoes. A sandal of llama skin protects their feet on the rough trails as they go to market.

HUANCAYO IS A FAMOUS MARKET TOWN

Indians from Huayao and other towns come in great numbers to the Sunday market of Huancayo. It is also a popular place for tourists because it is on the railroad from Lima. On the main street of the town all kinds of goods are for sale. There are rugs and ponchos of intricate designs

THE INDIAN WOMEN in this picture have a variety of merchandise for sale: baskets, small chairs, clay animals, sandals, and jewelry of silver. They are from Oroya, high in the Andes, as their felt hats show.

made by the men of some highland village; from another village there is pottery made with clay from the same pits which were worked by the Incas. The craftsmen of today, however, do not know how to sift and wash the clay nor make the beautiful designs their ancestors made. There may also be blankets of the silky wool of the vicuña, that rare animal which lives in the heights of the Andes. So difficult is it to hunt this creature that its long fine wool brings a high price. In the markets, too, are sold pigs, corn, beans, potatoes, toy llamas for lucky tokens, dolls, hides — everything which is grown or made.

At Huancayo, Indians who wish them can buy store-made things: bolts of factory calico, American ten-cent-store beads and earrings. Compared to the silver filigree work made by Indian silver workers, these baubles seem very cheap indeed.

The market is the only pleasure the Indians have outside of the *fiestas*. They go to see their friends, to gossip, and to drink *chicha*. If you were to stop an Indian on the trail outside Huancayo and offer to buy all his load of goods at a high price, he would probably refuse you. The market is the high point of the week for the Indians and they do not want to miss it.

ANDEAN INDIANS HAVE THE DRUG HABIT

Also for sale in the market are large piles of leaves from the coca shrub. This shrub should not be confused with cacao or coconut; it is the plant from which the drug, cocaine, is derived. Cocaine is used to deaden pain, but it is so dangerous that we have laws in this country against its use without a doctor's prescription. In ancient times, the Indians learned that the leaves of this plant when chewed produced a dreamlike feeling and gave the user a sense of extra strength. They allowed the plant to be used only on special occasions when they were subject to unusual exertions. Today almost all Andean Indians from Colombia to Chile chew coca leaves continually. Children of ten or twelve are seen with wads of the leaves in their cheeks.

Coca is so much in demand that it has become the chief crop on the eastern slopes of the Andes, in Peru and Bolivia. It grows wild in the forests of the *montaña*, but most of the coca comes from plantations. The Indians will make almost any sacrifice to get coca leaves. The cocaine in the leaves gives them great resistance to fatigue and lessens the pangs of hunger. An Indian can walk the mountain trails all day without food if he has his wad of coca in his mouth. But coca keeps the user dull and stupefied. Probably a great deal of the stupidity which white men complain of in the Indian is due to the fact that he is in a drugged condition most of the time. Certainly the chewing of coca leaves is one of the greatest hindrances to progress among the Indian people.

MOST OF THE INDIANS LIVE AS PEONS ON THE LARGE ESTATES

The inhabitants of Huayao and other *ayllus* are called "free Indians." Only about a third of the Andean Indians are fortunate enough to be free Indians. The rest live for the most part on the enormous landholdings which take up most of the good land of Ecuador, Peru, and Bolivia. The landowners seldom live on the *haciendas*, preferring the more social atmosphere of Lima or Quito or Europe. Their estates are run by *cholos*, who are often neglectful and inefficient.

The Indians who live on the land are allowed a piece of ground to cultivate and a hut to sleep in. They also keep a few llamas or sheep. They are required to work a certain number of days each year for the landlord and to buy their supplies from him. In spite of recent laws forbidding the holding of Indians for debt, the Indian is considered part of the estate and must remain on it even when it is sold. The estate Indian lives a hopeless life of poverty and ignorance. He is silent and obedient to his white master, but has no feeling of friendship or loyalty toward him.

QUECHUAS AND AYMARÁS LIVE IN THE HIGHLANDS

The Quechua Indians form the largest group in the highland region of Ecuador, Peru, and Bolivia. The Quechuas are small, about five feet in height and of stocky build. They are so serious by nature that even the babies and children never smile!

Many of the Indians of the *altiplano* in Bolivia are Aymarás (eye-mah-rahs'), who are larger and heavier than the Quechuas. They are also less docile and submissive than the other Indians. They live a much harder life than the Indians of Ecuador and Peru, for they must struggle continuously against cold and hunger on the bleak plateau. The Aymarás live in stone huts without windows; a hole in the top lets out the smoke

Lanks

THESE BOLIVIAN INDIANS on the shore of Lake Titicaca are dancing a strange, whirling dance in honor of the grain harvest. Don't the two women look like enormous tops in their many skirts?

from the dung fire which burns in the middle of the floor.

Since wheat and corn will not grow well at great altitudes, the Aymará lives chiefly on potatoes. Dry, frozen potatoes are made into a dish called *chuño* (choo'nyoh). The potatoes grown on the *altiplano* are small, round ones, not at all like the Burbank, Idaho, or Maine variety which we are used to. They are spread out on the ground and allowed to freeze during the cold nights. During the day, the potatoes are stamped out by barefooted children into a pulpy mass. This freezing and stamping process is repeated until all the juice is squeezed out. When the sun comes out, the pulp dries. This is used instead of bread and will keep for years. The Aymará eats little meat or bread, but sometimes the *chuño* is cooked with mutton or llama meat as a *fiesta* dish.

Living as he does, it is little wonder that the Aymará is sullen and defiant.

The Indians of Bolivia who own their own land in villages love it deeply. In fact, it is said that an Indian would rather sell his child than give up his land. Nothing will make him leave his humble hut where he and his father before him were born. If his village is taken over by a neighboring *hacienda*, the Indian goes with it, still clinging to his ancestral soil.

INDIAN EDUCATION IS AN IMPORTANT PROBLEM IN PERU, BOLIVIA, AND ECUADOR

Tourists may see the Andean Indians as picturesque and interesting people, but they are much more than that. Their backwardness is a serious hindrance to the development of the countries in which they live. Imagine what the United States would be like if half our population were made up of

310

Indians who lived as did the North American tribes of four centuries ago! It is easy to see why these Andean countries have not made such rapid progress toward modern civilization as Colombia and Costa Rica, for instance, where few Indians exist. Half of the people of Peru, Ecuador, and Bolivia live in another cultural age and take no part in the national life. They do not speak Spanish, and do not wish to learn. They know nothing of sanitation and cleanliness. Food production in the highlands depends entirely upon the labor of the Indians, yet they refuse to change their primitive methods.

The only solution of the Indian problem is a long and uphill program of education such as Mexico has started. Peru has made a little progress toward improving the lot of the Indians. The Bureau of Indian Affairs in Lima has sent out "cultural brigades" like the cultural missions of Mexico. Into highland villages trucks carry books, sanitary equipment, and motion pictures showing the cause and cure of diseases. The program works especially well where the villages own their own land. A certain village in Peru has built a rural school. With the help of trained leaders that same village has built an electric light plant, a flour mill, and a long irrigation canal. Of course, this is an unusual example, but it does show what the Indians can accomplish if they are encouraged to improve their lives.

At one time during the 1500's, the Pope sent word to the Spanish priests and landowners that the American Indian was human and was not to be treated like an animal. Certainly few landowners ever took this statement seriously; for four hundred years the Indian has been treated as little better than an animal. Indeed today, drugged with coca and often drunk from *chicha*, he is not much better off than many animals.

Recently there has been a definite movement toward bettering the condition of the Indians. New political parties, such as the Apra in Peru, are demanding not only education for the Indians, but a share in the government. But the spirit of consideration for the Indian people which we saw in Mexico is still lacking in the Andean countries of South America. It may be years before Peru, Bolivia, and Ecuador establish a widespread program to help the Indians. However, dull-witted and stupid as they may seem, it is well to remember that the humble people of the Andes are the sons of a great race which once had the most advanced civilization in the Americas.

Are You a Careful Reader?   Test Yourself!

I. Can you supply the correct word for each blank?

1. The ancestors of the Andean Indians were the cultured . . . . .

2. A powerful modern drug called . . . . is manufactured from the leaves of an Andean shrub. The Indians chew these . . . . leaves which are said to give great . . . . , but which make the user . . . . .

3. The Andean Indians live in deepest . . . . and suffer from many . . . . .

4. Their greatest need is for . . . . .

5. Expeditions sent to Indian villages to carry motion pictures and sanitary equipment are known as . . . .

II. Can you match the following words and statements?

1. Quechuas	*a.* frozen, dried potatoes
2. chuño	*b.* large market town of Peru interesting to tourists
3. Aymarás	*c.* shawls worn by Indian women
4. "free Indians"	*d.* tribe descended from the Indians of the Inca empire
5. chicha	*e.* Indians of Bolivia
6. cacique	*f. mestizos* or half-breeds
7. Huancayo	*g.* village owning land in common
8. ayllu	*h.* high priest at *fiesta*
9. mantas	*i.* beer made from fermented corn
10. Huayao	*j.* Indians living in *ayllus*
	k. typical highland *ayllu*
	l. chief chosen by free Indians

Food for Thought and Discussion

1. Compare the Mexican village of Santa Cruz Etla with the Peruvian village of Huayao. In which has more progress been made? Why?

2. In what ways are the Andean Indians worse off today than they were in the days of the Incas?

3. If you had charge of the government of an Andean country, what would you do for these millions of poverty-stricken and ignorant Indians?

Interesting Things to Do

1. Find out all you can about the new Simón Bolívar Highway from Caracas to Quito and report on it to the class.

2. Learn more about one of the interesting men mentioned in this part of the book and tell the class about him.

3. Look up information on one of the following subjects and report to the class: the Barca oil pipeline in Colombia; the construction of the Guayaquil to Quito Railroad, or the Central or Southern Railroad of Peru; the Cerro de Pasco copper mine in Peru; Simón Patiño and the tin industry of Bolivia; the oil industry at Lake Maracaibo.

4. Tell the class about the Chiclín sugar estate in Peru and its model workers' village.

5. Look up *National Geographic* articles on the Aymará, Quechua, or Otavalo Indians. Give a talk on one of these tribes, showing pictures if possible.

6. Check the Pan American Union Bulletins for up-to-date information on Indian schools.

7. Look up the cacao industry and tell the story of a chocolate bar from its beginning to its end!

8. Make cartoons of Juan Bimba and his reactions to the New Deal in Venezuela.

9. Draw and color pictures of the gay clothes of the Andean Indians, or make a sketch of an Indian market or *fiesta*.

10. Write a story about a boy or girl living in an Indian village in the Andes.

Interesting Books to Read

For Further Information

Clark, Sydney A., *The West Coast of South America*. Prentice-Hall. A travel book emphasizing Andean geography.

Fergusson, Erna, *Venezuela*. Knopf. Comments on present conditions and recent history.

Franck, Harry, *Vagabonding down the Andes*. Grosset. A travel story containing much factual material.

Niles, Blair, *Colombia, Land of Miracles*. Grosset. Past and recent history.

Witherspoon, Anna, *Let's See South America*. Southern Publishing Company. Easy and interesting travel story written in the first person.

For Pleasure

Dickey, Herbert Spencer, *My Jungle Book*. Little Brown. Travels in the Orinoco Basin.

Niles, Blair, *Peruvian Pageant*. Bobbs Merrill. A novelist's search for material about the Indians.

Overbeck, Alicia, *Living High*. Appleton-Century. Adventures of the wife of a mining engineer in Bolivia.

Thomas, Margaret Loring, *The Packtrain Steamboat*. Bobbs Merrill. Easy-reading fiction about the boat on Lake Titicaca.

Part Seven · THE NATIONS OF

ARE VIGOROUS

Tropic of
Capricorn

B O L I V I A

P A R A G U A Y

B R A Z I L

ASUNCIÓN ⊙

Paraná River

C H I L E

A R G E N T I N A

SANTIAGO ⊙

URUGUAY

BUENOS ⊙
AIRES

⊙ MONTEVIDEO

Río de la Plata

P A C I F I C   O C E A N

A T L A N T I C

O C E A N

THE TEMPERATE COUNTRIES OF SOUTH AMERICA

0   200   400
SCALE IN MILES

TEMPERATE SOUTH AMERICA

AND PROGRESSIVE

In Part VII we shall visit the countries which enjoy June weather in December — the republics of temperate South America, where the seasons are the reverse of ours. These countries are entirely different from the other nations we have studied. The climate is cool and the people are vigorous. There were no large Indian civilizations in these southern countries, so there was no problem of assimilating millions of native peoples. Immigrants from Europe have come by the thousands to the rich lands of Chile, Argentina, and Uruguay. Today these countries are predominantly white with people much like our own.

Paraguay, the fourth country in southern South America, cannot be classed with the other three. It is partly in the Tropics and partly in the Temperate Zone. It is not an Andean country, nor is it a typical Temperate Zone country. The story of Paraguay, however, is told with that of Uruguay, since they are the two smallest countries in South America.

On the opposite page is a map of the four southern countries of South America. Note their boundaries and give their capital cities. To what region in North America would the southern part of Chile and Argentina correspond (compare latitudes, using classroom map)? To what region in North America would the northern part correspond? How does the location of Paraguay make it different from the other countries?

Now you are ready to get acquainted with countries in which you will feel at home. As you read the next few chapters, keep your attention on these questions:

1. In what ways are Chile and the United States alike?

2. Why is Argentina one of the most important nations in Latin America?

3. Why is Uruguay considered one of the most democratic countries in the world?

4. What is the explanation for the backwardness of Paraguay and the progressiveness of Uruguay?

Chapter 28

Changing Chile Takes Her Place Among Democratic Nations

It is five years since I came from the provinces of Peru as directed by the Governor Marquis D. Francisco Pizarro, to conquer and settle these provinces... called Chile.... We went through the first two [years] in very great want, so great that I could not describe it; and many of the Christians had to go sometimes to dig up roots for food,... and now from henceforward there will be a great abundance of food in this land, for there are two sowings in the year.... For this land is such that there is none better in the world for living in and settling down.[1]

THIS IS PART of a long letter written four hundred years ago to the King of Spain by the *conquistador* who founded Chile, Captain Pedro de Valdivia (vahl-dee'vee-ah). In addition to the starvation he speaks of, the colonists suffered Indian attacks. Valdivia himself was tortured to death by the fierce Araucanian Indians who inhabited southern Chile, but his settlement in Santiago survived to become part of the Chilean nation.

His letter shows that he realized the wealth of Chile lay, not in precious metals, but in her rich soil and warm climate. Little did he dream, however, that the copper and nitrates of northern Chile would one day produce wealth beyond even a *conquistador's* dreams.

CHILE'S GEOGRAPHY DIVIDES HER LAND AND UNITES HER PEOPLE

Travelers find that Chile is one of the pleasantest of all the lands in South America. This long stringbean of a country is bounded by the Andes on the east and the Pacific Ocean on the west. Wherever you look in Chile you see the Andes, either silhouetted against the distant sky or looming up close by. The coastal range runs parallel to the Andes and further narrows the land of Chile. Yet it is not a mountain country.

We have already learned in Part One that Chile is divided crosswise into three distinct regions.[2] The heart of Chile is the sunny central valley between the Andes and the coastal range. Here are most of the farms, industries, and cities. It rains in this valley only in the winter months, but the rivers rising in the Andes furnish water for summer irrigation just as they do in the coastal valleys of Peru. When we speak of Chile we usually mean this central region which

---

[1] R. B. Graham, *Pedro de Valdivia, Conqueror of Chile*. The Society of Authors, London.

[2] Before reading farther, turn to pages 25–28 and review Chile's geography.

is home to four fifths of the Chileans.

Chileans do not feel at home in the region which lies south of the musical-sounding Río Bío Bío (bee′oh). In spite of its beautiful lakes, its forests, and its deep fiords, the southern country is too cold and too wet for the average Chilean. The sunbaked region of northern Chile also attracts few people. For the most part only those employed in mining nitrates or copper live in this parched and barren land.

Although geography divides the land, it has united the Chilean people. Isolated by Nature's barriers the Chileans, like the Colombians, have had to learn to shift for themselves. In colonial days they were separated from their neighbors by desert and mountains which made travel difficult. Ships from Europe had to make the long trip around the Horn to reach Chile. Furthermore, settlers not only had to fight for every acre of land, but they had to defend it against the warlike Indians who occupied the country. They had to harness mountain streams to get water for irrigating their farms. Chileans were forced to be tough in order to survive. It is no wonder that, shut within their narrow boundaries, they became a strong and self-reliant people with a deep feeling of patriotism.

WHO ARE THE CHILEANS?

The 150 settlers who accompanied Valdivia to Chile have increased until today Chile has nearly 6,000,000 inhabitants. It was a hundred years before the Spaniards succeeded in subduing the hostile Araucanian Indians. Unlike the Incas, they refused to submit to the white men. They fought so fiercely for their cherished

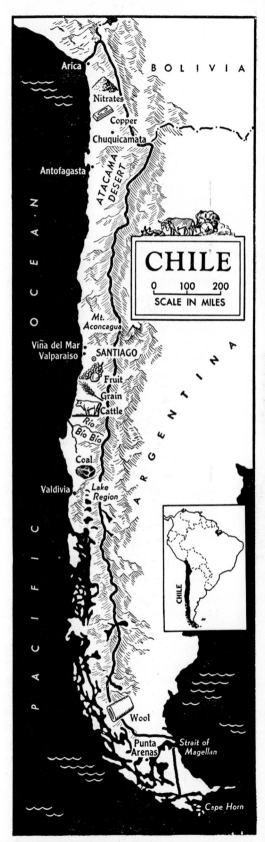

liberty that they won the admiration of their Spanish enemies. Finally the Araucanians agreed to accept as their own all the land south of the Bío Bío River. Although many immigrants have since settled in the Indian lands, there are still several thousand pure-blooded Araucanians living in southern Chile.

In spite of the years of warfare between Indians and whites, many Spaniards married Indian women and a new *mestizo* race grew up in Chile. Most of the upper-class Chileans are white people, but the majority of the working classes have a mingling of Indian blood. Much of the energy and aggressiveness of the Chileans is due to their Araucanian heritage.

Immigrants from Europe have come to Chile ever since colonial days and have intermarried with the Chileans. Bernardo O'Higgins, you remember, was the son of an Irish immigrant. Today there are many Chileans with English, Irish, German, and other European names who speak no language but Spanish. But regardless of their ancestry, people born in Chile are Chileans first of all, just as we are Americans.

VALPARAISO IS AN IMPORTANT PORT

When Valdivia reached the green valley of the Aconcagua River after his grueling march through the Atacama Desert, he is said to have cried, "*El valle del paraiso!*" meaning, "The valley of paradise." As a result, the settlement he founded on the Pacific coast became known as Valparaiso (vahl-pah-rah'ee-soh). Today it is not only the chief port of Chile but the largest American seaport on the Pacific south of California. Of the fifty ports in Chile, Valparaiso has

the only harbor where ships are adequately protected from the open sea. In peace times, ships of many nations are in the harbor and the wharves and docks are busy.

The city is built on the shore of a handsome semicircular bay and up the sides of the coast range. It is a beautiful sight at night to see the lights of the city and its suburbs sparkle in a great jeweled arc. To the traveler there seem to be two cities, the business section along the waterfront, and the residential section built on the heights overlooking the bay. Cable cars, which are called *ascensores* (ah-sen-soh'rays) and which look like elevators, take the Valparaisans up to the hilltop communities.

Valparaiso has several times been almost destroyed. It was rebuilt after it was bombarded by a Spanish fleet in 1866, and in 1906, the year of the San Francisco earthquake, a destructive earthquake shook Valparaiso to ruins.

Travelers in Valparaiso remember it as the city where women run the street-cars. During the war with Peru sixty years ago, women replaced men who went to war, and women conductors became the custom.

You may take an automobile or an electric train from Valparaiso to one of the famous summer beach resorts near-by. The best known of these is Viña del Mar (veen'yah del mahr), which has as fine hotels, casinos, and facilities for sports as you might find at any fashionable resort. The people of Chile's inland cities like to spend the hot summer months of January, February, and March at one of the beaches. Strangely enough, other sports are more popular than swimming. This is because the Humboldt

Black Star

VINA DEL MAR is a favorite summer resort of rich Argentines as well as Chileans. If you wish to see the wealthy and aristocratic upper class of Chile and Argentina, Viña del Mar is the place to visit.

Current keeps the waters along the coast too cold for swimming.

SANTIAGO IS THE HEART OF CHILE

Santiago, capital of Chile, is in the green valley of the Mapocho (mah-poh'cho) River about 75 miles inland from Valparaiso. Its million people live in the shadow of the Andes, and the majestic snow-crowned peaks form an eternal background for the city. Santiago is a friendly city which visitors remember with pleasure. North Americans feel at home in the business section where newsboys rush through the streets selling extras, and billboards carry many advertisements familiar to people from the United States. It is a modern capital, and in recent years fine public and office buildings as well as apartment houses have replaced the older buildings in the center of the city.

The visitor notices that the people walk much more rapidly in Santiago than they do in tropical Lima or Guayaquil, where there is no hurry. There are no picturesque Indians on the street such as you find in La Paz and Quito. The people are dressed like people in any big city and have much fairer complexions than any Latin Americans we have seen so far. Taxis are old and driven with little regard to safety. The shops carry hand-made Chilean silver and copper pots to tempt the visitor. There is a handsome, broad boulevard, called the Avenida de las Delicias (Avenue of Delights) which runs through the

Black Star

YOU ARE LOOKING DOWN upon Santiago from Santa Lucía Park
in the very heart of the city. This unusual hill is a tremendous mass
of rock rising from the flat plain on which Santiago is built.

center of the city. An open flower market sells quantities of beautiful flowers for a small price.

Santiago has kept some of its Spanish charm. The older homes of the well-to-do are square, one-storied houses of Spanish style with large patios within. Young men and girls still follow the custom of promenading around the central plaza in opposite directions while chaperons watch from benches.

In 1941, Santiago celebrated its 400th anniversary. A pageant depicted Valdivia riding into the city on a white horse carrying a small Madonna, as he is said to have done in 1541. The ancient Madonna can be seen today in the old church of San Francisco.

The most historic spot in the city is the hill called Cerro Santa Lucía. It was at the top of this natural fortress that Valdivia built his fort, and here that the inhabitants of the town ran for safety when the Indians attacked. Today the hill has become Santa Lucía Park. In it are flowers and garden paths, chapels, fountains, and statues. The top of the hill affords a fine view of the city, the surrounding valley, and the mountains. A marble Pedro de Valdivia, sword in hand, looks down upon the great city which he founded.

THE CENTRAL VALLEY IS A RICH AND OLD AGRICULTURAL REGION

From Santiago you may make a tour of Chile's beautiful central valley.   As you ride south through this lovely land in the shadow of the Andes, you look upon farms that have been worked for hundreds of years. Chile is a land of large estates. Many of the land grants of Valdivia's time have been handed down from generation to generation in the same family. Poplars and eucalyptus trees line the roads and mark the boundaries of the fields.   Luxuriant   vineyards   and fields of grain alternate with green meadows where cattle and horses graze. Orchards are heavy with fruit in summer.   The central valley furnishes food for all of Chile.

CHILE HAS THE FIRST ORDERLY GOVERN- MENT ON THE CONTINENT

Chile has the distinction of being the first country in South America to work out a stable government after gaining independence.   While neighboring republics were passing through years of revolution or enduring the rule of tyrant dictators, Chile was establishing herself as a strong and progressive nation. How can this be explained?   For one thing, Chile has her geography to thank. She had no far-off provinces unwilling to submit to authority.   Mountains, desert, and sea protected her from interference by her neighbors. But, more important, the republic soon came under the control of a wealthy landed aristocracy which was able to prevent ambitious soldiers from seizing the government.   Thus Chile was saved from the revolutions and military dictatorships, which, as we have seen, kept many of the new Latin American

CAN YOU GUESS which of the three people in this restaurant in Santiago, Chile, is an American? If you pick the girl at the left, you are wrong, for she is a native Chilean. The young man is an American lawyer.

Black Star

un par de Banderillas

Hispanic Foundation, Washington, D.C.

BERNARDO O'HIGGINS, son of an Irishman, is called "Oeegins" by Chileans. Like Bolívar, this handsome and fearless youth was inspired by the great Miranda to work for Chile's independence.

nations from making peaceful progress.

O'HIGGINS IS THE GEORGE WASHINGTON OF CHILE

Let us turn back to the year 1818 in Chile. In that year the Spanish armies were driven from Chile, and Bernardo O'Higgins was made "Supreme Director." You remember that O'Higgins was one of the Chilean revolutionists who crossed into Chile with San Martín's army in order to defeat the Spanish forces there. This great patriot had been educated in England and had come under the influence of Miranda and Bolívar. While he believed in the ideals of democracy, he was practical enough to see that his people were not ready for self-government, and he ruled with a strong hand.

O'Higgins, like Bolívar and Sucre, met with a great deal of opposition and jealousy. He tried to modernize the country and gave much attention to education. But many of his reforms were unpopular, and there was fear that he might become a permanent dictator. After a serious uprising, he resigned his office and went to Peru where he died twenty years later. Like other patriots of South America, his services were not appreciated until after his death. Today the Chileans are proud to recognize him as the founder of their nation. Almost every town in Chile has a plaza or street named for him.

THE CONSERVATIVES GAIN CONTROL OF THE CHILEAN GOVERNMENT

After the exile of O'Higgins, there was a struggle between the Conservatives and the Liberals for the control of the government. We have met these political parties before, but in Chile they were given nicknames. The Conservatives were called *Pelucones* (pay-loo-coh'nays) or "bigwigs" because of their fine dress. The Liberals were known as *Pipiolos* (pee-pee-oh'lohs) or "greenhorns" because of their noisiness and ignorance.

The *Pelucones*, who were largely the landowning class, wanted a strong president who would run the government to suit the landowners. The *Pipiolos* demanded more power for the congress and laws to aid the common people. When the elections of 1829 showed that the Liberals were strong, the *Pelucones* organized an uprising and seized the government by force. They then made their position secure by drawing up a new constitution which gave the president very great authority. He appointed and removed practically all officials without the consent of the people. In time of public disturbance he could take over complete control of the government. No one was allowed to vote unless he owned property and could read and write; the Catholic Church was made the state church. The most remarkable fact about the constitution is that it lasted almost 100 years, which is most unusual in Latin America.

ORDERLY GOVERNMENT BRINGS A
"GOLDEN AGE" TO CHILE

For the next thirty years Chile prospered under strong and able presidents. The first steamship route on the Pacific coast was started between Valparaiso and Callao, Peru. Railroad-building began, and telegraph lines connected the chief cities. Agriculture was greatly stimulated by the California gold rush, since boats carrying the "forty-niners" around the Horn or through the Straits of Magellan stopped at Chile's ports for wheat and flour. Immigration was encouraged by the government, and many Germans settled in Valdivia and the lake region of the south. Several presidents paid particular attention to establishing schools.

The presidency of Manuel Montt (mohnt), in the years 1851 to 1861, has been called the "Golden Age" of Chile. Chile prospered not only in commerce and agriculture, but also in education and literature. Montt was unusual because he did not belong to the rich landowning class as other presidents of Chile had. He was a man of humble family who had risen in the world through his own ability. However, he was a strict Conservative who believed in law and order and

had no use for the ideas of the Liberals. In fact, he dealt harshly with an uprising of Liberals which followed his election.

Montt is especially known for his support of education. As Minister of Education for Chile under a former president, he had founded about 300 primary schools and several secondary schools. Because the teaching methods were very poor in Chile's schools, he established the first normal school for training teachers. It was headed by Sarmiento (sahr-myen'toh) who later became the "schoolmaster president" of Argentina. Montt was also responsible for founding the University of Chile in Santiago. While he was president, he not only opened 500 more schools, but also established public libraries in several towns.

LIBERAL GOVERNMENTS BRING REFORMS
TO CHILE

In the years following the presidency of Montt, political power gradually slipped from the hands of the old-fashioned *Pelucones* into those of the younger generation of Liberals. Chile's leaders were changing. Men were no longer powerful merely because they were of noble birth and had inherited great estates. Wealthy merchants and miners and the intellectual leaders of the country were taking the place of the nobility and the clergy of colonial times.

The Liberals gradually increased the powers of congress and lessened those of the president; they also reduced the privileges of the powerful Church. A spirit of religious toleration was growing. Protestants were at last permitted to conduct church services and schools in accordance with their own religious beliefs. For the first time marriage by civil authorities as well as by Catholic clergy was declared legal. Up to this time the Church had controlled all cemeteries and had refused to allow non-Catholics to be buried in them. Cemeteries were now provided for people of all creeds, and births and deaths were registered by the state.

A PERIOD OF UNREST FOLLOWS THE WAR OF THE PACIFIC

You remember that the War of the Pacific was fought over the question of the nitrate fields of Peru and Bolivia. It was a test of Chile's strength as a nation. Her well-trained army and navy easily defeated Peru and Bolivia on land and sea, and she established herself as the most important country on the Pacific coast of South America. The nitrate fields

THE OPENING OF THE CHILEAN CONGRESS on May 21st is accompanied by much pomp and ceremony. This beautiful building with its huge columns is the national capitol where the two houses of congress meet.

Black Star

which passed to her brought a new industry and easy wealth, but they did not bring peace in politics.

The president elected in 1886 was José Manuel Balmaceda (bahl-mah-say'dah). He was rich, intelligent, handsome, and one of the most brilliant orators of his generation. Sale of the nitrates brought a great deal of money to the government and Balmaceda started a program of public improvements. He built roads, bridges, buildings, and founded schools and hospitals. For the first time pure drinking water was supplied to many Chilean cities. But he quarreled with congress over his rights as president. The long struggle by congress to reduce the powers of the president finally came to a climax in his administration. The result was a bloody civil war. In 1891, the congressional group rebelled, supported by most of the navy, and after eight months of fighting defeated the president and his army. On the day when his term ended, President Balmaceda committed suicide. After the civil war, presidents played a less important rôle in the political history of the republic.

THE YEAR 1920 OPENS A NEW ERA FOR CHILE

The year 1920 is an important one in Chile's history because it marked a great peaceful revolution by the middle class against the old rule. A new group had been forming in Chile, made up of small landowners who were the sons of European immigrants, of school-teachers, lawyers, doctors, businessmen, and storekeepers. They belonged neither to the Spanish upper classes nor to the peasant class which worked their land. They were the middle class without which no country can become a democracy.

In the election of Arturo Alessandri (ah-leh-sahn'dree) in 1920, the democratic forces of the nation for the first time captured not only the presidency but the lower house of congress as well. The Conservatives had steered a wise and safe course through the first century of Chile's independence, but their period of usefulness was over. Changes were taking place in Chile which required new leadership. Alessandri, son of an Italian immigrant, was definitely a man of the people. So overjoyed were the Chileans at his election that they staged a wild celebration outside his home and carried away from his house pieces of plaster and stone as souvenirs.

Alessandri came into office with a large program of reform, including laws to improve wages and hours of work. But the Conservatives still held a majority in the Senate. They hated Alessandri sincerely and refused to approve his reform measures. In the lower house of Congress, too, the election had introduced a new lot of men without political experience and with little sense of public responsibility. Many political crises followed and the president was forced to resign in 1924. He was recalled, however, and through his efforts a revised constitution was adopted for Chile. This constitution of 1925 is still in force today. The president is elected for six years by direct vote of all men over twenty-one. Congress has been deprived of its power to interfere with the executive branch of the government. Primary education is made compulsory for every child. The Catholic Church is no longer the state church.

Black Star

NEWSSTANDS IN CHILE are not very different from newsstands in New York or Chicago or Los Angeles. This one is in Santiago.

CHILE IS A DEMOCRACY IN THE MAKING

Today the majority of liberal Chileans belong to the Radical and Democratic parties. The term "Radical" has a different meaning in Latin America from that in the United States. The Radicals of Chile correspond to the New Deal Democrats in the United States. They are middle-class liberals. In 1938, Radicals united with other democratic political parties to form what is called a Popular Front government, the first in South America.

Pedro Aguirre Cerda (ah-gee'ray sehr'dah), an outstanding Radical, was elected to the presidency as the Popular Front candidate. The new president belonged to the middle class, and was a well-known writer, teacher, and champion of the "underdog." Although he started life as a poor boy, he became a millionaire vineyard owner. Aguirre's government was interested in helping the common people of Chile. Unfortunately for Chile, however, he died in the fall of 1941. His successor also died in office.

In 1946 a man famous for his liberal ideas, Gabriel González Videla (gohn-sah'lays vee-day'lah), was elected president. In 1950 President Videla came to Washington, D.C. to visit President Truman.

Chile's peaceful revolution has been accomplished by ballots instead of bullets. Chile deserves our admiration because it is one of the few countries in Latin America which are building a democratic nation upon the old institutions inherited from Spain. Chile is still a democracy in the making with many problems to solve, which are like the problems of our own democracy.

This chapter has dealt largely with Chile's political history. In the next chapter we shall read about the industries and the farms and the people of Chile.

Are You a Careful Reader?   Test Yourself!

I. Can you complete the following statements?

1. Chile achieved an .... before any other South American republic.
2. In Chile's "Golden Age," progress was made not only in commerce and agriculture, but in .....
3. By 1920, a new group had come to power, known as the .... class, without which no .... can exist.
4. In Chile today a party called .... resembles the New Deal Democrats.
5. The president of Chile is elected for .... years.

II. Match the following words with the correct statements:

1. Araucanians
2. Valparaiso
3. Alessandri
4. Balmaceda
5. Santiago
6. Montt
7. Viña del Mar
8. O'Higgins
9. Pelucones
10. Valdivia

a. early name for liberal party
b. undefeated Indians of Chile
c. conservative wealthy party
d. present day labor party
e. principal seaport of Chile
f. founder of the Chilean republic
g. fashionable seaside resort
h. conqueror and colonizer of Chile
i. capital of Chile
j. president during "Golden Age" who encouraged education
k. recent reform president who was the son of an Italian immigrant
l. defeated in civil war between president and Congress

Food for Thought and Discussion

1. Compare the history of Chile since independence with that of Peru. Does the difference account entirely for Chile's greater progress or are there other reasons? If so, what are they?
2. How did the middle class of Chile achieve a peaceful revolution against the wealthy, landowning Conservatives? Could Mexico have done the same? Why?

Chapter 29

Chileans Develop Their Resources and Improve the Lot of Their Workers

ALTHOUGH the political story of a nation is important to know, it tells us little of the people who go about their work day after day regardless of what party is in power or who is president. While the *Pelucones* and the *Pipiolos* struggled for control of the government, while the War of the Pacific was fought and won, and while the Liberals slowly grew to power, the country was developing and expanding. Immigrants were settling new land, mines were being worked, crops were planted and harvested.

NITRATES PAY CHILE'S BILLS FOR FORTY YEARS

When Valdivia led his Spanish horsemen across Chile's northern desert, they raised a white dust which choked and nearly blinded them. Three hundred years later a Scotchman noticed that when he used the white desert soil to bank up his flower beds, the plants in those beds grew amazingly. He sent some of this soil to Scotland to be tested, and it was found to contain nitrate of soda. This substance is valuable as a fertilizer, and the nitrogen gas obtained from it is used in the manufacture of explosives.

The War of the Pacific gained for Chile the richest nitrate region. Soldiers released from the army went to work in the nitrate fields, and before long millions of tons of nitrate of soda were being shipped to Europe and the United States. This was a period of easy money for the government. Although the mines were worked by foreign companies, Chile's royalties amounted to $30,000,000 a year, almost enough to pay all the government expenses. After the first World War, however, a discovery by a German chemist brought forty years of Chilean prosperity to a close; a process had been developed to obtain nitrogen from the air. From 1920 on, Chile's nitrate trade began to decline. Competition with the artificial nitrate caused the price to drop to one fourth of its former level. Miners lost their jobs, the government lost its income, and the "nitrate depression" was on in Chile.

The industry did not die out entirely. There were still tons of nitrate to be sold if they could be mined more cheaply. A new process was invented which cut by one half the cost of producing the mineral, and today the sales of nitrates are increasing. Most of the production is in the hands of companies from the United States.

but the Chilean government takes 25 per cent of the profits and regulates the sale of the nitrates.

MODERN NITRATE PLANTS ARE COMMUNITIES AS WELL AS FACTORIES

The two most modern nitrate plants are the Pedro de Valdivia and the Maria Elena, both owned by United States companies. They are called *oficinas* (oh-fee-see'nahs). A visit to an *oficina* is a most interesting experience. A four-hour trip from the coast by car across the cheerless nitrate desert brings you to the mine. Besides the low factory buildings, there are houses for the workmen, stores, a school, a hospital, and a church. Everything is covered with a thick coat of fine white dust which sparkles like new-fallen snow. The mine workers are tough, hardy men, known for their independence, but exceedingly hard workers if treated right.

At the mines the ore, which is close to the surface of the ground, is loosened by dynamite blasts and dug out with great mechanical shovels. Electric engines haul the ore to the *oficina* where it is crushed fine. It is then thrown into large tanks and dissolved in hot water. When cooled, the nitrate forms crystals which are dried and hauled to the nearest port. From the liquid remaining in the tanks, iodine can be extracted. Chile till recently furnished about 90 per cent of the world's supply of iodine.

CHILE HAS THE LARGEST COPPER MINE IN THE WORLD

Although Chile has long been known for its nitrates, copper is actually her largest and most valuable export. Some copper was mined in colonial days, but it was not until the age of electricity called for miles of copper wire that Chile's copper mines came into their own. Today Chile

WHITE NITRATE CRYSTALS are drying in the troughs above the tanks. These tanks are used to hold the nitrate solution, but in this picture the crystals have been removed and the tanks drained.

Galloway

ranks next to the United States as the world's greatest producer of copper. If all the copper that Chile has produced were made into wire one sixteenth of an inch thick, it would reach to the sun and back with about 3,000,000 miles left over!

One of the largest single copper deposits in the world lies in the great mine at Chuquicamata (choo-kee-cah-mah'tah) in the heart of the nitrate desert. The American mining company which runs the mine has established a model camp for the 15,000 workers. Comfortable living quarters, medical service, movie theaters, and even a football team are found at Chuquicamata. Drinking water is piped in from the high Andes.

Throughout the copper region are many small mines owned and operated by Chileans. They haul in food and water by mule cart or truck and ship their ore out the same way. They produce little copper, but they are important to Chile because they are native undertakings.

MANUFACTURING IS INCREASING IN CHILE

Chileans like to buy goods bearing the label "Fabricación Chilena" (Made in Chile) because they are supporting their own manufacturing industry. When the world depression hit Chile, she was already suffering from the loss of her nitrate markets and could no longer buy in foreign markets the manufactured goods she needed. One of the most important policies adopted by the government was to encourage the manufacture of needed goods at home. Thousands of new factories have been started since 1932. Many Chilean factories are small and poorly equipped compared with those of the

United States, and their goods are not always equal in quality to imported goods. But articles like matches, shoes, paper, woolen and leather goods which were formerly imported now bear the label "Fabricación Chilena."

Many Chileans believe that the day is coming when Chile will not only manufacture her own goods, but will be able to supply manufactured articles to other nations of South America. In fact, Chile is now exporting considerable glass to Peru. She has plenty of coal to run her factories, and has iron for steel and waterpower from swift mountain rivers for electricity. Electric plants are being built by the government. One drawback is the lack of capital to finance large manufacturing plants, and Chile may not be willing to have industries controlled by foreign companies as her mines are. Foreign capital, on the other hand, may not be willing to invest in a country whose government might any day follow Mexico's example of expropriation. At present, at least, Chile has plenty of markets at home to keep her factories busy.

CHILE'S LAWS AID INDUSTRIAL WORKERS

The mines and factories have gradually been drawing workers from the farms until today there are 600,000 people in mining and industry. This is almost half of all the working people of Chile. No other country in Latin America has such a large proportion of industrial workers. These people are called rotos (roh'tohs) or "ragged ones." It is the rotos who have given strong support to recent democratic government. It is for them that child-labor laws, housing laws, and social security laws have been passed by the Chilean congress.

The *rotos'* friend, Alessandri, organized for them benefit organizations called *cajas* (cah′hahs). The employer, the government, and the worker each contributes funds somewhat like our social security fund. From this money pensions are paid to the workers when they retire and insurance if they are killed or injured. In addition it provides free medical and hospital care. The *cajas* also operate workingmen's restaurants where food is cheap and good. Modern tenements are being built and day nurseries set up for children of working mothers.

The laws for Chile's workers are new and by no means perfect. Thousands of *rotos* live in crowded tenements in Santiago and other cities and work for wages too small for decent living. Nevertheless, Chile has made a start that may well be a guide to some other countries in South America.

CHILE'S GREATEST PROBLEM IS HER AGRICULTURAL WORKERS

Unfortunately, half of Chile's workers are not affected by the new laws. These are the farm laborers or *inquilinos* (een-kee-lee′nohs) who live in poverty on the great estates in the fertile central valley. These estates

THIS BEAUTIFUL SCENE is not a movie set, but the grounds of a fine home on a *fundo* in Chile. The huts of the *inquilinos* are probably some distance away from the owner's home and grounds.

Black Star

fighting has never been popular in Chile. Today people much prefer a good game of soccer, football, or tennis. On Sunday afternoon the band plays in the plaza and promenaders crowd the streets.

The graceful *cueca* (cway'cah), the national dance of Chile, is danced by all classes of people whenever there is a celebration. It is especially popular in country districts. The couples face each other, the man dressed as a Chilean cowboy with a white kerchief in his hand. As they go through the intricate steps, the spectators hum and clap their hands solemnly to the lively rhythm of the guitar and the harp.

The rodeo is the great sport of the country people. It is held in November, which is springtime in Chile, and people come for miles around to see the cowboys perform. A number of range cattle are driven into one part of a great semicircular corral. The *huasos* (whah'sohs), as the Chilean cowboys are called, gather on the other side of the corral. They are mounted on fine horses with fancy saddles and wear bright-colored ponchos. *Huasos* do not use ropes as our western cowboys do, but work in pairs and cut an animal from the rest of the herd by using only their horses. The animal is then caught between the horse's shoulder and the brush fence of the corral. This feat requires great skill on the part of both horse and rider.

CHILEANS LIKE GOOD FOOD

A Chilean dish of which foreigners become fond is *cazuela* (cah-sway'lah). This is a delicious soup made with mutton or fowl and many kinds of vegetables cooked together. *Cazuela* is served as the first course for any meal, but always appears for the midday meal or *almuerzo* (ahl-moo-ahr'so). In fact, a luncheon without *cazuela* would seem a very poor meal in Chile.

Chilean bread looks like what we call French bread, except that it is heavier and made of darker flour. The poor people eat a great deal of bread. It is the main item in their diet just as beans are the chief food in Mexico.

A favorite dish of the visitor to Chile is the delicious lobster from the Juan Fernández Islands, 400 miles off the coast of Chile. These lobsters are so much in demand that they are even shipped by plane over the Andes to restaurants and hotels in Buenos Aires. It was on one of the Juan Fernández Islands that a young British sailor, Alexander Selkirk, was marooned in 1703. When he was rescued and returned to England after four years, Defoe wrote his story and called it "Robinson Crusoe." He changed the setting to an island in the Caribbean and introduced a "man Friday," but it is actually Selkirk's story.

We now leave Chile and her charming and energetic people. They have been called the "Yankees of South America." Perhaps that is why the visitor from the United States feels at home there. Certainly this temperate country is much more like our own than any other Latin American country we have studied.

Weimer

THIS FATHER AND SON belong to an old Chilean family and own a great *fundo* in southern Chile. The son wears a country squire's outfit with black hat, striped poncho, and a sheepskin across his saddle.

government of Chile today is waging war on illiteracy by building schools in city and country. A recent build-ing program calls for 600 new ele-mentary schools. There are new high schools, trade schools, normal schools. Adults who cannot read are enrolling in night schools. Like the schools of Mexico, Chilean schools must teach health and sanitation as well as read-ing and writing. At present over two thirds of the children of primary age are attending school, but the govern-ment will not be satisfied until there are schools enough to provide educa-tion for every child.

One of the greatest strides made so far has been in rural education. For the first time thousands of *inquilinos* and small farmers in remote country districts are being reached through the Institute of Rural Education. Simple books with bright pictures on the covers were sent to thousands of families over the country. They contain simple history, advice to farmers, information on the care of babies, all written in story form. No sooner had these books been sent out than the Institute was flooded with requests from other families who wanted the books. The country peo-ple are learning that the government is their friend and they write about their problems to the civil authorities. When they read that Aguirre Cerda had been a poor boy and had gone to a rural school, they were proud that he had become president and wrote many friendly letters to him. Those who work with Chile's humble people realize that all they need to become alert and intelligent citizens is op-portunity.

CITY AND COUNTRY PEOPLE ENJOY THEMSELVES

Life is not all serious in Chile, and the traveler finds that the Chileans play as well as work. In the cities people amuse themselves much as they do in our cities. They go to the movies or to the beaches or up into the mountains for winter sports. Bull-

333

the owner at wages less than a dollar a day. He seldom leaves the *fundo*. There is a church and a school for his children with a teacher furnished by the government. The *inquilino* can call no part of the *fundo* his own; yet he is today the mainstay of Chile's agriculture as he has always been. The more progressive landowners have taken an interest in their *inquilinos* and furnished them with better homes, larger wages, and more food, but others close their eyes to the poverty of the worker and claim that he is better satisfied when he has less.

While the only real solution to Chile's problem of rural workers would be the breaking-up of the great estates, not even the Popular Front government has dared to take such a step. Recent laws make it possible for the government to purchase estates whose owners are willing to sell and divide them into small farms. The government in this way has established a few agricultural colonies on former *fundos*. Irrigation canals have been built, and schools and doctors have been furnished the workers by the government.

EDUCATION IS REACHING THE COMMON PEOPLE OF CHILE

When Aguirre Cerda was president of Chile, he said: "If I had the power, I would strew Chile with schools as a farmer sows wheat on rich land." The

THESE BAREFOOT CHILEAN CHILDREN are interested in their book on the adventures of a monkey. They probably learned to read at one of the new schools which the government has established.

Black Star

Weimer

A CHILEAN FARMER returning from town with his oxen and cart crosses rivers in a barge. Do you see the tow ropes by which horses pull the barge across? This is not a wealthy *fundo* owner, but a poor small farmer of southern Chile.

are called *fundos* (foon′dohs), and are a heritage from colonial days when lands and Indians were allotted to the Spanish conquerors. The Chilean *inquilino* was not a slave, but because he had to work or starve, he was practically bound to the land as his descendants are today. Even though often both master and *inquilino* have Indian blood in their veins, there is a great gulf between them. There is no middle class in rural Chile; there are only owners and workers.

In Chile's rich valley more than one half the land is owned by about 500 families living on the great *fundos*. Some of these *fundos* are as large as 100,000 acres, but the average is about 27,000 acres. As those of us who live in farming communities

may know, 27,000 acres is a great deal of land. All the farms owned by small Chilean farmers amount to no more than one tenth of the land. The *fundos* are beautiful to see. The owner's house is surrounded by trees and flower gardens, and on all sides are fields of grain, orchards, and green pastures. The road to the estate is shaded with tall poplars or eucalyptus.

Often several hundred people, including the *inquilinos* and their families, live upon a *fundo*. The *inquilino* has a little cottage of one or two rooms, often a dark adobe hut, and an acre or two of land on which he can raise his food. The cottage has only an earthen floor, and furniture is of the most primitive sort. The *inquilino* must work from sunrise to sunset for

II. Can you match the following words and statements?

1. *provinciano*   a. worker on *estancia* who replaces gaucho
2. *estancia*   b. delicatessen and tea shop
3. peon   c. prize-winning steer at livestock show
4. *domador*   d. family gathering including all relatives
5. *caballo*   e. Argentine barbecue
6. *asado*   f. cowboy who breaks horses
7. *estanciero*   g. gaucho cook
8. *asadero*   h. large estate on the pampa
9. *confitería*   i. native dance which originated on the pampa
10. tango   j. Argentine who lives in the provinces
          k. Spanish word for horse
          l. member of the landowning aristocracy

Food for Thought and Discussion

1. Why do you suppose the small landowners on the pampa have not prospered like our mid-Western farmers who began in a small way?

2. What is the difference between the peon and the tenant farmer on the *estancia*?

3. Would the girls in the class be contented to be daughters of an upper-class Argentine family? Why?

Chapter 33

Paraguay and Progressive Uruguay Are South America's Smallest Countries

---

IN SOUTHERN SOUTH AMERICA are two small countries named Uruguay and Paraguay. They are much more different than their names suggest. Their people are different; their government, their products, and their customs are different. Uruguay is one of the most progressive democracies in the world; Paraguay is a back-ward country with a tragic history of bloody wars and cruel dictators. Uruguay is populated by white people, over three fifths of whom can read and write; Paraguay's inhabitants are *mestizos* and Indians, three fifths of whom cannot write their names or read a newspaper. Most people have enough to live on in Uruguay; almost everyone is poor in Paraguay. Uruguay's capital is a modern city with paved streets, automobiles, fine shops and hotels; Paraguay's capital is a sleepy, colonial city where donkeys still carry loads over cobbled roads.

Why are these two countries, which started out as independent nations at about the same time, so entirely different today? This chapter will help you to answer that question.

Uruguay

República Oriental del Uruguay (Eastern Republic of Uruguay) is one of the most interesting and remarkable little republics in Latin America. It is named after the Uruguay River which separates its territory from that of Argentina. The early Indian inhabitants gave it this name, which means "River of Birds," because of the myriads of swans and flamingos which lived upon its banks. Tucked in between Brazil and Argentina, Uruguay is the smallest of all South American nations. It has 700 miles of coast which stretch along the Atlantic to the east and the Plata River to the south. Its land is for the most part a rolling, grassy plain, less flat than the pampa of Argentina and well suited to cattle-grazing. Its climate is delightful with mild, snowless winters and cool sea breezes to temper the summer heat.

The traveler who has seen the magnificent scenery of the Andean countries may find Uruguay somewhat disappointing. There are no breathtaking scenic views nor picturesque Indian people. As a modern guidebook says, "It is less a place to see than a place in which to live." Life is pleasant in Uruguay.

MONTEVIDEO IS THE HEART OF URUGUAY

It takes seven hours to go by steamer from Buenos Aires on the west bank of the Plata to Monte-

video (mohn-tay-vee-day'oh) on the east bank. As the boat approaches the capital city, the famous *Cerro* (say'-roh) or hill can be seen rising above the flat shores of the river. There is a legend that a Portuguese sailor on one of Magellan's ships saw the hill in early dawn and cried, "*Monte vide eu!*" or "I see a mountain!" This lone hill served as a landmark for ships thereafter. When a city was founded at its foot 200 years later, it was called Montevideo. The *Cerro* appears on the Uruguayan coat of arms.

The steamer from Buenos Aires docks at a modern wharf in a fine horseshoe-shaped harbor. Ships flying the flags of many nations crowd the harbor in normal times. There are also many boats that have come down the Uruguay River from the interior, carrying hides and lumber to be loaded into ocean freighters.

Montevideo is the home of 850,000 people, or about a third of the inhabitants of Uruguay. It has beautiful parks and gardens, clean, tree-lined streets, and fine public buildings. The new capitol building, of which Uruguayans are very proud, is one of the most beautiful in South America. There are modern houses as well as dignified old Spanish homes. The suburbs are charming with white houses set in gardens of gorgeous flowers.

Montevideo is a restful city with

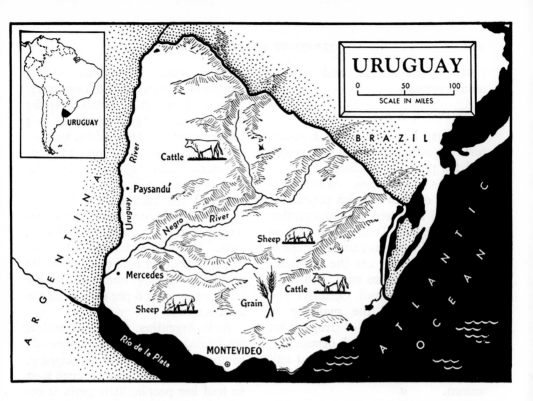

little of the rush and activity that the traveler notices in Buenos Aires. Business houses are closed for an hour and a half at noon so that people may eat lunch. The Uruguayans, like the Argentines, have a pleasant custom of drinking their coffee at sidewalk cafés which remind one of Paris and Vienna or other European cities. People on the streets are well dressed and prosperous-looking. We do not see evidences of great wealth and social position as in the Argentine capital nor do we see the poverty-stricken people so common in Buenos Aires and in Santiago.

According to Latin American custom, streets and plazas are named after great men and great days in Uruguay's history. The main street is named Avenida 18 de Julio (18th of July Avenue) in honor of their independence day. The oldest plaza, Plaza de Constitución, is in the center of the city with the ancient cathedral on one side. Beyond the old plaza is the Plaza de la Independencia which is one of the main centers of Montevideo. From here buses will take you to any part of the city. For a small fare you can go to one of the famous bathing beaches which are so popular with the people of that city. Fine hotels and summer cottages house the many summer visitors who come from Brazil and Argentina, and the sands are dotted with gay umbrellas and dressing tents.

On the outskirts of the city and on the country roads you can see the high-wheeled farm carts and pack mules still used for transportation. Countrymen on horseback drive cattle to the packing houses at the foot of the *Cerro.* Five thousand miles of improved roads radiate from the city to the towns in the interior. These towns, like Montevideo, have electric

367

lights, paved streets, and modern sewage systems.

URUGUAY IS A MINIATURE ARGENTINA

Uruguay has been called a miniature Argentina because the people and the products of these two countries are so much alike. As in Argentina, the original Spanish population has been increased by immigration from Europe. Today nine out of every ten Uruguayans are of European blood. Spaniards are the most numerous, Italians are next, and there are several thousand Germans and Brazilians. Like the majority of Argentines, the people of Uruguay are energetic, vigorous, and democratic. Travelers admire the spirit and animation of the dark-eyed Uruguayan women.

Uruguay is even more a cattle country than Argentina. Three fourths of her land is used for grazing; there are four cattle and ten sheep for every human being in Uruguay. It is not necessary to grow alfalfa because the natural grass on the plains fattens the cattle without special fodder. Although there are large cattle ranches, much of the land is held in small farms. The government encourages farmers and ranchers to buy their own land. Uruguay is fortunate because 87 per cent of her land can be used for pasture or farming; compare this with Chile where only 8 per cent of all the land is usable.

As in Argentina, *frigoríficos*, owned by English, American, and domestic companies, prepare meat for shipping. Although Uruguay grows enough food to feed her people, little grain is exported. Her best customer is Eng-

MONTEVIDEO'S DOWNTOWN DISTRICT with the harbor and the *Cerro* in the background. In the foreground is the Plaza Independencia, bus and streetcar center. The statue is of José Artigas, national hero of Uruguay.

Sawders

land. As far as trade with the United States is concerned, she is in the same position as Argentina. Her beef is quarantined because of hoof-and-mouth disease. In spite of this, Uruguay is one of the most co-operative of the American family of nations, and one of the best friends we have.

URUGUAY STARTS LIFE AS AN INDEPENDENT NATION

Uruguay has not always been the orderly and progressive state that it is today. As we know, it was called the *Banda Oriental* or Eastern Bank in colonial days, and was part of the viceroyalty of Buenos Aires. In 1810, when Buenos Aires severed its connection with Spain, the Spanish royalists made their headquarters in Montevideo, and it was not until four years later that the creoles from the two sides of the Plata were able to drive them out. Meantime a creole soldier, José Artigas (ar-tee′gahs), had become the leader of the Uruguayan creoles and after a falling-out with his allies in Buenos Aires he seized control of the Eastern Bank. But the Portuguese in Brazil also wanted to annex the country, and in 1820 a Brazilian army drove Artigas into exile in Paraguay. Although like San Martín and other early leaders, Artigas died in exile, his patriotic services were later recognized by the country. Today he lies buried under a great monument bearing the words, "The Founder of the Uruguayan Nation."

"THIRTY−THREE IMMORTALS" BRING INDEPENDENCE TO URUGUAY

From 1821 to 1825 the *Banda Oriental* was a province of Brazil. But the Uruguayan patriots resented Brazilian rule. A group of thirty-

Black Star

THIS CARICATURE OF A GAUCHO has become as popular in Uruguay and Argentina as Juan Bimba is in Venezuela. It is really the ad of a big shoe factory.

three, living as exiles in Buenos Aires, determined to drive out the invader. One dark night, they crossed the Plata and landed on the shores of Uruguay. Their forces were increased by hundreds of their countrymen and bloody fighting followed. Argentina, eager to have the little country out of Brazilian control, sided with the revolutionists. The result of the war between Argentina and Brazil was the creation of the independent nation of Uruguay. Each country was satisfied as long as the other could not have the territory. July 18, 1830, is the date of the adoption of the country's constitution, a landmark in Uruguayan history.

POLITICAL FACTIONS STRUGGLE FOR CONTROL OF URUGUAY

Independence did not bring peace to Uruguay. At first her powerful neighbors interfered in her affairs. Rosas of Argentina came to power just as the new nation was formed and for over ten years was at war with the government at Montevideo. Brazil also wanted to control the affairs of the little republic. Even when Uruguay was safe from outside interference, there was strife within the country itself. Fighting had become a habit with the hardy Uruguayans, and they seemed unable to stop and settle down to build a stable government.

Two political parties fought for the upper hand, the *Blancos* (blahn'cohs) or Whites, and the *Colorados* (coh-loh-rah'dohs) or Reds. As the *Colorados* were continuously in power after 1865, they came to be associated with the progressive merchant and professional people of the capital, Montevideo. The *Blancos* on the other hand, always excluded from the government, became a sort of country party, supported by the clergy and the conservative rural population. They did not fight over important national problems, however, like the Federalists and Unitarians in Argentina. It was the old story of personal ambition and greed. Their quarrels were like the feuds in some sections of our own country; unreasoning hatred for the other side was passed on from generation to generation.

The history of Uruguay from 1830 to 1904 was a struggle between the *Blancos* and the *Colorados*, with Argentina or Brazil often supporting one side or another. Rosas of Argentina was thrown out of power largely as a result of his interference in Uruguay. A dictator of Paraguay caused a great war by siding with the *Blancos* while Brazil aided the *Colorados*. One president declared Uruguay was ungovernable; another was assassinated.

A GREAT LEADER BRINGS PEACE AND PROGRESS TO EMBATTLED URUGUAY

In 1903, one of the greatest statesmen in Uruguay's history was elected president of the republic. José Batlle y Ordóñez (bat'yay ee ohr-dohn'yays) was president for two terms between 1903 and 1915, and was a strong influence in his country until his death in 1929. He was a farsighted and resolute leader. His first job was to restore order after seventy years of disorder. Then he set about developing Uruguay into a modern nation. He believed that the government should give every citizen equal opportunity to get an education and to make his own living.

Under Batlle's influence many new schools were opened, modern methods of teaching were introduced, and compulsory attendance at school began to be enforced. Children's playgrounds were established in nearly every village.

Under presidents who supported his program, laws to aid the poor were passed which were more advanced than those of any country except the Scandinavian countries. Uruguay had the eight-hour day and minimum-wage laws long before the United States. Child labor, not yet abolished in our country, has been outlawed in Uruguay since the time of Batlle. Workers of Uruguay got old-age pensions twenty years before the Social Security Act was passed in the United States. Many countries have minimum wages for industrial workers, but probably no other government in the world protects farm workers with a minimum-wage law. These are not just paper laws, but are actually enforced by the government.

Batlle also believed that the government should take a hand in business and industry for the benefit of the people. In Uruguay the government controls banking and the insurance companies, owns the street-car lines, and is buying back the railroads owned by British companies. Homes are built for workers and loans are made on homes under a plan similar to that of our Federal Housing Administration. Government restaurants in Montevideo offer clean and nourishing food at cheap prices.

These reforms are Uruguay's answer to the grave problems that every nation faces today. One writer has said that only the fact that Uruguay has so few people prevents her from being the most talked-of country in America. Her people take great interest in their democratic government and cherish their many freedoms just

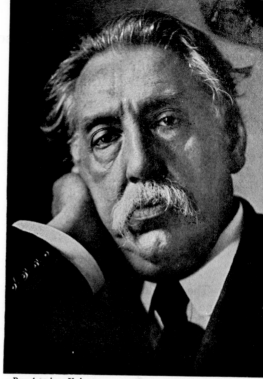

Pan American Union

DR. JOSÉ BATLLE Y ORDÓÑEZ, the great leader of modern Uruguay, lived to see his country become one of the most progressive in the world.

as we do. Uruguay has been active in the affairs of the United Nations and of UNESCO.

Paraguay

Few people realize that deep in the heart of South America is a beautiful and interesting country with a tragic history. There are several stories about the origin of Paraguay's name. One is that Paraguay is the Indian name for the parrots that come to this country by the millions during mating season. Another story is that it is named for an Indian tribe that once inhabited the region. Surrounded by her larger neighbors, Argentina, Brazil, and Bolivia, Paraguay appears tiny on the map, although it is as large as Kansas and Nebraska combined. It is the second smallest nation in South America, and has the smallest population.

Notice on the map that Paraguay is almost encircled by rivers. The upper Paraná forms its south and east boundary. The Pilcomayo (peel-coh-my'yoh) on the southwest border joins the Paraguay which in turn flows south to join the Paraná and complete the river boundary of the country. Notice also that the Paraguay River divides the country from

371

north to south into two sections. These are very different in climate and in geography. West of the river is the Gran Chaco with rolling plains and unexplored jungle which are alternately dry and flooded. Eastern Paraguay is the real Paraguay. It is here that most of the million inhabitants live and that most of the crops are grown. It is here that the capital city of Asunción is located.

THE RIVER TRIP TO ASUNCIÓN REVEALS THE PARAGUAYAN COUNTRYSIDE

The traveler can reach this remote land either by steamer up the Paraná and Paraguay Rivers or by railroad. The four-day trip to Asunción in one of the large white steamers that travel from Buenos Aires gives one a chance to see the country. For the first three days the boat follows the winding, shifting course of the Paraná River. The shallow channel is often clogged with sand bars. When the river is in flood, the banks are inundated, and débris comes floating down, carrying marooned snakes and other creatures to sea.

On the fourth day the Paraná turns sharply eastward, and the boat continues the trip north to Asunción by the Paraguay River. There is a great deal of traffic on the river. Boats carrying bales of cotton or tobacco or *maté* leaves pass by on the way down to Buenos Aires. The boat docks at Asunción opposite the mouth of the Pilcomayo. Piers are built far out into the river so that the ships may dock when the dry season lowers the water level.

ASUNCIÓN WAS OLD WHEN BOSTON WAS FOUNDED

The capital is a quiet little city

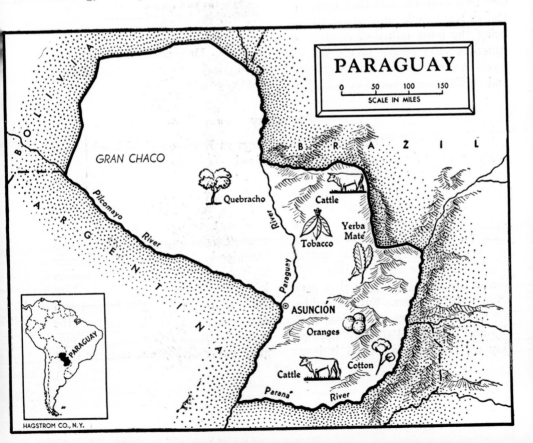

Three Lions

THE MAIN STREET of the quiet little capital of Paraguay is Calle Palma. The pedestrians seem to prefer the street to the sidewalk! Notice that this is a modern street with autos and a car track.

located on a high bank above the river. You remember that it was founded by settlers from the abandoned colony of Buenos Aires. By the time the Massachusetts Bay Colony was founded Asunción was already a hundred years old. It became for a time the most important town in the southeast in colonial days, while Buenos Aires was just a convenient stopping-off place for colonists of Asunción on their way to and from Spain.

On a plaza near the river is the old cathedral surrounded by low stone houses whose moss-covered tiled roofs and thick walls are a heritage from colonial days. The older streets are still paved with cobbles worn smooth over the years by donkeys and oxen. Everywhere in the city flowers bloom in a riot of color. The flaming poin-

settia, jasmine, hibiscus, and roses remind one of Southern California. The modern capitol building and railroad station and even the few automobiles seem out of place in this ancient town.

In the streets of Asunción the traveler finds the color that is lacking in Montevideo. There is a native market with piles of golden oranges and other fruits. Women walk in bare feet, with head and shoulders wrapped in a white shawl which looks like a sheet. They are often seen smoking big black cigars! We notice two things in particular about Paraguay. There appear to be many more women than men, and the women seem to do most of the work. The reason for this will appear when we read about the history of this interesting little country.

THIS GUARANÍ INDIAN BOY lives in a thatched hut in the Paraná River Valley. Like others of his race he works at gathering and drying maté.

and on the streets. It makes one wonder who conquered whom in Paraguay! A story is told about a Paraguayan army officer who went to France to learn to speak the French language. It is said that within a few weeks all the Frenchmen in the small village where he lived were speaking Guaraní!

PARAGUAY LIVES ON THE PRODUCTS OF HER FERTILE LAND

The rich, red earth, *tierra colorada*, and the climate of eastern Paraguay are ideal for growing cotton and tobacco. Cotton has in recent years become the chief crop of the country. If there were enough laborers, an enormous acreage could be cultivated. The government encourages cotton-growing by distributing free seed to farmers. Tobacco ranks second as an export crop. In the fall months the country people who live in the hilly region east of Asunción bring in the dried leaf to the warehouse. It is carried in oxcarts, by horseback, and even on the heads of the women. Smoking is very common in rural Paraguay. Not only the women, but the children, can be seen puffing cigars. Home-made cigars can be bought for a few cents a dozen.

PARAGUAYANS ARE A MIXED RACE

When the Spaniards came to Paraguay they found the Guaraní (gwah-rah-nee′) Indians living there. They were a peaceful agricultural race without the culture and the wealth of the Incas. The Spaniards exploited the Indians as they did elsewhere in America, but as very few European women ever came to this remote region, they also married Indian wives. Today, although many Indians survive, there are few pure-blooded Spaniards in the country. The majority of the people are *mestizos*.

Although Spanish is the language of the educated people, almost every Paraguayan speaks the melodious Guaraní. Paraguay is unique because it is the only country in Latin America in which the upper classes use an Indian language in their homes

Paraguay used to be almost entirely a cattle country, and hides and meat are still important exports. In the forests along the upper Paraguay River millions of *quebracho* trees grow. Both tannin and logs are exported. We have already mentioned the *yerba maté* which is a favorite drink of South Americans. It is said to be rich in vitamins and is made like tea with hot water. It is surprising that vitamin-conscious North Americans have not become *maté* drinkers! The traditional way of drinking the *yerba maté* is through a tube from a gourd or bowl. The gourd and the drink are both called *maté* and the tube is called a *bombilla* (bohm-bee'yah). The tree from which the *yerba* leaves are picked is a member of the holly family and grows wild in Paraguay. The *yerba* pickers dry the leaves over a fire, then beat them into pieces with wooden paddles. They are then taken to the warehouse for shipment.

Travelers remember the juicy oranges which grow everywhere in Paraguay. Planted by the Jesuits 300 years ago, they are now so plentiful that they cannot all be used. Part of the crop is sent to Uruguay and Argentina, but in some places oranges are fed to the hogs. If this industry were well managed, it might become as important as the orange industry in California and Florida.

PARAGUAY WINS INDEPENDENCE AND FALLS UNDER THE RULE OF A DICTATOR

Paraguay has perhaps the most colorful and tragic history of any country in South America. Like Uruguay it was part of the viceroyalty of Buenos Aires. In 1811, independence was achieved without bloodshed. The people declared themselves free of Spain and invited the Spanish governor to resign, which he did peacefully. The Paraguayans refused to ally themselves with Buenos Aires because they feared the power of that city. For the next sixty years Paraguay was under the yoke of three dictators. When Doctor José Gaspar de Francia (frahn'see-ah) became the dictator of the new nation, Paraguay started on a strange quarter of a century. Of all the picturesque and despotic dictators of Latin America,

Francia heads the list. He was a stern, lonely, and suspicious man without family ties and with few friends. He not only shut himself away from the people, but he shut his country away from the world.

We have heard of isolationists, but never of so thoroughgoing an isolationist as Francia was. Fearing his powerful neighbors, he attempted to play safe by isolating his country. He kept troops along the border and allowed few people to enter or leave the country. He stopped the mails and forbade all trade with the countries down the river. Paraguay was forced to support itself by increasing its crops and growing and manufacturing cotton.

El Supremo (suh-pray'moh), the Supreme One, as he was called, used torture and murder against those

MATÉ is drunk everywhere in southern South America, sometimes with lemon and sugar. This man seems to have poured the hot water from a thermos jug!

Lanks

THIS OLD JESUIT MISSION in Paraguay is a reminder of the missionaries who labored there for 160 years. Under their rule the savage Guaranís became prosperous and peaceful farmers. Paraguayan villages are still built on the Jesuit plan.

C. H. Haring

whom he suspected of opposing him. So great was the fear of him, it is said, that when he walked through the streets of Asunción people hid in their houses. Like Gómez of Venezuela, Francia lived to be an old man. In spite of his cruelty he had aided Paraguay, for at his death he left a united, self-supporting nation untouched by the civil wars that afflicted its neighbors.

PARAGUAY PROGRESSES UNDER DICTATOR NUMBER TWO

Francia was followed by Carlos Antonio López. Although a dictator, he was sincerely fond of his country. To make his rule legal, he called a congress to draw up a constitution providing for a president with dictatorial powers. He then had himself elected president which made his office entirely constitutional! When López opened Paraguay to trade and immigration, it began to make some progress after its long isolation. The first newspapers were published, the telegraph was introduced, and a short railway was built. López wanted every man in his country to learn to read and write and established a primary school in every town and village. By the end of his rule he had succeeded in his ambition. To be able to read was so unusual among the common people of South America that Paraguayans proved their nationality by proudly stating that they could read. Under López the country was kept continually prepared for any hostile moves by Brazil or Argentina.

DICTATOR NUMBER THREE BRINGS A DISASTROUS WAR UPON PARAGUAY

López's greatest mistake was in spoiling his son whom he had trained to be his successor. The young man had been made the head of the army when only nineteen, and later was sent to travel in Europe. When his father died, a congress elected Francisco López as president. It is probable that the presence of López at the congress and the presence of his army outside the building had something to do with his election.

This spoiled young man was conceited, cruel, and erratic. He had delusions of grandeur and believed that he could conquer South America as Napoleon had conquered Europe. He went so far as to have a copy of Napoleon's crown made and sent from Europe. López never wore the crown nor did he even see it because the Argentine customs authorities seized the royal emblem and refused to send it on. Apparently they did not sympathize with this would-be Napoleon! The crown can still be seen to this day in a museum in Buenos Aires.

Francisco López spent three years developing his country and building up a fighting machine so that he might make Paraguay a great military power. In 1864, when Brazil invaded Uruguay to aid the ousted *Colorados*, López sided with the *Blancos* and sent troops into Brazil. When other Paraguayan troops attempted to cross Argentine soil to reach Brazil, he found himself at war with two powerful countries. Uruguay later joined them in a triple alliance to defeat the dictator.

Common sense should have told Paraguayans how foolish this war was. But they were intensely patriotic and had been taught unquestioning obedience for fifty years. The people scarcely knew what they were fighting for. Their banners said "*Vencer o morir*" (Conquer or die). Most of them died. So great was the slaughter that toward the end of the war boys of ten, old men, and even women were fighting. Famine and disease spread, but still the loyal people fought on. The war did not end until 1870 when López himself was surrounded by a squad of Brazilians and stabbed to death. The population of Paraguay was reduced to one third its size before the war; there were seven times as many women left as men. López had almost wiped out a whole nation. The brave people turned back to their wasted fields and towns; all the progress made under Carlos López had been lost. When we judge Paraguay, we must remember that she started anew in 1870 to rebuild a ruined country.

THE GRAN CHACO WAR BRINGS FURTHER DESTRUCTION TO A BRAVE NATION

In 1870, a new constitution was framed which attempted to prevent the rule of dictators by limiting the president's term to four years. But dictatorships did not end; they merely became shorter. With no competent leaders to guide the unfortunate country, many years of disorder followed. By 1921, however, the country appeared to be heading for progress and stability under an able president. But a long-standing boundary dispute with Bolivia led to a war over the Gran Chaco region in 1932. The story of this tragic and disastrous war has already been told in Chapter 26.

Since the end of the Chaco War in 1935, the valiant nation has been struggling to get on its feet once more. But there have been a number of revolutions and several presidents in recent years. There seems little hope of a more democratic government in Paraguay for some time.

* * *

PARAGUAY has been called a backward nation. In spite of its rich land

and pastures, it is a poor country. It is true that most of its people cannot read or write and that the standard of living is very low. But we must remember that this little nation has endured two destructive wars. There has been little opportunity for peaceful development. Not only did the wars prevent progress; they destroyed man-power. Paraguay lacks people, but its remoteness prevents a large amount of immigra-tion. Add to this the fact that it is an inland country which must depend on slow and expensive river traffic to get its exports to market. Furthermore, its exports are small. For example, while Uruguay in 1940 exported $58,000,000 worth of goods, Paraguay's exports were worth only $7,000,000. When we consider the obstacles facing this country, we wonder, not that it is backward, but that it has survived at all.

Are You a Careful Reader?   Test Yourself!

I. Supply the correct word for each blank:

1. .... , capital of Uruguay, is a prosperous modern seaport; .... , capital of Paraguay, is an old river port many miles inland from the sea.

2. The "Thirty-Three Immortals" are famous because they led the fight against .... and brought .... to Uruguay.

3. The great progress of Uruguay is due largely to one man, ...

4. The most important export of Uruguay is .... ; the exports of Paraguay are .... , ... , and .... .

5. Paraguay's lack of progress is due to the rule of .... and to .... disastrous ...

II. Match the following words and statements:

1. yerba	*a.*	red earth of Paraguay
2. Batlle	*b.*	general in Gran Chaco War
3. Blancos	*c.*	Uruguayan president elected in 1938
4. Pilcomayo	*d.*	Indian language spoken by most Paraguayans
5. Guaraní	*e.*	language of Uruguayans
6. Francia	*f.*	isolationist dictator of Paraguay
7. López	*g.*	family name of two dictators of Paraguay
8. tierra colorada	*h.*	tree whose leaves are used for drink
9. Baldomir	*i.*	river flowing into the Paraguay River
10. Artigas	*j.*	father of progress and democracy in Uruguay
	k.	conservative rural party of Uruguay
	l.	patriot Uruguayan soldier, leader of *Banda Oriental*

Food for Thought and Discussion

1. How much of Paraguay's backwardness can be traced to war?

2. Compare Uruguay and Costa Rica as to democracy and social reform. Which one do you consider most progressive? Why?

3. List all the differences between Uruguay and Paraguay that you can. Do these differences explain the difference in progress?

Interesting Things to Do

1. Read and tell the class about one of these trips: through the Chilean Lake region to Lake Nahuel Huapi in Argentina; south from La Paz to Córdoba; up the Paraná to Iguassú Falls; from Buenos Aires into the Gran Chaco of Argentina.

2. Learn more about such men as: Montt, Rosas, Sarmiento, Rivadavia, Artigas, Irigoyen, Batlle, Carlos López, Doctor Francia, Alessandri.

3. Draw a plan of an Argentine *estancia*; sketch old-time gaucho costumes from the *National Geographic* or *Américas*.

4. Learn about the semi-civilized Indians of today such as the Guaraní of Paraguay, the Patagonians, or the Araucanians.

5. Find out all you can about the nitrate industry of Chile; the refrigeration of meat; or the story of *quebracho* bark from the tree to its final use.

6. Write the story of a boy or girl immigrant to Argentina as a homesteader on the pampa; write a diary of a Paraguayan soldier in the Chaco War; tell the story of a day at an *estancia* or a *fundo* as the guest of the owner. Write a poem about the pampa, the air trip over Uspallata Pass, or the Christ of the Andes.

7. Read and tell the story of the Christ of the Andes.

8. Bring to class newspaper clippings on Chile, Argentina, Uruguay, and Paraguay. Let a committee present a radio news broadcast on current happenings in these countries.

9. Find records of the national anthems of the countries in Part Seven and play for the class; play an Argentine tango on the piano or phonograph.

10. Read any letters received from pen-pals.

11. *For the whole class:* Make a chart comparing two of the most democratic and progressive republics of Latin America with two of the most backward. List the countries and rate them under the following headings: (1) Government — president or dictator? (2) Population — large or small native group? (3) Land — large estates or small farms? (4) Middle class — large or small? (5) Schools — few or many? (6) Transportation — good or poor roads?

Interesting Books to Read

For Further Information

Clark, Sydney, *The East Coast of South America.* Prentice-Hall. Chapters on Argentina and Uruguay.

Fodor, Laszlo, *Argentina.* Hastings House. Beautiful photographs with factual description.

Hanson, Earl P., *Chile: Land of Progress.* Reynal Hitchcock. Best reference work

Weddell, Alexander, *Introduction to Argentina.* Greystone. A guide for tourists written by one of our ambassadors.

For Pleasure

De Sherbinin, Betty, *Wind on the Pampas.* A novel of life on an *estancia.*

Duguid, Julian, *The Cloak of Monkey Fur.* Appleton-Century. A story of the Spanish settlement of Paraguay.

Frank, Waldo, ed., *Tales from the Argentine.* Farrar and Rinehart. Translations of good stories.

Williamson, T. R., *Last of the Gauchos.* Bobbs-Merrill. A boy's life on the Argentine plains.

CARIBBEAN SEA

CENTRAL
AMERICA

ATLANTIC

VENEZUELA

COLOMBIA

THE
GUIANAS

OCEAN

Equator

ECUADOR

Nuts

Rubber

Pará
(Belém)

Manaus

River

Wax

Amazon

Belterra

Fordlandia

Sugar

Cotto

P E R U

Pernambu
(Recife)

Rubber

Cattle

Hardwood

São Francisco

Baía
(Salvador)

Quartz

Cacao

O C E A N

River

Diamonds

Manganese

BOLIVIA

Gold

Iron

Cattle

River

MINAS

Coffee

Tropic of
Capricorn

PARAGUAY

Paraná

GERAIS

Coffee

Coffee

São Paulo

RIO DE JANEIRO

C H I L E

Cotton

Santos

A R G E N T I N A

RIO GRANDE
DO SUL

P A C I F I C

Cattle

URUGUAY

BRAZIL

0   300   600   900

SCALE IN MILES

BRAZIL FACES A FUTURE OF PROMISE

OUR LAST VISIT in Latin America will be to our largest neighbor, Brazil. We shall find this country quite different from the others we have visited because it was settled not by Spanish people but by Portuguese. As we shall see, Brazil's background, language, and customs are largely Portuguese. For this reason we shall find it one of the most interesting of our American neighbors.

First we shall travel through the settled part of this great land, looking in upon gay and enchanting Rio, watching the endless streams of coffee bags pour into the holds of waiting ships at Santos, and visiting old and interesting colonial cities farther north. Next we shall trace Brazil's history from colonial times to the present, and see a royal court move from the Old World to the New.

We shall visit the workers of Brazil and learn of government plans to improve their lot. We shall see factories run by hydro-electric power in a bustling modern city, and in contrast see huge areas unchanged since the days when Orellano sailed down the Amazon. Finally, we shall get acquainted with the daily life of the Brazilians and learn, perhaps to our surprise, that they read our cartoons and enjoy our movies.

Before starting the story of Brazil, let us look at the map on the opposite page. In what zone is most of Brazil located? Find the Amazon River. Where are the Brazilian Highlands? Where in Brazil would you expect the climate to be hot? Where would it be cool? What products would you expect to find in the southern states bordering on Argentina and Uruguay? What important cities can you name?

While you are reading the story of Brazil, keep in mind the following questions:

1. Why has Brazil's government in the past been more stable and orderly than that of most of the Spanish republics?

2. Why can Brazil be called a real melting pot of races?

3. What are some of the important problems which face the government of Brazil?

Chapter 34

We Become Acquainted with the Land and Cities of Brazil

I've never sailed the Amazon,
I've never reached Brazil;
But the *Don* and *Magdalena*,
They can go there when they will!

Yes, weekly from Southampton,
Great steamers, white and gold,
Go rolling down to Rio
(Roll down — roll down to Rio!)
And I'd like to roll to Rio
Some day before I'm old!

I've never seen a Jaguar,
Nor yet an Armadill —
O dilloing in his armour,
And I s'pose I never will,

Unless I go to Rio
These wonders to behold —
Roll down — roll down to Rio —
Roll really down to Rio!
Oh, I'd love to roll to Rio
Some day before I'm old! [1]

THESE LINES express the feelings of Rudyard Kipling when he saw the steamers *Don* and *Magdalena* leave Southampton, England, bound for far-off Brazil. The poem is full of the lure of that tropical country.

Most of us know little about Brazil. We may remember that Theodore Roosevelt explored the River of Doubt, or that Brazil nuts and coffee

[1] From *Just So Stories* by Rudyard Kipling, copyright 1902, 1907, 1935. By permission A. P. Watt & Son, Doubleday, Doran & Co., Inc., and The Macmillan Company of Canada.

grow there. We may have read of Rio de Janeiro and its beautiful harbor, and more recently, of Brazil's part in the second World War. But it is important that we know something about the land of Brazil, about its people, its history, and its form of government. Not only is it one of the richest countries of South America, but it is the nearest one to Africa and Europe. Today Brazil not only supplies the United States with needed raw materials, but she is also one of our best friends in the American family of nations. It is important to the safety of the Western Hemisphere that Brazil remain a good neighbor.

BRAZIL IS BIG, RICH, AND EMPTY

What is Brazil like? To answer this question is as difficult as trying to tell what the United States is like. What we might say about the Middle West would certainly not be true of the South, and a description of the Pacific Northwest would hardly fit the East. But in Brazil, as in the United States, there are certain facts that are true of the whole country.

The most overwhelming fact about Brazil is its size. It has 3,286,000 square miles of territory. Or, if figures do not mean much to you, it is bigger by the whole state of Texas than the United States; it is as big as all the rest of South America; it covers one fifth of the land of the entire Western Hemisphere. There is a single island in the mouth of the Amazon River larger than the states of Vermont and New Hampshire combined! If a steamer traveled all the navigable rivers of Brazil, it would have covered a distance equivalent to crossing the Pacific eight times.

A second overwhelming fact is the richness of Brazil. On her fertile soil from tropical north to temperate south can be grown almost every crop known to mankind — cacao, cotton, sugar, coffee, tobacco, cereals, fruits, nuts of all kinds. Her vast tropical forests yield almost every kind of wood known to man, as well as the rubber for which she may again become famous. Brazil has no deserts and no waste mountain land; rainfall is plentiful. In her eastern plateau region untold wealth in minerals lies under the soil. Brazil has perhaps the greatest quantities of iron ore and manganese in the world, as well as other valuable minerals. Gold, diamonds, and other precious and semi-precious stones are mined. In addition to all of these resources, Brazil has many fine landlocked bays to serve as harbors for her trade.

No other country in the world has so much land that will support human beings. It is said that several hundred million people could live in Brazil. Yet two thirds of this great land is unoccupied and only three per cent of the arable land is cultivated. Brazilians live for the most part in a strip of country along the coast about the size of Argentina. In this section of coast and cool plateau, lying between the mouth of the Amazon and the border of Uruguay, are the chief cities and most of the cultivated lands of Brazil. In fact, this is all of Brazil that matters today, and this is the Brazil we shall learn about. The rest is for the most part empty, untamed wilderness waiting for science to solve the problems of heat and tropical disease before it can be inhabited by civilized man.

BRAZIL AND BRAZILIANS ARE DIVIDED

Brazil is divided into twenty states. We need not learn the names of all the states, but there are several that are important to know if we wish to understand the country. In the northeast are nine states. The two most important are Baía (bah-ee'ah) and Pernambuco (pair-nahm-boo'-coh) where cacao and sugar are grown. These states are in the tropics and the majority of the population are Negroes and mulattoes.

The heart of Brazil includes the important states of São Paulo [1] (sow pow'loo), Minas Gerais (mee'nahs zhay-rah'eesh), and Rio de Janeiro (ree'oh day zhah-nay'roh), all three inhabited largely by whites. These states are the wealthiest and most powerful politically of the entire nation. Within their borders lie the coffee and one of the principal cotton regions of Brazil.

The southern section of Brazil lies in the Temperate Zone and is a con-

[1] Although Portuguese is a first cousin of Spanish, there are several differences which confuse the Spanish-speaking visitor. For instance *San* (saint) becomes *São*, pronounced *sow* with a slightly nasal sound as in French. The final *m* as in Belém is also nasal: *Beleng*. *De o* (of the) becomes *do* and *de a* becomes *da*. The Spanish *ñ* becomes *nh* in Portuguese, as in senhor. The Spanish *z* as in *plaza* is written as *ç*.

AVENIDA RIO BRANCO has a decided roll! Believe it or not, the building in the background has been in the U.S.A. It held Brazil's exhibit at the St. Louis Exposition and was later rebuilt in Rio.

Gendreau

tinuation of the rolling grasslands of Uruguay. Of the three southern states, Rio Grande do Sul (ree'oh grahn'de doh sool) is the most important. It is a cattle- and sheep-raising state.

The states of Brazil differ as greatly from one another as do Nevada and Georgia, or California and Maine. Likewise, the Brazilians themselves differ just as the Nevadan differs from the Georgian. But the man from Nevada is first of all a citizen of the United States. In Brazil, it is the other way around, for the Brazilian is very apt to think first of his loyalty to the home state. For instance, if you meet a group of Brazilians in Rio de Janeiro, the man from the state of São Paulo will make a point of telling you

that he is a *paulista* (pow-lees'tah). He who hails from the cattle-raising state of Rio Grande do Sul calls himself a gaucho (gah-ush'oh), while a native of the mining state of Minas Gerais is a *mineiro* (mee-nay'roh). You will learn the reason for this strong local feeling when we come to the history of Brazil.

In the most important states, cities have grown up which differ greatly from north to south. There are certain of these cities which everyone should know something about.

WE "ROLL DOWN TO RIO"

The traveler who enters the great bay of Rio de Janeiro has the feeling that he must be dreaming, so fantastic and unbelievable are the jagged peaks and pinnacles which form the natural skyline of the city. It looks as though some giant child had dropped his great blocks, piling some topsy-turvy on the shore and tipping others into the water at all angles. In the background above the city rears the Corcovado (cohr-coh-vah'-doh) or "Hunchback" peak with its statue of Christ on the summit. From the blue outline of the distant Organ Mountains another peak, the "Finger of God," stretches a mighty finger up into the heavens. As the ship steams toward the harbor entrance, the beautiful crescent of Copacabana (coh-pah-cah-bah'nah) Beach curves to the left and the famous bald cone of the Sugar Loaf rises up ahead. If you remember the bullet-shaped native sugar of the tropical countries, you will understand why this peak is so named.

When the ship enters the turquoise waters of Guanabara (gwah-nah-bah'-rah) Bay, the city can be seen spreading out over the narrow coastland and reaching up into the hills. Everywhere in the harbor steep, rocky spurs reach out into the blue water forming beautiful bays and inlets which are fringed with shining sand. The steamer is parked as though it were a car, at the very foot of Avenida Rio Branco (brahn'-coh), the main street of the city!

This street, only a mile and a half long, cuts across the peninsula of land which forms the heart of the city and ends at the waterfront on the opposite side. It was built in 1904 when the city was modernized. The traveler is fascinated by the famous black and white mosaic sidewalks of Rio Branco which were copied from the streets of Lisbon. The most common mosaic is a "rolling wave" pattern which is apt to make the pedestrian feel he is still on the bounding sea. In front of buildings and in some of the squares, or *praças* (prah'sahs), as they are called in Brazil, other patterns trace the shapes of sea-horses, anchors, butterflies, and flowers.

The Avenida is lined with fine buildings, theaters, and shops to tempt the tourist. There are many sidewalk cafés where people sit drinking the very strong, very sweet coffee of Brazil. The National Library, one of the largest in South America, and the Municipal Theater can be seen on one of the *praças*. Near-by is Cinelandia, a group of moving-picture theaters where movies from the United States are shown. Crossing the Avenida about in the middle is the famous shopping street, Rùa do Ouvidor (ruah do oo-vee-dohr'). Built when the city was still young, it is so narrow that no vehicles are allowed on it and people walk in the street as well as on the sidewalks.

The people of Rio are called *cariocas* (cah-ree-oh'cahs), which is a name given by the Indians, meaning "white man's house." They are a leisurely people, courteous and friendly. Although many of the upper class are white, the majority of *cariocas*, like most Brazilians, are *mestiços* (mes-tee'sohs), or people of mixed race. The visitor from the United States notices how freely they mix without the prejudice found in our country.

The *cariocas* are proud of their clean and healthful city. Streets are scrubbed every night, and all food sold in the city is carefully handled in the most sanitary manner. Rio was not always like this. At one time it was considered the "pest-hole of the east coast." Malaria and yellow

COPACABANA BEACH on the Atlantic is the playground of Rio. Notice the skyscraper hotels and apartment houses and the long promenade of black and white tile.

Lanks

C. H. Haring

RIO AT NIGHT is a sight never to be forgotten. Not only is the city lighted, but the drives along the beach are illuminated for miles. The lights stay on all night, going off only when the sun rises.

fever were rampant. Doctor Oswaldo Cruz is responsible for cleaning up the city. After Doctor Gorgas had rid Cuba and the Panama Canal Zone of mosquito-borne diseases, Doctor Cruz set to work in the early 1900's to stamp out disease in Rio. Constant watchfulness keeps the city safe.

TIME GOES FAST IN RIO

There are many fascinating sights to be seen in Rio. The visitor may take the marine drive along the waterfront over miles of scalloped beach, passing the marble palaces of the rich, hotels, churches, and apartment houses. There is a tunnel through a rocky ridge which leads to Copacabana Beach, one of the most famous in the world. Mosaic walks border the white sands, and ultra-modern apartment houses and hotels are built in this fashionable suburb. *Cariocas* love their beaches and may be seen at all seasons sun-bathing and swimming.

The visitor may go to see the Botanical Gardens started by a former emperor. They have specimens of every kind of tropical plant in the world. Here also is the mother palm from whose seed grew all the royal palms which line the streets of Rio. There is a story that when a king of Portugal was in Brazil, he received seeds of the palm from the West Indies. He planted the seeds with his own hands and ordered that when the trees grew, they were to be kept for his gardens alone. Hence the name, royal palms. One of the finest sights in the gardens is the radiating avenues of palms, with each tree a hundred feet high and a hundred years old.

The adventurous person can take the dizzy trip by aerial cable-car up to the summit of the Sugar Loaf, 1300 feet above the sea. It is worth swinging through space to look down upon Rio and its curving bays with the purple mountains beyond. The scene is especially beautiful in the evening as darkness falls. One by one the crescent shores become gleaming necklaces of jeweled lights casting their glimmering reflections across the water. The city streets are outlined in brilliance and lights twinkle up the dark hillsides. Last of all, the statue of Christ on Corcovado suddenly gleams white against the velvet blackness as though it were descending from heaven. Looking at this sublime scene, it is easy to understand the expression heard in Rio, "God is a Brazilian."

A beautiful trip visitors often take is the journey to the old town of Petropolis north of Rio. It is amazing how soon one reaches the jungle after leaving Rio. Vines and tangled creepers wind around great trees, and brilliant blue butterflies, gaily colored birds and flowers make vivid splashes of color against the green jungle. The Petropolis road winds up the Organ Mountains back of Rio, furnishing enchanting glimpses of Rio Bay and the shimmering city in the distance. Forty miles from Rio over the summit of the mountains is the quaint old town, once the summer home of the rulers of Brazil. Situated in the cooler air of the plateau, Petropolis is still a summer resort for *cariocas*. There are beautiful homes and gardens, and the streets are shaded with flowering trees.

THIS MODERN ELECTRIC TRAIN will take you from Rio to São Paulo at a price much lower than you would pay in the United States. Many government-owned Diesel and electric trains connect nearby districts with Rio.

Weimer

SÃO PAULO IS THE CHICAGO OF SOUTH AMERICA

São Paulo is about 300 miles west of Rio and 40 miles inland from the sea. It can be reached by plane, fast train, or automobile. Coming from beautiful Rio, the visitor may be disappointed in São Paulo, for it looks a great deal like the industrial cities of the United States. Factories and skyscrapers, electric signs, streets crowded with traffic, all remind the North American of home. The *paulistas* consider their city and their state the most important in Brazil and hope to make São Paulo a world metropolis. They boast that the city has grown forty times its size in sixty years and is the fastest-growing city in the hemisphere. They point proudly to the magnificent public buildings, the beautiful residence districts, and the new stadium which is one of the most enormous and elaborate in the world.

Not only is São Paulo the largest manufacturing city in South America, but it lies in the heart of the richest agricultural district of Brazil. While its factories pour out textiles, leather goods, and other manufactures, the surrounding region pours into the city coffee, cotton, fruits, and vegetables.

Only the ancient center of the town, called the "Triangle," reveals that São Paulo is not a young and modern city. A network of narrow and crooked streets laid out hundreds of years ago still forms the business and shopping center of the city.

It has been said that Rio is a city to play in, while São Paulo is a city to work in. Certainly the busy and energetic *paulistas* who throng the streets of the city are quite unlike the leisure-loving *cariocas*. *Paulistas* do not pass the afternoon drinking coffee at sidewalk cafés, but drink it hurriedly as they stand at a counter. Factory workers and businessmen do not stop for the customary Latin American siesta. Few Negroes and *mestiços* are seen on the streets; like the people of Buenos Aires, the *paulistas* are mostly white. In fact the people are much like those in any big city of the United States, for immigration has brought Italians, Germans, Portuguese, and Spaniards. Almost any language may be heard on the streets of São Paulo.

Everyone who goes to São Paulo visits the famous snake farm, the first of its kind in the world. It is called the Instituto Butantán, and is run by the Brazilian government. Here are kept poisonous snakes from all over Brazil, and serums are made from their venom to prevent death from snakebite. A Brazilian named Doctor Vital Brazil has given his life to this work, and has been able to reduce the number of deaths from snakebite to only three per cent of those bitten. Any native of Brazil may send snakes to Butantán free of charge, and receives a vial of serum for every snake he supplies.

SANTOS IS THE COFFEE PORT OF THE WORLD

All the products which pour into São Paulo are exported by way of Santos, a seaport forty miles away. The railroad which connects them is a marvel of engineering; it is one of the steepest in the world. Cars are pulled up and down the steep slopes of the hills by cables. Because much of the exports and imports of São Paulo go over this road, it makes an

Weimer

SÃO PAULO, Brazil's great industrial city, handles its traffic in a modern manner. Note the wide tree-lined boulevard with its several zones of traffic and the traffic bridge above.

enormous profit and is known as the richest railroad in the world.

Santos is located on an island at the mouth of a river three miles from the open sea. Coffee has made Santos famous. Almost everyone in the city makes his living from coffee in one way or another, by buying and selling it, by carrying, storing, or shipping it. Indeed, the whole city smells of coffee.

The waterfront of Santos is an interesting sight. Great warehouses hold millions of sacks of coffee; rat-proof concrete wharves are equipped with modern loading machinery. In peace times, ships from all over the world line up along the four miles of docks, waiting their turn to be filled with bags of fragrant coffee beans.

At many docks, conveyor belts carry the sacks into the holds of the ships; at others, an endless procession of Negro laborers, each with a sack on his back, moves from warehouse to ship. At present, 9,000,000 or 10,-000,000 sacks leave Santos every year, and over half of this amount goes to the United States. In a narrow street in the center of town is the coffee-trading center of the world. Here the coffee brokers transact the world's coffee business, and the coffee tasters sip coffee all day to determine its quality. Many a fortune has been made and lost in this coffee market.

Away from the waterfront, Santos is more like a typical Portuguese colonial town than any other we have seen thus far. Spanish colonial towns, as you know, were built about a central plaza with straight streets crossing at right angles. The Portuguese built towns with winding streets and high houses decorated with blue and white tile or with gay painted scenes. In the old quarter of Santos, the pink, yellow, and blue plaster houses with brightly painted walls give a quaint air to the town. Miles of broad, white beaches with playgrounds and parks make Santos a popular vacation city for Brazilians during the winter months. For centuries this city was avoided because of the epidemics of yellow fever. A sanitary campaign fostered the draining of the swampy, malarial lowlands of the coast, and today Santos is a safe city in which to live.

BAÍA IS AN ANCIENT CITY

Seven hundred miles up the hot coast from Rio is one of the oldest cities and first capital of Brazil, Baía.[1] Baía means bay, the complete name being *Baía de São Salvador de Todos os Santos* or the Bay of the Holy Savior of All the Saints. The town was originally called São Salvador, but we commonly call it Baía. Two arms of land enclose the bay and form a gateway into the harbor. The town is a picturesque sight,

[1] Baía was originally spelled Bahía. A few years ago a system of reformed spelling was introduced in Brazil, which changed the spelling of many proper names.

THE UPPER TOWN OF BAÍA looks down upon its busy waterfront. The buildings are in soft pastel colors and the little boats with their odd sails skim in and out over the turquoise water of the harbor.

Gendreau

built half on the narrow shore and half on the bluff that rises from the bay. The lower town is given to docks, warehouses, shipping offices, and the homes of the poorer inhabitants. In the upper town are the residences, the government buildings, the schools, and the many churches. To reach the upper town you can climb or drive 300 feet up the narrow streets, or you can take one of the four elevators for a few pennies.

One of the first things the traveler notices is the many Negro people in Baía. This city was once the largest slave market in the world and 90 per cent of all Baianos (bah-ee-ah'nohs) are descendants of Negro slaves brought to work in the sugar plantations. Not all Baianos are Negro. Some Portuguese families are proud of their unmixed blood and their names which date back for many centuries. Life is easy for the Negroes of Baía. Food may be had for the picking in this tropical land; the sea provides fish in abundance. Most of the Negroes are gay and irresponsible and work only enough to supply their few needs.

Lower Baía on the waterfront is a busy and colorful place. Bright-colored sailboats come down the rivers from the interior loaded with sugar cane, tobacco, cacao, and other tropical products. People idle about the docks watching the activities of the harbor. The native market swarms with children. Vendors carry their wares upon their heads. There are baskets of fish, trays of fruit and sweets, earthenware jars — all balanced on the heads of the men and women. Some clop-clop in the wooden sandals worn in Brazil, others are barefoot.

Guillumette

GAY BAIANA DOLLS, looking for all the world like the Negro women of Baía even to the baskets on their heads, can be bought in the native market.

The picturesque Negro women, with their long, full, flowered skirts and their turbaned heads, are called *Baianas.* Many of them are descendants of Negro women who were the pampered favorites of wealthy Portuguese, and they walk majestically along the streets carrying their burden aloft. In the native market one can buy dolls dressed like these stately Baianas, and carved hands to ward off the "evil eye." The Negroes still practice the ancient customs and cults of their African ancestors, and in interior villages strange and weird dances take place.

UPPER BAÍA IS A BIT OF OLD PORTUGAL

In upper Baía, life is leisurely and pleasant. There are many reminders that this is an old Portuguese town. Houses, painted in bright colors and decorated with tiles or gay scenes, are almost buried in luxuriant tropical gardens.

Baía, like Quito, is a city of many churches. They are built in a highly ornate style and interiors are decorated with gold leaf and carved wood. The church of São Francisco, built in the 1500's, is paneled over the whole interior in the carved wood of the jacaranda tree. Images of angels, cherubs, birds, and flowers, painted in bright colors or covered with gold, stand out in elaborate confusion.

PERNAMBUCO IS THE FOURTH LARGEST CITY OF BRAZIL

The port of Pernambuco is located on the bulge of Brazil (see map, page 380). This is another city with two names. The Portuguese named it Recife (ray-see'feh), or "reef," because of the coral reef on which the old part of the city is built, but it is commonly called by the Indian name of the little state in which it is located. Pernambuco is the most important seaport north of Baía, and is one of the closest to Africa in the hemisphere. Sugar and cotton grown in the region are shipped from Pernambuco.

During colonial days, the Dutch once gained possession of Pernambuco. Many of the old houses are tall and narrow, with gabled roofs like Dutch houses. The island on the reef is connected with the mainland by bridges, and there are bridges across the two rivers which flow through the town. The many waterways and the picturesque bridges have caused the city to be called the "Venice of Brazil." Many boats go back and forth through the city carrying freight and passengers.

THE RIVER BANK AT MANAUS, which, although no longer a boom town, is still doing business as this picture indicates. Manaus is not located on the Amazon, but nine miles up river on a branch called the Rio Negro.

Guillumette

JUNGLE AND CIVILIZATION MEET AT PARÁ AND MANAUS

We ought not to leave Brazilian cities without mentioning the Amazon ports of Pará (pah-rah') and Manaus (mah-nah'ush). Pará or Belem (be-leng') is ninety miles from the sea on the River Pará which forms one of the mouths of the great Amazon delta. One thousand miles up the river by steamer is Manaus. Electric lights, street-cars, mosaic sidewalks, and taxis surprise the visitor to this jungle city. Both Pará and Manaus were boom towns when the Brazilian rubber trade was at its height in the early 1900's and both cities became fabulously wealthy. Fortunes were spent on magnificent public buildings, homes, and luxuries imported from Europe. For instance, the white marble opera house at Manaus cost $10,000,000! Famous singers traveled up the Amazon to entertain the wealthy families of the rubber town. Whole families, including uncles, aunts, and cousins, traveled to Europe; sons were sent to England for their education. When the rubber bubble burst, these cities collapsed almost overnight.

Today these handsome cities are by no means ghost cities, as they are sometimes called. The products of the rich Amazon basin pass through their ports. Rubber is still exported,

Sawders

THE MARBLE OPERA HOUSE in Manaus is quite a contrast to the primitive port. Who knows but that one day this former rubber metropolis may again grow up to its opera house?

together with many tons of Brazil nuts and other tropical products.

* * *

THESE ARE the cities of Brazil. Each one is different, from sophisticated Rio to the one-time rubber metropolis in Amazonia. Except in the south, the cities are not connected by road, but only by boat, which helps to explain the sectional feeling existing among the people of Brazil.

Are You a Careful Reader?   Test Yourself!

I. Can you supply the correct word for each blank?

1. The language spoken in Brazil is . . . . .
2. . . . . of Brazil is empty; only about . . . . per cent of its arable land is cultivated.
3. Brazil is divided into . . . . states.
4. Residents of Rio call themselves . . . . ; residents of the state of São Paulo call themselves . . . . .
5. The capital of Brazil is . . . . ; the chief manufacturing city is . . . .

II. Can you match the following words and statements?

1. Copacabana   *a.* summer resort in mountains near Rio
2. Corcovado   *b.* coffee port
3. Sugar Loaf   *c.* fashionable Rio beach
4. Pernambuco   *d.* cattle-raising state of the south
5. Baía   *e.* inhabitant of Minas Gerais
6. Rio Grande do Sul   *f.* main street of Rio
7. Rio Branco   *g.* mountain peak behind Rio
8. Petropolis   *h.* port near mouth of the Amazon
9. Santos   *i.* coast city built on two levels
10. Pará   *j.* landmark of Rio's harbor
                       k. northern coast city also called Recife
                       l. famous shopping street of Rio

Food for Thought and Discussion

1. Do residents of certain states in our own country give themselves names as the Brazilians do? What are some of these names? Do you think any Americans give their first loyalty to their native states rather than to their country?

2. Under what conditions could Manaus and Pará become the thriving cities they once were?

3. Do you believe the Amazon region will ever be opened to settlement, with great tropical plantations and air-cooled cities?

Chapter 35

Brazil Progresses from Colony to Empire to Republic

PORTUGUESE BRAZIL has a story quite different from that of her Spanish neighbors. No bold *conquistadores* march across the pages of Brazil's history; nor are there tales of buccaneers lying in wait to seize treasure galleons bound for home. Brazil had no great Indian peoples to conquer and her wealth was in sugar and dyewoods, poor booty for a buccaneer. No heroic campaigns were fought to win her independence; it was established with little bloodshed. Brazil is unique because for almost seventy years she was an empire ruled by sovereign princes. There was a royal court in Rio, with all the pomp and ceremony of European court life.

The history of Brazil falls naturally into three parts — Brazil as a colony, Brazil as a kingdom, and Brazil as an independent republic. Her early history, like that of the other Latin American republics, begins in the Old World. Let us turn back to the kingdom of Portugal in the 1400's.

Brazil Becomes a Portuguese Colony

PORTUGAL ACCIDENTALLY SECURES A FOOTHOLD IN SPAIN'S NEW WORLD

As we know, Spain was not the only country whose navigators sailed unknown seas in search of new lands. From the little kingdom of Portugal facing the Atlantic, many a bold mariner set forth into unknown waters. You remember that in the 1400's the Portuguese had discovered and colonized not only the Madeira Islands and the Azores, but also the Cape Verde Islands far to the westward in the Atlantic.[1] Under the inspiration of Prince Henry the Navigator, Portuguese sailors had ventured farther and farther along the west coast of Africa, seeking a way to India around that vast continent.

Before any Portuguese reached India, the news of the amazing discoveries of Christopher Columbus under the flag of Castile electrified the two courts. When at the request of Ferdinand and Isabella the Pope established the line of 1493, the king of Portugal was dissatisfied with the decision. He appealed to the Spanish rulers, who agreed to move the line several hundred miles farther west with Portugal taking all territory to the east. It was later found that the new line cut through the bulge of eastern South America. Thus Portugal was able to claim that vast land of great rivers, jungle forests, and cool plateaus known today as Brazil.

BRAZIL IS CLAIMED AND NAMED FOR PORTUGAL

Da Gama's discovery in 1499 of a route to India by way of Africa turned the attention of the king of Portugal to the rich East. In the year 1500, a fleet of thirteen merchant ships under Pedro Alvares Cabral (cah-brahl') set out from Portugal to follow da Gama's route to India. The explorer had advised Cabral to sail far to the west to avoid the calms off the coast of Africa. Either by accident or intention, he sailed so far westward that he reached the bulge of the New World that lay nearest to Africa. He thought it was an island, and since it lay east of the Pope's line, he officially claimed it for Portugal.

Later expeditions along the coast of the new land brought back to Portugal a wood which, when boiled with cloth, dyed the cloth a fiery red. This wood, already known in Europe, was called *brasil* (brah-seel') after *brasa*, the word for red-hot coals. Thus the new Portuguese territory came to be known as the land of the red dyewood, or *Terra do Brasil*. Brazil is the English spelling for Portugal's New World possession.

For thirty years after the claiming of Brazil, the Portuguese were too

[1] To refresh your memory on the early Portuguese discoveries, read pages 86–87 in Chapter 8.

much interested in their rich trade with the East Indies to pay much attention to the wild land on the western ocean. French as well as Portuguese fleets visited Brazil's coast to get shiploads of the valuable dyewood. At this time Spanish explorers were telling tales of great Indian cities and fabulous treasure in gold. The first visitors to Brazil brought back word of brown and naked natives who lived in mud huts, and grew cotton, corn, and cassava. The earliest settlers on the coast of Brazil were shipwrecked sailors, or convicts marooned there and forced to survive as best they could.

THE PORTUGUESE ESTABLISH A COLONIAL SYSTEM IN BRAZIL

By 1525, tiny settlements were

IN BAÍA this steep and narrow cobbled street is a main thoroughfare between the upper and lower town. Note the large basket on the man's head and the shoes beside the door of the shoe shop.

Black Star

scattered along the coast particularly where the present cities of Baía and Pernambuco are located. The French also established trading posts on the coast, for they had designs on this rich land which Portugal was neglecting. The Portuguese finally became concerned for the safety of Brazil and sent an official expedition under Martim de Sousa (mahr-teeng' duh soh'oo-sah). In 1532, he founded the first official colony of Brazil, São Vicente (sow vee-sen'teh), near the present city of Santos.

Portugal did not establish viceroyalties and *audiencias* in her territory as did Spain. Instead, the coast of Brazil was divided into fifteen strips of land fifty leagues wide called *captaincies*. These were offered to Portuguese noblemen if they would colonize and develop the country at their own expense. Six or seven grants north of São Vicente were soon taken up and settled. In their territories the captains were given almost complete authority over the colonists. The captaincies were separated by mountains, forests, and jungle, so that there was little communication between them. For this reason there grew up in these local settlements a strong feeling of independence which has lasted to this day.

In 1548, the king appointed a governor-general over all the separate captaincies. Tomé de Souza (tohmay' duh soh'oo-sah) arrived with six shiploads of soldiers and colonists and anchored in the great Bay of All Saints. On the high bluffs above the bay the settlers laid out a *praça* and started a town of adobe huts. This was the first capital of Brazil, the city of Baía or São Salvador. Baía grew rapidly. In its third year a group of orphaned girls were sent by the queen of Portugal to be wives for the colonists.

Rio de Janeiro was not important in the early colonial period. In 1502, Portuguese explorers sailing along the coast on New Year's Day had entered a magnificent bay south of Baía. Believing it to be the mouth of a great river, they named it Rio de Janeiro (River of January). No Portuguese settlement was established there, but a French Protestant colony later settled on the bay shore. Although the Portuguese governor sent soldiers to drive out the French, they did not succeed until 1567. No one dreamed that the little settlement built by these soldiers and called São Sebastião do Rio de Janeiro (Saint Sebastian of the River of January) would one day become a great and famous city.

MISSIONARIES BRING EDUCATION AND RELIGION TO THE INDIANS

The Portuguese did not forget that there were souls to be saved as well as land to be settled. Missionary priests came over with the settlers and carried on their unselfish work of converting and educating the Indians. They not only founded schools for the Indians, but they learned their language and tried to write a Bible in their native tongue. Like the priests who penetrated into Paraguay, the brave fathers ventured far into the interior to found missions for the Indians. The Indians, usually hostile to the whites, became used to the black-robed fathers who came into their villages. It is said that many a candidate for a cannibal feast was rescued by the fathers before he was put into the cooking pot!

The present town of São Paulo grew up around the Indian school which the priests founded on the high plateau. Colonists from São Vicente left the hot, malarial coast below and settled on the rich red soil of the cool highland region.

Churches for the settlers were also established by priests throughout the separated colonies, and became the center of many towns and villages. In Baía and Recife the colonists were so religious that their towns became noted for their many beautiful churches.

SUGAR AND SLAVES BRING WEALTH TO COLONIAL BRAZIL

Green shoots of the sugar cane brought from the Madeiras proved more valuable to Portugal than all the silver mined in Peru. Sugar was first planted in the captaincy of Pernambuco and grew so amazingly that great tracts of land were taken up for sugar plantations by noblemen and settlers. Baía became another rich sugar region. All along the coast forests were cleared and sugar fields planted, until by 1600 Brazil's crude sugar mills were producing most of Europe's sugar.

Who did the work on the great sugar plantations, or *fazendas* (fahsen'dahs), as they were called? Sugar, as well as cotton, required thousands of cheap laborers. Like the Spaniards, no Portuguese above the peasant class would lift a hand to do any manual labor. The Portuguese at first tried to force the Indians to work for them, but the enslaved Indians would do little work in spite of the overseer's whip. They either escaped into the forests or died of enforced labor like the Indians on Española.

The Portuguese began to import shiploads of slaves from the African coast to replace the Indians. These unhappy humans were torn from their homes and packed like animals in the foul holds of the slave boats. In the 1600's, Baía became the largest slave market in the world, where strong Negroes were bought and sold to labor for the white man. In this land of few whites, Negroes became as important in the production of sugar as the Negroes in our own South were important to the cotton industry.

A RACIAL MIXTURE BEGINS IN BRAZIL

Since few Portuguese women came with the early settlers, the men mated with the Indian women. The half-breeds, who soon became numerous in Brazil, were called *mamelucos* or mamelukes. In São Paulo, where the climate is more stimulating, the mamelukes were a fierce and fearless breed. They became famous for their love of hardship and for their bold explorations into the interior of Brazil. Like the brave frontiersmen of our early days, they subdued or enslaved warlike Indians and explored far into the heart of the continent, claiming new regions for Brazil. In the 1600's these bold souls became known as *bandeirantes* (bahn-day-ee-rahn'tesh) because they carried a flag or *bandeira* in their expeditions. The later claims of Portugal to a territory far west of the Line of Demarcation were based on the explorations of the *bandeirantes*.

As the slaves increased, the Portuguese and Negro mixtures became more numerous. Like the Spaniards,

the Portuguese were used to the dark-skinned Moors and had no prejudice against the Negroes. Thus mulattoes and Negroes became the largest group in Brazil, a situation which was true of only one other region of Latin America — the islands of the West Indies. The mulatto people became small tradesmen, or overseers on the *fazendas*.

As in Spanish America, the Indians and Negroes were the lowest class, but the division was not nearly so strict. In Brazil people were classed according to wealth and position rather than color. It was not at all unusual for the upper classes to marry people of mulatto blood. When white women in larger numbers came to Brazil, people of pure Portuguese strain became more numerous in the colony. Thus, in colonial Brazil was laid the foundation for the Brazilian people of today.

BANDEIRANTES DISCOVER GOLD AND DIG THEIR OWN GRAVES

During the early 1600's some of the *bandeirantes* of São Paulo made a living by seizing jungle Indians to sell as slaves to the plantations at Rio and Baía. They often raided Indian missions in Brazil and near-by Paraguay. When slave raids ceased to be profitable, they turned to seeking gold. At the end of the century, the first important mines were discovered in the wild region back of Rio. The mines were so numerous in the 1700's and so general that the district was called *Minas Gerais* or "General Mines" (see map, page 380). As if gold were not enough, diamonds were later discovered in the same region.

These discoveries of the *bandeirantes* soon led to their own undoing,

Guillumette

THE CITY OF A HUNDRED CHURCHES might be a good name for Baía. The most famous is the Church of São Francisco. Every square inch of its interior is carved, tiled or inlaid with gold leaf!

for the news of gold brought a stampede of gold hunters much like the California gold rush. Cane fields and sugar mills were abandoned as the colonists rushed to the mines. Ships from Portugal were filled with fortune hunters. Mushroom towns grew up everywhere in the gold regions, and Minas Gerais, which had been almost uninhabited, soon boasted a population of a quarter of a million.

The *bandeirantes* resented the intrusion of Portuguese adventurers into mines which they had discovered, and they fought fiercely to keep them out. Government troops from Rio de Janeiro were sent against them and civil war lasted for two years.

The *bandeirantes* were finally defeated, and some of them moved away to create settlements still farther inland where the states of Goiaz and Mato Grosso are today.

THE MINES ARE REGULATED BY THE PORTUGUESE KING

The Portuguese rulers had long been envious of the riches that had reached Spain from the mines of Peru and Mexico. When gold was at last discovered in Brazil, the Portuguese king, like the king of Spain, demanded a fifth of all the precious metal. So that no other nation could profit from the mines, laws were passed forbidding any but Portuguese and Brazilians to mine the gold. Roads and rivers were guarded to keep foreigners out. Hundreds of slaves were sent to labor in the diggings. But the Brazilians resented having to pay the royal fifth to Portugal and much of the gold was smuggled out to avoid this tax.

Brazil in the 1700's became the leading producer of gold and diamonds in the world. The gold was sent on muleback along rough trails down to Rio de Janeiro. This city hummed with activity because it was the gold port. From there the royal fifth, when it could be collected, crossed the sea to the Portuguese king. In 1763, the capital was changed from Baía to the more important city of Rio de Janeiro. But the mines were worked so continuously that by the middle of the 1700's the richest deposits had been exhausted. By 1800, the flow of the treasure was much diminished, and the miners deserted by the thousands. Many who came to mine remained to farm. The gold rush had brought a huge immigration to the colonies. By 1808, there were about 3,000,000 people in Brazil. In 1820, Rio was the largest city with about 100,000 inhabitants. Baía had a population of about 70,000, while Recife and São Paulo were smaller.

LIFE IN COLONIAL BRAZIL WAS PRIMITIVE

Before we leave the colonial days in Brazil, let us look at life on the sugar *fazendas* and in the towns. The huge *fazendas*, with their miles of sugar cane, their sugar mills, and slave huts, were communities ruled over by the owner. The master and his family lived in the *casa grande*, a thick-walled, one-story dwelling with great rooms, heavy, carved furniture,

and a chapel. The women led an idle and secluded life, seldom appearing even when there was company. Slave women waited on them and often took charge of all household affairs. Babies were turned over to Negro nurses and every child had his own slave.

The sugar grown on the plantation was generously used in little cakes and sweet desserts. Since colonial women did not count their calories, they must have had many more curves than present standards of beauty would allow! So idle a life did the upper classes live that when master or lady went out they were carried in chairs by slaves. A woman or girl going to Mass had to be accompanied by husband or father or a trusted slave. Curtains over the canopied chairs shut them off from staring eyes.

The town of Rio, unlike the modern city, was like an ugly blot in its beautiful setting. Filth and refuse rotted in the unpaved streets and epidemics of typhoid and yellow fever were frequent. Swine were driven through the streets in the hope that the plague might infest them instead of humans, but no one thought of cleaning up the town. Street vendors, slaves, priests, and beggars swarmed in the streets. Men rode their horses on the narrow sidewalks.

The rich dressed in elegant clothes and ate from gold plates, but they had few conveniences. All were extremely religious and stopped several times a day to go into a church and pray. For amusement they attended the religious festivals of the Church. Colonial Brazil, as we have seen, was made up of a number of isolated provinces or captaincies from the Amazon to São Paulo. Although we know there were a few cities, most of the population lived in the country, on the great sugar plantations of the north or the cattle ranches of the south. There was little travel except by sea because of the wild country separating the colonies and the lack of roads.

In many ways colonial Brazil was far behind the Spanish colonies. You recall the fine universities in Mexico City, Lima, and other parts of Spanish America. In Brazil there was not one university. Although Brazil had several fine writers, their works had to be printed in Portugal because no printing press existed in the colony. There were few artists in Brazil equal to the many well-known men in the other American colonies; and although there are many splendid churches dating from colonial times, the architecture of homes and palaces did not compare with the splendid buildings in cities like Lima and Mexico City. This is because Brazilians did not have Indians to work on their buildings such as the skilled craftsmen of Peru and Mexico. On the whole, life was more primitive in colonial Brazil than in most of the Spanish colonies in the New World.

Brazil Becomes an Independent Empire

BRAZIL RECEIVES THE ROYAL FAMILY OF PORTUGAL

In 1808, the colonists had some startling news which was to change the course of their history. They learned that the royal family of Portugal was coming to live in Brazil! You remember that early in the 1800's Napoleon marched on Spain, captured the king, and put his own brother on the Spanish throne. When his armies advanced upon Portugal also, Dom João (zho-ow′), the acting king, did not wait to be captured, but fled with his family and hundreds of Portuguese nobles across the sea to Brazil. The people of Brazil were overjoyed to have the royal family in their midst. But the Portuguese aristocrats were disgusted to find that the colonial capital was a dirty city with unpaved streets and uncomfortable stone houses. They looked down upon the native aristocrats with the greatest scorn.

BRAZIL MAKES PROGRESS UNDER THE KING'S RULE

Dom [1] João, at first only regent for his mother, the queen, became king at her death in 1816. During his rule the group of isolated provinces which had made up Brazil became more united. Dom João pleased the Brazilians by raising their country to equal importance with Portugal. More important to the development of Brazil, he opened the ports to European trade. Up to this time the trade of the colony, like that of the Spanish colonies, had been restricted to the mother country, and there had been little development of commerce or industry. Now merchants from England and France flocked to open businesses in the capital. New roads and port works were constructed. Brazilian women were thrilled by Parisian styles and perfumes; for the first time European

[1] *Dom* is the Portuguese form of the title *Don*.

goods could be had in great variety and abundance.

The Portuguese government had tried to keep Brazil isolated from European influence in intellectual matters as well as in trade. As we have seen, colonial Brazil boasted no university nor even a printing press. Sons of the upper classes were sent to Portugal for education. Dom João, however, had brought sculpture, paintings, and family art treasures which he put in museums and galleries for the benefit of the people. The Royal Library of 60,000 volumes was opened to the public. A few printing presses began to print books and papers. He also founded the famous Botanical Gardens of Rio, where he planted palms which became the famous royal palms. Dom João encouraged music and the theater by importing musicians and actors from Portugal. For the first time, the women of Brazil, imitating the Portuguese ladies, appeared at the Royal Theater with beautiful clothes and with faces uncovered. It is said that the king was responsible for ending the seclusion of the colonial women.

Much was done to improve the capital city. Streets and *praças* in Rio were cleaned and some of the worst dwellings torn down. French artists and architects were invited to come to Rio to build a city worthy of the Portuguese court.

THE MOVEMENT FOR INDEPENDENCE GROWS IN BRAZIL

The king did not find all smooth sailing in his government of the colony. News of the French and North American Revolutions had trickled into Brazil and for some time there had been a growing sentiment for independence. There was little love for Portugal among the scattered provinces of Brazil. They had felt, although not so strongly, the same grievances as did the Spanish colonies toward the restrictions of the mother country.

One attempt at independence had already been made by a group of young patriots. They were led by an ardent young man known as Tiradentes, the "Tooth-Puller." The plot was discovered, and in 1792 Tiradentes was hanged before great crowds in Rio. Considered a martyr to the cause of independence, Tiradentes's name has been given to many parks and streets in Brazilian cities. Another attempt at independence might have taken place when the Spanish colonies were revolting if it had not been for the coming of the royal family. But in spite of King João's reforms the desire for independence was growing. The native Brazilians did not like the favoritism shown the Portuguese subjects of the king. These overbearing nobles were not only given gifts and titles, but also most of the important colonial offices. Furthermore, the cost of keeping the royal court in luxury had greatly increased the taxes which the colonists must pay.

While revolts threatened in Brazil, trouble was brewing across the sea in Portugal. After the French had been driven out in 1814, the king and his court might have returned to Lisbon. But Dom João liked his pleasant existence in Brazil and did not want to leave. In 1821, however, after a revolution in Portugal demanded his return, the king of two countries sailed from Rio with his family and his nobles and most of the money in the treasury. He appointed his son to rule Brazil in his place, and before he left, gave him some advice: "Pedro, if Brazil is to separate herself from Portugal, let her be for you who respect me rather than for any of these adventurers."

BRAZIL GAINS HER INDEPENDENCE AS AN EMPIRE

Dom Pedro was a handsome and headstrong prince, but he was intelligent and was loved by Brazilians for his interest in their country. When the government of Portugal ordered the crown prince also to return home and withdrew all the privileges that had been granted to Brazil, Dom Pedro was very angry. When thousands of Brazilians signed a petition begging him to remain with them, he answered, "Tell the people I remain."

When Portuguese troops tried to oppose his decision, he forced them to embark for Europe. On September 7, 1822, while he was visiting the province of São Paulo, news was brought to him that Portugal had rejected his claims for Brazil. Beside the little stream of Ypiranga (ee-pee-rahn'gah) outside São Paulo, Dom Pedro tore his Portuguese colors from his uniform and cried, "It is time! Independence or Death!" This declaration of independence is called the *Grito de Ypiranga,* or "Cry of Ypiranga." September 7 is celebrated in Brazil as the "Day of the Cry" just as September 16 marks the "Cry of Dolores" in Mexico.

The people of Rio and São Paulo went wild with delight when Pedro defied Portugal. A few months later the prince was crowned Pedro 1, Emperor of Brazil. He and his young empress rode in their coach through the narrow streets of Rio which were decked with flowers in his honor, while lovely ladies tossed bouquets to them from their balconies. Portuguese troops which were in northern Brazil were driven out by 1823, and two years later Portugal was forced to acknowledge Brazilian independence.

BRAZIL'S FATHER OF INDEPENDENCE FEARS THE PORTUGUESE

Although Brazil needed no great soldier like Bolívar or San Martín to secure independence for her, she did have a leader who is honored today as her national hero. José Bonifacio de Andrada (boh-nee-fah'shee-oh duh ahn-drah'dah) was not a politician, but a learned man educated in Europe. He had returned to his native land when he was 57 years old expecting to carry on scientific research, and had become interested in the political affairs of his country. He wisely saw that Brazil was not ready to be a republic. He had encouraged the break with Portugal, but wanted a monarch at the head of the government. As the chief adviser of Dom Pedro, he had urged him to take a definite stand for independence. Later he became a minister in the young emperor's cabinet.

Bonifacio soon incurred royal disfavor because of his opposition to the native Portuguese in the court who had a strong influence in Dom Pedro's government. When he and his two brothers became delegates to a convention called by the emperor for the purpose of drafting a constitution for Brazil, they openly worked against the power of the Portuguese aristocracy. Dom Pedro finally dissolved the convention and exiled the Andrada brothers. Then Dom Pedro himself directed the drawing-up of a liberal constitution which remained the law of the land for 65 years.

DOM PEDRO'S POPULARITY WANES AND HE DEPARTS FOR PORTUGAL

In spite of his liberal tendencies, the emperor began to lose his popularity with the people. They were suspicious of him because he was Portuguese-born, and they resented his favoritism to the native Portuguese in his court. When old King João died and Dom Pedro became Pedro IV of Portugal, as well as Emperor of Brazil, people feared that he might return to Portugal like his father. Although Dom Pedro renounced the throne of Portugal in favor of his seven-year-old daughter, suspicion continued and uprisings threatened. The war with Argentina in 1825 over Brazil's province of Uruguay ended in the loss of that territory. This added to the emperor's unpopularity. Finally, after a revolt of the people in Rio, the emperor abdicated the throne. He departed with his wife and oldest daughter for Portugal, leaving his five-year-old son Pedro to rule in his stead. He asked the scholarly Bonifacio, who had returned to Brazil, to act as tutor for his son until the boy was grown.

In spite of the conflicts during Dom Pedro's reign, Brazil was much more advanced politically than any other republic in Latin America. He had given the country a liberal constitution providing for religious freedom and making no distinctions against color or race. There was freedom of speech and press not to be found in other parts of the continent. When we remember the revolutions, the as-sassinations, the dictators, and the religious intolerance in the other countries of South America, we realize that Brazil was fortunate.

DOM PEDRO II RULES FOR FIFTY YEARS

While the blond and handsome little Pedro was being educated to assume the burdens of government, the regents who ruled for him had a difficult time holding the provinces together. Many Brazilians wanted a republic instead of the monarchy, and in both the north and the south, provinces seceded and governed themselves independently. After ten years the regents tried to restore unity by placing the young prince on the throne. When the slim, serious boy of fifteen was asked if he would head the government, he replied, "*Quero já*" ("I wish to do so at once"). In 1841 he was crowned Pedro II, Emperor of Brazil.

When he was eighteen, Princess Theresa Christina of Sicily was chosen as his bride. One of his nobles describes the eagerness with which the lonely boy went to meet the ship which brought his bride to Rio. Although her pictures had shown a beautiful princess, the girl who disembarked from the ship was not only homely, but lame! The young emperor covered up his disappointment and greeted her with a smile. She proved to be a devoted wife and a fine, warm-hearted woman who won the hearts of the Brazilian people.

Dom Pedro II was a dignified and simple man who was anxious to rule his subjects wisely and justly. He was a serious student of art and science and could read fourteen languages and speak eight. Although he believed in ruling with a strong hand, he chose the most capable men as his ministers, regardless of their politics. He had the welfare of his humble people at heart. Once a week his subjects, even the poorest slaves and Indians, could go to him with their troubles and complaints. Soon the tall emperor with his kindly face became known and trusted throughout the land. Indeed, Dom Pedro II of Brazil won the respect and admiration of the world.

During the emperor's reign the disorganized provinces were united into a nation which made steady progress through the years. Only two wars disturbed the peace — when Brazil helped Uruguay and Urquiza defeat the Argentine dictator, Rosas; and when she joined the Triple Alliance to fight the dictator, López, in Paraguay. Dom Pedro was eager for the advancement of his country and established many primary and secondary schools in provincial towns. He encouraged trade and manufacturing. He went to Europe to study schools and factories, asking hundreds of questions. When he visited the United States, he went sightseeing alone in New York every morning at six o'clock. It is said that before he left he knew more about the city than the chief of police! He visited for hours with Longfellow, Emerson, and Whittier, and when he returned home, translated many of their poems into Portuguese. He encouraged immigration, and during his reign many Germans, Italians, and Portuguese settled in southern Brazil.

Up to this time, transportation between the provinces had been by sea from one port to another; travel between the coast and the inland plateau was very difficult. In Dom

Keystone

DOM PEDRO THE MAGNANIMOUS, as he has been called, was six feet four inches tall. Although simple and democratic in his daily life, he looked every inch an emperor.

Pedro's reign, railroads were built connecting several of the seaports with the interior of the country. A famous cable railroad was built up the mountains from Santos to São Paulo to aid in the transportation of coffee to the port.

THE SLAVES ARE FREED AND DOM PEDRO II LOSES HIS THRONE

It seems strange that such a man as we have described should be forced to abdicate, but that is what happened to Dom Pedro. The trouble was caused largely by the slavery question. In 1850 perhaps one third of the population of Brazil was made up

405

of slaves. The emperor himself was deeply opposed to slavery and had freed all the slaves on his own estates. But he knew that immediate abolition of slavery would ruin the cotton and sugar planters. He planned a gradual freeing of the Negroes so that free labor could be substituted for slave labor. In 1871, a law was passed declaring that all Negro children born after that year should be free. This angered the planters, but did not satisfy the group who wanted immediate freedom for all slaves.

In 1888, while Dom Pedro was in Europe for his health, his daughter, acting as regent, signed a bill providing for immediate abolition of slavery. Many of the planters were ruined when the Negroes left their work to go to the towns or to take up land of their own. Angry landowners and businessmen blamed the emperor and joined the party which was demanding a republic for Brazil. When the ill and aged emperor returned from abroad, proud of what his people had done, he had no idea of the true state of affairs. A year later a group of conspirators, discontented republicans and army leaders, declared Brazil a republic and Pedro was informed that he must abdicate.

He and his family were hustled away on a ship before the common people could learn what had happened to their beloved rulers. There was no bloodshed. The empire died and a republic was born while people were still confused over the rapid course of events. Exiled from the land they loved, both emperor and empress died broken-hearted within two years. Thirty years later their bodies were returned to Brazil and buried with honor in a beautiful church in Petropolis.

Brazilians still regret the cruel banishment of their rulers who had given their lives to serving Brazil. When we look back on a half-century of wise and tolerant government enjoyed by the Brazilians under Pedro II, it is easy to understand why he is revered today as the greatest Brazilian.

Brazil Becomes a Republic

BRAZILIANS FIND THE PATH OF DEMOCRACY DIFFICULT

The new republic inherited the weaknesses of the colonial period and of the empire. The provinces were still isolated units with local loyalties; the illiterate people were used to the strong paternal rule of a monarch. As politicians struggled to gain control of the government, Brazil at last experienced the revolutions that had torn her neighbor republics. The two most powerful political groups proved to be in the progressive provinces of São Paulo and Minas Gerais. From 1889 until 1930, most of the presidents of Brazil were either *paulistas* or *mineiros*.

A new constitution in 1891 united the former provinces into a union of twenty states called the United States of Brazil with a president and a national congress. The organization of the government was much like that of the United States, with certain powers delegated to the federal government and others to the states. But few people were represented in the government since only those who could read and write were allowed to vote.

The honor of being founder of the republic went to General Deodoro da Fonseca (day-oh-doh'roh dah fohn-say'cah), because as head of the army he proclaimed Brazil a republic and because he was elected the first president. Like many military men with thousands of soldiers behind him, the general became a high-handed dictator with little regard for the constitution. When he was forced to resign, the vice-president, another military man, continued the same type of arbitrary government. Revolts became the order of the day. He did not choose to become a permanent dictator, and in the next election a civilian was chosen president. From that time on until 1930, the republican governments were for the most part orderly and constitutional.

GETULIO VARGAS SEIZES THE GOVERNMENT OF BRAZIL

By 1930, people were beginning to resent greatly the domination of the government by the powerful states of São Paulo and Minas Gerais. There was a serious crisis in the coffee in-dustry on which Brazil had chiefly depended for its wealth, and politicians bitterly blamed the government. In the same year, Getulio Vargas (gay-tool'yo vahr'gahs), Liberal candidate for president, was defeated by a *paulista*. He claimed the election was fraudulent and started a revolt in his cowboy state of Rio Grande do Sul. The revolt spread to other states, the president was deposed, and Getulio Vargas was made temporary president of the republic. In 1934, under a new constitution, he was elected president for four years more, but remained in power until 1945. When it came time for another election, Vargas acted quickly, cleverly, and unconstitutionally. In November, 1937, he put the country under martial law, called off the elections, dissolved the congress, and set up a dictatorship before people realized what was happening.

THE IRON HAND OF VARGAS IS COVERED BY A VELVET GLOVE

President Vargas immediately proclaimed another constitution, but it was not put in force. Under Vargas's *Estado Novo* (New State), therefore, Brazil had no congress and the president had supreme authority. The

GETULIO VARGAS, the President of Brazil, is shown here in three candid camera shots. Does Vargas look like a typical dictator to you? At the right he is drinking the customary small cup of coffee served in Brazil.

Black Star

states no longer elected their own governors, but were governed by men called *interventors* who were appointed by the president.

Although Vargas was a dictator who suppressed all opposition, he did a great deal toward uniting Brazil and inspiring national patriotism. On the other hand, he deprived the people of the freedom of speech and press which they had enjoyed for more than a century. Brazilians finally became so discontented with the lack of free elections and other rights that they forced Vargas to resign in 1945. When elections were held a short time later, however, Vargas's friend, General Enrico Dutra (doo'trah), was chosen

president, and Vargas himself was made senator from his home district. The Brazilians tried to protect themselves from another military dictatorship by making a new constitution in 1946. In the fall of 1950 Vargas again headed the government. He was chosen president in a free election, to succeed Dutra.

Brazil has followed a policy of friendliness and co-operation toward the United States. In both World Wars she was quick to join the Allies against Germany. Today Brazil is an active member of the United Nations. She also served as one of the first eleven nations on the Security Council.

Are You a Careful Reader?   Test Yourself!

I. Can you supply the correct word for each blank?

1. . . . . claimed Brazil for . . . . .
2. Brazil was divided for colonial government into . . . . strips of land called . . . . .
3. The Portuguese imported many . . . . to work on the . . . . plantations.
4. Today the majority of Brazilians have . . . . blood.
5. Much of the progress of Brazil in the 1800's was due to . . . .

II. Which statements are true and which are false?

1. The difficulties of communication between the various settlements of Brazil caused strong local patriotisms which have prevented Brazil from becoming a united nation.

2. The great cotton plantations of northern Brazil were producing most of Europe's cotton by 1600.

3. The mameluke of Brazil would be called a *mestizo* in Colombia.

4. The first capital of Brazil was Rio de Janeiro.

5. The *bandeirantes* were mamelukes from the state of São Paulo who explored far into the interior of Brazil.

6. When gold was discovered in Brazil, men from many nations rushed in and began to mine gold.

7. Colonial Brazil was much further advanced in architecture, education, and art than were the Spanish colonies.

8. Brazil gained her independence at about the same time as the Spanish colonies.

9. Bonifacio objected to the influence of the native Portuguese in the government of Dom Pedro I.

10. Dom Pedro II signed a bill calling for the immediate abolition of slavery.

11. A republic was declared in Brazil while the aged Dom Pedro was still emperor.

12. The people of Brazil enjoyed freedom of speech and press under their emperors which they did not have when Vargas came into power.

Food for Thought and Discussion

1. Do you believe that a dictatorship is better for Brazil at present than a democratic government would be? Why?

2. Why does a dictator seldom allow freedom of speech and of the press?

3. Compare the government of Brazil in the 1800's with the government of Mexico. Do you think Bonifacio was right in believing that Brazil was better off as an empire under a wise monarch than as a republic under a selfish dictator? Why?

Chapter 36

Brazil Develops Her Rich and Enormous Resources

Gold, tobacco, and diamonds;
Manganese, mahogany, and monkey fur;
Orchids and butterflies;
Rosewood, emeralds, and chrysoberyls;
Babassu and sesamum oils;
Black diamonds and asbestos;
Arrowroot and ipecac;
Wax from the palms of Ceara.

THESE romantic-sounding items are not from a tale of the *Arabian Nights*; they are a list of some of the exports of Brazil. In addition to these items, Brazil exports great quantities of more commonplace goods. Just imagine 17,000,000 sacks of coffee; 400,000 tons of cotton; 260,000,000 pounds of cacao; 10,000,000 stems of bananas; 150,000,000 coconuts; and 30,000 tons of Brazil nuts! This is only a partial list of the exports of this vast country.

The three "C's," coffee, cotton, and cacao, lead in value.

BRAZIL IS AN AGRICULTURAL COUNTRY

In addition to exporting enormous quantities of food, Brazil feeds her own 50,000,000 people. Three fourths of all Brazilians live on the manioc and beans and potatoes which they raise in their own gardens. They do not depend for their living on the export of cash crops. The people who profit from the coffee, cotton, and cacao of Brazil are the planters and the shippers and the businessmen who are a small but important part of the population of Brazil. These are the men who have developed the agricultural resources of Brazil.

Throughout her history, Brazil has

concentrated on first one major crop and then another. Sugar, as you know, was the important crop in colonial days. More recently, coffee has been the chief product of Brazil. Today, cotton is becoming an important crop. Since it is unwise for a nation to put all her eggs in one basket, Brazil is working today toward the development of several crops instead of depending upon one.

SUGAR IS A STAPLE CROP IN BRAZIL

The discovery of gold by the *paulistas* in the 1700's ended the colonial reign of King Sugar. Planters abandoned their plantations and hurried south with their slaves to the gold fields of Minas Gerais. Brazilian sugar production declined, and the sugar islands of the West Indies came to be the chief suppliers of Europe. Once the world's chief exporter of sugar, Brazil was no longer able to sell at a profit.

Today sugar production is again increasing and Brazil is fifth of the world's sugar-producing countries. All of the sugar is used at home, to sweeten the millions of little cups of coffee sold on the sidewalks of Rio and other cities and to sweeten the desserts of which Brazilians are so fond. Millions of acres could be planted in Brazil, but the industry is not profitable unless efficiently run like the coffee industry. Although sugar is grown in most parts of Brazil, Pernambuco is the chief sugar-growing state.

COFFEE BECOMES KING IN PLACE OF SUGAR

According to one story, in 1727 a young man from Pará went to French Guiana to settle a boundary dispute between that colony and the neighboring Dutch Guiana. While there, he was served a beverage called coffee which he found very delicious. Although to carry even a tiny coffee berry out of the colony was punishable by death, the young man managed to smuggle out some seeds and plants which he planted in Pará. Three years later, the first Brazilian coffee reached Portugal, and the coffee trade of Brazil had begun.

Coffee had been known for many centuries in the Near East. It is said to have been discovered in the 800's by monks in Abyssinia. They noticed that goats and camels who had eaten the branches of a certain tree ran about all night instead of sleeping. A drink made from the berries of the plant proved useful in keeping monks awake when they must say prayers at night. In time coffee reached Europe, and became popular in England and France. Enterprising Dutch merchants planted the berries in Dutch Guiana whence they were smuggled into French Guiana, where our story began.

The most important coffee plantations have developed in São Paulo where the red soil and the mild climate of the plateau are especially suited to coffee culture. By 1860, Brazil was becoming the world's chief producer. The freeing of the slaves ruined many plantations, but São Paulo advertised for farmer immigrants to take the place of the Negroes on the coffee *fazendas*. Italians came over in great numbers. By the early 1900's, São Paulo had become the greatest coffee region in the world, growing three fourths of the world's coffee. In 1930, the biggest year, 28,000,000 sacks were produced. That is about

Galloway

COFFEE IS BEING LOADED into this ship at the coffee port of Santos. Twenty or more 132-pound sacks are ready to be lowered through the open hatch. In normal times more than 3000 ships are loaded every year.

3,700,000,000 pounds or 26 pounds apiece for every man, woman, and child in the United States! Coffee-growers, like the earlier sugar barons, became the wealthiest and most powerful group in Brazil.

DESPITE DIFFICULTIES, COFFEE IS STILL KING IN BRAZIL

While *fazenda* owners continued to plant more coffee, Venezuela, Colombia, and the Caribbean countries were also selling their fine coffees on the market. The *paulistas* were then inspired to raise the price of coffee by controlling the output; but by 1929, they found themselves with more coffee than they could ever hope to sell, and prices began sliding downhill. To keep down the surplus, the government destroyed millions of tons of coffee. Some of this oversupply was tossed into the harbor at Santos, but it poisoned the fish, so it was then destroyed by fire. Great mountains of the inferior grades of coffee were kept burning day and night for years — over 80,000,000 sacks in all!

The end of the coffee story is not yet known. The world's production continued high and the price continued to go down. Then came the second World War which destroyed some of Brazil's best European mar-

kets. To meet the problem of over-
production of coffee, the Brazilian
government now tries to control the
amount of coffee grown. This helps
to maintain prices. Much of the loss
of European trade has been made up
by the enormous increase in trade
with the United States since 1945.
We buy over half of all Brazil's exports, and two thirds of all her coffee.
The little brown bean makes up about
57 per cent of all Brazil's exports.
Brazil ranks first in coffee production.

THE COFFEE FAZENDA IS A COMMUNITY IN ITSELF

Two thirds of the world's coffee is
grown on territory equal to one fourth
of the state of Indiana. The chief
coffee belt of Brazil is located in northern São Paulo and southern Minas
Gerais. This region has all the requirements for successful coffee-growing: rich, red soil; a hot and wet growing season; and a cool, rainless harvesting season. From planting to
shipping, coffee production, like the
banana industry in the Caribbean,
has become a great, efficiently run
business.

When young coffee plants are set
out, they require 5 or 6 years of care
and weeding before they bear. The
trees then yield for 30 to 40 years
without replanting. Coffee trees
grow from 18 to 20 feet high, and produce a small white bloom that looks
something like a spray of orange blossoms. When the berries appear, they
resemble cranberries. Inside the yellow pulp of each berry are two green
seeds. Picking begins about the first
of May. Hand-pickers strip the berries from the trees and let them fall
on cloths spread upon the ground.
Then they are gathered into baskets
and hauled by mules or on trucks to
washing tanks. From the tanks the
berries are carried by running water
to a mill where the red skin and yellow
pulp are removed. The green seeds
are spread out on tile or cement floors
to dry for two or three weeks in the
sun. They are next piled up and allowed to cure for another week. Rain
would spoil the crop, for acres of drying yards are found on the large
fazendas. Finally the coffee is taken
to a mill where it is cleaned, graded,
and sacked. It is then ready to ship
to Santos.

There is a large fazenda in northern
São Paulo that covers 30,000 acres
and employs 5000 people. Its 5,000,-
000 trees produce 7,000,000 to 10,000-
000 pounds of coffee every year! A
private railroad connects the fazenda
with the main Santos line. Enough
corn, meat, and beans are produced on
the fazenda to provide food for all the
workers. The corn is ground in the
fazenda mill; the cattle are killed by
the fazenda butcher. A general store
sells supplies to the workers which
they buy on credit until the harvest
is over. A school, a church, and a
hospital are provided for the workers.

The coffee colono (coh-loh'noh) or
colonist who works on the fazenda is
something like the sharecropper in
parts of the United States. He lives
with his family in a two- or three-
room house and works from sunup
to sundown. The colono agrees to
care for as many trees as he and his
family can handle. One man can look
after 2000 or 3000 trees. If he has
several children he may contract for
as many as 8000 trees. As soon as a
child is old enough to pull weeds, he is
set to work even though he is of school
age. The yearly wage of the colono

is about $17 for every 1000 trees. When he settles with the overseer, he often finds that he has no money coming at all because of the bill at the *fazenda* store. The colonist is usually ignorant and a dishonest overseer can take advantage of him.

COTTON RANKS SECOND AMONG THE EXPORTS OF BRAZIL

Within recent years the government has urged the planting of cotton instead of coffee. Many planters have pulled up their coffee trees and planted their red acres to cotton. When the United States reduced cotton production to raise the price on the world market, Brazilians planted cotton to take advantage of the higher prices! In the cotton zone of São Paulo, the fertile soil yields twice as much ordinary cotton to the acre as the land in our own South. In the northern cotton region of Brazil there is a cotton tree which grows five to fifteen years without replanting.

Cotton has been grown in Brazil since colonial times. Brazil was the first country in the New World to send unspun cotton as cargo to Europe. But cotton never became important because sugar pushed all other crops into the background. With the invention of the cotton gin in 1793, the United States was able to produce far more cotton than Brazil. During our War Between the States there was a cotton boom in Brazil. The southern states had been unable to export their usual amount of cotton and prices soared on the world market. So Brazilians planted more cotton to take advantage of the demand. After the war, planters returned to coffee and sugar which paid best in the long run. Today cotton is again important.

Gendreau

BLOSSOMS AND BERRIES often appear at the same time on the branches of the coffee tree. The flowers are fragrant white clusters; the berries are shiny red when ripe.

CACAO IS BRAZIL'S THIRD CROP

Ecuador, you remember, used to lead the world in cacao production until she lost her markets to the Gold Coast of Africa. Today she is only seventh in rank, but Brazil is second to Africa in the production of the little brown beans. Brazilian cacao is grown chiefly in the state of Baía. This crop makes much less profit per acre than coffee or sugar, so there are few large plantations. It is generally grown on small farms run by natives who are satisfied with the living it brings. Since the easy-going people of Baía give little care to the trees, Brazilian cacao has not the fine quality of the cacao found in Venezuela and Colombia.

THE RUBBER BUBBLE EXPANDS IN BRAZIL

The story of rubber in Brazil is the

413

story of men rushing to the Amazon, of dreams of quick riches, of cities built in the jungle, of the bursting rubber bubble, and collapse.

Rubber was known in America long before the Spaniards came. You remember the rubber balls used by the Aztecs in their games. It was also known in Europe in the 1700's, but there was no great demand for it until Charles Goodyear discovered that rubber could be made to withstand extremes of heat and cold by heating. When the vulcanizing process was perfected, the demand for rubber began to grow.

The first shipload of rubber to Europe was a cargo of overshoes made by the Indians at Pará. In the 1880's came the use of rubber for bicycle tires, for everyone who could afford to was riding that "new-fangled contraption," the bicycle. English and American companies went up the Amazon 900 miles from Pará to the old town of Manaus. In the jungles up the river from Manaus millions of rubber trees grew wild. Jungle Indians were forced to work practically as slaves, tapping the trees, collecting the sap, and smoking the rubber. Manaus became the collecting center for Brazil's rubber, because the navigable rivers made it possible for the rubber-gatherers to ship the rubber by boat to Manaus. Thus labor and transportation were cheap.

The population of Manaus increased rapidly. By 1912, the rubber exported from Brazil was worth almost as much as the coffee. Rubber contractors were making fortunes. As you know, a $10,000,000 opera house was built in Manaus, streets were paved, hotels and government buildings constructed. Money became so plentiful

that it lost its value. The story goes that the rich men of Manaus lighted their cigarettes with folded bills equal to $20 in our money! One man is said to have displayed his wealth by running champagne instead of water through his fountain. It looked as though the boom times would go on forever, and the rubber bubble swelled larger and larger.

THE RUBBER BUBBLE BURSTS

Meanwhile, in another part of the world trouble was brewing for Brazil. A botanist sent from England had collected seeds of the rubber trees. Although it was forbidden, he took them to London where they were planted in hothouses and nursed along until they sprouted. Cuttings from these tiny trees were taken to the British colonies in the Malay States in the East Indies. There they were set out into plantations with thousands of natives to tend them. When the automobile increased the demand for rubber, the eastern product began to steal Brazilian markets because it was cheaper and the supply could be depended on. After the first World War, Brazilian rubber dropped from about $1 to 20 cents a pound. The bubble had burst.

Rubber companies went out of business; rubber-gatherers left for the coast; Indians returned to their jungle villages. Weeds grew in the streets of Manaus and Pará, and the opera house closed. Manaus and Pará became ghost cities. By 1930, 95 per cent of the world's rubber was coming from the East Indies, and only 1½ per cent from Brazil.

RUBBER IS NOT DIFFICULT TO PRODUCE

The best tree for producing rubber

YOUNG RUBBER TREES beginning to bear on one of Ford's plantations
on the Amazon. This tree is ready to give sap. Except on plantations,
labor is hard to get because workers dislike living in the jungle.

is the *hevea braziliensis*. It grows as high as 100 feet and has a diameter of 3 to 4 feet. The wild trees are scattered through the forest so that a worker has to walk long distances from tree to tree. On a plantation, of course, the trees stand in rows, but the process of collecting the sap is the same. Spiral gashes are cut through the bark and a cup is clamped at the base of the cut to catch the white milk which drains out. One cutting will give about four gallons of sap. If the trees are bled for only part of the year, they will produce rubber for half a century.

Wild rubber is made solid by smoking it on paddles over a fire. The collector of wild rubber dips a wooden paddle in the sap and holds it over a fire to thicken it. By continuous dipping and heating, a large, round ball of rubber forms on the paddle. This is sold, paddle and all, to the rubber contractors. On the plantations in the Orient, the sap is turned into large vats where it is made solid by treating with formic acid. The moist, sticky sheets are smoked until dry and spongy, then wrapped in bales for export.

BRAZILIAN RUBBER AGAIN BECOMES IMPORTANT

Henry Ford established an experimental rubber plantation in Brazil, which he called Belterra. In 1949, when the five million rubber trees began to produce, the plantation was sold to the Brazilian government. It is free from malaria, and the workers have clean houses, running water, and good schools.

When the Second World War stopped imports of eastern rubber, the United States contracted for all of Brazil's supply of wild rubber. This was only a drop in the bucket compared to our war needs. We were forced to expand our synthetic rubber industry enormously. When the war ended, we began again to import rubber from the Malay States and continued to manufacture synthetic rubber as well. Each kind has its special use. It would seem wise to continue the development of natural rubber in this hemisphere. If plantations can be established by the Brazilian government or outside companies, and sufficient cheap labor secured, enough rubber might ultimately be produced to supply the Western Hemisphere. At any rate, whether we use natural rubber or synthetic rubber, or both, the countries of this hemisphere need not depend upon markets across the Pacific for their rubber supplies.

BRAZIL IS RICH IN MINERALS

Much of Brazil's vast wealth lies under her soil. You have read about the gold mines in Minas Gerais which caused a mad rush in the 1700's. The mines are not yet exhausted and are still producing about $6,000,000 worth of gold a year. The diamonds which were discovered soon after gold was found have also had their heyday. There are many stories of the diamond mines in the early days, stories of murder and stolen diamonds and intrigue. The largest diamond ever found in

Brazil was discovered by an old Negro woman who was washing clothes in a river. She gave it to her master to buy her freedom. The "Southern Star" was later sold to an Indian raja for half a million dollars. In 1938, a diamond was found which was named after President Vargas. It was cut up into 23 different jewels worth altogether $2,000,000!

Today the diamond output is small compared to that of South Africa. Most important are the hard, black diamonds which are used in cutting instruments in machine tool factories.

Brazil has metals badly needed in time of war. She has mountains of high-grade iron ore which have scarcely been touched. The region is estimated to contain billions of tons of ore, amounts beyond our power to imagine. Plans are being made to develop the mines and provide Brazil with a steel industry of its own. Brazil also has large supplies of manganese which is necessary in making steel, as well as other minerals which are needed in the United States.

TRANSPORTATION IS IMPROVING IN BRAZIL

Nature has given Brazil her best transportation system — the Amazon River and its tributaries. As we know, steamers can travel from the mouth of the Amazon for 2500 miles to Iquitos in Peru. There are 10,000 miles of waterways for large steamers, and 20,000 to 30,000 miles open to smaller boats. If it were not for her rivers, the interior of Brazil would be almost unknown and her tropical products could not reach a port.

Railroads extend inland from the seaports of Brazil and there are roads connecting the coffee districts in São Paulo, but there is no connection be-

Weimer

MODERN MACHINERY is used on this rice plantation in southern Brazil. At present there is a large demand for machinery of all kinds from the United States.

tween the cities of the northeast except by boat. You have read of the famous São Paulo railroad which hauls the country's coffee to the seaport. São Paulo is also connected with Rio and Montevideo by railroad, but there is no continuous railroad system in Brazil.

MANUFACTURING IS INCREASING IN BRAZIL

Although Brazil is largely an agricultural nation, she is turning more and more attention to manufacturing. As in Chile and Argentina, when the first World War cut Brazil off from foreign manufactured products, she began to make her own. Like Argentina also, she manufactures her cotton into cloth and her leather into shoes. Foods such as coffee and sugar are prepared for home consumption. The city of São Paulo has become the chief manufacturing center in all South America, while Rio is second in importance in Brazil.

Brazil, like Argentina, has little coal, and what she has is of inferior quality. But Brazil has many rivers which drop from the plateau to the coast and furnish enormous water-power for generating electricity. Hydroelectric power runs not only the factories and street-cars of São Paulo and Rio, but also supplies the lights in these cities. In the state of São Paulo, the cities, towns, and even the *fazendas* have electric lights. Thus Brazil has an advantage over Argentina and Chile in the matter of manufacturing. Not only has she cheap power to run her factories, but the power is easily available from near-by rivers.

Are You a Careful Reader?   Test Yourself!

I. Can you supply the correct word for each blank?

1. Three quarters of all Brazilians do not depend upon the country's .... for their living, but upon products of their .... .

2. Brazil's chief exports are the three C's, ... , ... , and .... .

3. Coffee plants were first smuggled into Brazil from ....

4. .... of the world's coffee is grown in the São Paulo region on large plantations called .... . Coffee workers are called .... .

5. Brazil was the greatest .... producing country in the world in the early 1900's.

II. Which statements are true and which are false?

1. Since World War II the Brazilian government has attempted to control the amount of coffee produced in that country.

2. The United States buys about one third of Brazil's coffee export.

3. The coffee *colono* and his family work long hours at a small wage.

4. Brazil could easily outdistance our southern states in cotton production because her rich soil yields more cotton per acre and because she has a variety of cotton which produces for several years without replanting.

5. Brazilian cacao is grown on large plantations in southern Brazil.

6. Brazil lost her rubber market because the Malay States had a tree which produced much finer rubber than the Brazilian rubber tree.

7. Brazil is supplying the United States with metals needed for war industries.

8. Brazil has a railroad system which connects all of her chief cities.

9. Like Argentina, Brazil is increasing her home manufactured products, but does not have enough coal of her own to run many factories.

10. Brazil cannot operate her factories by electricity because the rivers which can furnish waterpower are too far inland to be of any use.

Food for Thought and Discussion

1. Can laws of a country keep any commercially valuable plant within the borders of that country? Give two examples to prove your answer.

2. If you were president of Brazil, would you develop manufacturing to the point where Brazil would not need to import any manufactured articles? Why? Give a good reason for your answer.

3. Would you plant large rubber plantations in the Amazon region? Why?

Chapter 37

Brazilian Customs and Culture Are Unique in Latin America

IN 1938, Señorita Gabriela Mistral of Chile, well known as a writer and leader among Chilean women, visited schools in many countries of Latin America. When she went to Brazil, she was as much a stranger as you or I would be. She was a visitor from a temperate country where Spanish language and Spanish blood prevail. The Portuguese language was new to her. She visited a primary school in Rio de Janeiro, where the majority of children had Indian or Negro blood or both in their veins. Her letter of farewell describes so well the Brazilian people that it was printed by the Pan American Union.[1] This is part of her letter:

I am grateful to you for the day I spent in the Antonio Delfino School ... we exchanged stories of your childhood and mine, tossing them from hand to hand like playthings, as we chatted together like members of one family.... Children of Brazil, heirs of the Portuguese who doubled our geographical knowledge, you were the first (from the Western Hemisphere) to venture to offer to the world your own music, at once abrupt and slow, harsh and gentle,

[1] From *El Mercurio*, Santiago, Chile, June 5, 1938. Quoted in *Bulletin of Pan American Union*, October, 1938.

like your forests, your wilderness, and your parks. Moreover, children of Brazil, you have unwittingly created something which is no longer respected in other parts of the world. You have created a Christian melting-pot of races at the very moment Christianity is being hacked to pieces or disfigured in other parts of the world.

WHAT IS A BRAZILIAN?

The children visited by the lady from Chile were probably of all shades of skin, from black and brown to white, yet she found no feeling of race prejudice among them. These children are typical of all Brazil. We know that for centuries the whites, reds, and blacks have been mixed in Brazil's great melting-pot to produce the Brazilian people. Today, as in colonial days, the majority of them are *mestiços* or men of color. Very few pure-blooded Indians remain and most of them live in the interior. About 14 per cent of the people are Negroes, who live for the most part in the northern states. Probably a third of all Brazilians are white, but many of these have a Negro strain. While in the United States no one is considered white who has Negro blood, this is not true in Brazil. As in all Latin American countries, there is in Brazil a small group of families proud of their unmixed white blood, but these are too few to be important.

Far from being concerned about their mixed race, Brazilians believe that the Portuguese race has benefited by the blood of the Negro and the Indian. There is no color prejudice in politics or society. One president of Brazil spoke with pride of his Negro blood. No one is barred from business or political office because of his race. Residence districts, cafés, street-cars, and theaters are open to people of all colors. On the beaches white children and black play together without a thought for the color of their skins. Brazil is indeed, as Señorita Mistral wrote, "a Christian melting-pot of races."

Although Brazilians differ in different localities just as North Americans do, there are certain national characteristics which differentiate them from their Spanish-American neighbors. They have not the pride of the Argentines nor the energy of the Chileans nor the class consciousness of the Peruvians. They are a charming, easy-going people with a love of music which may be a gift of the Negro race. It is said that they dislike cruelty in any form and would rather see a football game than a bullfight. Brazil does not use the death sentence. As in other Latin American nations, dangerous political enemies of the government are generally sent abroad to "promenade," as Brazilians call it, while lesser ones are merely put in jail for a short time.

IMMIGRANTS HAVE POURED INTO BRAZIL'S MELTING-POT

Since 1820, over 4,000,000 Europeans have migrated to new homes in Brazil, the land of opportunity. By far the most numerous have been the Portuguese and Italians. As you know, when the Negroes were freed, they left the coffee plantations by the thousands. Most of them went north to the tropical regions where they could make a living with little effort. Italian peasants came to take their places, and today, as you know, Italian is heard as often as Portuguese on the streets of São Paulo. A few have made fortunes, many others own their own coffee plantations, most of them are workers on *fazendas* or in factories.

New immigration laws encourage immigrants to become Brazilians. Eighty per cent of the immigrants in any year must be "farmers or technicians in rural industries." All immigrants must settle in towns or districts in which 30 per cent of the people are Portuguese-speaking Brazilians. All teachers must be Brazilian by birth and no foreign-language lessons can be taught to children under fourteen, except in the approved foreign-language classes of the secondary schools. Thus President Vargas hopes to create a unified Brazilian nation with its loyalty in this hemisphere.

WEALTHY BRAZILIANS LEAD A PLEASANT LIFE

The well-to-do people of Brazil are an intellectual and cultured people. They read widely in several languages and are interested in the arts. Their wealth comes from cotton and coffee and textile mills. They live in palatial homes in Baía, Rio, or São Paulo, or in skyscraper apartment houses along Copacabana Beach. Before the war they spent their winters in the fashionable resorts of southern France. Their sons were educated in European universities, their daughters in select

Galloway

SIDEWALK CAFÉS, seldom seen in the United States, are common in Rio. *Cariocas* can sit outside drinking their coffee and watching the passers-by.

seminaries. They amuse themselves as sophisticated people do everywhere, at the Jockey Club races and the smart casinos, at the theater and the movies. But the rich are only two or three per cent of the people of Brazil.

THE LABORERS OF BRAZIL ARE POOR

The middle class of Brazil has a hard time making ends meet. Clerks, bookkeepers, and teachers get salaries too small to live comfortably. A teacher in Rio makes about $87.50 a month, a department store clerk about $50 a month. Although food is cheap in Brazil, such salaries are not enough to provide a decent livelihood.

The workers of Brazil in both city and country live very poorly. On the hills behind Rio are the city's slums, poor huts of tin and scraps of wood where the laborers make their homes. In São Paulo there are back streets full of miserable tenements where factory workers live with their families in hopeless poverty. Even on the coffee and cotton *fazenda* the worker has a tiny hut without water or plumbing and barely makes a living for all his hard work. Few of the workers get enough to eat, and what food they have is poorly balanced. Black beans, rice, manioc, bananas, and sometimes jerked beef make up the Brazilians' diet. They do not get the milk, fruit, or vegetables which we know are important to health. They are afflicted

421

Weimer

THESE HOMES OF FACTORY WORKERS in Petropolis are a great contrast to the wretched slums of São Paulo and Rio. President Vargas plans to establish more factories outside of large cities where workers can get fresh air and sunshine.

with tuberculosis, rickets, typhoid, and hookworm. Many children die at birth or in early childhood from poor food and lack of medical care.

The Brazilian worker has been called lazy, but his lack of energy probably comes from years of too little food and too much illness. He needs medical care and proper food and sanitary houses. Money which has been spent to beautify Rio's waterfront or to build magnificent government buildings elsewhere might better have been spent in improving the condition of Brazil's workers. The present government realizes the needs of the common people. President Vargas has passed laws providing for a minimum wage for workers, old-age pensions, and the eight-hour day, but

these laws are difficult to enforce. At best, they apply only to industrial workers, and do not affect the countless agricultural laborers who live in poverty and debt.

BRAZIL NEEDS MORE AND BETTER SCHOOLS

Probably 55 per cent of Brazilians cannot read or write. Although Vargas has increased the number of primary schools, there are still not enough for over half Brazil's children. In São Paulo and Rio de Janeiro, most of the grown people and all of the children can read and write, because those progressive modern cities have always had good schools. On the *fazendas*, and in rural communities, schools have been provided by law. But children are not forced to attend, and boys and girls old enough to work in the coffee or cotton fields have been kept out of school by their parents.

Teachers are not only poorly paid, but often poorly trained; the subjects taught in the schools are not very valuable to the barefooted, happy-go-lucky Brazilians. It does not help them to learn the names of the kings of Portugal when they do not know the importance of milk and fresh vegetables or sanitary living. Brazil needs schools like those of Mexico where pupils learn healthful living along with their a b c's.

Secondary schools in Brazil are modeled after the Colegio Pedro II, a high school founded by the last emperor. These high schools are also college preparatory schools, but are all too few in number. Most of the secondary schools are private. There are professional schools of law, medicine, and engineering in the more important cities. Only recently have they been brought together and organized as universities. Brazil has sent students of forestry, chemistry, electricity, medicine, and plant culture to state universities in the United States, so that they can come back and help solve the problems of Brazil.

BRAZILIAN WOMEN HAVE MORE FREEDOM

Brazilian women are more privileged than some in Latin America. Their constitution states that both men and women may vote at the age of eighteen. Girls, especially in Rio and São Paulo, enjoy considerable social freedom. They play on the beach, go out to golf or tennis clubs, and attend theaters at night without chaperons, a proceeding frowned on in Bogotá or Caracas, La Paz or Quito. Many women in Rio hold positions in the government or in business which is most unusual in Latin America. Spanish American girls would miss the Sunday evening promenade around the plaza, but they would find a daily promenade on the boulevards of Rio, Baía, or Santos between three and five o'clock in the afternoon. The young ladies walk up and down the black-and-white mosaic sidewalks and stop for little cups of thick sweet coffee. They can also buy ice cream or American magazines. Both young men and young women are becoming more and more interested in football and modern sports.

VISITORS ENJOY BRAZILIAN FOOD

The first thing a visitor to Brazil notices is that Brazilians like to drink their own coffee. They stop many times a day and drink a *cafezinho* (cah-fay-seen'yoh) or small cup of very sweet coffee. As in all South American countries, breakfast is served to hotel guests in their rooms and consists of fruit, delicious crisp rolls, and *café au lait* or coffee and hot milk. The staple soup of Brazil, called *canja* (cahn'zhah), is a delicious combination of chicken and rice. Many little special restaurants feature the favorite food of that particular region. In Rio the special dish is *feijoada* (fay zhoh-ah'dah). It is made of black beans fried with spices and chunks of bacon or pork, and covered with rich gravy. Served with rice, it makes a complete meal. In the north the favorites are *pitú* (pee-too') and *vatapá* (vah-tah-pah'). *Pitú* is a shrimp dish with a tangy sauce; *vatapá* is a fish dish made of many kinds of fish and shellfish and served with a sharp custard-colored sauce.

Brazilians' meals contain few vege-

Guillumette

AT CARNIVAL TIME in Rio *cariocas* dance everywhere, even in the streets. Notice the man in the background celebrating carnival in a woman's costume.

tables, but many meat dishes. One standby served at both lunch and dinner is *farinha* (fah-reen'yah) or ground manioc root. It is sprinkled on beans, meat, or in soup, and visitors find it not unlike sawdust. A favorite dessert is guava jelly and cheese, but there are also ice cream, *pudim* (pudding), and fruits of all kinds.

COINS AND CUSTOMS DIFFER IN BRAZIL

When the traveler from our country used to find that his hotel room cost 100,000 *reis* (race) a day and a newspaper cost 200 *reis*, he used to wonder how long his money would last. However, he soon discovered that his room is about $5 in our money and the newspaper only one cent, for the *rei* was about one two-hundredth of a cent! The unit of exchange used to be the *milreis* (meel'race) or a 1000 *reis*, only five cents in our money.

Very recently, however, Brazil has given new names to its coins. The *milreis* is now called the *cruzeiro* (kroo-zay'ee-roh), and is divided into 100 cents or *centavos* (sayn-tah'vosh), like the money used in the Spanish republics. There is also a larger unit called a *conto* or 1000 *cruzeiros*, worth about $50.

Among the many Brazilian customs which are new to North Americans, there is one which may catch an unsuspecting visitor unawares. That is the rule that men on the street or in public conveyances must wear a coat and tie. One traveler tells a story of how he got on a bus in Rio nattily attired in a sport shirt and slacks. Imagine his embarrassment when the conductor pointed to his shirt and stopped the bus for him to get off! In Brazil, as in other Latin American countries, a coat and tie are a badge of respectability.

ALL RIO CELEBRATES CARNIVAL

The great celebration of the year for Brazilians is carnival, which takes place during the three days before Ash Wednesday. Everyone, young or old, rich or poor, forgets his troubles and throws himself into the gaiety and fun. In Rio the carnival reaches its maddest and gayest form. Months before the celebration, mulatto tunemakers from the hill shanties of Rio begin to make up tunes for carnival. Out of the hundreds of tunes there are three or four which become the "hits" of the season. Long before carnival you hear the favorites hummed on the street, sung over the radio and in night clubs.

When carnival comes, the streets are a mass of dancing, singing people all in costume. There are Pierrots and Pierrettes, soldiers, sailors, Hawaiians, fantastic animals, princesses, buccaneers, Indians — all dancing to the rhythm of drums and tambourines. Crowds dance happily in and out of strange houses where orchestras are playing. Everyone carries a small squirtgun of perfume and ether, gaily squirting bald heads and bare necks. Tons of confetti and serpentine are thrown. For four days no one does any work. The entire population of the city is on the streets, yet there are few arrests and no rowdies! The day after carnival is a holiday until noon, while everyone from the president to the street-sweeper gets some sleep for the first time in four days.

MOVIES AND MAGAZINES CAUSE INTEREST IN THE UNITED STATES

Brazilians are interested in the United States. They feel that they know us because they read our magazines and see our movies. Brazilians from rich to poor, like all other Latin Americans, are movie fans. Well-to-do people go several times a week and know the stars as well as we do. *Gone With the Wind* and other historical pictures have made our history and the sections of our country very real to them. In fact, *Gone With the Wind* made such a deep impression that one of the favorite songs of the carnival was given that name. *Popeye* and *Donald Duck* are as great favorites in Brazil as in the United States. The pictures have Portuguese captions, but many young people have learned English and get the conversation first

hand. When we think of some of the exaggerated and lurid movies our Brazilian neighbors must have seen, we can only hope they do not form all their ideas of us from them!

Educated Brazilians read our books and magazines. They like *Life* and *Vogue* and the *Ladies' Home Journal.* It is said that the women are fascinated by North American kitchens as well as by the freedom of North American women.

Moving pictures and magazines have bridged the gap between Portuguese Brazil and the United States. Brazilians like us, not because we buy their goods, but because they believe they know our country and our people. This is the kind of friendship worth having because it comes from the heart, not the pocketbook.

THIS FATHER AND BABY are both dressed in carnival costume. The poorer classes look forward all year to this gala season, and save their money for the gay celebration.

Guillumette

Are You a Careful Reader?   Test Yourself!

I. Can you supply the correct word for each blank?

1. The largest number of immigrants in Brazil are .... and .... who settled largely in the state of ....

2. Many of Brazil's children die from poor .... and lack of a .... when they are sick.

3. .... workers in .... must often support their families on very small wages.

4. Only about .... per cent of all Brazilians can read and write.

5. Brazilians laugh over .... and .... cartoons just as Americans do.

II. Can you match these words and statements?

 1. carnival
 2. farinha
 3. Colegio Pedro II
 4. cruzeiro
 5. mestiço
 6. conto
 7. fazenda
 8. canja
 9. feijoada
10. cafezinho

   a. coffee plantation
   b. model for Brazilian high schools
   c. small cup of strong, sweet coffee
   d. tasty dish made of shrimp
   e. soup made with rice and chicken
   f. most common unit of money
   g. college established by Pedro II
   h. Rio's favorite dish — black beans with meat
   i. three-day annual celebration
   j. Brazilian money worth about $50
   k. Brazilian of mixed race
   l. flour-like substance sprinkled on meat dishes

Food for Thought and Discussion

1. It has been said that socially Brazilians are more democratic than we are. What do you think this means? Do you agree that it is true?

2. If you were planning a program to aid the agricultural and factory workers of Brazil, what are some of the things you would do first? What advantage has Venezuela in her new program for the workers?

3. Why do you think Brazilians like us better than the Argentines do? Give as many reasons as you can for your answer.

Looking Backward

You have read the story of our friendly and likeable neighbors, the Brazilians. Now turn to the questions at the beginning of Part VIII which you were asked to keep in mind while you read the chapters. How many of them can you answer? These are questions which every citizen should know about Brazil and they should be easy for you now.

Interesting Things to Do

1. Make a map of Brazil and locate on it all the places mentioned in the text. Sketch in the products of the various regions where they belong.

2. Make a time-line chart of Brazilian history, using dates from 1492 to the present. List important events in Brazilian history with the dates on which they occurred, and in a parallel column list important events in Mexican or Argentine history for the same dates.

3. Find out more about such famous Brazilians as: Tomé de Sousa, Mem de Sa, Tiradentes, Bonifacio, Emperor João, Pedro I, Pedro II, Princess Isabel, Vargas, Oswaldo Cruz, Doctor Vital Brazil.

4. Read and make a report on one of the following: the Indians of the Amazon valley; the São Paulo snake farm and the uses to which the snake venom is put; the story of coffee from berry to bag; cafelite, the coffee plastic.

5. Make a report to the class on the wild life of the jungles of Brazil, showing pictures of specimens from nature-study books and magazines to illustrate your talk.

6. Write imaginary letters from a tourist in Rio. Tell the story of a girl or boy living on a coffee *fazenda*, of life on a colonial sugar plantation. Imagine yourself a member of the royal court of Portugal and write a letter back home telling of your arrival in Rio, and describing the city and the people.

7. Secure records of some of the Brazilian carnival tunes sung by Carmen Miranda or others and play them for the class.

8. If anyone has been corresponding with a pen-pal in Brazil, read the letters to the class.

9. Choose a member of the class to organize a spell-down on the Spanish and Portuguese words and phrases which you have in your notebooks.

Interesting Books to Read

For Further Information

Fodor, Laszlo, *Brazil*. Hastings House. Beautiful photographs with factual explanation.

Gibson, Hugh, *Rio*. Doubleday. A guide to the city, written by an American ambassador.

Kelsey, Vera, *Seven Keys to Brazil*. Funk and Wagnalls. One of the best reference books on Brazil.

Roosevelt, Theodore, *Through the Brazilian Wilderness*. Scribners. Jungle description by a famous American.

For Pleasure

Bowman, Heath, and Dickinson, Sterling, *Westward from Rio*. Willett Clark. Adventurous travel story with interesting woodcut illustrations.

Fleming, Peter, *Brazilian Adventure*. Grosset-Dunlap. A fumbling search for a lost aviator.

Harding, Jack, *I Like Brazil*. Bobbs-Merrill. Travel story of carnivals, river trips, and strange foods.

Weise, Kurt, *Parrot Dealer*. Coward-McCann. Boy's story of Brazilian Indians.

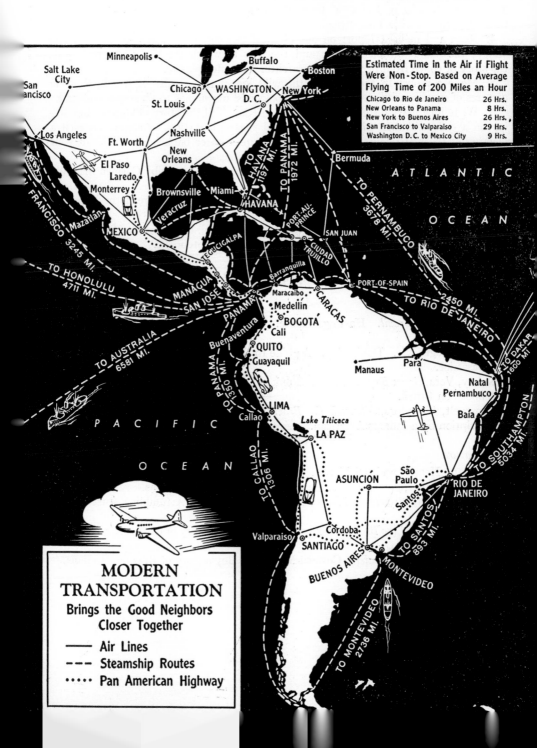

Estimated Time in the Air if Flight Were Non-Stop. Based on Average Flying Time of 200 Miles an Hour

Chicago to Rio de Janeiro	26 Hrs.
New Orleans to Panama	8 Hrs.
New York to Buenos Aires	26 Hrs.
San Francisco to Valparaiso	29 Hrs.
Washington D.C. to Mexico City	9 Hrs.

MODERN TRANSPORTATION
Brings the Good Neighbors Closer Together

—— Air Lines
--- Steamship Routes
••••• Pan American Highway

WORK TOGETHER TOWARD A FINER

A PERMANENT PEACE

Do you like the kind of neighbor who interferes in your affairs, who steps into your house and tells you what to do? Of course you do not. Nations do not like such a neighbor, either, but unfortunately that is the kind of neighbor that the United States has sometimes been in the past. In this last part of our book we shall learn how our country earned for herself the name of "Colossus of the North." We shall also learn that since the United States changed her policy to that of a good neighbor, she has enjoyed the willing co-operation of those who formerly disliked her.

We shall learn about various conferences which have been held, as well as the organization through which the twenty-one American republics work together. Finally, our last chapter will tell us about the famous people who have contributed to the culture of Latin America. It will also help us to understand the courtesies and social customs which make our Latin American neighbors such charming and cultured people.

Modern transportation will bring us even closer to these good neighbors of ours. On the map opposite trace some of the chief transportation routes: the Pan-American Highway, the important airlines and steamship routes. Today we do not yet have the fast schedules which are indicated in the corner of the map and which are possible with the speed of modern planes. But tomorrow, with faster planes and express service, even this schedule of "time-in-the-air" will seem slow indeed.

As you turn now to the last chapters in this book, try to find answers to these questions:

1. What proof have we that the attitude of the Latin American countries toward the United States has changed?

2. What effect will the Pan-American Highway have on the twenty-one American republics?

3. What are the chief contributions of Latin America to the culture of the Americas?

4. What can the United States do to keep the friendship and co-operation of her neighbors?

Chapter 38

The United States Changes from Policeman to Good Neighbor

SIMÓN BOLÍVAR was more than a great soldier; he was a farseeing statesman. He planned not only for the liberation of the countries of Spanish America, but for the days ahead when they would be infant nations in need of protection. It was his dream to establish a league of "majesty and greatness" among the American nations. There was to be a central court for the settlement of disputes between them, and an army for their defense made up of at least 100,000 men.

On the eve of the battle of Ayacucho he invited the Spanish American states to attend a congress to be held at Panama City in 1826. Later the United States, Brazil, and England were also invited. The exchange of plans and letters took so long and there was so much jealousy between the new states that some governments either refused to send delegates or did not act in time. One of our delegates arrived too late; the other died on the way. When the congress met, only four Spanish American states and England were represented and very little was accomplished. Bolívar's plans died with him and it was to be a long time before his dream of a league of New World nations would become a reality. But the congress was not in vain, for the idea of an inter-American union had been planted and was not forgotten.

PRESIDENT MONROE WARNS EUROPE TO KEEP HANDS OFF THE AMERICAS

When the weak little republics of Latin America set out on the path of independence, they were eager to have their new governments recognized by their more powerful neighbor to the north. The people of the United States had sympathized with the rebellion of Spain's colonies, and by 1826, President Monroe had officially recognized all the new republics as well as the new empire of Brazil. Yet this was not enough to make them feel secure, for Spain refused to recognize their independence and a group of strong European nations was threatening to help Spain get back her colonies. The United States government was opposed to any such action on the part of European nations. At this same time, Russia, which had made settlements in Alaska, was claiming the right to the whole Pacific coast north of 51 degrees north latitude. It was time for the United States to take action of some kind.

In December, 1823, President Monroe in his message to Congress let the world know how the United States felt about European interference in the Western Hemisphere. He said that our government would regard any attempt on the part of European powers to establish colonies in any part of the Western Hemisphere as dangerous to our peace and safety. He said also that the United States would not interfere with any existing European colonies in the New World (such as the Guianas), but warned European powers against interfering with the new republics whose governments had been recognized by the United States. This statement, which was soon called the Monroe Doctrine, has served ever since as the guide for our dealings with European countries.

Naturally the European powers referred to by Monroe were indignant at the warning of the bold young republic across the ocean. A German statesman called the speech an "international impertinence." However, the Monroe Doctrine would not have been regarded very seriously if the powerful English government had not also opposed interference in Latin America. Latin Americans were generally pleased, because they believed they would be protected against European schemes. None foresaw what trouble it would cause in the Western Hemisphere itself.

THE UNITED STATES BEGINS TO AROUSE SUSPICION

As time went on it proved to be the United States, not Europe, who encroached on Latin American territory. The new republics watched with alarm as their huge neighbor gobbled up Texas in 1845 and, a few years later, all of Mexico's territory north of the Rio Grande.[1] Suspicion grew when William Walker raided Nicaragua and actually gained control of the government, and the United States took no steps to stop him.[2] The Central American states naturally believed our government encouraged his outrageous activities.

About this time, you remember, France had established Maximilian as emperor of Mexico, supported by French troops.[3] The fears of Latin America were partly erased when the United States threatened France with war if she did not remove her troops from Mexico. When the United States Senate in 1870 refused to consider annexing the Dominican Republic, this fact also made a good impression on Latin America.[4] Suspicion of us died down until the end of the 1800's.

AMERICAN REPUBLICS ORGANIZE A PERMANENT UNION

When James G. Blaine was Secretary of State in the 1880's, he realized that trade with the southern republics would be increased if friendlier relations could be established with the United States. Invitations were sent out to a conference of American states to be held in Washington. In 1889, the first International Conference of American States took place with delegates from every state but the Dominican Republic. A permanent "Union of American Republics" was formed with a central bureau at Washington to distribute information on trade and commerce. Although

[1] See pages 145–46 to refresh your memory of the annexation of Texas and the Mexican War.
[2] See page 211. [3] Turn to page 149.
[4] See page 233.

this was not the political union of "majesty and greatness" dreamed of by Bolívar, it was the first time in the world's history that eighteen nations had met to promote peace and encourage trade.

Since 1890 a number of important conferences have been held in the capitals of the various American states. They were known as Pan-American conferences ("*Pan*" is the Greek word for *all*) until the 1940's when the official name became Inter-American conferences. With the years, the work of these conferences and of the Organization of American States (as the organization which sponsors them is now called) has greatly increased. Almost a hundred special conferences have been called to deal with such problems as highways, child welfare, Red Cross, health and sanitation, education, radio communications, and arbitration of disputes.

The Inter-American conferences have had three chief aims: (1) to bring about the peaceful settlement of disputes between nations; (2) to encourage inter-American trade; (3) to promote cultural bonds among American republics.

THE UNITED STATES BECOMES A POLICEMAN TO LATIN AMERICA

At the turn of the century, several events took place which caused resentment toward the United States to flare up again. When we fought the Spanish-American War to free Cuba, the Spanish republics forgot their old grievances against Spain and bitterly criticized the United States. When we came out of the war with new possessions, Puerto Rico and the Philippines, they were convinced our main purpose had been to win more terri-

tory. The fact that we gave Cuba her independence made matters no better, because our Senate passed the Platt Amendment providing for interference in case of disorderly government in Cuba.[1] The Venezuelan poet, Rufino Blanco Fombona, warned Latin Americans that the Yankees were the enemies of their civilization and of their independence.

What created more fear and suspicion than anything else was the encouragement given by Theodore Roosevelt in the Panama Revolution.[2] Some of the best writers of Spanish America wrote bitter denunciations of the "Colossus of the North." Rubén Darío, famous Nicaraguan poet, dedicated a defiant poem to Roosevelt. The following is part of it:[3]

You are the United States,
You are the future invader
Of that ingenious America of native blood,
That prays to Jesus still and still speaks
    Spanish. . . .
You hold that life is a fire,
And progress an eruption;
That where your guns can reach,
There you control the future. No!
. . . Beware, for Spanish America lives!
The Spanish lion has a thousand cubs.
'Twere needful, Roosevelt, to be, . . .
The terrible rifleman and the hunter strong,
Ever to keep us in your iron grasp.

It was in the early 1900's, you remember, that Haiti, the Dominican Republic, and other Caribbean countries were on the verge of ruin because of their dishonest and disorderly governments.[4] European governments

[1] Re-read the story of the Spanish-American War, pages 238–239.
[2] Turn to page 220.
[3] G. Dundas Craig, *The Modernist Trend in Spanish-American Poetry*. University of California Press.
[4] Re-read page 190.

were threatening to come over to collect debts owed them.

Theodore Roosevelt declared in 1904 that under the Monroe Doctrine the United States might be forced to exercise a police power over countries too weak to keep order or pay their debts. It was the same as saying that if neighboring countries did not behave themselves and maintain a responsible government, the United States would step in to see that they behaved. As you remember, that is just what we did, sending Marines into Haiti, the Dominican Republic, and Nicaragua. Regardless of how much good may have been accomplished, we were guilty of interfering in the affairs of independent nations. We were accused of protecting the investments of our businessmen in these countries by what Latin Americans bitterly called our "dollar diplomacy." Altogether we put in a bad quarter of a century as far as Latin American friendship was concerned.

LATIN AMERICAN NATIONS FOLLOW THE LEADERSHIP OF IDEALISTIC WOODROW WILSON DURING THE FIRST WORLD WAR

The United States realized the damage being done to trade and to the position of the United States in the eyes of the world. When Woodrow Wilson became President, he assured Latin Americans that he did not consider the Monroe Doctrine to mean that the United States must act as guardian over the American nations. He emphasized the fact that they were all friends, not hostile rivals, and said that the United States did not want even a foot of Latin American territory. Wilson's new interpretation of the Monroe Doctrine was favorably received. The Latin American states recognized Wilson's sincerity and idealism even though he did later intervene in Mexico. When the United States declared war against Germany, eight of them followed suit (although only Brazil had a grievance against Germany), and five others broke off diplomatic relations.

When the League of Nations for which Wilson worked so hard was established, all the Latin American countries joined, probably hoping to be protected against the aggression of the United States. But Wilson lost his leadership in his own country and the United States herself refused to join the League. Disappointed in their hopes of the League, Latin Americans looked again at the Caribbean and found some of the states still occupied by United States Marines. By this time the Latin American states were ready to take action to stop United States aggression.

When the fifth Pan-American conference met in Santiago, Chile, in 1923, a proposal was made that all the states approve the principle of the Monroe Doctrine. This would have given them all a share in enforcing it. But the United States opposed this idea and no action was taken. At the sixth conference in Havana in 1928, the Latin American republics tried in vain to pass a resolution condemning intervention on the part of any state. Debate was hot and heavy, but the United States won out and the resolution was not voted on. (The conferences at that time were under the control of the powerful United States and were not co-operative undertakings among equal states.) However, the conference did provide for treaties calling for the settlement of inter-American disputes by peaceful means.

Keystone

UNITED STATES AND CUBAN REPRESENTATIVES are shown here signing a treaty to encourage trade after the repeal of the Platt Amendment. Cordell Hull, who was Secretary of State at that time, is signing the document.

THE GOOD NEIGHBOR POLICY CHANGES ENEMIES TO FRIENDS

The Good Neighbor policy actually began under President Coolidge, although it was Franklin Roosevelt who gave it that name. When Coolidge became President, the United States was involved in a serious quarrel with Mexico over the rights of American oil companies. Coolidge wisely sent as ambassador to Mexico Dwight Morrow, who, by taking a friendly attitude, completely changed the strained relations between the countries. Friendly feelings were increased when Charles Lindbergh, who had recently made his sensational trip across the Atlantic, made an air trip to Mexico. After Herbert Hoover was elected President, he made a visit to South America where he spoke in favor of better understanding between the United States and Latin America. When he became President he recalled the Marines from Nicaragua.

In his inaugural address in 1933, Franklin Roosevelt pledged himself to be a "good neighbor" toward Latin America:

"In the field of world policy I would dedicate this nation to the policy of the good neighbor — the neighbor who resolutely respects himself and, because he does so, respects the rights of others — the neighbor who respects his obligations and the sanctity of his agreements in and with a world of neighbors."

THE UNITED STATES PROVES THAT ACTIONS SPEAK LOUDER THAN WORDS

At the seventh inter-American conference at Montevideo late in 1933, there was for the first time a feeling of friendliness and cordiality among the delegates. This was due largely to Secretary of State Cordell Hull, whose quiet, gentlemanly manner and tactful statements caused the old bitter feelings to disappear. He soon won the respect and confidence of all the delegates by his sincerity and his willingness to discuss any question.

All nations, including the United States, signed a declaration that "no state has the right to intervene in the internal or external affairs of any other state." By this declaration the United States recognized the equal rights of all American nations. The United States showed her sincerity by immediately repealing the Platt Amendment and recalling the last Marines from Haiti. There have been many opportunities for the United States to intervene in recent years, but she has remained true to her pledge.

In 1936, President Roosevelt called a special conference of American nations at Buenos Aires to take steps toward safeguarding peace on the American continents. Roosevelt himself opened the conference and was greeted with great enthusiasm by all the delegates. He told the delegates, "Each one of us has learned the glories of independence. Let each one of us learn the glories of interdependence." The conference agreed that if the peace of the Western

THE PAN-AMERICAN CONFERENCE at Buenos Aires in 1936 was opened by President Roosevelt. Important Latin American officials are on the rostrum with him. These conferences have done much to foster co-operation among American nations.

P. A. Inc.

Camera Clix

MEXICO PROVED HER LOYALTY to American interests by declaring war on the Axis in June, 1942. Former president Cárdenas was made commander of the Mexican army, whose well-trained machine gun units are shown here.

Hemisphere were menaced, the twenty-one republics would consult together with regard to the problem threatening them. The friendly spirit and confidence felt toward the United States at Buenos Aires was the direct result of President Roosevelt's and Secretary Hull's new policy of neighborliness.

Later conventions have bound the American republics closer together. At Lima, Peru, on Christmas Eve of the year 1938, Cordell Hull again opened the eighth conference of American nations. The peace of Europe was threatened. Germany had recently invaded Austria and Czechoslovakia, and Japan was invading China. Fascist countries were filling American republics with propaganda. In the Declaration of Lima, the twenty-one republics announced they would stand together in the face of any attempt at aggression.

When war broke out in 1939, the sincerity of the nations was put to a real test. At a meeting in Panama every representative voted for a 300-mile zone of safety around the Americas south of Canada. Warring nations were asked to avoid fighting in this neutrality zone. At Havana in 1940, the Americas again bound themselves to united resistance against aggression toward any American republic.

AMERICAN NATIONS STAND TOGETHER IN THE FACE OF WAR

When the United States declared war on the Axis Powers on December 8, after the Japanese attack on Pearl Harbor, it meant that declarations of American solidarity would soon be tested. The peace of the Western Hemisphere was threatened, one of the American republics had been attacked, and neutrality was a thing of the past. Foreign ministers of the republics met in January, 1942, at Rio de Janeiro during hot midsummer.

As a result of the conference, all but four of the nations broke off relations with the Axis Powers. Most went a step farther to prove their solidarity with the United States by passing declarations of war that same year. Chile and Argentina, however, remained neutral for many months and did not declare war until 1945.

Another conference of American nations was held in February, 1945, in Mexico City's Chapultepec Palace. Argentina had not been invited because of her pro-Nazi sympathies. The nations discussed what their policy would be toward the new world organization to be formed in San Francisco in April. All agreed to support an organization which would work for world peace. They also declared that no country should be allowed to join the United Nations unless it had declared war on Germany. Under this pressure, Argentina declared war on the Axis, signed the Act of Chapultepec (as the agreements made in Mexico were called), and was able to attend the San Francisco meeting as one of the United Nations. In 1948 the ninth Inter-American Conference met at Bogotá, Colombia. Here the twenty-one nations took a most important step. In the Pact of Bogotá they not only agreed to settle all international disputes peacefully, but to follow the definite steps for arbitration set down in the treaty. In Washington, D.C., in 1951, the American nations pledged co-operation in defending the hemisphere from the danger of Communism.

Latin American nations have also been active in the United Nations and the United Nations Educational, Scientific, and Cultural Organization. Dr. Jaime Torres Bodet (boh-dett') of Mexico became the head of UNESCO. The Latin American republics are taking their place today not only in their own hemisphere but in the world.

Are You a Careful Reader? Test Yourself!

I. Can you supply the correct word for each blank?

1. President .... 's message to Congress in 1823 warned .... governments against interfering with the new .... in the Western Hemisphere.

2. Some of the events which caused Latin America to consider the United States a menace to their security were: the annexation of .... ; the huge territory granted to the United States by .... after the Mexican War; the cession of .... and the .... after the Spanish American War.

3. Dislike for the .... was further increased by the attitude of .... Roosevelt toward the revolution in .... and by our intervention in the affairs of .... republics.

4. Although Coolidge and Hoover worked toward a better understanding with .... , credit for the .... policy belongs to ....

5. At a conference of American nations in Lima in 1938, the twenty-one republics pledged themselves to .... against .... .

6. By 1944 .... Latin American republics had broken off relations with the .... Powers.

7. By the Act of .... Argentina was forced to declare war in order to join the United Nations.

Food for Thought and Discussion

1. Do you think that some day the twenty-one American nations may establish a league such as Bolívar planned, with a court to settle disputes and a common army for defense?

2. Why are the Organization of American States and its conferences an advantage to the United States as well as to the republics of Latin America? Do the agreements at Lima, Havana, and Rio bind the United States to go to the defense of any American nation attacked by a foreign power?

3. Do you think the Latin Americans have entirely forgotten our unfriendly acts of the past? Could any President change Franklin Roosevelt's Good Neighbor policy?

4. If you were President or Secretary of State, what would be your policy toward Latin America? List several definite steps you would take.

Chapter 39

Co-operation Is the Keynote of American Friendship

IF SIMÓN BOLÍVAR could visit Washington, D.C., today, he would be delighted to see the beautiful white marble palace which is the headquarters of the Pan American Union. This building is the gift of Andrew Carnegie and was completed in 1910. In the magnificent central hall are the flags of all the American nations and the busts of their national heroes. The offices are built around a tropical patio full of palms and flowers in true Latin American style. This impressive building is a fitting home for the great organization which represents the union of the twenty-one American republics.

THE PAN AMERICAN UNION IS A CENTRAL CLEARING HOUSE

The name Pan American Union refers not only to the building but to the secretarial organization which does much of the work of the Organization

Pan American Union

THE PAN AMERICAN UNION in Washington, D.C., stands as a symbol of the friendship and co-operation existing between the 21 American republics. The statues on each side of the door represent North and South America.

of American States. The Union keeps on file documents and treaties of the Organization, and helps to plan the conferences. It also carries out many projects dealing with such matters as law, music, agriculture, education, economic life, labor and social information, cultural affairs, and exchange of students and teachers between the United States and Latin America.

One of the purposes of the Union is to serve as a central bureau of information about anything connected with the American nations. If a Peruvian government authority wants to establish schools for the Indians, he writes to the headquarters for information regarding types of rural schools. If an automobile exporting company wants to know just how many miles of concrete highway

there are in Argentina, the Pan American Union knows the answer. If a student in a university of Colombia wants information on the best course on tropical agriculture, the Union can tell him not only where such a course is offered, but how much it will cost. The director-general of the Pan American Union writes, "The Union answers thousands of letters of inquiry from citizens of all the American nations every year, from commerce to sanitation, from orchestra music to hotels, from municipal government to blast furnaces."

A most useful service of the Union is to publish a monthly magazine formerly called *The Bulletin of the Pan American Union*, but now known as *Américas*. It is a popular magazine in three editions, one English, one Span-

Pan American Union

IN THE BEAUTIFUL PATIO of the Pan American Union a fountain plays under a glass roof. There are gay-colored parrots and macaws, and flowers and plants from every nation.

ish, and one Portuguese. *Américas* furnishes news about the affairs of the Union. For example, one issue contains an article about tours through Chile's lake region, a story about silkworm culture in Brazil, letters from a school-teacher in Costa Rica, reports of improved conditions for miners in Peru, notices of meetings about mosquito control, reprints of a speech by the president of Paraguay, and the account of a rare new orchid from Colombia. An American student who reads *Américas* regularly is able to keep up with what is going on in Latin America.

In addition to publishing *Américas* and to answering all kinds of letters asking for information, the Pan American Union publishes reports of the many meetings held under its auspices. It prints much material for use in schools, pamphlets about each country, lists of Latin American music, pageants on Latin American history, and titles of new books students would like.

Pan-American Day is celebrated throughout the Western Hemisphere on April 14. In 1951 it was estimated that 14,000 clubs and patriotic groups observed this day with various celebrations. Schools in many American cities give plays and programs on Pan-American topics, often written by the students themselves. Pan-American clubs in Latin American schools also hold special exercises. In sections of our country where there is a large Mexican population, programs are made more colorful by children dressed in gay fiesta costumes.

Each year on April 14, in Washington, D.C., speakers and musicians from the American republics do honor to Pan-American Day. In the evening a musical program is held in the beautiful Hall of the Americas. Recently a famous trio of Peruvian Indians, dressed in gay costumes, entertained the audience with ancient songs and dances. Another year the well-known Brazilian singer, Olga Coelho (kwel-yu), sang melodies of her homeland. This kind of program has been held each year since the first Pan-American Day in 1931.

THE PAN AMERICAN UNION ENCOURAGES CO-OPERATION IN THE FIELD OF AGRICULTURE

One part of the work of the Union is in the field of agriculture. Its magazine is full of notices about all kinds of meetings between delegates of the Americas. Specialists meet to talk about rubber, quinine, forest conservation, vegetable oils, and plant pests. On the whole subject of agriculture there are perhaps more meetings than in any other one field. The Pan American Union keeps track of 700 agricultural societies in the Americas, knows the work done at the 200 experimental stations and the 250 agricultural training stations throughout the Latin American republics.

You know the need for modern scientific agriculture throughout Latin America. Anything that the agricultural scientists of one nation know, the Pan American Union passes on to the others, or calls a meeting so everyone can find out. The United States has developed the finest agricultural colleges in the world, and its Department

A GOOD NEIGHBOR PARADE stops at the statue of Simón Bolívar in New York City to honor the man who dreamed of Pan-American friendship. Flags of all the American republics led the parade which opened Pan-American Week.

CIAA Photo

of Agriculture has the most up-to-date information on how to raise livestock, kill locusts, stop plant diseases, fertilize barren ground, or build irrigation projects. For this reason, young Latin Americans are encouraged to come to American agricultural colleges to study. Also, North Americans graduating from these colleges are encouraged to go as specialists to Latin America. An Institute of Tropical Agriculture has been established in Costa Rica where students can take courses in the problems of agriculture in the tropics, which are not given in the United States.

INTERNATIONAL CO-OPERATION PROMOTES HEALTH

The Pan American Sanitary Bureau, which co-operates closely with the Pan American Union, has saved hundreds of thousands of lives. Malaria and yellow fever, first controlled by the United States in the tropics, have been checked by government health services everywhere. A series of sanitary conferences have been held to control the spread of mosquitoes and to provide for inspection of ships, trains, and airplanes from one country to another to make sure that mosquitoes which carry these diseases were not crossing borders. Ten conferences have met to consider public health, sanitation, surgery, tuberculosis, and a number of other subjects.

In the past twenty years the work has been helped by the Rockefeller Foundation in the United States, which has provided money and men to fight hookworm and other diseases in the tropics. The Red Cross has worked with the Pan-American health committees in cases of earthquakes, floods, and hurricanes. Airplanes today carry serums or oxygen tents from one American country to another. Public water supplies have been improved in many places, thus cutting down deaths from typhoid fever. Inspection of factories is becoming more common. As factories are built in Latin American countries, governments, under pressure from their doctors who attend sanitary conferences, are forcing factory owners to provide healthful working conditions. Hospitals are increasing. Today Brazil has 2600 hospitals, while Mexico has over 400. Standards of training nurses and doctors have improved. There are training schools for the study of tropical diseases in Bogotá, Rio de Janeiro, Mexico City, Lima, and Caracas.

The average Latin American's chance to live has greatly increased in the forty years since the establishment of the Pan American Sanitary Bureau. It reports encouraging figures on disease control. The dread cholera has disappeared from South America. All West Coast South American ports are now free from plague and yellow fever. Bolivia, Chile, and Guatemala report the number of cases of typhus cut in half by campaigns against lice. These pestilential diseases, as the epidemic diseases are called, cannot be controlled without international co-operation, without treaties calling for quarantine of ships and inspection of ports. A branch of our State Department and the World Health Organization of the UN are also working on this program.

THE AMERICAN NATIONS PROMOTE CULTURAL EXCHANGE

The Department of Cultural Af-

THESE LATIN AMERICAN STUDENTS have won scholarships given by New York City entitling them to advanced training in a profession or in industry. The late Mayor La Guardia greets students representing eleven of our neighbor republics.

fairs handles such matters as the exchange of ideas on education, the visits of students, scientists, and men of letters back and forth, the encouragement of traveling art exhibitions, and the translation and publication of books and articles which will help the American nations to understand and appreciate one another. Volumes could be written about the work the Pan American Union and other agencies have accomplished in this field. Among other measures, the organization of cultural institutes has been encouraged in Argentina, Brazil, Chile, and other countries. English is taught in these institutes, American books are lent out, lectures are given, and American art is often displayed.

The Pan American Union has encouraged Latin American writers. It has collaborated with an American publishing house in arranging a series of important literary contests for the best writings by Latin American authors. The winners receive a large money prize from the publishing house, and the winning works are translated and published in English. In 1941, for example, the prize for the best novel was won by a Peruvian, and honorable mention was awarded to an Ecuadorian, a Brazilian, and a Mexican. The winners came to New York to receive their prizes at a brilliant literary gathering and banquet in their honor. In 1943, the prize was won by two brothers from Haiti, and honorable mention was awarded to an Argentinian and a Colombian.

Since it has been very difficult to buy English books in Latin America or Latin American books here, traveling exhibits of books have been arranged. Recently the American Library Association sponsored a traveling exhibit of four hundred volumes of the best new Latin American books. These were shown in the United States at libraries, teachers' and textbook meetings, and women's clubs. In return an exhibit of books from the United States, selected and arranged by American publishers, was sent to South America. The Pan American Union reported that the exhibit of beautiful modern American books for children was the most popular of all, and that many school-children in South American cities had come to see them. They enjoyed the pictures whether they could read the stories or not.

Many art museums in the United States have in recent years arranged important exhibitions of the work of Latin American artists, and some have created permanent collections. A magnificent exhibit of contemporary Mexican painting was recently held by the Philadelphia Museum of Art, and the Brooklyn Museum possesses a large permanent collection of the colonial and folk arts of Latin American countries, including painting, sculpture, textiles, pottery, and glass. The Museum of Modern Art in New York possesses over three hundred paintings from Latin America, more than those from Europe. Several traveling exhibits of contemporary United States paintings have also been shown in the principal cities of Latin America. This interchange is only a beginning. The artists themselves have come to visit us. Diego Rivera, Clemente Orozco, and Candido Portinari have painted murals for American buildings. Recently a young Bolivian woman woodcarver, Marina Núñez del Prado, received a fellowship for study in the United States, and her fine carvings were on display in Washington.

MOVING PICTURES ARE VALUABLE IN PROMOTING FRIENDSHIP

The influence of our movies in Brazil has been mentioned. Every town in Latin America of average size has a motion-picture theater, although it may be made of galvanized iron, filled with backless benches, and show a movie only once a week. The great majority of these movies are from the United States. The talking is in English, but across the bottom of the photograph a translation of the conversation is flashed in Spanish or Portuguese in white letters. These movies encourage a great many people in remote villages to learn to read, and certainly everyone hears a great deal of English.

There are many stories about the effect of movies on the ignorant peons who come to see them. In one theater in a little town, an audience of peons was watching a movie. When a speeding train appeared to be rushing toward them from the screen, they took to their heels! Only when the manager assured them it was not real and let them feel the screen would they return to their seats. Movies are so real to these people that when an actor who has died in one picture appears in another, they are greatly perturbed, for is not the man dead?

Good pictures can spread much information about us and our customs. Bad pictures can do much harm by giving false impressions of us. A few years ago a well-to-do young Chilean lady, returning from the United States, was questioned by her friends as to how she had survived the custard pie-throwing which was a sport of Americans! A young Mexican teacher from Oaxaca in southern Mexico was asked in Los Angeles how she could live in Mexico where there were so many bandits. She replied that her family had very much disapproved of her visit to the United States because they doubted if she would return alive from gangster-ridden America! Today we are sending "four star" rather than "B grade" pictures to Latin America. A few good pictures will do more toward making friends than many good-will tours.

STUDENT EXCHANGE PROMOTES FRIENDSHIP

The Pan American Union handles much correspondence concerning schools and interchange of students and teachers between North and South America. Latin American students are coming in great numbers to study in the United States, especially since the second World War. For instance, a student from Honduras won a scholarship to study for two years at the University of Alabama. A group of boys from nine different countries attended the Merchant Marine Academy on Long Island at the expense of our government. Hundreds of other Latin Americans study at our universities every year. They are studying chemistry, plant culture, electric railway construction, veterinary medicine, and mining engineering. In 1936, a treaty was signed by twenty-one republics providing for the exchange of one teacher and two university students between each country every year. Scholarships or free schooling for Latin Americans to study in the United States are provided by American colleges and private companies up to a total of $260,000.

On the other hand, American students and teachers are traveling and going to school in Latin America. Many American universities send students and professors on tours and hold classes on the way. For example, a Texas teachers college took a group of students to Oaxaca, Mexico, for summer study. The University of San Marcos in Lima, South America's oldest university, offers special summer school classes in Spanish and South American history and geography. The University of Mexico City offers courses for American students in summer school. Costa Rica and Guatemala have invited student tourists to their universities and arranged with American universities for summer school credit.

Even students of high-school age are visiting Latin America. Two groups of high-school students organized by the Experiment in International Living at Putney, Vermont, spent an enjoyable summer in Mexico and in Peru, traveling in trucks equipped with camping outfits and chaperoned by teachers and camp counselors. One American girl reported learning to play the guitar while she in turn taught a Peruvian girl to play the harmonica. All these young people continued to correspond with their Latin American friends.

Other groups of young people travel yearly to Mexico and Guatemala as members of the American Youth Hostels. Each group of ten has a trained leader. They travel over Mexico by bicycle, covering as much as forty miles a day. They carry their own sleeping bags, eating utensils, and food. Long distances are covered by train or on buses with the bicycles strapped on top. These young people have an excellent chance to get acquainted with the geography and the people of Mexico. They are often entertained in the homes of the hospitable Mexicans. These young Americans often do a great deal toward building friendship and understanding between the people of Mexico and the United States.

We are also improving our friendship with Latin Americans by means of sports. Latin American nations have taken part in the Olympic games for years. In 1951 the first regional Latin American Olympic games were held in Buenos Aires. The United States sent a team of its best athletes — swimmers, track stars, tennis players, wrestlers. The expenses of the team were paid by American companies which do business in Latin America. Every nation in the Western Hemisphere sent athletes to compete in the games. Argentina won the competition by several points, chiefly because of its excellent polo team. Sports events such as this one do a great deal to bring about good-will among the American republics.

INTER–AMERICAN TRADE STRENGTHENS THE AMERICAN NATIONS

Although the improvement of trade relations between the American states has always been a large part of the inter-American program, trade has become particularly important today. The American nations have repeatedly pledged military co-operation in case of attack. But defense of the Western Hemisphere also requires economic co-operation. We need raw materials from Latin America for our defense; Latin America needs military and economic aid from us. We have pledged our help in increasing trade between the United States and Latin America and in developing the resources of all the American nations. This is not a temporary defense program, but a permanent policy designed to give Latin American states a sounder and better balanced economy.

The second World War brought about better trade relations. We needed many things that Latin America produced; Latin America needed help in disposing of the large surplus of goods that had formerly gone to the European markets now shut off by war. Wheat and corn piled up in enormous quantities in Argentina; coffee and cacao filled the warehouses of Brazil. Latin America could no longer buy manufactured goods from Europe. The United States, on the other hand, could no longer buy rubber and tin from the Malay States, silk from Japan, or manganese from Russia. We were able to exchange manufactured goods for badly needed raw materials from Latin America.

Our post-war trade has increased amazingly. In 1938 we bought over five hundred million dollars' worth of goods from Latin America, while at the mid-century our purchases amounted to about two and one-half billion dollars or about five times their former value! In fact thirty-five per cent of all our foreign purchases came from Latin America. We buy ninety-five per cent of our coffee, eighty-five per cent of our cane sugar, about twenty-five per cent of the metals, and about fifty per cent of the wool from our neighbors to the south.

Of our six chief imports, the only one we do not buy in large part from them is paper. On the other hand, we sold to Latin America about three billion dollars' worth of farm machinery, automobiles, electrical appliances, cloth, and chemicals. Argentina, Brazil, Colombia, Cuba, Mexico, and Venezuela are our most important customers. We buy more from Brazil than from any other country except Canada, while the best customer for our goods is Mexico.

The United States, through loans and technical aid, is helping Latin American nations to develop their resources. In Mexico and Brazil great dams and irrigation projects are being built. The largest steel mill in South America has been completed in Brazil, another huge new steel mill is operating in Chile. Countries are being encouraged to grow tropical products which we can use, such as rubber, quinine, hemp and sisal, spices and oils.

Manufacturing of commodities by Latin American countries is encouraged because it lessens dependence on imports; selling cheap raw materials and buying expensive manufactured goods leaves a country owing a trade balance. Home manufacture of essential commodities will mean fewer imports and a better trade balance. The loans for industrial development made by our government are on a partnership basis and not in any sense an attempt to gain control of industries or trade. We furnish the money and trained experts, Latin America furnishes the resources, and both partners benefit by this co-operative arrangement. This policy has fostered a greater feeling of equality among the American republics.

THE PAN–AMERICAN HIGHWAY BINDS THE AMERICAN NATIONS TOGETHER

One of the greatest aids to trade, to friendly relations, and to defense is the Pan-American Highway. The idea for this highway goes back to 1923 when a resolution was brought up at the Pan-American Conference at Santiago to "study motor highway possibilities." This was at a time when few country roads were paved in the United States and Latin America was in the oxcart era of travel. The possibilities were looked into, and, in 1928, at the Havana Conference, a committee of highway engineers offered a resolution that a continuous highway from Alaska to Buenos Aires be built. President Coolidge sent a message to the conference that the United States would send highway engineers to help build the road in Latin American countries. We have also helped with large financial appropriations.

Surveying of the road took several years because of the many stretches of difficult terrain. The Latin American section of the highway begins near Laredo, Texas, on the Mexican border. If you will turn to the map on page 428, you can trace the highway route through Panama to Colombia. In South America, the road runs from Medellín to Cali and thence to Quito, from Quito to Lima and south to Santiago, then across the Andes to Buenos Aires. As you can see, there are branches of the highway connecting other countries with the main road. We have mentioned the road from Caracas to Bogotá in an earlier chapter. Another route leaves the main highway in southern Peru, goes to Lake Titicaca and La Paz, crosses Bolivia and northern Argentina to

Sawders

THIS IS THE PAN-AMERICAN HIGHWAY leading to Mexico City, which is 52 kilometers or about 33 miles ahead. As you look at this picture do you feel an urge to follow the road "over the hills and far away"?

Buenos Aires. Other branches go to Asunción and to Santos and Rio de Janeiro by way of Montevideo.

The standard requirements for the Pan-American Highway called for a graded road paved with asphalt or concrete. It was to be 28 feet wide with no grade greater than 7 per cent. When we think of the jungles and the mountains which this highway must pass through, this standard seems difficult to maintain. Each country was to be responsible for the amount of highway passing between its borders. With the co-operation of the Latin American republics, our army engineers undertook the gigantic task. By 1952 the highway was completed through Mexico and Central America

to the Panama Canal, except for two very difficult stretches. The Guatemalan section does not meet the Mexican section at the border; in Costa Rica there remain many miles of mountain terrain to conquer. When these stretches are finished, travelers can drive through to the Canal.

Beyond the Canal in eastern Panama lies a jungle so impenetrable that it is doubtful whether a road will soon be attempted there. Instead, travelers on the Pan-American Highway may be carried with their cars by ship from the Canal to one of the port cities of Colombia or Venezuela, where they could pick up the highway again.

In South America, it is now possible

to drive from Caracas to Buenos Aires. Although portions of the highway are still unpaved and very rough, every year sees more miles improved. Sometime in the near future American motorists will follow the Pan-American Highway from the United States to Buenos Aires. This will be another tie to bind us to our neighbors south of the Rio Grande. When we can get better acquainted with our Latin American neighbors, better understanding will develop between the peoples of the Western Hemisphere.

Are You a Careful Reader? Test Yourself!

I. Supply the correct word for each blank:

1. The ... ... Union is the central bureau of the ... ... Conferences of all nations meet every .... year°

2. The official magazine of the Union is .... .

3. The headquarters of the Union are in .... , ...

4. ... ... Day is celebrated by all the American republics every year on ....

5. When completed, the Pan-American Highway will reach from .... to ... .

II. Which statements are true and which are false?

1. The Pan American Union gives advice on political affairs.

2. Inspection of ports and quarantine of ships are necessary to control epidemic diseases in Latin America.

3. Books written by Latin Americans are for sale in almost any book store in the United States.

4. Difficult parts of the Pan-American Highway in Central America have been built by United States Army engineers with the co-operation of Central American republics.

5. No part of the Pan-American Highway in South America can be used for travel.

Food for Thought and Discussion

1. There is a saying, "Seeing is believing." How does this apply to movies sent to Latin America from the United States? In what way can our movies be a strong influence toward a better understanding between us and our Latin American neighbors?

2. Name some of the ways in which you think exchange of students would promote friendship and understanding.

3. Why must political friendship be backed up by an increasing amount of trade between the United States and Latin America?

Chapter 40

Latin Americans Make Their Own Contribution to American Culture

WE HAVE READ of military heroes of Latin America, of presidents, of dictators, and of emperors, but greater than their contributions to civilization are those made by the artists, the writers, the musicians, and the scholars of Latin America. They have created something which wars and dictators cannot destroy. Governments, good and bad, may come and go, but a beautiful poem, an exquisite painting, or music that stirs men's souls live on forever.

Our neighbors south of the Rio Grande are building a Latin American culture of their own. It is neither Spanish nor Portuguese, Indian nor Negro, but something of all of these. It is a new culture with the vigor of the New World and the rich heritage of the Old. It is to our discredit in North America that we know so little of the men who have created the art and literature of our southern neighbors. If we would be good neighbors, we should know their great men as they know ours. In this short chapter we cannot tell the whole story of Latin American culture nor of all the men who helped to create it. The men mentioned here are merely representative of the many who have made their contribution to civilization in the Americas to the south.

LATIN AMERICANS LOVE POETRY

All educated Latin Americans read poetry, and almost all of them write it. Many presidents of Latin American countries have been well-known poets. Bartolomé Mitre, president of Argentina, and Rafael Nuñez, president of Colombia, were poets, and José Martí, leader of Cuban independence, published two volumes of delightful poetry. At first, when the republics were young, writers turned to Europe, and France in particular, for their models and their inspiration. Much of their work was in imitation of French, Spanish, and Portuguese writers. In the latter part of the 1800's, however, the poets of the New World began to find inspiration in the splendors of their own land and their own people. Gradually they broke away from Old World traditions and for the first time wrote freely and naturally.

DARÍO IS THE GREATEST POET OF LATIN AMERICA

The leader of the new movement in writing was Rubén Darío (roo-bane' dah-ree'oh), a Nicaraguan poet. This talented man, who is considered one of the greatest masters of the Spanish language, is little known in the United States. This is partly because few of us read Spanish and partly because we have not been interested in the literature of our Latin American neighbors. Darío's life reads like a novel. He was born in Nicaragua in 1867, of Spanish and Indian blood. When he was three years old, he was able to read, and at five or six this precocious boy was writing verses. By the time he was thirteen, he was known in Central America as the "boy poet." While still a young man, he went to Chile and Argentina where he wrote for the newspapers. Later he traveled in Europe and North America as a newspaper correspondent, and also served as representative of several Latin American governments. Wherever he was, he continued to write poetry.

Darío, sensitive and brilliant, was always in the heights of happiness or in the depths of despair. He had one unhappy love affair after another, and as he grew older he drank too much. He spent money as fast as he got it and was often reduced to real want. In 1915, worn out and ill, he returned to Nicaragua, where he died in poverty the following year at the age of forty-eight. Nicaraguans are proud to claim the birthplace and tomb of this famous poet.

Darío is noted for his clear and beautifully simple style. His first famous book of poems and prose published when he was twenty-one was called *Azul* ... (ah-sool') or "Blue ..." It not only brought him fame as a master of the Spanish language, but it influenced the whole history of writing in Latin America. Darío became known as the leader of the modern style of writing. We have already read one of his poems on page 432. He published many other poems and

Pan American Union

RUBÉN DARÍO, great modern poet, lived in so many lands that no one country can claim his genius. His life ended where it began, in León, Nicaragua. His tomb can be seen in the cathedral there.

prose works. Today his poems belong not only to Latin America, but to the world.

OTHER MODERN POETS FOLLOW IN DARÍO'S FOOTSTEPS

Mexico's greatest modern poet was influenced by Darío's natural and sincere style of writing. Amado Nervo (ah-mah'doh nair'voh), who lived from 1870 to 1919, also wrote verses as a small child. His poems are simple and strong, and often express a deep faith in mankind. His well-known poem, called "Miraculous Bird," was written in 1910 after a flight in an airplane, which he compares to a white bird. Over thirty years ago this poet wrote that the "celestial bird" was "born as a messenger of friendship" and begged the nations not to stain it with "missions of war." Little did he know that birds more miraculous than he had ever seen would one day swoop down from the skies to drop death and destruction upon mankind.

Rufino Blanco Fombona (fohm-boh'nah) is one of the great modern Latin American writers. He has written novels and essays as well as poems. His works reveal the fearless independence of his nature. Born in Caracas in 1874, he became involved in the politics of his country. His courageous denunciation of conditions in Venezuela led to imprisonment and exile. Some of his finest poems were written in the dungeons of Caracas while he was a prisoner there. This collection is called *Songs of Prison and Exile*. In the following poem called "The Flight of Psyche," Blanco Fombona tells how he escapes the prison chains.[1]

The prison crushes me. Dark fancies haunt me;
They wander through my mind, in sleep or awake.
My poet's wings, when I would fain unfold them,
Against the walls I break.

Buried and yet alive! The nights are endless,
Endless the days, that used to glide so fleet.
The Griefs keep with me. There are spies around me,
And fetters on my feet.

But when I close mine eyes — light, landscape, heaven!
The fetters break; the daylight grows serener;
On my love's arm I breathe a garden's fragrance —
Magnolia and verbena.

[1] Alice Stone Blackwell, *Some Spanish American Poets.* University of Pennsylvania Press.

I revel in the breeze, the clouds, the fountain,
A cool air like my love, that soothes my pains.
This is a joy no tyrant can take from me,
Nor keep it bound in chains.

Among the many other poets of Latin America is Gabriela Mistral, who, you remember, visited the schoolchildren of Brazil. This outstanding woman is a poet of international fame. We mention her because it is unusual for a Latin American woman to become famous. She is well known by her Chilean countrymen whether they can read her poems or not, because she has been a teacher and a leader among women as well as a poet. Many of her lovely lyrics are about children, as we would expect. Here is one called "Everything Is a Dance," which you will like: [1]

The stars are children in circling dance,
At watching the earth they play.
The wheat-ears are figures of little girls,
Their sport is to sway — to sway.

The rivers are children in circling dance,
They meet in the sea, with mirth;
The waves are dances of little girls,
They play at embracing the earth!

JOURNALISTS, PROSE WRITERS, AND NOVELISTS INCREASE THE LITERATURE OF LATIN AMERICA

Latin Americans, with their creative minds and desire for expression, turned also to all kinds of prose writing. One of the most popular forms of writing in Latin America is journalism or newspaper writing. Newspapers in the large cities such as Buenos Aires, give more space to literature and science and less to sports and comics than do the papers of North America. People enjoy reading political or philosophical essays and

[1] *Ibid.*

humorous articles as much as they do the news. Many fine writers interested in political writing have been journalists or editors on a large paper.

A great writer of South America with whose name we should be familiar is José Enrique Rodó (en-ree'-kay roh-doh') (1872–1917), a brilliant philosopher and poet of Uruguay. He has been called a master of style, and, like Darío, had much influence on young writers who followed him.

Novels and poems about the days of the gaucho in Argentina enjoyed much popularity. Two of these have become classics in South American literature. One is the long epic poem dealing with Indians and gauchos written by José Hernández (1834–1886) and called *The Return of Martín Fierro*. It tells of the ruin of a gaucho family when the father was forced to join the army, and it became so popular that it made gaucho stories fashionable. The other gaucho classic is a famous novel called *Don Segundo Sombra* by Ricardo Guiraldes (gee-rahl'dace) (1886–1927). The romantic novel *María*, written by the Colombian Jorge Isaacs (hohr'hay ee'-sahks) in the late 1800's, is another classic which is still read a great deal. It is a sentimental love story of the Cauca Valley near Medellín where Isaacs spent his childhood.

Today, however, the writing of romantic novels has gone out of style. Many authors are interested in their lands and in the humble people who live and work upon the land. For instance, scholars and artists as well as writers have been inspired by the ancient culture of the Indians. A movement called *Indianismo* has grown up in the Andean countries among those who are interested in the cultural contributions of the Indians and in bettering their miserable existence.

A MODERN ARCHEOLOGIST AND A MODERN SOCIOLOGIST STUDY INDIAN AND NEGRO CULTURES

In Peru, a Quechua Indian spent much of his life unearthing the ancient culture of his own ancestors. This man was Doctor Julio Tello (hoo'lee-oh tay'yoh), eminent archeologist. He was born and brought up with twelve brothers and sisters in a tiny Indian village high in the Andes. Because of his intelligence, his father sent him to Lima for an education. It is said that when he saw pictures of ancient Indian skulls in the National Library, he determined to devote his life to learning more about his Inca ancestors. At San Marcos he studied Quechua, Spanish, and foreign languages as well as medicine and science, then went to Harvard University and to Berlin for additional study. Until his death recently, he was director of the archeological museum of San Marcos University in Lima.

Doctor Tello also discovered many ancient burial places and a rich store of pottery, tools, and sometimes mummies, preserved in the dry air of the Peruvian desert. All of these discoveries add another link to the history of the ancient peoples of Peru. Doctor Tello did much more than increase archeological knowledge; he is an outstanding example of the fact that the Andean Indian can be educated and take a place in national life.

In Brazil the gifted sociologist, Gilberto Freyre (fray'ray), has made a study of Negro slavery in colonial Brazil. Gilberto Freyre was born in Pernambuco of Spanish, Portuguese,

Hispanic Foundation, Washington, D.C.

CÂNDIDO PORTINARI'S PAINTING called "Loading Coffee" is a good example of his style. Notice the great feet and hands of the workers. Today this picture is at the Carnegie Institute in Pittsburgh, Pennsylvania.

and Dutch ancestry. He has studied at Columbia University in New York and is now professor of sociology in the normal school at Pernambuco. Freyre strongly favors the mixing of races that is taking place in Brazil. He believes that the addition of Indian and Negro blood forms a valuable contribution to the Brazilian race which is in the making and claims that Brazil, not the United States, has true democracy.

PAINTERS OF LATIN AMERICA INTERPRET THE SOUL OF THE PEOPLE

North Americans are better acquainted with the artists of Latin America. Art exhibits from Latin America often appear in museums and art galleries of our cities. In the story of Mexico we mentioned the great modern painter, Diego Rivera. In South America there is an artist who is often called the Diego Rivera of Brazil. This man is Cândido Portinari (cahn-dee'doh pohr-tee-nah'ree). Like Rivera he portrays the workers of his homeland in magnificent frescoes and is known as one of the finest mural painters of the day. Indeed, Portinari is said by some to be a greater artist than Rivera himself.

Portinari was born to humble Italian *colonos* on a coffee *fazenda* in São Paulo. He showed his talents when he decorated the village church near his home. When he was fifteen years old, he left home and managed by sheer persistence to get into the Academy of Fine Arts in Rio. Later he won a traveling scholarship to Europe. He became known in New York by his murals in the Brazilian Pavilion at the World's Fair. For the new building of the Ministry of Education and Health in Rio de Janeiro, Portinari is creating twelve great murals to represent the "twelve cultures" of Brazil — sugar, cattle, mining, tobacco, cotton, maté, coffee, cacao, iron, rubber, woods, and the "primary school."

In spite of his reputation in the United States and Europe, some of the aristocrats of Brazil dislike Portinari's work. The enormous, earthy figures in his murals, with their great feet and bulging muscles, are distasteful to many Brazilians. You may recall that some Mexicans feel the same about the work of Rivera.

In Argentina, the gauchos of the 1800's are portrayed by the gifted painter, Cesareo Bernaldo Quirós (key-rohs'). Quirós was well acquainted with these half-savage horsemen, for he had lived among them on his father's *estancia*. His pictures portraying the life of the gaucho are colorful and vivid.

In the slums of Buenos Aires, is a district, called *La Boca*, where the dock workers live. Here is one of the most famous art studios in Latin America where the great Argentine "maestro," Quinquela Martín (keen-kay'lah mahr-teen') lives and paints. He was a poor orphan boy working on the docks as a "wharf rat" when he began to make sketches with charcoal on the sides of packing boxes. Today

QUINQUELA MARTÍN is shown here in his studio finishing a painting called "Fire on a Boat." His studio looks out upon the busy docks of Buenos Aires which he has known and loved for many years.

Black Star

his murals are on the walls of many public buildings in Buenos Aires. They show the lives of the dock workers, fishermen, and sailors of the port.

Quinquela Martín insists on working and teaching among the people of the slum in which he was born. His students are from the second generation of Buenos Aires "wharf rats." He encourages them to paint the workers of Argentina. Like Rivera and Portinari, he wants to interpret the life of the common people of his country. His exhibits have been enthusiastically received in the United States.

MUSIC IS PART OF LIFE TO LATIN AMERICANS

Everyone in the United States recognizes the music of Latin America. We have all heard the "Rancho Grande," "Cielito Lindo," and "Estrellita," and other popular Mexican songs. We know the slow music of the Argentine tango and the gay rhumba of Cuba. It is not surprising that Latin Americans love music when we think of the people who make up their races. Spaniards, Portuguese, Indians, and Negroes are all music-lovers. What a rich heritage of music belongs to our southern neighbors! Gay dance music and folk songs of Spain and Portugal, the rich music of the Catholic Church, plaintive melodies of the Indians, and melodious Negro tunes — all form a great reservoir of music for Latin American composers to draw upon. In the 1800's, Latin Americans looked to Europe for their music, but it was not long before native composers turned to the rich musical resources of their own countries. Modern musicians began to compose orchestra and other music based on folk music.

The greatest composer of Latin America and one of the greatest in the world, is Heitor Villa-Lobos (vee'-lah loh'bosh) of Brazil. He is famous not only for his beautiful compositions, but because he uses fascinating rhythms and folk themes borrowed from the Indian and Negro. Many high-school students know the music of Villa-Lobos through his recordings. He has written over 1400 compositions, from light fantasies for the piano to operas and symphonies. One of his compositions, a fantasy for piano and orchestra, interprets the carnival in music — gay crowds, the cries of children, popular snatches from the bands, the cheers that greet the king of the carnival.

Villa-Lobos is not only a composer, but is also director of music for the schools of Rio de Janeiro and all Brazil. This energetic man works constantly with school groups. His gigantic music festivals in which as many as 30,000 pupils take part are claiming the attention of musicians and educators everywhere. Perhaps his work of teaching the children of Brazil to sing and love music may be a greater contribution to the world than his great compositions.

Interest in native music is everywhere prevalent in Latin America. You remember the Mexican composer and conductor, Carlos Chavez, who had collected Mexican Indian melodies. In Panama, Narciso Garay (nar-see'soh gah-rah-ee') has also made a collection of Panama's folk music. In Chile, a leading educator and composer named Carlos Isamitt (ee-sah-meet') has studied the life and music of the Araucanian Indians. Humberto Allende (ah-yen'day) of Chile is famous for his use of native rhythms.

Students who play the piano know Ernesto Lecuona (lay-kwo′nah) of Cuba who wrote the popular *Malagueña* (mah-lah-gay′nyah). His music is based on Spanish dance themes.

While country people of Latin America enjoy their *fiestas* and folk songs and dances, the more sophisticated people of the cities enjoy operas and orchestra concerts. For many years European singers, opera companies, and orchestras visited important Latin American capitals, such as Buenos Aires and Rio de Janeiro. The brilliant musical season is one of the important social events. Today many of Europe's finest musicians have taken refuge in Latin America because of the war. Their talents have enriched the musical life of Latin America and greatly improved the native symphony orchestras.

Buenos Aires is one of the important musical centers of the world. We have mentioned the fine Teatro Colón and the opera season there. The productions at this theater rank with those of the Metropolitan in New York. Two of Argentina's most interesting composers are the Castro brothers, José María Castro and Juan José Castro. In addition to composing, they have done a great deal to encourage the love of good music in their country. Juan José Castro is also a famous conductor, and in 1941 he came to the United States and conducted the NBC Orchestra in a series of radio concerts.

The Latin American boy or girl in primary school does not have music and art classes such as our children do. Although many schools are beginning to give more attention to these subjects, regular instruction in music and art is almost unheard of. However, in some countries talented young students are given free training in conservatories sponsored by the government. It was in one of these free academies that Portinari got his start.

WOMEN OF LATIN AMERICA ARE TAKING THEIR PLACE IN NATIONAL LIFE

One of the most interesting features of life in Latin America today is the change taking place in women's lives. Women of Latin America have always lived in a man's world. They were considered inferior to men, were given little education, and were never allowed to vote or enter into life outside the home. If they didn't find husbands, they usually became nuns, because life held little for a single woman in Latin America. They were, and still are, controlled by their husbands or fathers in a way American women find it hard to understand.

But in the 1900's, a gradual change began to take place. Immigrant women were coming to countries like Argentina, Chile, and Uruguay. These women and their daughters belonged to the new middle class and were not bound by Spanish ideas of what was proper for women. Protestant schools established in Latin America offered secondary education to women; girls sent abroad to school enjoyed the freedom given women and often returned home anxious to take part in the life of the nation.

It was in Chile that women first began to get jobs and train for professions, and the woman's movement spread to other countries. By 1937, women were admitted to universities in all Latin American countries, and what is more, were excellent as scholars and successful in the law and medical professions. Brazil is known

Pan American Union

THIS WOOD CARVING OF AN INDIAN HEAD was done by a present-day sculptress of Bolivia named Marina Núñez del Prado. It is typical of the growing interest in the Indians and their culture.

for the number of women engineers trained by her universities.

Women also became interested in the welfare of women and children. It was not until the 1920's that Paulina Luisi (loo-ee'see), a woman doctor of Uruguay, began to speak and write for social reform and for woman's right to vote. In 1922, many Latin American women attended a Pan-American conference for women in Baltimore, Maryland, and returned to form organizations to work for greater rights for women. They wanted better educational facilities, more protection for working women, and, of course, the right to vote. Today five of the countries of Latin America have woman suffrage. Women are doing much to help children

and mothers. Clinics and health centers, juvenile courts, visiting nurses, model tenements — all these are being established through women's efforts. But in spite of these activities, only a beginning has been made in a national life for women.

WOMEN ARE REPRESENTED IN THE ARTS

A few women of Latin America are well known in the United States and Europe. Gabriela Mistral, poet, educator, woman's leader, has been mentioned. Juana Ibarbourou (ee-bar-boo'roo) of Uruguay and Clorinda Matto de Turner of Peru are well-known women writers. Brazil has two fine women musicians, Guiomar Novaes (gee-oh-mar' noh-vah'esh), the pianist, and Bidú Sayão (bee-doo' sah-yown'), the opera singer, who are well known to North Americans. The fiery Carmen Miranda from Rio is as well known to people in the United States as she is in South America. She first appeared in the United States as a singer and dancer with her own band, and became so popular that over 300 recordings of her songs have been made. They are native songs often based on Negro music.

We must remember, however, that women are only beginning to share in life outside the home. Most upper-class women live restricted lives as they always have, especially in such countries as Ecuador and Colombia.

COURTESY AND FORMALITY ARE IMPORTANT TO LATIN AMERICANS

This chapter would not be complete without a brief glance at the gracious Latin American way of life, which North Americans seldom take the trouble to understand. We are such energetic and practical people that we fail to appreciate the importance placed by our Latin American neighbors on courtesy and formality. What may seem time-consuming and even insincere to us is second nature to them. When one of our Latin American neighbors says, *"Es su casa"* (My house is yours), he is entirely sincere even though he does not expect you to move in. It is his natural way of showing friendliness and hospitality. Visitors to Latin America hear constantly such gracious phrases as "How glad I am to see you!", "Goodbye until tomorrow," "The pleasure is mine," "I am your humble servant," and "I am at your service." Spoken in the melodious Spanish tongue these expressions are in great contrast to the abrupt "hellos," "good-byes," and "O.K.'s" of North America.

The Latin American takes time to be polite. He shakes hands with the clerk before buying goods at the store. He would never think of rudely breaking up a conversation with a friend even to keep an engagement. Our hurried good-byes when time is pressing would offend him. Regardless of his haste, he would courteously carry out all the customary formality of leave-taking. Even business letters are filled with polite phrases and always end with such courteous expressions as "I remain your attentive, very affectionate and constant servant." A business conference begins with a polite inquiry about the health of the respective families and a general conversation about topics of the day. The American salesman who neglects these formalities will do little business. This may seem foolish to us, but it is not foolish to the Latin American, and if we desire friendly relations with him, we must respect his customs when in his country.

One of the reasons we have been disliked south of the Rio Grande is that our business representatives and travelers have not made the effort to observe customary courtesies or even to speak the Spanish language. The Latin American has a name for the friendly, courteous, and understanding person. He is *simpático* (seem-pah′tee-coh). The North American who is *simpático* finds the Latin a charming friend and good neighbor.

BIDÚ SAYÃO, charming and talented soprano, is called "Brazil's Singing Ambassador" by President Vargas. She is shown here in a role in the opera "Don Giovanni," produced by our Metropolitan Opera Association.

N.Y. Times

Are You a Careful Reader?   Test Yourself!

I. Can you match these names and statements?

1. Rubén Darío	*a.* Brazilian sociologist
2. Amado Nervo	*b.* famous woman opera singer
3. Blanco Fombona	*c.* eminent Indian archeologist of Peru
4. Gabriela Mistral	*d.* present-day Brazilian composer and director of music
5. Villa-Lobos	*e.* famous Chilean poet and teacher
6. Julio Tello	*f.* artist who paints Indians of the Andes
7. Gilberto Freyre	*g.* modern Venezuelan writer who wrote poems in prison
8. Portinari	*h.* modern Mexican poet
9. Bidú Sayão	*i.* master of modern style of writing who wrote *Azul...*
10. Quinquela Martín	*j.* mural painter of Brazil who portrays the humble man
	k. Latin American dancer
	l. painter of Buenos Aires who portrays the people of the slums

II. Can you supply the correct word for each blank?

1. Latin Americans are especially fond of reading and writing ......
2. *The Return of Martín Fierro* is the story of a ..... family
3. Quirós was a painter who portrayed the ..... of Argentina.
4. Ernesto Lecuona is a ..... of Cuba.
5. Bidú Sayão is a famous woman ..... of Brazil.

Food for Thought and Discussion

1. The greatest painters of Latin America today are those who portray the humble people. Do you think this is evidence of a new attitude toward the worker?

2. Would a better knowledge of Latin American music and musicians create a better understanding of our neighbors? Why?

3. What advice would you give to a person who plans to visit in Latin America to help him be a welcome guest? What advice would you give to a businessman who is going to live in Latin America as a representative of his firm?

4. Would most of us profit by a greater use of courtesy in our everyday life?

Looking Backward

In this last part of the text you have learned how the republics of America are working together. You have also learned something about their great men and their customs which are so different from ours. The questions on page 429 will have more meaning to you now. Can you answer them readily?

Interesting Things to Do

1. Plan a trip on the Pan-American Highway from San Antonio, Texas, to Buenos Aires. If possible, check what parts of the highway are open to travel at present.

2. Read about these men who are pioneers of the route of the Pan-American Highway: Aimé Tschiffely, Herbert Lanks, Richard Tewksbury. Report to the class.

3. Make cartoons of one or more of the following situations: show Uncle Sam and the Monroe Doctrine; Uncle Sam and the Mexican War; our interference in Haiti and

Nicaragua; the liberation of Cuba; the founding of the Pan American Union; the Good Neighbor policy and Franklin Roosevelt; Pan-American solidarity.

4. Learn more about the men who were good friends of the Good Neighbors: Sumner Welles, Cordell Hull, Nelson Rockefeller, Oswaldo Aranha, Ezequiel Padilla.

5. Look up the Committee on Inter-American Affairs and report on its work.

6. Read reports on the conferences at Havana, Lima, Buenos Aires, and Rio from issues of *Américas* of the last few years.

7. Report on what the Union has done to improve public health in such matters as control of tropical diseases, training of doctors and nurses, quarantine of ports and inspection of ships, etc. Use back issues of *Américas*.

8. Find and show to the class colored reproductions of the work of the famous artists mentioned in Chapter 40. See *Américas*.

9. List motion pictures you have seen which give either a correct or a false impression of Latin America. What impressions of the United States would Latin American students receive from any five pictures you have seen in recent months?

10. Write an essay on the importance of sending motion pictures to Latin America which give a true picture of the United States.

11. Sum up your semester's work of Latin America by doing one of the following:

Plan a play or pageant on the history of Latin America from the Spanish conquest through independence, or a pageant in which each of the 21 republics is portrayed. Committees should plan the scenery, costumes and staging. If you cannot write your own play, send to the Pan American Union for materials. Give the play for other history classes or for the entire school.

Plan a public exhibit of all art projects, maps, and cartoons made in your class, as well as paintings or travel pictures collected.

Prepare a portfolio of letters to students in some Latin American country describing your semester's work on Latin America and your school. The Junior Red Cross in your city will send it to a Latin American secondary school for you.

Interesting Books to Read

For Further Information

Aikman, Duncan, *The All-American Front*. Doubleday, Doran. Problems of inter-American relationships.

Duggan, Stephen, *Two Americas, an Interpretation*. Scribners. A comparison between our life and theirs.

Martin, Percy Alvin, *Who's Who in Latin America*. Stanford University. The only reference for short biographies of present-day leaders.

Williams, Mary Wilhelmine, *People and Politics of Latin America*. Ginn. Good chapters on cultural contributions.

For Pleasure

Blackwell, Alice Stone, *Some Spanish American Poets*. University of Pennsylvania Press. Translations of well-known poems.

Flores, Angel, and Poore, Dudley, *Fiesta in November*. Houghton Mifflin.

Helm, MacKinley, *Modern Mexican Painters*. Harpers. Illustrated.

Torre, Emilio, *The Latin American Song Book*. Ginn. Seventy songs with English words and piano accompaniment.

Gallego, Rómulo, *Doña Barbara*. Cape and Smith; Guiraldes, Ricardo, *Don Segundo Sombra*. Farrar and Rinehart; Isaacs, Jorge, *Maria*. Harpers. Translations of the best-known South American novels.

To You Who Have Read This Book

LATIN AMERICA is no longer a vague term to you; it has a definite meaning. Now that you have read this book, an item you see in the newspaper about Chile or Costa Rica or any country of Latin America takes on new significance, for you have become acquainted with these countries — with their people and their politics, with their culture and their customs.

In this book you have followed the story of Latin America through four and one half centuries. You have seen the great Indian civilizations conquered by the men of Spain; you have seen the New World colonized and governed by Spain and Portugal. You have read about the struggle for independence and the new nations which emerged from that struggle, inexperienced in democracy and unfitted to govern themselves. You have watched their slow development from military dictatorships and revolutions toward a stable government. You know their great men and you know their humble people.

You have learned how our past mistakes in dealing with the nations of Latin America resulted in fear and distrust of the United States, and how the Good Neighbor policy has done a great deal to restore good feeling toward us. Today the United States is genuinely interested in gaining the co-operation of the Latin American republics. They, in turn, are convinced for the first time that we are sincere in our desire to be a good neighbor. They have proved their own sincerity by giving wholehearted support to the policy of hemisphere solidarity. Today, for the first time in their history, the American nations stand together.

But what of the future? An important part of our destiny lies with the republics of the New World. We must continue our co-operation with these republics. We have made a good beginning. Let us improve our American league of nations until it becomes that union of "majesty and greatness" of which Bolívar dreamed. Let us show to a war-weary world that twenty-one nations can work together in peace and friendship. Then, indeed, will the New World fulfill its noble destiny!

Index, Guide to Pronunciation, and Glossary

To THE READER: *This alphabetical list will tell you where to find the important things mentioned in this book, what they mean, and how to pronounce them.*

Christophe, Henri (ahn'ree crees-tof'), emperor of Haiti, 230–231

chuno (choo'noh), dried potato, 310

Ciudad Bolívar (see-oo-dahd' boh-lee'vahr), town in Venezuela, 275

coca, shrub producing cocaine, 308–309

Coelho, Olga (kwel-yu), Brazilian singer, 441

coffee: in Guatemala, 194; in Costa Rica, 213–214; in Colombia, 262; in Venezuela, 263; in Ecuador, 283; in Brazil, 410–413

Collas, ancient Peruvians, 53

Colombia, 255–266: from the air, 18–19; geography of, 255–256; history of, 248–250, 256–258; democracy in, 258; cities of, 258–263; transportation in, 18, 263–264; oil in, 264–265; land system in, 265–266; life and customs of, 265–266

Colon (coh-lohn'), city in Canal Zone, 223–224

colonies, Spanish, 107–119; classes in, 107–108; Indians in, 108; government of, 109–110, 113; position of Church in, 110–112; life in, 113–114; cities of, 114–116; agriculture and industry in, 116–117; control of trade in, 117–118

colono (coh-loh'noh), coffee worker of Brazil, 412

Colorados (coh-loh-rah'dohs), political party of Uruguay, 370

Columbus, Christopher, 87–90; tomb of, 234

Comodoro Rivadavia (coh-moh-doh'roh ree-vah-dah'vee-ah), town of Argentina, 343

confitería (cohn-fee-tay-ree'ah), candy store, 361

conquistador (cohn-kees-tah-dohr'), Spanish conqueror, 94

Conservatives, Argentine political party, 350

Coolidge, Calvin, and relations with Latin America, 434

Copacabana (coh-pah-cah-bah'nah), beach at Rio, 384, 386

copper: in Peru, 290; in Chile, 328–329

Corcovado (cohr-coh-vah'doh), mountain in Rio, 384

cordillera (cohr-dee-yay'rah), mountain chain, 9, 18, 23. *See also* Andes

Córdoba (cohr'doh-bah), city in Argentina, 342

Coronado, Francisco de (frahn-sees'coh day cohr-roh-nah'doh), Spanish explorer, 100

Cortez, Hernando (air-nahn'doh cohr-tays'), conqueror of Mexico, 95–100

Costa Rica (cohs'tah ree'cah), 212–217: geography of, 212; life and customs in, 212–213; coffee in, 213–214; democracy in, 214–216; education in, 217

Cotopaxi (coh-toh-pahk'zee), peak in Ecuador, 20, 280

cotton: in Peru, 290; in Brazil, 413

criollo (kree-oh'yoh), American-born Spaniard, 107

Cristóbal (krees-toh'bahl), city in Canal Zone, 223–224

Cruz, Dr. Oswaldo, and sanitation in Rio, 386

cruzeiro (kroo-say'roh), Brazilian coin, 424

Cuba, 235–243: from the air, 39; geography of, 235; cities of, 235–236; and Spanish American War, 237–238; agriculture and industry in, 241–242; history of, 236–240; life and customs in, 242–243

cueca (cway'cah), Chilean dance, 334

Cuernavaca (cwair-nah-vah'cah), town in Mexico, 140

culture of Latin America, 450–460

Cuzco (coos'coh), Inca city, 54–55; city of Peru, 293–294

Darío, Rubén (roo-ben' dah-ree'oh), poet, 450–451

David (dah-veed'), town in Panama, 224

de Lesseps, Ferdinand, and Panama Canal, 219–220

Dessalines (dess-ah-leen'), ruler of Haiti, 230

Díaz, Bartholomew (dee'ahs), Portuguese explorer, 87

Díaz, Bernal (behr-nahl' dee'ahs), early historian, 75

Díaz, Porfirio (pohr-fee'ree-oh dee'ahs), president of Mexico, 150–151

Dolores (doh-loh'rays), and Mexican independence, 120, 122

Dom Pedro, *see* Pedro I

domador (doh-mah-dohr'), Argentine horseman, 359

Dominican Republic, 233–234: Marines in, 233

don and *doña*, Mexican titles, 164

Don Segundo Sombra, novel of gaucho life, 453

Dos Bocas (dohs boh'cahs), Mexican oil well, 158

Drake, Sir Francis, English buccaneer, 185–186

Dutra, Enrico (en-ree'coh doo'trah), president of Brazil, 408

Ecuador, 280–286: from the air, 19–20; geography of, 280–281; history of, 281–282; industry in, 282–284; cacao in, 282–283; and boundary dispute with Peru, 282; cities of, 284–286; railroads in, 286

education: in colonies, 115–116; in Mexico, 161–166; in El Salvador, 203; in Costa Rica, 217; in Venezuela, 271–272; in Peru, Ecuador, and Bolivia, 310–311; in Chile, 332–333; in Argentina, 363–364; in Brazil, 422–423; of women, 262, 467

ejido (ay-hee'doh), Mexican co-operative village, 161

El Brujo (el broo'hoh), name for Venezuelan dictator, 270

El Dorado (el doh-rah'doh), legend of, 105

El Salvador (el sahl-vah-dohr'), 200–203: geography of, 201; agriculture in, 202; education in, 203

El Supremo (el soo-pray'moh), name for dictator of Paraguay, 375–376

El Tigre (el tee'gray), resort in Argentina, 341

encomienda (en-coh-mee-en'dah), allotment of Indians, 108

encomiendero (en-coh-mee-en-day'roh), colonist in charge of Indians, 108

Equator: crossing of, 19–20; in Ecuador, 286

Estado Novo (ay-stah'doh noh'voh), "New State" under Vargas, 407–408

Española (es-pahn-yoh'lah), *see* Hispaniola

estancia (ay-stahn'see-ah), estate in Argentina, 342, 352–353; 357–359

estanciero (ay-stahn-see-ay'roh), estate owner, 357–359

Everything is a Dance, poem, 452

Fabricación Chilena (fah-bree-cah-see-ohn' chee-lay'nah), made in Chile, 329

farinha (fah-reen'yah), food of Brazil, 424

fazenda (fah-sen'dah), plantation of Brazil, 397–398; 412–413

Federalists, political party in Argentina, 346–347

feijoada (fay-zhoh-ah'dah), Brazilian dish, 423

Ferdinand I, king of Spain, 85

fiesta (fee-es'tah), holiday: in Mexico, 168–170; in Guatemala, 200; in Panama, 235; in Peru, 305–306